SECULARIZATION, RATIONALISM, AND SECTARIANISM

SECULARIZATION RATIONALISM AND SECTARIANISM

Essays in Honour of
Bryan R. Wilson

EDITED BY

EILEEN BARKER, JAMES A. BECKFORD,
AND KAREL DOBBELAERE

CLARENDON PRESS · OXFORD
1993

Oxford University Press, Walton Street, Oxford OX2 6DP

Oxford New York Toronto
Delhi Bombay Calcutta Madras Karachi
Kuala Lumpur Singapore Hong Kong Tokyo
Nairobi Dar es Salaam Cape Town
Melbourne Auckland Madrid
and associated companies in
Berlin Ibadan

Oxford is a trade mark of Oxford University Press

Published in the United States
by Oxford University Press Inc., New York

British Library Cataloguing in Publication Data
Data available

Library of Congress Cataloging in Publication Data
Secularization, rationalism, and sectarianism: essays in honour of
Bryan R. Wilson/edited by Eileen Barker, James A. Beckford, and
Karel Dobbelaere.
p. cm.
Includes bibliographical references and index.
1. Religion and sociology. 2. Secularization (Theology)
3. Rationalism. 4. Sects. I. Wilson, Bryan R. II. Barker,
Eileen. III. Beckford, James A. IV. Dobbelaere, Karel.
BL60.S43 1993 200'.9'04—dc20 92–41458
ISBN 0–19–827721–0

1 3 5 7 9 10 8 6 4 2

Typeset by Cambrian Typesetters, Frimley, Surrey
Printed in Great Britain
on acid-free paper by
Biddles Ltd., Guildford and King's Lynn

Preface

These specially commissioned essays have been written by a diverse group of scholars who all share at least one thing—respect, admiration, and affection for Bryan Wilson, the doyen of sociological studies of religion in Britain. All the contributors are, in the broadest sense of the term, his colleagues; some of them have been privileged to be his students. In honouring Bryan Wilson in this *Festschrift*, they represent thousands of other scholars around the world who owe him an enormous debt of gratitude for the enrichment that he has brought to our understanding of modern societies.

Bryan Wilson spent his undergraduate years at University College, Leicester, obtaining a B.Sc. (Econ.) with First Class Honours from the University of London in 1952. He continued his studies under the supervision of Donald MacRae at the London School of Economics, where, in 1955, he completed his doctoral thesis which was revised for publication under the title *Sects and Society* in 1961. Wilson then took up a lecturing post at the University of Leeds until 1962, when the University of Oxford awarded him an M.A. and appointed him as a Reader in Sociology. A year later he became a Fellow of All Souls College, Oxford, the home to which he has continued to return after each of his many sojourns in Europe, America, Africa, Asia, or Australia as a researcher or Visiting Professor. In 1984, the University of Oxford conferred upon him a D.Litt. In 1992, as the high point of its celebration of 100 years of social sciences, the Catholic University of Leuven, Louvain (Belgium) conferred upon him the degree of *Doctor Honoris Causa* in recognition of his outstanding contribution to the sociology of religion.

A scholar of indubitable integrity, Wilson displays a scrupulous attention to detail within a broad theoretical approach that not only educates and illuminates, but also stimulates his readers. Rarely does one find someone engaged in original research who is so influential theoretically. His lectures and writings, full of nuances and subtleties, are models of clarity and elegance.

The scope of Wilson's scholarship and erudition defies brief summary. His discussions of fundamental concepts of sociology, his analysis of social roles, his diagnosis of modern cultural trends, and his discernment of the processes of rationalization and societalization all represent distinguished contributions to scholarship. Noteworthy for their defence of discriminating taste and civilized values in education are an early article on the role of the teacher (first published in 1962) and his edited collections on *Youth Culture and the Universities* (1970) and *Education, Equality and Society* (1975). But pride of place must be given to his many and varied contributions to the sociology of religion.

Wilson's first major publication in the sociology of religion was *Sects and Society*, a meticulous study of the Elim Pentecostal Church, the Christadelphians, and Christian Science. At the time of publication in 1961, it was the first sociological analysis of religious sects in Britain. This pioneering work set high standards of descriptive accuracy and sociological insight. It subsequently served as a model for the research of the many graduate students who have been inspired by Wilson's scholarship to conduct their own studies of other sectarian movements. Indeed, the variety and richness of the research that he supervised on this topic are evident in *Patterns of Sectarianism*, the collection of his doctoral students' essays that he edited in 1967. It is a tribute to his skill and sensitivity as a teacher that, while there has never been a 'Wilson school' of sociology, his students have frequently made effective and inventive adaptations of his typologies and classifications of religious sects—as, indeed, has Wilson himself in publications such as *Religious Sects* (1971), which offers a wealth of information in a form that is readily accessible not merely to the student of religion, but also to the general reader.

With its publication in 1966, *Religion in Secular Society* laid the foundation for many subsequent elaborations of the theory of secularization; Wilson's definition of secularization as 'the process whereby religious thinking, practice and institutions lose social significance' was to form, and (as can be seen in some of the contributions to this volume) still functions as, a basis for the continuing 'secularization debate'. Twenty years later, Wilson was chosen to provide the 'lead article', 'Secularization: The Inherited Model', for *The Sacred in a Secular Age* (1985), the volume edited by Phillip Hammond for the Society for the Scientific Study of Religion's official appraisal of the current status of its field of inquiry. In that paper, as elsewhere, Wilson cogently argues that, despite the fact that religion may remain as an alternative *culture* in modern society, the social *system* becomes secularized.

Questions about the logic of social science explanations are rarely far from the surface of sociological analyses of religious and other belief systems. The collection of essays on *Rationality* that Wilson edited in 1970 brought a number of philosophical and broadly anthropological issues into sharp focus for the first time. This volume was an indispensable guide to discussions about the proper approach for social scientists to adopt towards the understanding of religion, magic, and superstition. A closely related aspect of Wilson's interests emerged in *Magic and the Millennium* (1973). This was a densely reasoned and amply illustrated study of the processes whereby the cultures of some pre-industrial societies have adapted to the influence of modern Western ideas and ways of life. It was a magisterial survey of anthropological and sociological arguments about the attenuation of magic, prophecy, and millennialism in developing societies. Related themes were central to *The Noble Savages: The Primitive Origins of Charisma and its Contemporary Survival* (1975). This was another timely study of the processes whereby the charisma which pervades institutions in many pre-industrial societies undergoes transformation in the course of exposure to the rationalizing effects of Western cultures and social organizations.

The Riddell Lectures, delivered at the University of Newcastle upon Tyne, gave Wilson the opportunity to take stock of post-war changes in religion, and to interpret these changes for a non-specialist audience. Published as *Contemporary Transformations of Religion* in 1976, these lectures were a skilful synthesis of his own and other scholars' writings about religious decline and religious renewal within the general framework of the secularizing process. His unrivalled grasp of the complex issues concerning new religious movements was further evident in the collection of essays that he edited in 1981 under the title of *The Social Impact of New Religious Movements*.

The wide range of Wilson's interests in the sociology of religion was clearly reflected in the topics of the lectures that he delivered in Japan in 1979, which were published in 1982 as *Religion in Sociological Perspective*. Reflections on the development of theory in the sociology of religion are juxtaposed with critical insights into the familiar concepts of sects, new religious movements, and secularization—but with the added spice of examples drawn from non-Christian religions and cultures.

The extent of continuity and consistency in Wilson's writings is remarkable. Even more impressive, however, are the subtlety and creativity with which he has explored, and continues to explore, the implications of sectarianism and secularization in the modern world. His latest collection of old and new essays, *The Social Dimensions of Sectarianism* (1990), is proof that his uninterrupted concern over more than thirty years with the historical development, cultural significance, and social composition of marginal religious movements is still responsive to new problems. In particular, questions about the relations between the state, the law, and the fortunes of religious minorities which do not conform with modern morality, manners, or materialism are a *Leitmotiv* of his most recent writings. While these questions were implicit in his earliest articles on the varieties of sectarian responses to the world, they have now become explicit in his discussions of the legal and political controversies surrounding some religious movements. Wilson has, moreover, been prepared publicly to defend the rights to a fair hearing for groups and individuals whose beliefs, values, and behaviour differ radically not only from those of the majority of people in their own society, but also from his own.

Despite the prodigious quality and quantity of his research and writing, Wilson has always played a prominent role in servicing the community of which he is a part. His involvement in the life of All Souls is well known to all who have enjoyed his hospitality within its hallowed walls. He was a founding member of the University Association for the Sociology of Religion. From 1971 to 1975 he was President of the CISR (now known as the International Society for the Sociology of Religion or SISR), and has faithfully attended its biennial meetings, taking upon himself the task of ensuring that international scholars are greeted and made welcome. At the 1991 conference he became the first scholar to receive an honorary presidency from the Society. He has also taken on and judiciously carried out editorial duties—as European editor of the *Journal for the Scientific Study of Religion*, sitting on the editorial board of the *Annual Review of the Social Science of Religion*, and sharing responsibility for the English-language papers of SISR issues of *Social Compass*.

Generations of students and internationally renowned sociologists, historians, anthropologists, and many others have given papers and joined in the discussions presided over by Wilson at the Thursday afternoon Sociology of Religion Seminars at All Souls; recently Bellew Publishing asked him to edit a selection of papers delivered at the Seminar. In his role as a teacher, Wilson commands respect and gratitude; his students have the opportunity to benefit from an extraordinary and all too rare combination of accessibility, reliability, and erudition. Always supportive, his gentle criticisms sound as though they were but tentative suggestions or innocent enquiries; yet these can save the foolhardy from exposing rash enthusiasms and, at the same time, alert the student to new avenues for further investigation and analysis.

Many of his colleagues too, be they at the start or the pinnacle of their careers, have benefited from the generous advice and time that he has devoted to their work. And, at a more personal level, they have found him a discreet, loyal, and generous friend who can be relied upon to listen sympathetically and to select without fail the best claret from any cellar.

The early planning for this *Festschrift* took place when the three editors met with Roy Wallis in Tübingen during the 1987 conference of the CISR. Wallis was a member of that band of Wilson's students who went on to join the ranks of internationally renowned sociologists of religion. One of the last pieces of writing that he completed before his tragic death in 1990 was his contribution to this *Festschrift*. The dedication that Wallis penned in his book *The Elementary Forms of the New Religious Life* cannot be improved upon for this collection:

> For Bryan R. Wilson,
> teacher and friend.

Eileen Barker
James A. Beckford
Karel Dobbelaere

Contents

Contributors

SABINO ACQUAVIVA is Professor of Sociology at the University of Padua. He has contributed to numerous scientific and cultural journals and is the author of *Eclipse of the Holy in Industrial Society* (1979) and *Eros, morte ed esperienza religiosa (Eros, Death and Religious Experience)* (1991).

EILEEN BARKER is Professor of Sociology at the London School of Economics. Her publications include *The Making of a Moonie: Brainwashing or Choice?* and *New Religious Movements: A Practical Introduction* (1989), a number of edited books, and over a hundred articles. She is the founder and Honorary Director of INFORM, a charity supported by the British Government to provide information about new religious movements. She is currently president of the Society for the Scientific Study of Religion.

JAMES A. BECKFORD is Professor of Sociology at the University of Warwick. His main publications include *The Trumpet of Prophecy* (1975), *Religious Organization* (1975), *Cult Controversies* (1985), and *Religion and Advanced Industrial Society* (1989). He is the editor of *New Religious Movements and Rapid Social Change* (1986) and co-editor with Thomas Luckman of *The Changing Face of Religion* (1989). He was editor of *Current Sociology* from 1980 to 1987 and president of the Association for the Sociology of Religion in 1988–9.

LORD BRIGGS is Chancellor of the Open University and was formerly Provost of Worcester College (1976–91). He was a colleague of Dr Wilson at the University of Leeds, where he was Professor of Modern History from 1955 to 1961. He is the author of four volumes of *The History of Broadcasting in Britain* and *Governing the BBC*.

KAREL DOBBELAERE is Professor of Sociology and Sociology of Religion and Culture and Dean of the Faculty of Social Sciences at the Catholic University of Leuven. He is also Professor of Sociological Research at the University of Antwerp. His publications include six books, four edited volumes, and over a hundred articles. His main research interests are currently secularization, pillarization, and religious involvement. He is a past president of the International Society for the Sociology of Religion and a member of the Academia Europaea.

RICHARD FENN is Professor of Christianity and Society at Princeton Theological Seminary. He has published several works in the sociology of religion, including *Toward a Theory of Secularization, Liturgies and Trials: The Secularization of Religious Language, The Dream of the Perfect Act: An Inquiry into the Fate of Religion in a Secular World*, and most recently *The Death of Herod* and *The Secularization of Sin*.

RICHARD GOMBRICH has been Boden Professor of Sanskrit at Oxford University and Fellow of Balliol College since 1976. His publications include *Buddhist Precept and Practice, Theravada Buddhism*, and, with G. Obeyesekere, *Buddhism Transformed: Religious Change in Sri Lanka*. He is honorary secretary and treasurer of the Pali Text Society. He is interested in all aspects of the empirical study of Buddhism and is sorry that so few people study the subject, which suffers from a dearth of ideas.

PHILLIP E. HAMMOND is Professor of Religious Studies and Sociology in the Department of Religious Studies at the University of California, Santa Barbara. He received his Ph.D. in Sociology from Columbia University, then taught sociology, specializing in the study of religion, at Yale, the University of Wisconsin, and the University of Arizona. He is author or editor of over a dozen books, most recently *Religion and Personal Autonomy: The Third Disestablishment in America* and *The Protestant Presence in Twentieth Century America*. He was editor from 1978 to 1982 of the *Journal for the Scientific Study of Religion*, and served a term as president of its sponsoring association, the Society for the Scientific Study of Religion.

MICHAEL HILL has been Professor of Sociology, Victoria University of Wellington, New Zealand, since 1976. He was a sociology under-graduate at the London School of Economics (Hobhouse Memorial Prize, 1965), then did his postgraduate work at Wadham and Nuffield colleges, Oxford. From 1967 to 1975, he was a Lecturer in Sociology at the L.S.E. His publications include *A Sociology of Religion* and *The Religious Order*, the co-editorship of *Shades of Deviance* (1983), and contributions to Frank Whaling (ed.), *Contemporary Approaches to the Study of Religion*, and Mircea Eliade (ed.), *The Encyclopedia of Religion*. He was associate editor of the *British Journal of Sociology* from 1975 to 1976, and editor of *A Sociological Yearbook of Religion in Britain* from 1970 to 1975.

DAVID MARTIN is Professor Emeritus of the University of London (L.S.E.); Visiting Professor, King's College, London; and International Fellow, I.S.E.C. (Institute for the Study of Economic Culture), at Boston

University. He is the author of numerous books, including *A Sociology of English Religion, A General Theory of Secularization, The Breaking of the Image, The Dilemmas of Contemporary Religion,* and *Tongues of Fire: The Explosion of Protestantism in Latin America.*

J. D. Y. PEEL is Professor of Anthropology and Sociology at the School of Oriental and African Studies, University of London. He has also held posts at Nottingham University, the London School of Economics, and the universities of Ife, Liverpool, and Chicago. His main works have been *Aladura: A Religious Movement among the Yoruba* (1968), *Herbert Spencer: The Evolution of a Sociologist* (1971), and *Ijeshas and Nigerians* (1983), and he is at present working on a study of the encounter of religions in nineteenth-century Yorubaland. He was elected a Fellow of the British Academy in 1991.

PHILIP RIEFF is Benjamin Franklin Professor of Sociology and University Professor at the University of Pennsylvania, as well as Professor-Elect of Psychiatry at the Medical College of Pennsylvania. He is the author of *The Feeling Intellect* (1990), *Fellow Teachers: Of Culture and its Second Death* (1984, first published as *Fellow Teachers* in 1973), *The Triumph of the Therapeutic: Uses of Faith after Freud* (1966), and *Freud: The Mind of a Moralist* (1959; 3rd ed., 1979).

ROLAND ROBERTSON is Professor of Sociology and Religious Studies at the University of Pittsburgh. He is the author of books and articles in the sociology of religion, sociological theory, and the analysis of globalization, including *Globalization: Social Theory and Global Culture* (1992). He has also recently co-edited *Religion and Global Order* (with W. R. Garrett) and *Talcott Parsons: Theorist of Modernity* (with B. S. Turner).

DR JEAN SÉGUY is Senior Research Fellow at CNRS (Centre National de la Recherche Scientifique), Paris. He belongs to the 'Groupe de Sociologie des Religions', and is a former editor of *Archives de sciences sociales des religions.* He is interested in Christian sectarianism and associated topics, and also has an interest in Max Weber and Ernst Troeltsch. He has published seven books and more than 230 articles in scholarly journals (so far).

MARK A. SHIBLEY is a doctoral student in Sociology at the University of California at Santa Barbara. His publications include articles in *Sociological Analysis* and the *Pacific North-West Quarterly.* His dissertation is entitled 'The Southernization of American Religion: Mapping the Resurgence of Evangelicalism, 1970–1990'. He was the

1989 recipient of the Robert McNamara Student Paper Award presented annually by the Association for the Sociology of Religion for the best student paper in the sociology of religion.

SUSUMU SHIMAZONO received his M.A. from the Department of Religious Studies, University of Tokyo. Following research at the University of Tsukuba, he became an Associate Professor of the University of Tokyo. He has written extensively on Japanese religiosity and particularly on the new religions. His publications include *On Salvation Religion in Contemporary Society* (1992) and numerous articles. Many of his English publications are to be found in the *Japanese Journal of Religious Studies*. His recent research has focused on various new expressions of popular mysticism in Japan and Western countries.

ROY WALLIS was Professor of Sociology and Pro-Vice-Chancellor of Queen's University, Belfast, at the time of his death in 1990. His numerous publications include *The Road to Total Freedom: A Sociological Analysis of Scientology* (1976), *Salvation and Protest: Studies of Social and Religious Movements* (1979), and *The Elementary Forms of the New Religious Life* (1984).

1

Community, Society, Globality, and the Category of Religion

> Although nominally *religious* tolerance *per se* appears to have grown, paradoxically, the freedom to subscribe to the 'religion of your choice' is available on the implicit assumption that that choice has no particular social significance.
>
> (Wilson 1982: 155)

> The course of social development that has come, in recent times, to make the society, and not the community, the primary locus of the individual's life has shorn religion of its erstwhile function in the maintenance of social order.
>
> (Wilson 1973: 47)

> (J)ust as we imagine that modern individuals will make different choices based in part on what they choose to keep from childhood, so we can imagine that different societies will keep aspects of their traditional identities. ... Different societies might become the communal equivalent of different life styles, something like clubs one is free to join or leave.
>
> (Kolb 1986: 5)

> It seems correct to say that telic considerations do in fact *define* man's end ... , but this is not the same as saying that they *constitute* it.
>
> (Parsons 1978: 366)

I

My primary focus here is the basis of twentieth-century interest in religion, with particular reference to the work of Bryan Wilson. My intention is by no means to reduce religion to purely mundane aspects of social life. Rather, I am interested in the ways in which the general conception of religion has acquired significance across the twentieth-century world-as-a-whole; even though this has clearly been—from a different standpoint—a century of secularization. Far from wanting to reduce religion to something else, I seek to dereify *the idea of* religion: to expose the way in which it has become a procedure for the ordering of life in twentieth-century societies and the global human circumstance generally. In that respect one of my major concerns is to indicate the importance of understanding the specifics of the diffusion of the idea of religion (to use Hegelian terminology, but not in a Hegelian spirit).[1]

Bryan Wilson's contributions to this issue have been particularly subtle and complex; for he has in his work on religion attempted to distance himself from metaphysical, theological, and normative problems, yet, on the other hand, has displayed great moral compassion ever since his earliest sociological writings, particularly in terms of his claim that religion is 'the ideology of community'. Thus I want, in the first place, to draw attention to the link between the crystallization of Western intellectual concern with *Gemeinschaft* at the end of the nineteenth century and what I call the 'take-off period' of contemporary globalization, lasting from about 1870 until about 1925, when the present form of the twentieth-century shift towards a 'single world' was firmly established. Specifically, I argue that, from its modern beginnings, the concern with communality—as opposed to societality—has combined the idea of the primordial, local community, on the one hand, with the notion of the *global* community, on the other. The intellectual concern for community was partly a result of a paradoxically nostalgic encounter with 'the East', while in the West itself some of the more striking developments on the religious and quasi-religious fronts involved the interpenetration of communal and global orientations. For example, it was a period during which the modern ecumenical movement arose, combining communal with inter- and trans-communal interests. To invoke an even more specific example, this was the time during which the international youth hostel movement arose—very explicitly co-ordinating moral concern about 'international' fraternity and complexity with a 'back-to-nature' communalism and simplicity (Grassl and Graham 1988).

While the term 'religion' has a series of very long etymological histories and has played a significant part in the fates of a number of civilizations—with particular reference to ideas about bonds among human beings and/or between humans and gods—it has not acquired thoroughly contested public and global significance until relatively recent times. On the other hand, specialists in the study of religion—most particularly those who have claimed scientific status for their intellectual endeavours—have tended to overlook the significance of religion as a category of life, often seeking instead a stable definition applicable to all times and places. Only with the unignorable recent disputes about the boundaries between religious and non-religious practices which have occurred with respect to televangelism and new religious movements has the attention of scholars and academics been emphatically turned to that issue. But even in that regard the interest has been limited mainly to strictly legal and political matters within specific societal contexts, most frequently the USA.

The more general problems of the link between modernity and religion as a category and the ways in which the idea of religion has been involved in interactions between societies—and accordingly has constituted an aspect of recent processes of globalization—have thus been greatly neglected. A great irony in the latter respect is that at the very time that the basis for twentieth-century sociology of religion was being established in the works of Emile Durkheim and Max Weber, with considerable interest in the problems that arise in trying to compare Western and Eastern forms of religion in terms of 'universal' criteria, much intellectual and political debate was occurring *within* Eastern societies—notably China and Japan—as to the meaning and relevance of Western conceptions of religion. One specific problem which arises in that connection is that in East Asian societies there has traditionally been a close aligning of 'culture' and 'religion'. More specifically, in so far as religion was a relatively tangible concept, it tended to be particular rather than universal. Thus in China the Confucian understanding of religion (*tsung chiao*) traces communally shared rituals and beliefs back to distinctively Chinese worship, emphasizing social, cultural, and political implications over 'purely religious' matters. The encounter with the West, in the second half of the nineteenth century, created—or at least exacerbated—the problem of distinguishing between the social-communal and the more spiritual-supernatural aspects of religion, represented in China by Buddhism and Taoism respectively.

Thus, from the beginning the sociological study of religion has largely overlooked the issue of the degrees of reflexiveness involved in 'real' conceptions of religion, on the one hand, and the significance of differing conceptions of religion in the ordering of relationships between and within twentieth-century societies, on the other. As the leading proponent of the secularization thesis among sociologists of religion, Bryan Wilson has been very persuasive in speaking of the loss of the 'erstwhile function' of religion 'in the maintenance of social order'—in so far as one thinks only of what might be called the 'penetrative significance' of religious beliefs and practices *vis-à-vis* collective life. However, what has been overlooked by strong proponents of the secularization thesis (as well as by most of its opponents) is that religion has been a major ordering category of the twentieth-century world-as-a-whole.

Along such lines it could well be argued that religion has become more, rather than less, significant during the twentieth century, quite regardless of the issue of its penetrative significance. At the same time it could be argued that the commodification of religion under the umbrella of nominal religious tolerance—religion as purely private preference—is a social fact, consisting in the idea that such privatization is good for society. More specifically, the privatization of religion is an aspect of globally diffused ideas about individualism as an institution. As John Meyer has argued, modern individualism is sustained on a global scale in terms of two closely related dimensions of 'the public institutionalization of the life course'. Individuals operate in terms of instrumental rationality, on the one hand, and the publicly celebrated private or subjective individual who is free—is, indeed, expected—to find meaning and value as a self in relation to the rationalized environment, on the other (Meyer 1987).

The rise of the nationally constituted society was accompanied in many places by the notion that religion was to be regarded as separate from the systemic domains of state and economy. If one had to pinpoint a period when that development took off in earnest, it would be the late 1780s and early 1790s. In France and the newly born USA the claim that religion (as something supernaturally revealed and socially organized) is, at least potentially, destructive of society made considerable impact. Of course, there were great differences between the French and the American revolutions in that regard; but they do not seriously qualify the general thesis that after the early 1790s the desirability of the separation of 'Church and State' rapidly gained ground in much of Europe and in Latin America and laid the basis for the development of the idea at the end of the nineteenth century that religion could and should be studied as an isolable sphere of sociocultural life. In any case, during the nineteenth century the idea of the private, relatively sequestered status of religion was cultivated and widely diffused, some of the more important developments in that respect occurring, as I have already suggested, in East Asia.

There is thus a paradoxical relationship between modernity and religion. 'Religion' is largely a category and a problem of modernity, a motif which was produced in the circumstance of modernity—partly 'in order to' show what modernity was leaving behind. On the other hand, positive subscription to the idea of religion has largely constituted, in varying degrees, a critique of modernity itself. In those terms we may regard the comparative religion and history of religions 'movement' as having developed in opposition to *Gesellschaft* (Homans 1987). At the same time, the sociology of religion (as opposed to religious sociology) has become, particularly since the Second World War, a 'scientific' discipline torn between the modernist—historically Enlightenment—attempt to thematize the peripherality of religion (religion as a dependent variable) and the anti-modernist effort to give religion a privileged status as a supplier of meaning and/or social solidarity—hence the centrality of the problematic of secularization in the sociology of religion. The latter has two parents who are, or were, not very compatible: the modernity which issued from the Enlightenment and envisaged a world without religion, and the anti-modernity which has not been able to embrace that idea. The concern with secularization is largely an expression of the offspring's dilemma.

While 'societalization' has been regarded as the primary enemy of religion—most explicitly in the work of Bryan Wilson—it can, I think, be shown more precisely that it is 'institutionalized societal-ism' which has actually installed religion as a global *category*. As Frank Lechner has written, 'One of the puzzles confronting the classical sociologists was the peculiar presence of "the individual" in the new *Gesellschaft*-like society. They had to produce a non-individualistic theory of the new social order that would also account for individualism and individuation as social facts.' Now, a century later, we confront 'an analogous puzzle in the form of the empirical existence of independent societies in the new world-system. We have to produce a non- or trans-societal theory that also accounts ... for the presence of societies as constituent elements in the world-system [as] a global fact' (Lechner 1989: 16).

After the French and the American revolutions, the place of religion in 'duly constituted' societies became a widespread problem. While it is certainly true that the idea of religious tolerance was rather widely diffused in the Western world, the other side of that circumstance was the increasing emphasis on the conception of the homogeneous society in which individuals participated as nationally standardized citizens who were supposed to bracket their extra-societal commitments. A number of the newly independent societies of Latin America tried in various ways during the nineteenth century to promote a secular state alongside a sequestered sphere of religion. By the end of that period the principle of the freedom of religion, on the one hand, and the idea that religion should not be political, on the other, had spread eastwards from Europe—indeed, as far as Japan.[2] At the same time the insistence on societies having identities considerably blurred the issue of what was to count as religion; for the period lasting from about 1870 until the end of the first quarter of the twentieth century was one in which there was great emphasis across much of the world on national rituals, celebrations, traditions, and so on (Hobsbawm and Ranger 1983; Robertson 1990). Thus in Meiji Japan the idea of the 'national polity' (*kokutai*) was celebrated and disseminated by an allegedly dereligionized form of national Shinto. State Shinto was declared to be a moral, rather than a religious, institution, partly in order to conform to Western expectations concerning the sequestered status and freedom of 'real' religion. (Indeed, the standard Japanese translation of the Western term 'religion' as *Shukyo* dates from the early Meiji period.) Later in Kemalist Turkey a secular state was adamantly promoted during the 1920s in an Islamic religio-cultural setting; yet Durkheimian ideas concerning the need for modern societies to have some kind of civil religion were influential (Gokalp 1968). And so on—into the period of the post-1945 beginnings of the Third World, marked by India's political élite wrestling with the difficult problem of defining religion in order to establish a secular state. Thus the supposedly integrating—or, at least, identifying—functions of religion continued to be taken seriously, but 'real religion' was frequently considered to be an impediment to the secularization which, it was thought, was a desideratum of societalization.

II

The origins of a fully recognizable sociology of religion are typically traced to the declining years of the nineteenth century and the very early years of the present century, and two names usually figure most strongly in that attribution—those of Durkheim and Weber. Yet neither of these two men produced entirely new perspectives on the study of religion. While there was much originality in both cases, there was also considerable reliance on the writings of precursors, and both men in one way or another refracted particular features of the societies of which they were members (France in Durkheim's case, Germany in Weber's) (Robertson, 1985*a*). Moreover, as social scientists, their interests in religion were largely dictated by basically secular, sociocultural considerations. They were inspired to write about religion mainly in terms of their concern with the main features of what we have come to call 'modernity'.

Thus the two major leaders in the emergence of a specialized study of religion were not interested in religion intrinsically. Rather, their interest was a product of their diagnoses of the major trends and predicaments of Western societies in a period when it was widely believed that an old era was passing away and a new, 'modern' one was beginning. Neither believed that religion in the traditional Western sense of revealed, supernaturally oriented faith and attendant ritual had a significant future in the West or, in the longer run, in other parts of the world. On the other hand, unlike the vast majority of recent specialists in the study of modern religion, they did directly concern themselves with questions concerning, *inter re*, emergent forms of solidarity, ethics, morality, and meaning.

In that regard it should be said that, among prominent contemporary sociological students of religion, Bryan Wilson has been particularly conspicuous precisely because he *has* continuously addressed such matters. In fact, it would not be too much to say that they have constituted the core of his extensive work on religion in various places and periods. On the other hand, Wilson has, with equal consistency, insisted that his is fundamentally an analytical-empirical approach. As he wrote in the relatively early stages of his academic career, 'The sociological approach is not a polemic, an apologetic, or a therapeutic orientation, but rather a search for explanations of just how an institution functions, its focal points of tension and conflict, and its adaptability to change' (Wilson 1962: 109). None the less, there can be no doubt that in spite of this claim to 'value neutrality', Wilson has operated with a definite set of entry-points—with a solid 'hermeneutic'—in his numerous discussions of religious movements and trends. Among those have been a concern with 'the attenuation of pristine values' (in which he has followed such sociologists as Max Weber, Robert Michels, and Philip Selznick), the idea of religion as essentially 'the ideology of community', and the issue of the extent to which there has been a decline in civility—his interest in that regard possibly having developed in relation to the work of one of his earliest teachers, Norbert Elias (1978), on 'the civilizing process'. More generally, Wilson has been deeply concerned—and, from his own point of view, pessimistic—about the relationship between religion and morality, on the one hand, and the ways in which and the degrees to which groups of individuals have sought—particularly during the twentieth century—to promote and sustain resistance to the consolidation of Weber's 'iron cage', on the other. Indeed, it would not be too much to say that Wilson has written of modernity as a tragedy.

Thus Wilson's claims to analytical detachment have surely been embedded in 'a certain point of view'. He began his writings on religion at a time when 'functional analysis' was quite widely taken to be the ideal-typical style of sociological investigation—when, in a special sense, 'being a functionalist' was regarded as a form of detached but caring 'civility'. Being a functionalist meant care for what Talcott Parsons was, in the 1960s, to call 'the societal community'—obviously a deliberate and provocative combination of terms which, to this day, many consider to be polar opposites. As a 'pessimistic functionalist', Wilson, however, has developed much of his thinking precisely around the theme of a caesural break between *Gemeinschaft* and *Gesellschaft*. Let us, however, return briefly to classical sociology of religion.

Durkheim and Weber were differentially influenced by the sense of Western superiority and 'progress' which had gained considerable momentum during the nineteenth century, by evolutionary ways of conceiving of sociocultural change, and by a concern with the odyssey and future of reason and rationality. On the other hand, they wrote in a period when much of the optimism and rationalistic intellectualism of the earlier period was fading. The idea of taking a scientific approach to religion had been well established in Western Europe by the time that both Durkheim and Weber began to write in earnest in the 1890s. The most crucial period in that respect had been the decade of the 1860s, just before which Charles Darwin had (in 1859) published his *Origin of the Species*. Until then, as Sharpe has written, 'The student of the religions of the world, although he might have ample motive for his study, and more than enough material on which to base his researches, had no self-evident method for dealing with the material.' By the end of the 1860s, however, 'he had the evolutionary method' (Sharpe 1986: 27).

In speaking of the impact of the rise of evolutionism in both biology and the human sciences upon the Western study of religion (and Western religion itself), we must be aware of two relatively independent tendencies: the idea of evolutionism as a scientific challenge to religion, on the one hand, and the evolutionary method as a way of analyzing religious change, on the other. While there were those who saw biological evolutionism as a challenge to the very validity of any form of religion and yet saw the evolutionary method as the best way of analysing religions, there were others—most notably Max Müller—who found in evolutionism ways of comparing religions and analysing religion generally without adopting a negative attitude. Such considerations enable us to set the scene for distinguishing between the general points of view of Durkheim and Weber.

Weber was undoubtedly influenced by ways of comparing religions—particularly those of Hegel—which had been developed during the nineteenth century (Robertson 1985b). But he did not directly interest himself in the theme of the evolution of modern religion. Durkheim, on the other hand, believed that reason could and should be applied to religion, in order to enhance its survival in distinctively modern forms—mainly because of his commitment to the view that religion is the universal basis of morality and social solidarity and that without 'the seriousness' of religion human life would crumble (even though traditional forms of religious commitment were being steadily undermined, at least in the West). Weber centred much of his work precisely upon that process of undermining, and thus largely initiated the full-fledged modern concern with the phenomenon of secularization; whereas Durkheim was mainly interested in the social future of religion. Although much more could be said along these lines, as well as about the details of the different ways in which Durkheim and Weber have been influential in the twentieth-century study of religion in the sociological mode (centred upon concern with the social foundations and/or the social consequences of religion), I wish to dwell for a moment mainly on a single aspect of the sociology of religion since the period of Durkheim and Weber. This has to do with the distinctively American cast of the subdiscipline in recent decades.

Although the thinking of Durkheim and Weber has been heavily (but selectively) incorporated into America-centred sociology of religion, the latter has certainly manifested considerable autonomy. The kind of analysis which has crystallized under American influence has largely centred upon American concern with the separation of Church and State and the associated notion that religion is basically a private matter but one whose privacy has to be publicly cultivated. Thus in the USA the privatization of religion is a particularly significant social fact, in Durkheim's sense of that term.

More, perhaps, than anywhere else, the sociology of religion in the USA has occupied an interstitial position—between sociology as a very secular discipline and religious studies as both a defence of religion and a critique of Western secularity. To that extent, much of American sociology *of* religion might more aptly be described as sociology *and* religion—a seeking of a conciliation between sociological science and privatized religion, in parallel with, but less explicit than, the psychology and religion 'movement'. In any case, probably under American influence, the term 'religion' became prominent in the West during the nineteenth century, and was then diffused across the globe—in such a way and to such a degree that it has become a conspicuous component of twentieth-century public discourse. In that particular, but very important, sense, 'religion' is, as I have already emphasized, a distinctively *modern* phenomenon. More specifically, 'the problem of religion' is a problem of modernity. The sociological study of religion has, in spite of its secularity, promoted religion; yet, at the same time, it has—or so I would claim—irretrievably functionalized and relativized it. Religion as a category encapsulates the modern sense of 'what we have lost.' Much of it is part of modernity's nostalgia. This is most clearly true of the West and probably also of much of the Islamic world. It may also well be true of the East. But in the East, religion also enjoys a particularly prominent position in some intellectual circles as a form of critique of the West, in which regard it overlaps with a more subdued thrust of the Western religious studies movement.

III

The preceding considerations lead to the suggestion that we need to pay systematic attention to the manner in which religion as a concept or category has been invoked in intellectual and general-public discourse during the twentieth century. We need to know much more about what interest in religion represents. In order to address such issues, I maintain that we should be directly concerned with the comparative genealogy of religion. Comparative genealogy of religion should rest on Nietzsche's dictum that that which has a history cannot or should not be defined, a dictum that flies in the face of the conventional procedures of the social science of religion, which typically involve attempts to define a phenomenon of interest in such a way as to make the definition essentially applicable to an infinite variety of historical and sociocultural circumstances. Indeed, much of sociology has rested on the assumption that definitions have application, at least in principle, to *all* sociocultural circumstances; although it should again be noted that Max Weber introduced his own major set of reflections on the sociology of religion by directly invoking the Nietzschean principle. On the other hand, in recent years there has developed—partly under Nietzsche's influence—resistance to the essentialist tendency, most notably in and via the work of Michel Foucault.

As Merquior puts it, Foucault argued that 'the "what" of discourse does not antedate the emergence of discourse; rather, it is constituted by the complex set of relations obtaining between, in Foucault's own enumeration, institutions, socio-economic processes, techniques and modes of behavior, systems of classification and characterization, etc' (Merquior 1985: 15). There is, however, no need for us fully to embrace Foucault's negativism—that is, his subversive attempt to expose and render the categories and modes of discourse which have allegedly been crystallized by the human sciences as exploitative, power-linked forms of discipline—in order to implement the general idea that an important task for both the scientist and the humanist is to grasp systematically the different ways in which categories and concepts interpenetratively enter both disciplinary discourse and 'the real world'. In any case, as Merquior puts it on Foucault's behalf, 'The rules of discursive formation allow or forbid the what of knowledge; and the genealogist's eye seeks to pierce through the thickness of discourse to identify its historical routes—the "why" of that "what" ' (Merquior 1985: 152). Thus genealogy, in its most general sense, involves the tracing of lineages of modes and categories of discourse in relation to their sociocultural, historical, and global circumstances. As I use the term, 'comparative genealogy' shows particular interest in the systematic comparison of such lineages in different societies and, on a larger scale, different civilizations. Moreover, doing comparative genealogy in global perspective does not simply mean that one should reach for the largest range of comparison possible. It means, above all, that one takes carefully into consideration the phenomenon of globalization—namely, the processes that have been making the entire world into what I call a single place, even a world society.

Adding globalization to comparison—or, more accurately, doing comparative work globally—involves systematic attention to the ways in which modes and categories of discourse spread from one society or civilization to another and the global circumstances of such diffusion. In that regard we should be careful to avoid the trap indicated by Raimundo Panikkar when he argues that because the West is no longer able 'to dominate other peoples politically, it tries to maintain—most of the time unconsciously—a certain striving toward a global picture of the world by means of comparative studies' (Panikkar 1988: 116). We should also bear in mind Hajime Nakamura's suggestion that concepts such as 'philosophy' and 'religion' may well turn out to be 'provincial clichés that need to be carefully reexamined and reinterpreted from the perspective of a broadly based cross-cultural anthropology' (Nakamura 1988:

151). Thus I should make it as clear as possible that the global-comparative approach which I am advocating involves careful attention to the concreteness of the diffusion of categories and modes of discourse from one civilizational context to another, the relationship between diffused and indigenous patterns of thought and, not least, the ways in which participation in the global-human circumstance involves, in varying degrees, acceptance of globally structured categories and styles of communication.

I certainly cannot present here anything resembling a full-fledged global-comparative genealogy of religion as a category and, more diffusely, a mode of discourse. Nevertheless, some additional observations are possible. As I have said, the idea of religion began to assume a particularly public form in the West in the later part of the eighteenth century. Against a long-drawn-out historical background, which began in earnest with the Protestant Reformation—but which itself derived in large part from a deep-rooted ambiguous relationship between temporal and spiritual powers in predominantly Christian parts of the world since the earliest days of the Christian Church—there crystallized at the end of the eighteenth century a view of religion centred on the place of individual religious commitment in the nationally constituted society. Whereas the European feudal sociocultural formation had been closely integrated with what is often called 'the medieval Christian synthesis' and had involved the idea that it was, as Hansen says, 'the church's universal mandate to include all humanity within its scope' and that such a mandate 'imposed rights and duties on the heads of the spiritual and political institutions of Christendom', the Protestant Reformation (after much bloodshed in some parts of Europe) established the basis for deviation from the churchly orthodoxy which had been upheld by 'the combined legitimacy of the two swords' (Hansen 1987: 27).

With the rise in Europe of the strong, centralized, and increasingly secular state during the nineteenth century, there arose—against the background of the equally important, but very long-drawn-out 'discovery of the individual'—a distinctive problem of citizenship in nationally constituted societies (Abercrombie *et al*. 1986). The idea of citizenly involvement in and communal identification with a nation posed particular problems as far as loyalty to trans-societal doctrines and ways of life were concerned. Thus came to a head the general theme of religious toleration—that is, legally structured 'respect' for religious difference—and the notion that citizenship (indeed, civility) demanded limitations on the degree to which religious commitment could intrude on the secular affairs of public-governmental life.

As I have said, in a special but important respect 'religion' entered modern discourse largely in terms of its status as a sphere of modern societies. It became part of the way in which modern national societies are cognitively and politically ordered. As Europe-centred 'international society' expanded during the nineteenth century, new members—such as the newly independent nations of Latin America—struggled with the problems of separating the sphere of religion from the domain of politics. In Europe itself the diffuse question of the validity and legitimacy of religious belief and practice was frequently raised in revolutionary struggles against what were perceived to be strong remnants or reassertions of the old alliance between the temporal and the spiritual powers— the 'anti-supernatural' thrust of the French revolutionaries at the end of the eighteenth century being the matrix from which much of that activity sprang. At the end of the nineteenth century and the beginning of the twentieth century a number of non-European— mainly Asian—societies were constrained, with varying degrees of voluntariness, to join international society, and in so doing had to confront the expectation that a 'civilized' society was to be ordered in a way which, broadly speaking, conformed to the structural pattern of the older members of that 'society'.

That confrontation between West and East was complex, particularly with respect to the tension between the requirement that religion be, so to speak, kept in its place as a relatively sequestered domain of the national society and the more philosophical view that religion was essentially an all-embracing source of meaning and identity. Although the requirement of the new form of the national society was that religion be kept out of the secularized spheres of public life—that a progressive society, following Comte and Spencer, was one which was not in the thrall of theology or metaphysics—there was also a more than residual view that, even if modern society were necessarily marked by secularity, there was a need for 'something' which would perform the same functions that religion had allegedly performed in the past. Thus *the idea of* religion was spread Eastwards from the West in terms of its status as a way of categorizing and constraining beliefs and practices concerning the fundamental issues of human life and its significance as an all-encompassing orientation to life as a whole.

One particularly important aspect of this apparent contradiction—between 'a sphere of life' and 'a way of life'—was that while the structure of the modern form of national society sequestered religion or named a particular aspect of life as religion, the emergent structure of international society required each national society to have its own identity. (As Durkheim was to argue at length, some form of religion continued to be necessary as a way of binding individuals to national societies.) Thus it was almost inevitable that, with the growing presence of the West in the East in the second half of the nineteenth century, 'religion' would become a major reference point for—a vehicle for the expression of—such vital issues as the major differences between the East and the West and the problem of the degree to which collective identities (both of particular societies and of entire civilizations) could be 'invented' in the face of importation of Western means and techniques.

In emphasizing the importance of the processes in terms of which religion was 'discovered' and the ambiguous functions which that discovery performed from a sociological point of view, I do not seek to diminish the profundity of the issues which have come to be discussed under its aegis. Nor, in particular, do I wish, to undermine in any way whatsoever the significance of metaphysical ideas concerning the human condition which have been central themes of Asian societies for many hundreds of years. But the fact of the matter is that the concept of religion was alien to the East when it was first brought from the West, although since the late nineteenth century much attention has been devoted to reconciling Western conceptions of religion with Eastern notions of apparent 'family resemblance'. In the process there has been a strong tendency for some Eastern societies to feel constrained, nevertheless, to use the category of religion to reinterpret their traditions of thinking about 'ways of life'.

Thus 'religion' has become a globally diffused mode of discourse which plays an important part in the institutional ordering of national societies and international society, as well as a form of discourse concerning what Durkheim called 'the serious life'. However, there are currently signs of civilizations and societies reasserting their identities in terms of global categories—or at least attempting to restructure the dominant forms of discourse. Our consciousness of the relativity and historicity of the category of religion is itself a manifestation of that circumstance, and thus encourages us to enquire systematically into the genealogy of those categories in non-Western societies which appear to parallel Western categories. Thus we need not only to show how the Western concept of religion became globally significant, but also to insist that in all literate or partially literate civilizations there have been genealogies of dominant ideas. Attention to the latter will help to avoid the view that quintessential indigenous categories have simply been overridden by Western ones. It is not simply concepts of Western origin which have to be 'deconstructed'. At the same time it has to be recognized that in recent centuries the significant categories of human life have been increasingly subject to global constraints and what Parsons calls 'telic considerations'.[3]

Notes

1. Some parts of this discussion rest on Robertson 1988.
2. For the spread of the concept of 'civilization' in a manner that has some bearing on these matters, see Gong 1984.
3. I make some comparisons between the approaches of Bryan Wilson and Talcott Parsons in Robertson 1989.

References

Abercrombie, N., *et al.* (1986), *Sovereign Individuals of Capitalism* (London).
Elias, N. (1978), *The History of Manners* (New York).
—— (1982), *State Formation and Civilization* (Oxford).
Gokalp, Z. (1968), *The Principles of Turkism* (Leiden).
Gong, G. W. (1984), *The Standard of 'Civilization' in International Society* (Oxford).
Grassl, A., and Graham, H. (1988), *The Magic Triangle* (Bielefeld).
Hansen, E. O. (1987), *The Catholic Church in World Politics* (Princeton, NJ).
Hobsbawm, E., and Ranger, T. (eds.), (1983), *The Invention of Tradition* (Cambridge).

Homans, P. (1987), 'Psychology and Religion Movement', in M. Eliade (ed.), *Encyclopedia of Religion*, vol. 12 (New York), 66–75.

Kolb, D. (1986), *The Critique of Pure Modernity* (Chicago).

Lechner, F. (1989), 'Cultural Aspects of the Modern World-System', in W. Swatos Jr. (ed.), *Religious Politics in Global and Comparative Perspective* (New York), 11–28.

Merquior, J. G. (1985), *Foucault* (Berkeley, Calif.).

Meyer, J. W. (1987), 'Self and Life Course: Institutionalization and its Effects', in G. Thomas *et al.* (eds.), *Institutional Structure* (Beverly Hills, Calif.), 240–61.

Nakamura, H. (1988), 'The Meaning of the Terms "Philosophy" and "Religion" in Various Traditions', in G. J. Larson and E. Deutsch (eds.), *Interpreting across Boundaries* (Princeton, NJ), 137–51.

Panikkar, R. (1988), 'What is Comparative Philosophy Comparing?', in G. J. Larson and E. Deutsch (eds.), *Interpreting across Boundaries* (Princeton, NJ), 116–36.

Parsons, T. (1978), *Action Theory and the Human Condition* (New York).

Robertson, R. (1985*a*), 'The Development and Modern Implications of the Classical Sociological Perspective on Religion and Revolution', in B. Lincoln (ed.), *Religion, Rebellion, Revolution* (London), 236–65.

—— (1985*b*), 'Max Weber and German Sociology of Religion', in N. Smart *et al.* (eds.), *Nineteenth Century Religious Thought in the West*, vol. 3 (Cambridge), 263–304.

—— (1988), 'Modernity and Religion: Towards the Comparative Genealogy of Religion in Global Perspective', *Zen Buddhism Today*, 6: 125–33.

—— (1989), 'A New Perspective on Religion and Secularization in the Global Context', in J. Hadden and A. Shupe (eds.), *Secularization and Fundamentalism Reconsidered* (New York), 63–77.

—— (1990), 'After Nostalgia? Wilful Nostalgia and the Phases of Globalization', in B. S. Turner (ed.), *Theories of Modernity and Postmodernity* (London), 45–61.

Sharpe, E. (1986), *Comparative Religion* (La Salle, Ill.).

Wilson, B. R. (1962), 'Analytical Studies of Social Institutions', in A. T. Welford *et al.* (eds.), *Society: Problems and Methods of Study* (London), 99–110.

—— (1973), *Magic and the Millennium* (London and New York).

—— (1982), *Religion in Sociological Perspective* (Oxford).

2

Church Involvement and Secularization: Making Sense of the European Case

In his analysis of religion in the nine countries covered by the European Value Systems Study Group (EVSSG), Stoetzel suggests that France, Belgium, and the Netherlands form a 'laicized region', surrounded by Catholic (e.g. Italy), Protestant (e.g. Great Britain) and religiously mixed countries (e.g. the German Federal Republic) (Stoetzel 1983: 90–1). First, I shall describe the situation in the 'laicized region' and see if other regions develop along the same lines, using additional data from sources other than the EVSSG study. Then, I shall offer an explanation of the changes which have occurred in church affiliation and involvement in Europe.

1. A DESCRIPTION OF THE SITUATION

According to the EVSSG study, in the laicized region, the number of people having no religion was 26.4 per cent in 1981 (Stoetzel 1983: 113). This number has been growing in the last decades, with a greater proportion in younger age-categories (under 35) than in older ones.[1] According to sources referred to by Wallis, non-affiliation is also very high and growing in Britain; a recent study of a cohort of young people reveals an increase of 150 per cent in non-affiliation.[2]

Although in France and Belgium about three out of four people still declare themselves Catholic, the number of practising Catholics is very low and declining. The sharpest decline occurred in the late 1960s and the early 1970s. A similar trend was also recorded for Dutch Catholics.[3] In a comparative table, van Hemert (1980: 10–11) demonstrated that the decline was not limited to the Catholic Church, nor to the laicized region of Europe. This can be easily documented with data from the German Federal Republic.[4] Before the mid-1960s there were no indications of a weakening of ties to the Catholic and Protestant Churches. But the so-called stability reached since the early 1970s is only apparent; it masks the decline of church involvement in the younger generations (Köcher 1987: 174–7). As Köcher (1987: 176) clearly documents, in the 1950s and early 1960s in the German Federal Republic, 'There was a balance between the generations. Today the age composition of the congregations constitutes an inverted pyramid'.

Stoetzel (1983: 94–5) had established that this was the situation in all European countries covered by EVSSG. He suggested that it reflected a law of nature according to which the need for religion increased as one approached the end of life. However, the data from the German Federal Republic and other countries over the last thirty years run counter to that explanation, as most data pertaining to Europe confirm that the younger generations are drifting away from the churches.[5] Consequently, these data suggest that a new situation emerged in the 1960s and that—even if the life cycle still has some effect—the major explanation for the actual relationship between age and church involvement should be looked for in specific historical developments taking place in the late 1960s and early 1970s which shaped the religious outlook of the new European generations.

Church practice declined everywhere in Europe, most notably in the Catholic Church (Harding *et al.* 1986: 41–2).[6] In 1981, according to the EVSSG study, 37 per cent of Catholics and 9 per cent of Protestants still went to church weekly. However, this does not mean that people who do not attend weekly have severed all ties with their church. Only one-third of the self-declared Protestants and a little more than one-fifth of the self-declared Catholics never go, whereas the others go occasionally.[7]

Apart from going to church at weekends, many people go or are brought to church to sacralize important passages in their life: birth, entering adulthood, marriage, and death. The frequency of attendance at rites of passage is best recorded for Catholics in the European laicized region, and these data are often used by the Catholic Church to show that many people still behave religiously at important moments of their lives. Although the vast majority of the children of Catholics are still baptized in the laicized region of Europe, a serious decline set in in the 1960s. The number of religious marriages has also been going down since the 1970s.[8] This indicates that more and more young adults—i.e. those marrying[9] and those having children—not only refrain from going to church at weekends, but also no longer engage in religious activities on solemn occasions (Lambert 1988: 50–3). Consequently, more and more young adults have become a-religious. This is not the case for the older population: the number of Catholic burials has been very stable in the Netherlands and Belgium for the last twenty years.[10]

We may then conclude that, in Europe, young adults are not only becoming less involved in the churches, but there are also clear indications that more and more are not affiliated to a church. All the data that have been compiled underscore the results of the EVSSG study. In Europe, up to 20 per cent of people between 18 and 35 years of age declared that they did not belong to a church. In all the countries studied except for Northern Ireland and Eire this was markedly more than in the older age-categories (Harding *et al.* 1986: 42). Non-affiliation is especially marked in the laicized region. However, nearly 10 per cent of those living in Protestant and religiously mixed regions also declared themselves unconnected to a church, as did about 7 per cent in the so-called Catholic region (Stoetzel 1983: 113). Recently, an increasing trend towards non-affiliation among the young has been documented in the Catholic region.[11]

Some might object that our analysis up to now has been based only on self-declared church membership and ritual behaviour, but that beliefs and ethical practices are more important to an evaluation of a person's religiosity. However, the EVSSG study has shown that people's way of conceiving of God bears a strong relationship to the other beliefs that they hold and to church involvement. Belief in a 'personal' God correlates with traditional beliefs in life after death, a soul, hell, heaven, and sin. Again, the number of people accepting traditional Christian beliefs has declined, especially among the young.[12] Furthermore, the majority of those believing in a 'personal God' attend a church service weekly. Those conceiving of God as a 'spirit' or 'life force' and those who 'do not really know how to "conceive" him' attend less frequently. Finally, people who doubt God's existence or do not believe in him are overwhelmingly not involved in a church.[13] In Belgium, a person's conception of God is a better predictor of his or her participation in a church than vice versa.[14]

The diversity of reported beliefs about God also has implications for the ethical points of view that people take. Belief in a 'personal God' tends to promote the acceptance of absolute moral guide-lines as opposed to the notion that good and evil depend entirely upon the situation. A 'relativistic' perspective, by contrast, is more likely to be endorsed by those who believe in a 'spirit' or 'life force' and by those who either do not believe in God or are uncertain in their beliefs (Harding *et al.* 1986: 49).

Similar results arise from an examination of the relationship between affiliation to a church and degree of ritual participation, on the one hand, and acceptance of moral guide-lines, on the other. Those defining themselves as non-affiliated are less likely than Protestants or Catholics to say that the Ten Commandments are relevant for them today. Of course, there is a difference between the type of commandments: it is more true for the religious command-ments (the first three) than for the commandments relating to sexual matters, and the least so for the moral commandments (Stoetzel 1983: 119). However, as Köcher points out for Germany in particular and Europe in general, it even holds for those moral commandments (5 and 7) which are accepted by the largest number of Europeans (more than 80 per cent). This becomes even more apparent when the commandments are translated into everyday decision-making situations. Furthermore, the closer Protestants and Catholics are to their church, the more conservative are their ethical standards (Köcher 1987: 185–94 and 242–79). Phillips and Harding (1985: 108) speak about a pervasive effect of religion on moral values in Britain,[15] and de Moor (1987: 31) and Dobbelaere (1984: 89–94) found the same in the Netherlands and Belgium respectively. Again, as in the case of affiliation, involvement, and beliefs, moral attitudes varied with age in all nations studied by the EVSSG: the younger the population—affiliated or not—the less orthodox they were in moral matters.[16]

We may conclude our descriptive section, then, by stating that beliefs, church involvement, and ethical views are strongly connected and that all these dimensions reveal a clear difference between the generations. While it is correct to state that the Catholic faith, in general, is still sustaining a greater commitment among young people than is the Protestant faith (Harding *et al.* 1986: 70), it is also true to say that changes have been more pronounced within the Catholic population in the last decades. The EVSSG study also makes it clear that if gender differences exist, they are attributable to women who are not in paid employment; women in full-time employment display an outlook on religious and moral matters close to that of men (Harding *et al.* 1986: 63; de Moor 1987: 31; and Dobbelaere 1984: 104). All the other traditional social variables—such as level of education, income, social class, home ownership, and urbanization—have no impact or only an incidental one. No stable trends could be detected with regard to these variables,[17] which represents quite a change since the 1950s and 1960s.[18]

2. THE CHANGES EXPLAINED: SECULARIZATION AND POSTMODERNITY

2.1 Secularization

The data presented here indicate that the number of non-affiliated people has grown in Europe and that more and more people, even if they still consider themselves to belong to a church, have doubts about traditional beliefs and do not practise regularly. A large number of practising Protestants and Catholics doubt or reject some of the traditional beliefs and ethical standards of their Church. People, even those practising regularly, 'pick and choose' what to believe and what to practise. They no longer accept the 'set menu' of their Church, and this is most clearly seen in a Church with authoritatively given beliefs, practices, and ethics, i.e. the Catholic Church.[19] I think, to draw further on the menu analogy, that most people now practise a religion 'à la carte'. What does this mean?

It signals the individuation or privatization of religion: religion has become—in Danièle Hervieu-Léger's (1986: 59) terms—'*affaire d'option individuelle et non plus évidence collective*'. However, contrary to what Church leaders and religious people think, this is *not* an individual option. It is the particularization in the religious sphere of a more general structural characteristic of our societies: the '*Privatisierung des Entscheidens*', the individuation of decisions. As Luhmann has demonstrated, it is linked to functional differentiation and to the inclusion requirement, which can be met only if, in each and every subsystem, complementary roles emerge alongside the professional ones. In order to safeguard the functional segregation between subsystems on the level of the complementary roles (the so-called publics), the individuation of decisions serves as a functional equivalent—since a strict segregation of complementary roles at the individual level is difficult to enforce and to control. Indeed, if personal decisions are purely private, the chances are that a statistical neutralization of the consequences of such micro-decisions will occur, even if a lack of compartmentalization still exists on the micro-level equivalent to the differentiation on the societal level (Luhmann 1977: 232–48).[20]

Inclusion, of course, is based on the cultural value of 'equality' which Churches, especially the Catholic Church, seem unable to accept. The recent insistence of its hierarchy on discipline and religious submission negates equality. This is forcefully exemplified by the Vatican's demand that a loyalty oath be imposed on theologians teaching at Catholic colleges and universities. A century and a half ago, de Tocqueville (1986: 449) wrote that in an inequalitarian society, the legislators pretend to promulgate eternal laws, as they cannot imagine the conditions of future societies changing. This is exactly the perception that the Catholic hierarchy has of its Church and, to a lesser extent, that of the hierarchy of other Churches. Consequently, they want to eternalize their doctrines and laws.

The complementary process of the individuation of decisions, related to functional differentiation, is secularization. This means that on the *societal level*, 'Religion has lost its presidency over other institutions' (Wilson 1985: 15). The overarching and transcendent religious system of old is being reduced in a modern, functionally differentiated society to a subsystem alongside other subsystems, and religion's overarching claims are losing their relevance. As a result, religion has lost its societal significance, and is no longer backed by other subsystems, especially the polity. Consequently, it can no longer be imposed on citizens, and must now be marketed (Berger 1967: 135–7). On the market it is faced with other systems of meaning: religious and non-religious, indigenous and alien, and with people making their own 'bricolage' (Luckmann 1979: 135), their religion 'à la carte'. This is shown in the EVSSG results: in Western Europe 21 per cent believe in reincarnation, a concept alien to Christianity. Reincarnation is even integrated into the belief system of 20 per cent of practising Catholics in Belgium (Harding *et al.* 1986: 46–7; Dobbelaere 1984: 73).

Belief in a 'personal God' seems to be important in the conservation of traditional religion, as we have described it. This is linked to belief in most traditional tenets of Christian doctrine, and it ensures that traditional rites are practised and traditional Christian ethics accepted. Why has belief in a 'personal God' declined in our societies, dragging other traditional Christian beliefs, rituals, and ethics in its wake?

I have to return to Wilson's (1976a) seminal work on secularization in order to explain this. Wilson linked secularization to rationalization and to the societalization of our societies. Central to his work is the idea that—as Weber had already indicated—the world is more and more considered to be controllable and calculable, so things can be planned. This applies to the psychological and the social world, as well as to the physical world. This world was planned: societalization took place, destroying traditional communities. Communal relations were based on total personal relations, on trust, respect, and 'clear patterns of authority that build on biological determinants'. In society, role and performance matter more than persons and goodwill. Society is 'based on impersonal role relationships, the coordination of skills, and essentially formal and contractual patterns of behaviour, in which personal virtue, as distinguished from role obligation, is of small consequence' (Wilson 1982: 155). It follows that social control could no longer be moral or religious in such a society. Control had to 'become impersonal and amoral, a matter of routine techniques and unknown officials'—legal, technical, mechanized, computerized, and electronized (Wilson 1976b: 20, 102).

Young adults have always lived in a world conceived to be controllable and calculable: the economic, the educational, the domestic, and the procreative world.[21] Consequently, God is more and more removed from their world. Many can no longer believe in God, because '*they* have the whole world in *their* hands'. Middle-aged and older men and working women have also become progressively caught up in such a world. Only middle-aged and older housewives have been sheltered from this world and are, rather, familiar with a world based on values such as tradition, devotion, humility, and love, and on personal, total, and lasting relationships. This explains why employment and generational experiences are the only social variables which bring about significant variations in beliefs, ethical attitudes, and ritual behaviour. And if the notion of God still lingers on with some, he is more and more conceived of as a 'higher power', a 'spirit', 'something vague and general', rather than as a 'personal' God. How could he be thought of as a 'personal' God if people experience fewer and fewer 'personal' relationships in their public life? In a society in which impersonal, segmented, role relations prevail, belief in a 'personal' God, and consequently the celebration of a relationship with him in the Eucharist, seems an anachronism for many modern women and men.

My basic argument is that many people can no longer believe in God because not only the physical but also the psychological and social worlds are now seen as controllable and calculable. Consequently, human beings can manipulate these worlds: their actions become calculated, systematic, regulated, and routinized; they also become disconnected from religion and God. This has not only had an impact on church attendance and the desacralization of ethics; it has also desacralized the meaning of life, suffering, and death. Indeed, recent sociological studies in the Netherlands have documented the impact of the secularization of the social system on the meaning that people give to life, suffering, and death. 'An idea like Kluckhohn's that there are "sets of existential premises almost inextricably blended with values in the overall picture of experience" cannot be postulated any more' (Thung *et al.* 1985: 147). Value orientations seem to vary independently of beliefs and interpretations of life, suffering, and death; nor is a relationship established between such interpretations and people's beliefs.[22] These studies thus suggest that since the organizing principles of life have become detached from religious interpretations, there has been a process of 'secularization' at the level of the individual (Felling *et al.* 1986: 76 and de Moor 1987: 47). The differentiation of the personal life-world, which we can aptly describe as 'compartmentalization', results in the marginalization of religion in the personal life of the individual. This desacralization at the individual level often results either in the rejection of God or in his depersonalization. And, as Durkheim suggested, the more general, vague, and impersonal God becomes, the more removed he is from this world and the more ineffective he is. At the same time, such belief is very insecure. It is belief in an abstract notion without real impact on people's lives, and can easily be disposed of.

Finally, we have to explain why there was a drastic decline in church involvement in Protestant and Catholic Churches from about the mid-1960s until the early 1970s. Since the decline was not limited to the Catholic Church, it cannot be explained as just a Catholic phenomenon as is done by Greeley (1985: 56). His explanation—the papal encyclical on birth control—does not hold even for European Catholics, since the decline started before 1968. Rather, it should be explained as the collapse of traditional behaviour that was no longer supported by the belief in a 'personal God' and the traditional values proclaimed by the Churches. Under the growing impact of human capabilities, belief in a personal God and in other articles of faith had already been strongly undermined in the golden 1960s, but overt traditional behaviour simply persisted under the impact of social control. Sunday service became for many a duty, a tradition, not supported by belief in a personal God. However, as a consequence of public discussions about religion in the mass media—about, for example, Robinson's *Honest to God*, the underground churches, the Vatican Council and the so-called 'Protestantization' of the Catholic Church—individuals suddenly became aware in the mid-1960s that they were not alone in their doubts and disbelief, in their challenge to Church authority and so forth, and they adapted their *public* behaviour to their *personal* disbelief in the doctrines and values of their Church. Since then, social control has increasingly had a completely different impact in Europe: it has started to keep people out of the churches, whereas it had previously induced them to attend.

This alignment of public behaviour with personal conviction was also due to a structural change: an increase in leisure time, the development of leisure activities, and a 'leisure culture'. In the 1960s and 1970s, an increasing number of people had more and more leisure time. Consequently, in a period when Sunday service became a 'sheer duty' or an 'obligation of little substance', situated in a period of extended leisure time, the pleasure associated with leisure time—being primarily a time of 'freedom', of 'exemption from pressures'—aggravated the feeling of 'duty' associated with religious 'obligations' for a growing number of people.[23]

Of course, younger adults have been greatly influenced by the leisure culture, a culture which is based not on 'the word', as religion is, but on 'music', supported by video images. The generation of young adults '*s'est organisé musicalement, autour du rock*', Yonnet writes, and the rock-themes 'celebrate free time, exalt the end of the periods of constraint (school, work, family time)' and, we may add, church. 'Free time' is celebrated not in church but in discothèques and other recreation facilities '*par le vertige*' (Yonnet 1985: 156, 185). This is a type of recreation that underscores a structural characteristic of present-day society: individualism and massification (Balandier 1985: 186–91). Young people dance less as a 'couple', but on their own, losing themselves in the crowd. Bit by bit, a youth culture has emerged that conflicts head on with traditional religious culture, which legitimates a 'culture of duties and self-restraint' and is based on the notion of 'community'. Youth culture, on the contrary, stresses freedom and individualism, massification and emotionalism, pleasure and ecstasy—which some ultimately look for in drugs. Young people have also created their own rituals, international festivals like Live-Aid and SOS-Racism—and more local ones like Torhout-Werchter in Belgium. This culture is reflected in the clothing of the young, and has filtered up to the rest of society (Yonnet 1985: 297–366). We live in a 'consumer society', characterized by massification and individuation, supported by advertising which stresses novelty: new trends, new products, new fashions, and so on; church rituals, to the contrary, tend to 'repeat' and stress continuity and tradition.

What then is the residual function of religious rituals in society? Churches are invited to give an additional aura to national ceremonies, to underscore the continuity of the nation, to revivify its myths. Indeed, Churches still perform 'civil religious' functions, and, on the individual level, they continue to perform the same functions: they ritualize continuity in change (in baptism and marriage), and revivify the myths (finiteness is overcome by eternity). The compartmentalization of religion on the individual level seems to follow—albeit with some time-lag—the functional differentiation on the societal level.

2.2 Postmodernity

Secularization is the product of functional differentiation, with its accompanying processes of rationalization, mechanization, computerization, societalization, bureaucratization, and the segmentation of social relationships—all of which, at the individual level, produce individuation and compartmentalization. These processes are often referred to as 'modernization'. In the 1970s, however, a postmodern reaction emerged. It became apparent in the works of postmodernist architects who rejected 'absolute functionalism', stressed non-functional ornaments, and romanticized their constructions. Postmodernist thinking rejected '*les visions totalisantes*' and the elaboration of political or utopian projects. It is a movement of deconstruction. And painters and writers in this vein stressed, among other things, the naïve, the trivial, the emotional, and the fragmentation of the life-world (Balandier 1985: 138–40). With the disappearance of global ideologies, the militants vanished. They had to make room for technicians who try to solve particular, concrete problems: '*médecins sans frontières*', '*les îles de la paix*'. Some people, Voyé suggests, have called our epoch 'insipid and amorphous, resigned to the mediocrity of everyday life'. Indeed, everyday life is, as she points out, the centre of people's preoccupations. Contemporary social problems are not tackled from the point of view of global theories, but from the particular point of view of everyday life: unemployment is not analysed by reference to social class theories or to general theories of social justice, but as a threat to the social organization of daily life; and the anti-racist movement '*Hands off my buddy*' is successful since it situates the problem on the level of interpersonal relations (Voyé 1985: 269–71). The emphasis on interpersonal relations has also resulted in a re-evaluation of intermediate structures, the civil society, which may alleviate the shortcomings of an excessively bureaucratic public sector. This partly explains the stability and even the relative growth of some sectors, for example, of the Christian pillar in Belgium (Voyé and Remy 1985: 237–8), a country where church involvement has declined by 50 per cent in the last two decades.

To fight against the massification and the fragmentation of the life-world, individuals look for collectivities on the micro-level, where personal relations can flourish: small groups, primary groups, which emerge on the basis of 'elective affinity' rather than on the basis of ascription or locality (Balandier 1985: 193–4). People choose their personal, intimate relations—their *alter ego*, their friends and acquaintances—and create networks which give them socio-affective support. These small groups, '*ces niches individuelles*', are meeting-places where people may exchange and share visions and feelings.

From this perspective, the Churches—and especially the Catholic Church—emerge as structures based on other values. Leaders of the

Churches think about daily problems in terms of grand principles, and evaluate them from this vantage-point. This is true, for example, of their attitude to abortion, and particularly the Catholic Church's approach to *in vitro* fertilization and birth control. The mainline Churches are also bureaucratic, hierarchical, and eco-logically structured. This situation promotes anonymous social interactions. In many parishes of the Catholic Church in Belgium, I have observed that the 'habit' of wishing one another peace by shaking hands, which was introduced a couple of years ago, still has to be stimulated by the officiating priest, since one does not know who it is one is sitting next to in church. And the so-called expression of 'communal care' for worthy causes is expressed in terms of money, the most universal means of exchange and consequently the most impersonal expression of care.

Hence, from the postmodern perspective, one does not follow the road to church on weekends. On the contrary, people tend to favour folk religious practices—church burials, pilgrimages, and implorations of Jesus, the Holy Mother, and the saints with prayers and candle light, especially in the Catholic Church—to deal emotionally with their losses and pains. Such practices favour a certain 'polytheism', a *'retour des dieux'*, to follow Voyé's (1985: 271–2) line of thinking. A religion which offers a general theory of existence based on one God does not find a large echo with people looking for responses to the daily problems of their lives. In Belgium, churches are quite often crowded for funerals: not so much with people from the parish community, but with friends and acquaintances representing the networks associated with the deceased. And so one may see churches packed with strangers who have only one point in common: the deceased and his or her family. Consequently, these burials are social rather than religious rituals.

Some people are also drawn to small groups of like-minded people, such as Bible study groups, or to rituals that allow for greater emotionality, such as those organized by the Charismatic Movement. Some also find their way to sects and cults: to bury their loneliness and rejoice in the warmth of a small group (Wilson and Dobbelaere 1987 and Dobbelaere and Wilson 1980); to be able to manage the world 'out there' with the gnosis they offer; or to experience the 'other' world in 'incense and myrrh'. However, the number of cult and sect members does not in the least compensate for the decline in the number of church members (Wallis 1984: 61–2).

CONCLUSION

My conclusion is very straightforward: in Europe, I cannot see that the near future will bring a reversal of the trends described above. Rather, I see a consolidation on the individual level of the secularization of European society. One might, of course, ask what would happen if the Christian Churches adapted their vision and started talking about God and the Bible in a way that modern people could understand and accept (Dobbelaere 1988: 102–11). However, before venturing on such speculations, one would like some indication that the Churches might eventually go in this direction.

Notes

1. In 1984 the number of people with no religion was 31.3% in the Netherlands, nearly double what it had been in 1947. The number increases per cohort over the years for those born after 1940; see Dobbelaere 1988: 87 and Sasaki and Suzuki 1987: 1065–9. In France, 15.5% of the population reported having no religion in 1986, which was 5.5% more than in 1974; in 1983, about 20% of those younger than 35 years and less than 10% of those older than 50 years professed no religion; see Madelin 1988: 60–3. For Belgium, see Dobbelaere 1986–7: 297.
2. See Wallis 1984: 61 and Wadsworth and Freeman 1983: 422–3, who report an increase from 12.9% non-affiliated in childhood to 32.6% by 26 years.
3. Depending upon the sources, 71–83% of the French declared themselves Catholic in the early 1980s; 72% of Belgians in 1981. In France, according to national surveys, about 14% were regularly practising in 1986, 7% less than in 1974. In Belgium, according to official statistics published by the Catholic Church, regular church attendance during the weekends was down to 22.5% of the total number of inhabitants aged 5 to 69 years by 1985. This was a decline of 0.8 percentage points per annum in the last 12 years. However, the most dramatic decline in church attendance occurred in the preceding

period: 1.7 percentage points per annum from 1968 to 1973; it had previously been 0.6. In the Netherlands, church practice in the Catholic Church declined from 64.4% in 1966 to 17.6% in 1986 of all Catholics 7 years and older registered in the parishes. The most dramatic decline occurred between 1966 and 1973: 4.3 percentage points per annum. During the next 6 years it slowed down to 1.9, and from 1980 onwards to 1.2 percentge points per annum. See Madelin 1988: 60; Harding *et al.* 1986: 37; and Dobbelaere 1988: 94–5, 88–9.

4. According to Köcher 1987: 221, between 1963 and 1967/9 regular church attendance dropped 7%, from a high of 55% of Catholics aged 16 years and older to 48%. In the next 5 years it dropped 13% more to 35% in 1973; it subsequently went down to 32% by 1982. The figures for Protestants were a drop from 15% in 1963 to 10% in 1967/9, 7% in 1973, and even 6% in 1982.

5. See Köcher 1987: 177; Felling *et al.* 1982: 48–9; de Moor 1987: 30–1; Dobbelaere 1984: 103–4; and Harding *et al.* 1986: 40–41.

6. See also Furlong 1988: 121; Cipriani 1989; and Orensanz 1988: 138–9. According to Gabriel and Kaufmann 1988: 163, 'Participation in the (Catholic) Church seems to have regressed over the last twenty years (in Switzerland). In particular, the ties of the young to the Church have grown weaker.'

7. According to Stoetzel 1983: 120, 34% of Catholics and 40% of Protestants attend anywhere from once a month to once a year. The remainder go less than once a year.

8. In 1980, 66% of the children born in France were still *baptized* in the Catholic Church; in Belgium, the figure was 80%. However, in France since 1958 a decline of about 25% has taken place, and the decline is currently at least 1 percentage point per annum. In the Netherlands and Belgium, the decline is 0.8 percentage points a year since the late 1960s. For some years, the number of religious *marriages* was quite stable until the early 1970s: in France, it was 75%, and in Belgium more than 80% of the total number of marriages. Since then, it has gone down. Until the 1980s the rate of decline in France was more than 1 percentage point per annum; the available statistics for Belgian and Dutch Catholics confirm such a decline well into the 1980s. See Maitre 1988: 38, 36, and 35 and Dobbelaere 1988: 88–9 and 94–5.

9. This is also confirmed for Italy; see Cipriani 1989 and Furlong 1988: 121–2.

10. In Belgium, in the mid-1980s, 82% of the population was still buried by the Catholic Church; however, only 69% of marriages were conducted in church. I have pointed out elsewhere that this was not only because some partners were divorcees: the number of people who could have married in the Church but who did not has grown 2.6 times in the last 18 years in Belgium. See Dobbelaere 1987: 49–51.

11. See Cipriani 1989 and Furlong 1988 for Italy and Harding *et al.* 1986: 42 for Spain.
12. See Stoetzel 1983: 115; Felling *et al.* 1983: 70–72; Goddijn *et al.* 1979: 33 and 66; de Moor 1987: 39; Köcher 1987: 166–7 and 202; and Lambert 1988: 56–8.
13. See Harding *et al.* 1986: 48–9. A detailed analysis of Dutch data confirms this: Goddijn *et al.* 1979: 47 and de Moor 1987: 39.
14. Dobbelaere 1984: 82–4: Lambda participation/conception of God is 0.32 versus 0.23 for conception of God/participation.
15. For more details see Gerard 1985: 77–9.
16. See Stoetzel 1983: 253 and Harding *et al.* 1986: 66. See also Phillips and Harding 1985: 108, which describes the effect of age as 'pervasive'; Kerkhofs 1984: 53; Dobbelaere 1984: 87–9 and 92–3; and de Moor 1987: 30 and 44.
17. See Harding *et al.* 1986: 34–71 and Stoetzel 1983: 87–120. For national studies see de Moor 1987: 30–3; Gerard 1985: 68; and Dobbelaere 1984; 102–5.
18. See e.g. Voyé 1973 and Dobbelaere 1966.
19. See Harding *et al.* 1986: 45–9 and 55–62; Gerard 1985: 63; de Moor 1987: 24–5, 38, and 42–5; Dobbelaere 1984: 73 and 87–94; and Voyé 1988.
20. For a more detailed exposition of the ideas of Luhmann used here, see Beyer 1990 and Dobbelaere 1985.
21. The Catholic Church has also stimulated such thinking with its legitimation of the so-called natural method of birth control. This method in particular is based on observations, calculations, and planning.
22. See Thung *et al.* 1985: 157–9 and 194–5; Felling *et al.* 1982; 1983: 144–7.
23. For more elaborate argumentation, see Dobbelaere 1988: 98–100.

References

Balandier, G. (1985), *Le Détour* (Paris).
Berger, P. (1967), *The Sacred Canopy: Elements of a Sociological Theory of Religion* (New York).
Beyer, P. (1990), 'Privatization and the Public Influence of Religion in Global Society', *Theory, Culture and Society*, 7: 373–95.
Cipriani, R. (1989), ' "Diffused Religion" and New Values in Italy', in J. Beckford and T. Luckmann (eds.), *The Changing Face of Religion* (London), 24–48.

Dobbelaere, K. (1966) *Sociologische analyse van de Katholiciteit* (Antwerp).
—— (1984), 'Godsdienst in België', in J. Kerkhofs and R. Rezsohazy (eds.), *De stille ommekeer: Oude en nieuwe waarden in het België van de jaren tachtig* (Tielt), 67–111.
—— (1985), 'Secularization Theories and Sociological Paradigms: A Reformulation of the Private–Public Dichotomy and the Problem of Societal Integration', *Sociological Analysis*, 46: 377–400.
—— (1986–7), 'Vrijzinnigheid, kerkelijkheid en kerksheid in een geseculariseerde wereld: grensvervaging of nieuwe grenzen?', *Tijdschrift voor de Studie van de Verlichting en het Vrije Denken*, 14–15: 283–311.
—— (1987), *Het 'Volk-Gods' de mist in? Over de kerk in België* (Louvain).
—— (1988), 'Secularization, Pillarization, Religious Involvement, and Religious Change in the Low Countries', in T. Gannon (ed.), *World Catholicism in Transition* (New York), 80–115.
—— and Wilson, B. (1980), 'Jehovah's Witnesses in a Catholic Country', *Archives de sciences sociales des religions*, 50: 89–110.
Felling, A., Peters, J., and Schreuder, O. (1982), 'Identitätswandel in den Niederlanden', *Kölner Zeitschrift für Soziologie und Sozialpsychologie*, 34: 26–53.
—— —— —— (1983), *Burgerlijk en onburgerlijk Nederland* (Deventer).
—— —— —— (1986), *Geloven en leven* (Zeist).
Furlong, P. (1988), 'Authority, Change and Conflict in Italian Catholicism', in T. Gannon (ed.), *World Catholicism in Transition* (New York), 116–32.
Gabriel, K., and Kaufmann, F.-X. (1988), 'Catholicism in German-Speaking Central Europe', in T. Gannon (ed.), *World Catholicism in Transition* (New York), 147–68.
Gerard, D. (1985), 'Religious Attitudes and Values', in M. Abrams, G. Gerard, and N. Timms, (eds.), *Values and Social Change in Britain* (London), 50–92.
Goddijn, W., Smets, H., and van Tillo, G. (1979), *Opnieuw: God in Nederland* (Amsterdam).
Greeley, A. (1985), *American Catholics since the Council: An Unauthorized Report* (Chicago).
Harding, S., and Phillips, D. with Fogarty, M. (1986), *Contrasting Values in Western Europe: Unity, Diversity and Change* (London).
Hemert, M. van (1980), '*En zij verontschuldigden zich . . .': De ontwikkeling van het misbezoekcijfer 1966–79* (The Hague).
Hervieu-Léger, D. (1986), *Vers un nouveau Christianisme? Introduction à la sociologie du Christianisme occidental* (Paris).
Kerkhofs, J. (1984), 'Ethische accenten', in J. Kerkhofs and R. Rezsohazy (eds.), *De stille ommekeer: Oude en nieuwe waarden in het België van de jaren tachtig* (Tielt), 39–65.

Köcher, R. (1987), 'Religiös in einer säkularisierten Welt', in E. Noelle-Neuman and R. Köcher (eds.), *Die verletzte Nation: Über den Versuch der Deutschen, ihren Charakter zu ändern* (Stuttgart), 164–281.

Lambert, Y. (1988), 'Retour ou recul du religieux chez les jeunes?', *L'Année sociologique*, 38: 49–62.

Luckmann, T. (1979), 'The Structural Conditions of Religious Consciousness in Modern Societies', *Japanese Journal of Religious Studies*, 6: 121–37.

Luhmann, N. (1977), *Funktion der Religion* (Frankfurt).

Madelin, H. (1988), 'The Paradoxical Evolution of the French Catholic Church', in T. Gannon (ed.), *World Catholicism in Transition* (New York), 57–79.

Maitre, J. (1988), 'Les Deux Côtes du miroir: Note sur l'évolution religieuse actuelle de la population française par rapport au catholicisme', *L'Année sociologique*, 38: 33–47.

Moor, R. de (1987), 'Religieuze en morele waarden', in L. Halman, F. Heunks, R. de Moor, and H. Zanders (eds.), *Traditie, secularisatie en individualisering: Een studie naar de waarden van de Nederlanders in een Europese context* (Tilburg), 15–49.

Orensanz, A. (1988), 'Spanish Catholicism in Transition', in T. Gannon (ed.), *World Catholicism in Transition* (New York), 133–46.

Phillips, D., and Harding, S. (1985), 'The Structure of Moral Values', in M. Abrams, G. Gerard, and N. Timms (eds.), *Values and Social Change in Britain* (London), 93–108.

Sasaki, M., and Suzuki, T. (1987), 'Changes in Religious Commitment in the United States, Holland and Japan', *American Journal of Sociology*, 92: 1065–76.

Stoetzel, J. (1983), *Les Valeurs du temps présent* (Paris).

Thung, M., et al. (1985), *Exploring the New Religious Consciousness* (Amsterdam).

Tocqueville, A. de (1986), *De la démocratie en Amérique II* (Paris). First published in 2 vols. in 1835 and 1840.

Voyé, L. (1973), *Sociologie du geste religieux: De l'analyse de la pratique dominicale en Belgique à une interprétation théorique* (Brussels).

—— (1985), 'Au-delà de la sécularisation', in *Lettres pastorales: Informations officielles du diochèse de Tournai*, i. 253–74.

—— (1988), 'Du monopole religieux à la connivence culturelle en Belgique: Un catholicisme "hors les murs" ', *L'Année sociologique*, 38: 135–67.

—— and Remy, J. (1985), 'Les évolutions divergentes du monde catholique Belge', *La Revue nouvelle*, 81: 227–41.

Wadsworth, M., and Freeman, S. (1983), 'Generation Differences in Beliefs: A Cohort Study of Stability and Change in Religious Beliefs', *British Journal of Sociology*, 34: 416–37.

Wallis, R. (1984), *The Elementary Forms of the New Religious Life* (London).

Wilson, B. (1976*a*), 'Aspects of Secularization in the West', *Japanese Journal of Religious Studies*, 3: 259–76.

—— (1976*b*), *Contemporary Transformations of Religion* (Oxford).

—— (1982), *Religion in Sociological Perspective* (Oxford).

—— (1985), 'Secularization: The Inherited Model', in P. Hammond (ed.), *The Sacred in a Secular Age* (Berkeley), 9–20.

—— and Dobbelaere, K. (1987), 'Unificationism: A Study of the Moonies in Belgium', *British Journal of Sociology*, 38: 184–98.

Yonnet, P. (1985), *Jeux, modes et masses: La société française et le moderne, 1945–1985* (Paris).

3

When the Sacred Returns:
An Empirical Test

PHILLIP E. HAMMOND AND MARK A. SHIBLEY

INTRODUCTION

As the most articulate and prolific exponent of the secularization thesis, Bryan Wilson has been called upon to do battle with those for whom this thesis is unacceptable. 'Secularization', Wilson consistently maintains, is 'that process by which religious institutions, actions, and consciousness, lose their social significance' (Wilson 1966: xiv). Since, in the eyes of many, religion is still around, and in many places even vibrant, this thesis must be in error. Thus, for example, some point to the much greater church attendance in America than in Great Britain, and, averring the US to be the more secular society, challenge the notion that with secularization religious institutions lose their 'social significance'. Others see in the spate of so-called new religious movements emerging worldwide after the Second World War ample evidence not of secularization but of sacralization.

All this disagreement Wilson has met with equanimity but also a fierce defence. Perhaps his combative perspective was best evoked by Daniel Bell's 'The Return of the Sacred?' (Bell 1977), to which he responded in the *Journal for the Scientific Study of Religion* (Wilson 1979). 'Return' is not the proper concept, Wilson argues; a social pattern that may once have existed and then disappeared does not *reappear*, however prevalent may be some of the constituent elements of that pattern. In the process of retreating, the pattern plus the elements that comprised it will have changed. For Wilson, then, the sacred does not return in any usual sense, which would imply

a re-sacralization, a return to an apprehension of the supernatural, not only widespread in society but also having a profound effect on the culture. It implies new devotions and new dedication amounting to more than merely private sentiments, more than voluntary association of the like-minded for weekly acknowledgement of their shared intellectual, moral, and emotional disposition. And it suggests objective social legitimation of these apprehensions. (Wilson 1979: 279–80)

But in fact such a re-sacralization does not occur, Wilson insists. What happens instead is a change in meaning. Religious beliefs and practices may still obtain, but their relationship to the rest of social life will be different from the situation in the earlier pattern. New religious organizations may emerge, but they will not have the economic, political, legal, and cultural 'significance' that their predecessor organizations may once have had. Persons committed to such organizations may feel themselves just as committed as earlier generations did—and, in fact, may be just as committed— but their relationship to the organization cannot help but be altered in meaning because the meaning of that organization's relationship to the wider society has been altered. Secularization, Wilson argues, is a one-way process.

THE ISSUE IS JOINED

Opponents of the secularization thesis are thus obliged to show that, in 'returning', the sacred regains what it has lost. And the proponents of the thesis are obliged to show that, despite certain outward similarities between the old and the renewed, people's religious beliefs and practices do not mean what they once meant.

Despite the greatly circumscribed nature of our research data, we have an unusual opportunity to test almost exactly this issue. We have a sample of 645 persons reared as Roman Catholics of whom 407 have remained Catholic. Included also are 143 who, though reared Roman Catholic, dropped out of the church for a period of at least two years but have since 'returned'. Finally, this sample of persons reared Catholic contains 95 who not only dropped out of the Catholic Church but remain out and have not identified with any other religion.[1] We make the reasonable assumption that the act of dropping out of the Roman Catholic Church by persons raised in it is a reflection of 'secularization', and that returning is, in some sense, a 'reversal' of this secularization. Therefore, the group of 'returnees' is the critical population here: Do they resemble more the 'loyalists' who never left the Church? Or do they resemble the 'drop-outs' who left and never returned? That is the issue we address here.

ON RETURNING

As we shall now observe, returnees to the Catholic Church are, on most matters touched upon in the interview schedule, somewhere between those who never left the Church and those who left and never came back. Table 1 provides the evidence on an array of items, the first group reflecting what we can call 'attitudinal piety' the second group 'behavioural piety'. Of course, evidence of the sort contained in Table 1 does not directly address the issue of this essay. If loyalists are red-hot and drop-outs ice-cold, then returnees are lukewarm; while not surprising, these findings by themselves are therefore not very helpful in our quest. But they make the quest intriguing; what are we to make of this 'lukewarmness'?

The next table tells a different story, however, for it shows in what way returnees resemble loyalists far more than they do drop-outs. The items of Table 2 have to do with good and evil and

TABLE 1. *Loyalists, returnees, and drop-outs compared on piety issues (as percentages)*

Piety	Loyalists (n = 407)	Returnees (n = 143)	Drop-outs (n = 95)
Attitudinal. Agree that:			
Most churches today have lost the real spiritual part of religion.	41	56	76
The rules about morality preached by churches are just too restrictive.	34	43	62
The Bible is the actual word of God, and is to be taken literally.	33	25	9
Behavioural. Report:			
Weekly attendance at church	65	47	1
Reading the Bible at home within the past year	51	46	26
Always or usually saying grace at home before meals	35	24	9

transcendent reward and punishment. These would seem to be areas of concern largely left behind by those who dropped out and never returned but not really relinquished in the case of returnees. Such concerns may indeed be a factor in the decision to return.

The first two lines of the table are easy enough to interpret. Belief in eternal life and the Devil is the dominant position among loyalists and returnees, but is a minority position for the drop-outs. Something of the same message is contained in what we call the 'Morality Index', as a brief explanation will show. The Morality Index is the combination of people's answers to four questions: questions about premarital sex, homosexual relations, and abortion, to which people could respond that these things are always, usually, only sometimes, or never wrong, and a fourth question asking for agreement or disagreement with the idea that 'the husband ought to have the main say-so in family matters'. On this fourth item we counted agreement as indicative of a traditional moral position (+1) and disagreement as indicative of an alternative moral position (−1). Similarly, each 'always wrong' answer to the first three items was counted as reflecting a traditional viewpoint (+1), each 'never wrong' as reflecting an alternative viewpoint (−1), and other answers as reflecting an in-between (0). In Table 2, therefore, the category 'Traditional' includes those whose combined answers totalled +1, +2, or +3; the category 'Alternative' includes those whose combined answers totalled −1, −2, or −3; and the 'In-between' category includes persons who gave a mix of answers,

TABLE 2. *Loyalists, returnees, and drop-outs compared on beliefs and moral issues (as percentages)*

	Loyalists (n = 407)	Returnees (n = 143)	Drop-outs (n = 95)
Believe in:			
Eternal life	89	88	48
The Devil (Satan)	66	65	25
Morality index:			
Traditional	43	30	15
In-between	22	32	18
Alternative	35	38	67

or else consistently chose neither a + nor a − response and thus scored 0.

The central point is that returnees, while not as traditional in this sexual–family sphere as the loyalists, are just as *in*frequently found as the loyalists in the alternative camp. One can almost sense that, in dropping out, these returnees were showing some displeasure with the rigidity of their Church on these moral matters. But one can just as readily sense that, in coming back, they are registering dissent from the alternative moral perspective found outside the Church. Returnees therefore are far more likely to be in the in-between category. When looked at in combination with their responses to the questions regarding eternal life and the Devil, therefore, these once-lapsed Catholics do seem to resemble their never-lapsed counterparts.

If the above interpretation is correct—and proof would require time-series data we do not have—then returnees only *resemble* loyalists; they are not the *equivalents* of loyalists. Put another way, we can say that the 'lukewarm' answers given by returnees and reported in Table 1 are what they are because returnees share many of the beliefs and practices of the loyalists, but do not share the loyalists' *feelings* about those beliefs and practices. Those beliefs and practices mean something different to many, if not all, returnees.

Why this should be the case is the question we turn to next, where the social marginality of returnees' relationship to the Church will be examined. What we discover is that, in terms of social marginality, returnees look more like drop-outs than they look like loyalists.

BEING MARGINAL

Because our project anticipated the need for an index of primary-group ties, our interview asked people to think of their very closest friends, the people with whom they felt on most intimate terms. We then asked how many of their neighbours they felt this close to. How many of their relatives outside the immediate family? How many of the people they had grown up with and gone to school with? We asked about some other categories, too—workmates, fellow ethnics, fellow church members—but because not everybody has a job, identifies ethnically, or belongs to a church, we restricted our measure of primary-group ties to the first three questions: How many of their neighbours, relatives, and school chums did they feel close to? Their combined answers became our index of primary-group ties.

For the entire sample, this measure of friendship was found to be strongly related to involvement in a church, a finding that accords with general wisdom in the sociology of religion. Church-going is, among other things, a community matter, and the closer one is to one's community, the more likely one is to be associated with a church. This generalization held for the Catholics in our sample, but the question we now put was whether—as we would expect—such primary-group ties also served to inhibit dropping out and—an issue for which we would have no expectation—whether primary-group ties were related also to the phenomenon of returning.

The first question is easily answered. Nearly half the persons scoring at the low end of the index had dropped out. Approximately a third of those in the middle categories had dropped out. But fewer than a quarter of those with high index scores had done so. Clearly, being socially embedded in the network of nearby people inhibits dropping out of the Church. What was not so predictable is the fact that primary-group ties not only inhibit departure from the Church but also appear to encourage (though with less force) eventual return by those who do depart. This is to say that social network ties, the weakness of which apparently 'permits' dropping out, also help determine whether drop-outs will return.

Analysis showed some other characteristics that drop-outs were also likely to have: males dropped out more than females, the young (born since the Second World War) more than the old, and the better educated more than others. Also, those identifying ethnically with national origin groups having historic, monopolistic ties to Roman Catholicism (e.g. Italy, Ireland, Mexico, Spain, and Poland) remained loyal more frequently than those identifying ethnically with national origin groups having historic but not monopolistic ties to Catholicism (e.g. Austria, Belgium, Canada, France, and Germany), who were more loyal than those who identify with an ethnic group with no particular religious link, at least in America (e.g. China, India, Japan, and Yugoslavia) or those indicating no ethnic identity at all.

These four characteristics—being male, young, better educated, and having no ethnic identification with a Catholic culture—can be conceived as demographic predispositions to drop out or stay. Indeed, in combination, they show just this pattern, with those having none of these characteristics reporting only a 16 per cent drop-out rate, but those with more of the characteristics having close to a 50 per cent rate. What is worth noting, however, is that this set of demographic characteristics acts in a way analogous to the friendship index: among those with a low predisposition to drop out, the relatively few who did drop out returned at a sizeable rate (79 per cent). As people move up this predisposition scale, not only does their drop-out rate increase, but their return rate decreases (to a low of 40 per cent). In other words, the forces that encourage leaving also discourage returning.

MARGINALITY AND THE MEANING OF CHURCH INVOLVEMENT

We come, then, to the critical test. Returnees are midway between drop-outs and loyalists in Catholic beliefs and practices. In moral perspective they are closer to loyalists than to drop-outs. Where they differ most from loyalists—and resemble most their fellow drop-outs who never returned—is in their social ties to the Church. Table 3 provides the evidence.

The first three lines of Table 3 document what has already been implied. In terms of primary-group ties, returnees look more like drop-outs than they do loyalists. The second line of this table is, if you please, an independent confirmation of the earlier argument; not only are returnees less embedded in a close network of friends, but the friends they have are even less likely to know *each other* than the friends of either drop-outs or loyalists. The third is simply one specific indication of this marginal position; ethnic ties are important to returnees only to the same degree that they are important to drop-outs, which is less than their importance to loyalists.

The underlying issue of this investigation, however—whether, in returning, returnees recreate the prior relationship with the Church—is best answered in the last three lines of Table 3. The fourth line makes a fairly obvious point, that loyalists regard their

TABLE 3. *Loyalists, returnees, and drop-outs compared on social ties to the Church (as percentages)*

Social ties	Loyalists	Returnees	Drop-outs
High in primary-group ties	40	24	23
Most of one's close friends know each other	54	43	49
Most of one's close friends are of the same ethnicity	51	40	39
Membership in one's congregation is very important	42	27	—
Feel close to many of the people known at church	26	15	10
Regards oneself as a 'strong' Catholic	62	39	39

congregational membership as far more important than do drop-outs—who, by definition, have no congregational membership. In this context, for returnees to indicate a 'lukewarm' position is to recapitulate the earlier pages of this essay. It is really in the fifth and sixth lines of Table 3 that we see the most convincing evidence that bears on the theoretical question of the 'meaning' of returnees' return. The fifth line indicates that returnees resemble drop-outs in the matter of 'feeling close' to fellow church members, while the sixth line—probably the most telling of all—shows that, in terms of self-identity as 'strong' Catholics, the returnees are no more enthusiastic than the drop-outs. Both lag significantly behind the loyalists, and, perhaps more telling, the drop-outs continue to regard themselves as 'Catholic' at the same rate as returnees.

CONCLUSION

Without data drawn from different times in the lives of the same people, we are handicapped in inferring causation from survey data. Obviously, returnees' and drop-outs' answers to our questions are influenced by their actions, and thus may be as much effect as cause. Nevertheless, the portrait presented here has a coherence that fits better the Wilson than the Bell image of how the 'sacred' returns, if and when it does. Put succinctly, on the basis of these data on American Catholics in the late 1980s, 'returning' to the

Church after a significant period of non-involvement is far more a matter of assent to doctrine and resumption of pious practices than it is a resumption of social ties and thus the overlapping of one's religious identity with one's other identities. It is not, in other words, a resumption of the 'social significance' of religion.

In the debate in which Bryan Wilson has been so vigorous a combatant, therefore, we have to come down on the Wilson side. Yes, indeed, church membership and doctrinal assent can fluctuate, increase as well as decrease. But, while decreases may clearly signal secularization, increases are not exactly the reversal of that secularization. At least on the basis of the evidence here, the 'return' of the sacred is associated more with change than it is with the *status quo ante*.[2]

Notes

1. An additional 105, not included in the analysis here, are persons who were reared as Catholics but now identify themselves religiously with some non-Catholic group. The data are from telephone surveys with randomly selected adults (aged 24–60) in California, Massachusetts, North Carolina, and Ohio, conducted during October and November 1988. Approximately 650 interviews were conducted in each state.
2. The authors are indebted to the Lilly Endowment for the grant making possible the study on which this chapter is based.

References

Bell, D. (1977), 'The Return of the Sacred?' *British Journal of Sociology*, 28: 419–90.

Wilson, B. R. (1966), *Religion in Secular Society* (London).

—— (1979), 'The Return of the Sacred', *Journal for the Scientific Study of Religion*, 18: 268–80.

4

Some Reflections on the Parallel Decline of Religious Experience and Religious Practice

SABINO ACQUAVIVA

The substance of the criticism of some rather traditional empirical and experimental approaches to the sociology of religion is that religious practice is not a good photograph of religiousness or even an out-of-focus image of it. The criticism of this criticism is that it can be demonstrated that religious experience is closely correlated with liturgy and with religious practice. Until very recently, the former thesis seemed to be prevalent. But the progress that has been made in empirical and experimental research, especially in the psychology of religion, enables us to reconsider the problem again today after an interval of a few years. I will try to explain why.

Personally I tend to accept Wilson's definition of secularization (1985: 11–12) which holds that, 'In essence, it [secularization] relates to a process of transfer of property, power, activities, and both manifest and latent functions, from institutions with a supernaturalist frame of reference to (often new) institutions operating according to empirical, rational, pragmatic criteria.' By secularization Wilson means the process whereby religious institutions, actions, and consciousness lose their social significance. In short, Wilson (1985: 19) claims that 'The system no longer functions, even notionally, to fulfill the will of God.' Thus, what the ideas of salvation that are found in the universal religions now share is above all their reassurance (Wilson 1985: 14). But if religion reassures, it manifestly has psychological functions, and is destined to survive so long as society fails to satisfy human needs. To put it succinctly, society rejects religion intellectually without taking account of the cost of all this in terms of the emotional support which men need in order to live (Wilson 1976: 80 ff.).

This interpretation of secularization refers, at least implicitly, to the motives of action and to the type of experience that lies behind new (or old) patterns of action and the meaning attributed to reality. In fact, it is impossible to speak of secularization without asking questions such as: Is the secularization of institutions, powers, activity, and so forth, which Wilson discusses, a consequence of the change in motives of action or of organization—and, therefore, in religious experience? In short, is the secularization of society the product of a change in the motivation to act which is, in turn, influenced/motivated by the decreasing or increasing extent of religious experience (and vice versa)?

It seems possible to me to demonstrate that a theory of secularization presupposes a theory of action and that a theory of action in the religious field requires, in turn, a theory and analysis of religious experience as a profound motive for action, for interpretation, and for the generation of meaning. But in the context of a secularizing society, one of the reasons for having religious experience can be found in the sublimation of unsatisfied psychological needs as a function of the search for reassurance within the limits and with the characteristics that Wilson proposed above.

The question we are dealing with should, therefore, be discussed in this logical context. But a different question must be tackled first: If religious experience is the central nucleus of religion, in the sense in which it has been described above, are there still a considerable number of people who continue to have religious experiences and who, therefore, explain and interpret things religiously? If this is not the case, the problem I have raised would be practically irrelevant. It can be demonstrated roughly that the percentage of those who have had a religious experience during the last few years is quite large. Studies have shown that it varies from a minimum of 30–35 per cent (Greeley 1975; McCready and Greeley 1976; Wuthnow 1976; Gallup 1976) to a maximum of about 65 per cent, with a peak of 88 per cent according to a series of micro-sociological and psychological studies (De Sordi 1988; Ruzzon 1989; Battistin 1989; Faietti 1990; Acquaviva 1991).

Greeley (1975) asked interviewees if they had ever had the sensation of being near a power that projected them outside themselves. Thirty-three per cent answered this question affirmatively, whereas 34 per cent gave positive answers to a similar question in a study by Thomas and Cooper (1977). In studies by Hay (1979, 1987), at least 30 per cent of the respondents claimed that they had had such experiences. Nevertheless, on this point, we also need to take account of the findings by Glock and Stark (1965), Back and Bourque (1970), Greeley (1975), Wuthnow (1976), and Hay and Morisy (1978).

Hay (1979)—perhaps the most thorough among these scholars—put a question analogous to Greeley's, but slightly more limited, to a sample of postgraduate students. The question was: 'Do you feel that you have ever been aware of or influenced by a presence or a power, whether you call it God or not, which is different from your everyday self?' The percentages of affirmative answers were higher than those reported by other authors (Greeley 1975). But the reasons for the difference are clear enough, even if the influence of the different level of education in this sample compared with a random sample is discounted. Greeley, for example, writes of an experience that lifts one outside oneself. This question is thus more radical than that posed by Hay. So, pending further investigation, we can answer in the affirmative to the preliminary question: religious experience is fairly widespread in society, but we are often dealing with a sort of invisible religion. And up to this point, it seems to confirm some of the hypotheses related to the theory of secularization.

But, having verified the existence of a considerable degree of religious experience, we now come to the problem that interests me more. Some research in this field seems to demonstrate that religious practice, participation in liturgy, and religious experience are partially independent of each other. The analysis of some of this research—for example, Hay 1979 and Greeley 1975—tends in this direction. Nevertheless, in spite of these differences which are attributable to other factors, other analyses point to interesting relations between religiousness (in the form of religious experience), membership of religious groups, and participation in liturgy.

The proof of what I have affirmed is found in some of the results of Hay's research that are supported by others. Not least of these are the studies cited above which were conducted by my collaborators and me in Italy (De Sordi 1988; Ruzzon 1989; Battistin 1989; Faietti 1990; Acquaviva 1991). So, among denominational Christians the ratio between the 'aware' and the 'not aware' is approximately 4 to 1; among 'Christians' about 3 to 1; and among

TABLE 1. *Awareness*[a] *of a presence or power compared with present religious denomination or faith*[b]

	Aware	Not aware
Denominational Christian	11	3
'Christian'	16	5
Neither of these	38	21
Totals	65	29

[a] 'Awareness', in Hay's formulation, can be understood as an indicator of experience.
[b] Six cases excluded from table because 'not sure'.
$\chi^2 = 1.693 \ p > 0.03$
Source: Hay 1979

TABLE 2. *'Were or are there particular circumstances in which the experience is most likely to occur?'*

Alone or in silence	35
Times of severe distress or decision	34
Close to nature	26
With close or trusted friends	21
Times of great happiness or peace	15
During prayer or devotions	13
In darkness or dim light	12
At a church service	12
Before works of art; in old churches	10
No special circumstances	8

Source: Hay 1979

the others nearly 2 to 1. In addition, the conditions in which religious experience is verified are also significant, especially conditions that indicate a more or less consistent relation with the practice of worship or of prayer.

It emerges from the study, previously cited, of one of the Italian samples drawn from the region of Venice (De Sordi 1988: 91), but from others as well, that the most favourable circumstances for the occurrence of a religious experience were prayer (37 per cent) or participation in religious rites (26 per cent), even if the interviewees declared that the experience occurred in a secluded place (3 per cent), alone (20 per cent), or in silence (42 per cent). The latter circumstances are difficult to reconcile with being in a church during a service.

The feelings that appear in the English sample (Hay 1979, 1987) are typically associated with the experience of 'the radically other' (Acquaviva 1979, ch. 1). The interviewee, in fact, feels 'at peace' (62 per cent), 'ecstatic or joyous' (38 per cent), and so on. These data are also confirmed, on the whole, by the investigations—previously cited—that were conducted in Venice.

But let us try to take a step forward by looking in more detail at the social dimension, quantitative and qualitative, of religious experience and thus, at the dynamic of the phenomenon in question, precisely by evaluating the relationships between religious experience, church membership, religious practice, agnosticism, and atheism, while keeping the problem of secularization as a backdrop. Table 3 shows that the ratio of 'aware' to 'not aware' is about 7 to 1 for believers and about 1 to 1 for agnostics and atheists.

Hay's data are therefore clear: people who are members of an organized religious structure (Table 1) or who have a religious faith (Table 3) are more likely than others to have a religious experience. And those who are generally religious (or better Christians) have more intense experiences than those who do not fall into any of the above categories. This is true for Western industrial societies.

Moreover, these data are confirmed not only by Hay's comments in his most recent book (1987), in which the data are reported in less detail, but also by McCready and Greeley (1976: 144), who claim that the features which are associated to varying degrees with

TABLE 3. *'Awareness of a presence or power' compared with religious belief* [a]

	Aware	Not aware
Believers	40	6
Agnostics and atheists	25 (23 + 2)	23 (20 + 3)
Totals	65	29

[a] Six cases excluded because 'not sure'.
$\chi^2 = 34.6 \; p < 0.001$
Source: Hay 1979

membership in an organized religion are among the most important factors in stimulating religious experience, while other factors have little or no influence.

Furthermore, the connections between religious experience, religious membership, and participation in liturgy are confirmed by the fact that the four factors whose presence is very positively associated with religious experience are prayer, listening to a sermon or a lecture, attending a religious service, and reading the Bible. Clarifying the relationship between 'experience of a presence' and religious practice helps to throw further light on the phenomenon.

It should be clear by now that to understand secularization and the decline of religiousness, at least when looking at the evolution of the last few decades as well as considering the problem in a wider historical perspective, it is important and possible to know the trend of religious practice and of non-belief. This is because we are increasingly able to determine with greater precision what percentage of the various categories (religious practitioners, non-practitioners, agnostics, atheists) have religious experiences and perhaps invisible religion. It is not difficult to establish (precisely on the basis of the presumptive magnitude of experience for each category and of the way in which the categories change over time) the downward trend of religious experience, and therefore to measure the real process of secularization-desacralization.

The following series of findings largely confirm these conclusions. First, a 1985 Gallup poll on religious experience found that 45 per cent of respondents in the USA and 33 per cent in the UK reported

TABLE 4. *Awareness of a presence or a power compared with church attendance now*[a]

	Aware	Not aware
Regular or occasional attender	23	3
Seldom or never attend	42	24
Totals	65	27

[a] Eight cases excluded either because 'not sure' or because data on church attendance not known.
$\chi^2 = 5.544\ p < 0.02$
Source: Hay 1979

having these experiences. It is impossible not to see a connection between these two findings in the fact that religious practice in the USA is higher than in the UK.

Second, elderly people in the UK report much more intense religious experience than the young. By contrast, the difference between the old and the young in the USA is slight. This is probably because of the relative stability of religious practice in the latter country. With reference to the findings of the Gallup polls of 1975, 1976, and 1985 in the USA that the difference between the young and the old in religious experience is negligible, Hay notes: 'This is exactly what we would predict, because there has been no decline in church-going in the United States during the twentieth century comparable to the steep drop in Britain' (Hay 1987: 126).

Third, many studies find that a higher frequency of religious experience is found in areas in which the percentage of church-goers is greater. In short, the results of our research in Italy confirm that religious experience is strongly associated with church member-ship.

Fourth, if 43 per cent of 'churched' Americans claim to have had a religious experience, only 24 per cent of the 'unchurched' make the same claim.

If there is a difference, then, between the person who practises a religion and the person who is a religious being, the two phenomena are nevertheless in some way connected. And if the religious experience *per se* does not happen during liturgical practice, it is still more likely to occur among participants in the various churches. This, I repeat, is also found in the series of Italian studies some of which have already been cited (Garelli 1986; Piarotto 1987; De Sordi 1988; Ruzzon 1989; Battistin 1989; Faietti 1990; and Acquaviva 1990, 1991) which, except for Garelli's, have all been carried out in northeastern Italy by the Department of Sociology at the University of Padua. Battistin and Faietti worked with the same data, but whereas Battistin focused on a sub-sample of 100 individuals, Faietti's findings clearly demon-strate over a wide area that the Italian situation is analogous to that of other countries. Comparable results have emerged from other data which were extracted by a deeper analysis of the sample mentioned above (Acquaviva 1991).

To sum up, if we consider the occurrence and intensity of religious experience (moving in descending order from religious

TABLE 5. *Intensity of experience as a function of religious stance, as assessed by the individual concerned*

Religious stance	Intensity of experience							No answer	Total
	High intensity	Very intense	Intense	Low intensity	Not intense	Other[a]			
Practising believer	94	309	477	88	22	16	226	18	1250
	7.52	24.72	38.16	7.04	1.76	1.28	18.08	1.44	52.08
Non-practising believer	30	77	214	99	28	20	309	8	785
	3.82	9.81	27.26	12.61	3.57	2.55	39.36	1.02	32.71
Agnostic	1	12	23	18	13	2	153	2	224
	0.45	5.36	10.27	8.04	5.80	0.89	68.30	0.89	9.33
Atheist	2	5	10	4	0	2	112	0	135
	1.48	3.70	7.41	2.96	0.00	1.48	82.96	0.00	5.63
No answer	0	0	0	1	0	0	5	0	6
	0.00	0.00	0.00	16.67	0.00	0.00	83.33	0.00	0.25
Total	127	403	724	210	63	40	805	28	2400
Per cent	5.29	16.79	30.17	8.75	2.63	1.67	33.54	1.17	100.00

[a] They haven't lived the experience.
Source: Acquaviva 1991

practitioners to non-practitioners and from agnostics to atheists) (Hay and Morisy 1978; Hay 1979, 1987) and if we connect them to the data that the 'macro' indices offer (which show the collapse of regular practice, the loss of non-practising believers, and the growth of agnostics and atheists), we arrive at the conclusion that there is an association between secularization, the abandonment of religious practice, church membership, faith in a diversity of sacred cosmoi, and the decline of religious experience and finally of the presence—even if invisible—of religion in society. It follows that religious experience is closely connected to the mechanisms whereby religious meaning is attributed to reality in the manner suggested by Wilson (I use the term in the very wide sense in which it is used by Greeley and Hay). It is influenced by participation or non-participation and by declining rates of participation in church services. And this is so, regardless of the religion being considered.

It seems necessary, before going further, to review briefly the logical framework of my reasoning. First of all, I repeat that we are able to hypothesize fairly precisely that a relationship exists between participation in religious services and religious action (or more widely liturgy) on the one hand and religious experience on the other. We can, therefore, recover the significance of a large proportion of the studies (in the field) over the last thirty years which were tied to the use of indices of religious practice. In fact, as I have demonstrated, the use of the indices that were employed for the first phase of the crisis of religion in industrial and post-industrial, modern and postmodern society was correct, even if it was insufficient—especially in more recent years—for an exhaustive understanding of the phenomenon.

These conclusions confirm the view of past researchers, who always maintained that religiousness had been declining for decades, if not centuries. In addition, this decline was also allegedly demonstrated by the progressive and parallel decline of religious practice (Acquaviva 1979).

Anyone wishing to refute this hypothesis would have to do so by proving that the hypothesized relationship between religious experience and religious practice does not exist. That is, it would be necessary to demonstrate that it is untrue that religious experience is more frequent among practitioners than among non-practitioners, among believers than among agnostics, and among agnostics than atheists. This kind of argument can only be refuted by entering the 'game' with analogous empirical or experimental means. Consequently, attempts to refute the argument by inappropriate methods, as is often the case in the sociology (or philosophy) of secularization or the political sociology of religion, operate in a different dimension.

In these circumstances, perhaps it may now be possible to deal with the problem of secularization and desacralization in a new way which maintains firm connections between experience and behaviour, or between experience and attitudes towards institutions and the meanings attributed to them. This enables us to tackle the problem correctly by asking ourselves (by means of a strictly empirical and experimental approach) when, how, to what extent, under what conditions, and in what situations do individuals have (or no longer have) intense religious experiences. That is, we are able to establish, group by group, movement by movement, institution by institution, the extent, the conditions, and the meaning of a religious life for individuals and for society. Finally, we can therefore ask ourselves, but with good knowledge of the case and by using the instruments of experimental research, how far it makes sense (or nonsense) to talk of secularization.

But the search for the relationship described above between indices and religious experience shows that the experience is in decline. This does not simply change the way in which religious needs are met; it also changes the quantity and intensity of the supply and demand of satisfaction. Admittedly, charismatic and similar groups, new oriental religious sects and groups, astrology and modern satanism, have emerged in recent years, but, as the statistics demonstrate, these are minority groups which represent the rearguard, and they are extremely volatile (Wilson 1976). In addition, adherence to 'newly coined' religious groups (such as many sects and groups of oriental origin) is transitory. This fact is confirmed by some of the studies in the field (Bird and Reimer 1982: 14).

In conclusion, it seems to me that two solid points emerge from this argument. First, secularization is a complex process which is inseparable from the points that I have made above and cannot, therefore, be studied without taking account of the motivations to act which derive specifically from religious experience and without using the highly refined psychological means at our disposal.

Second, the relation between religious experience, faith, agnosticism, and atheism on the one hand and religious membership and practice on the other demonstrates that the crisis of religion, including invisible religion (and religious experience), is still in process. In short, religion (and religiousness), even considering their precise anthropological roots and given the sociocultural conditions, have diminished in contemporary society (and will probably continue to diminish), at least in the short and medium term.

In saying this, I am not contradicting the claim that I made in my earlier book that it was possible to discover 'an unconscious sacred motivation even in desacralized symbolism and myths' (Acquaviva 1979: 201). This claim is empirically supported by the opportunities offered more recently by the analysis of religious experience and of the relationship between religious experience and the religious sublimation of unsatisfied needs (Acquaviva 1991) which I have partially accounted for in these pages, albeit within the limits that I stipulated.

References

Acquaviva, S. (1979), *The Eclipse of the Holy in Industrial Society* (Oxford: Blackwell).

—— (1990), *Eros morte ed esperienza religiosa* (Eros, Death, and Religious Experience) (Bari: Laterza).

—— (1991), *Eros morte ed esperienza religiosa nell'Italia nord orientale. Risultati provvisori* (Eros, Death, and Religious Experience in Northeast Italy) (University of Padua).

—— and Stella, R. (1989), *Fine di un'ideologia: la secolarizzazione* (The End of an Ideology: Secularization) (Rome: Borla).

Back, K., and Bourque, L. B. (1970), 'Can Feelings be Enumerated?', *Behavioral Science* 15: 437–96.

Battistin, C. (1989), *Amore, morte ed esperienza religiosa: quale rapporto?* (Love, Death, and Religious Experience: How are they Related?) (University of Padua).

Bird, F., and Reimer, B. (1982), 'Participation Rates in New Religious and Para-religious Movements', *Journal for the Scientific Study of Religion*, 21/1: 1–14.

De Sordi, P. (1988), *Eros, paura della morte ed esperienza religiosa a Treviso* (Eros, Fear of Death and Religious Experience in Treviso) (University of Padua).

Faietti, S. (1990), *Amore, morte ed esperienza religiosa nel Trevento* (Love, Death, and Religious Experience in the Triveneto) (University of Padua).

Gallup, G. (1976), '31% Experience Religious Union', *Hartford Courant*, 11 December, 6.

Garelli, F. (1986), *La religione dello scenario* (The Religion of the Stage) (Bologna: Il Mulino).

Glock, C. Y., and Stark, R. (1965), *Religion and Society in Tension* (Chicago: Rand McNally & Co).

Greeley, A. M. (1975), *The Sociology of the Paranormal. A Reconnaissance* (Beverly Hills, Calif.: Sage).

Hay, D. (1979), 'Religious Experience amongst a Group of Postgraduate Students. A Qualitative Study', *Journal for the Scientific Study of Religion*, 18/2: 164–82.

—— (1987), *Exploring Inner Space* (Oxford: Mowbray).

—— and Morisy, A. (1978), 'Reports of Ecstatic, Paranormal or Religious Experience in Great Britain and the United States: A Comparison of Trends', *Journal for the Scientific Study of Religion*, 17/3: 255–66.

McCready, W. C., and Greeley, A. M. (1976), *The Ultimate Values of the American Population* (London: Sage).

Martelli, S. (1990), *La religione della società postmoderna tra secolarizzazione e desecolarizzazione* (Religion in Postmodern Society between Secularization and Desecularization) (Bologna: Dehoniane).

Piarotto, C. (1987), *Cultura e valori in evoluzione nel comune di Mirano* (Culture and Values in Evolution in the Commune of Mirano) (University of Padua).

Ruzzon, M. (1989), *Eros, morte ed esperienza religiosa nel Conselvano* (Eros, Death, and Religious Experience in the Commune of Conselve) (University of Padua).

Thomas, L. E., and Cooper, P. A. (1977), 'The Mystical Experience: Can it be Measured by Structural Questions?', paper presented at the annual meeting of the American Sociological Association, Chicago.

Wilson, B. R. (1976), *Contemporary Transformations of Religion* (Oxford: Clarendon Press).

—— (1985), 'Secularization: The Inherited Model', in P. E. Hammond (ed.), *The Sacred in a Secular Age* (Berkeley, Calif.: University of California Press), 9–20.

Wuthnow, R. (1976), 'Peak Experience. Some Empirical Tests' (Berkeley, Calif.: Survey Research Center Working Paper Series).

5

Buddhism in the Modern World: Secularization or Protestantization?

RICHARD F. GOMBRICH

If I have any claim at all to publish among sociologists of religion, it can only be because of the inspiration and direct help I have had from Bryan Wilson. In the late 1960s and early 1970s I regularly attended his seminars. I learnt so much from them that I like to regard myself as a pupil of his, a fellow pupil of that cohort of young scholars whom he trained in those days when our all-knowing central authorities still facilitated true scholarship and who then scattered to enliven and strengthen the sociology of religion in Britain and around the world. Unlike them, I never had the benefit of Bryan's supervision; but I have seen him as a model, both for the interest and cogency of his hypotheses and for the pains he takes to ferret out every relevant fact.

1. THE PROBLEM

Bryan Wilson's account of secularization in modern Western society is famous; like many other people, I have found it as eloquent in expression as it is convincing in substance. He has also turned his attention to the effects and varieties of Christianity in other changing societies, notably in Africa. But until recently he has said little about societies dominated by scriptural religious traditions other than Christianity or the impact of the modern world upon them. On 27 May 1988, however, he gave a remarkable lecture in the Nissan Institute here in Oxford on 'Japanese new religions'. So far as I know, the analysis he presented there of the religious movements which have arisen among Japanese Buddhists approximately since the end of the Second World War (though a few are slightly older) has not yet been published. Nevertheless, I would like to benefit from its stimulus and use this opportunity to react to it. My own knowledge of Japanese Buddhism is extremely slight and superficial—I do not know the language, I have spent only six weeks in Japan, and I have never studied the topic systematically—but that lecture gave focus to some of my musings on the resemblances and contrasts between religious developments in modern Japan and those in the Buddhist society with which I am familiar, Sri Lanka. Over a number of years Gananath Obeyesekere and I (he more than I) have investigated religious belief and practice among Sinhala Buddhists in Colombo and in other parts of society less conservative than the old agricultural villages typically frequented by anthropologists, and we have recently published a book, *Buddhism Transformed: Religious Change in Sri Lanka* (1988), which in my own work I think of as the second half of the diptych I began with *Precept and Practice: Traditional Buddhism in the Rural Highlands of Ceylon* (1971). For corroborative details of fact and argument which there is no room to supply here, I must refer the reader to *Buddhism Transformed*.

The term 'Protestantization' was introduced into the study of Sinhala Buddhism by Obeyesekere about twenty years ago[1] and has become quite common in studies of Indian religions. Obeyesekere, wishing to characterize the kind of Buddhism which arose in Ceylon from about the middle of the nineteenth century under European influence, chose the term for its double meaning: that the movement was both a protest against the Protestant missionaries (and the colonial power behind them) and in many ways a mirror image of their attitudes and activities. The protest element, a reaction to political circumstances, has virtually faded away; what is of lasting interest, and of value for comparative studies, is a cluster of features which resemble developments in the European Reformation. Obeyesekere and I have written:

The essence of Protestantism as we understand it lies in the individual's seeking his or her ultimate goal without intermediaries. In Christianity this means rejecting the priest and the saint as essential links between men and god; in Buddhism it means denying that only through the Sangha [the community of monks and nuns] can one seek or find salvation, *nirvāna*. The most important corollaries of this rejection are spiritual egalitarianism, which may or may not have consequences for practical life, and an emphasis on individual responsibility that must lead to self-scrutiny. Religion is privatized and internalized: the truly significant is not what takes place at a public celebration or in a ritual, but what happens inside one's own mind or soul. At the same time religion is universalized: its injunctions apply to everyone at all times and in all contexts. (Gombrich and Obeyesekere 1988: 215–16)

This formulation makes no reference to what Weber called 'the Protestant ethic' of 'this-worldly asceticism'. That ethic was not our main concern, but it did strike some Asians as an essential feature of Protestantism before they could have read Weber. To show that 'Protestantization' is no arbitrary academic construct, I give an example from India, dated 1916:

the Parsee race is now passing through *a period of transition* in this country at the time when the West is slowly pouring into the East and eddies and whirlpools in goodly numbers are created. A Protestant race is fast developing among the Zoroastrians of Western India, while their brethren in old Iran are still adhering to their ancient catholic ways. In spite of this if the community is renowned to-day for 'probity, high morality, truthfulness and charity', it does seem as though the whole body of Zoroaster's teachings is indeed a 'priceless treasure'. (Pithawalla 1916: 5)

In Christian societies of the West, including those which have remained Roman Catholic, Protestantization has apparently been a stage on the road to secularization. Of this latter concept I need only say that it refers to the diminution of the part played in people's lives by religion.

In this paper I shall look at Protestantization and secularization in Buddhist societies, using Sri Lanka and Japan as examples. I believe that Buddhist institutions and ideology require us to question some of the assumptions we may have acquired in learning about religious history and sociology by studying the Christian West. On the other hand, I think that both concepts have heuristic value elsewhere too. The most obvious form of secularization is the assumption by other institutions of functions that religious institutions used to perform—for instance, physical healing, formal education, care of the poor. A certain amount of such secularization can be seen throughout the world today, and in this sense both Japan and Sri Lanka are fairly secularized. If, however, we look rather at the part religion plays in people's hearts and thoughts and in their private rather than their public actions, the picture is quite different: Sinhala Buddhists are by no means secularized, and indeed are probably less so than they were fifty years ago, while

Japanese Buddhists are considerably secularized, but in a form rather unfamiliar to the modern West. To me it seems clear that secularization in the first, institutional sense depends largely on economic development (except when it is purely a political imposition, as it was in the Soviet Union. Where economic goods are not too scarce, the state or the market provides for most material needs). Whether the subsequent spread of secularization into private lives is equally dependent on wealth (of the society, not of each individual) I have not studied enough societies to say, but it seems to me plausible that it should be so.

What about Protestantization? Japan gave little scope to Protestant missionaries from the West; in fact, they were totally excluded until 1859 and not admitted freely until the 1870s. There were Protestantizing movements within Japanese Buddhism in the twelfth and thirteenth centuries, but the sects (Jōdo, Nichiren, and, above all, Jōdo Shin) in which these were embodied later reverted to the clerical pattern of the other sects; in that sense the early movements petered out, and did not directly affect modern developments. I believe that Protestantization has played little part in modern Japan, despite certain apparently Protestant features of the religious scene today, notably lay leadership; that turns out to be unremarkable when seen in the framework I propose. (The 'Protestant ethic' I shall leave aside; peasants change values when they become businessmen, and bourgeois values are widespread in Colombo and Tokyo, but how closely a high rate of reinvestment is linked to religious individualism has been disputed in studies of the Reformation as well.) Unlike the Japanese, very many Sinhala Buddhists of Sri Lanka have been Protestantized, but among them it has led to what I call a 'dual economy of the spirit'. If my analysis is plausible, it means both that secularization may occur without being preceded by Protestantization (Japan) and that even in the modern world Protestantization is compatible with increasing irrationality (Sri Lanka).

2. BUDDHISM'S DICHOTOMY BETWEEN RELIGION AND SECULARITY

The distinction between the things of this world and those of the next is fundamental to all the religions which began in ancient

India, though many thinkers, including the Buddha, regarded 'the next world' as a spiritual condition attainable in this life rather than a place or condition to be reached after death. It is tempting to identify this distinction with that in the Christian tradition between the religious and the secular (or between the sacred and the profane). However, such an identification would be seriously misleading, because the Indian religious traditions consign to the secular (Sanskrit: *laukika, aihika*) category a great deal of what Christians class as religious. For the Buddha and his followers (I shall now stick to them), salvation (*nirvāṇa*), which consists in the elimination of greed, hatred, and delusion, is attainable only by the individual on his own behalf, and is characterized as wholly other than phenomenal existence as we normally experience it. The latter is inherently characterized by impermanence, suffering, and lack of any enduring essence.

The world has neither a creator nor a beginning in time, and the gods (and other spirit beings) too are mortal; like all sentient beings, they die, and are reborn according to their moral deserts. Gods are powerful and on the whole good, but their power and goodness are finite. The benefits they can grant to human beings, such as health and wealth, are irrelevant to salvation. What Christians call 'petitionary prayer' is therefore a secular matter, like asking powerful people for help.

We human beings find ourselves in a world permeated by suffering, so that anyone who hopes to save himself must leave the world—i.e. society. The Buddha founded a community of monks and nuns, the Sangha, as a support structure for salvation-seekers. Members of the Sangha are supposed to take no part in worldly affairs; in particular, they are forbidden economic dealings (including the ownership of more than a few specified items of personal property) and all sexual activity. Bryan Wilson has written of religion that 'part of its business is to discipline the emotions' (Wilson 1976: 3); but it would hardly be an exaggeration to say that this is the *whole* business of early Buddhism. The only further element necessary for salvation is gnostic, the realization of impermanence, suffering, and non-self; and to this gnostic element the Mahayana, which developed at the beginning of the Christian era and then spread to China and Japan, gave greater emphasis. But in Theravada, the form of Buddhism which spread to Sri Lanka in the third century BC and has been there ever since, the original emphasis on emotional control has never faltered. Salvation requires total self-control. This is not to say that Buddhists cultivate impassivity, let alone catatonia; for, on the contrary, a Buddhist strives for omni-benevolence, but his emotions must be at his command.

For lay Buddhists too, their Buddhism was primarily a matter of socialization and self-control, but on a more modest scale. Lay Buddhism is a classic case of what sociologists since Weber have (perhaps unfortunately)[2] called an 'insufficiency ethic': the lay life was deemed inherently wanting, in that it did not provide the environment necessary for advanced spiritual progress. Since such progress depends on meditation, and that in turn on privacy, this judgement seems realistic. The laity were provided with a moral code, couched largely in prudential terms, which involved some self-discipline of a highly rational character; and the moral advice which the Buddha gave them, with its approval of diligence, thrift, and calculated generosity, has the distinctive flavour of Weberian 'this-worldly asceticism'. Meanwhile, social arrangements such as caste were considered as little the concern of Buddhism as the fulfilment of worldly wants; and the same goes for calendrical and life-cycle ceremonies. All these 'secular' affairs were left in place to proceed as before, providing only that they did not contravene Buddhist ethical principles—for instance, by taking life in animal sacrifice.

Buddhism thus sees itself purely as a soteriology. Salvation, the Buddha preached, is an individual achievement and essentially internal, a mental event. All that matters ultimately is to cultivate one's mind. The value of an act lies, accordingly, in the intention behind it. By a law of the universe (which one has to take on trust), good intention will ultimately be rewarded, and wicked intention punished; and this will continue through a series of rebirths until the mind has been so purified that there is no longer any desire left to fuel the process.

This doctrine has many characteristics of a Protestant reform.[3] By locating value in intention rather than in visible deeds, it substituted for the hierarchic particularism of caste society a religious egalitarianism: intentions are intrinsically good or bad, regardless of the intender's outward circumstances, and so all moral agents are on the same footing. This teaching made priests and their rituals irrelevant to salvation; conscience became the

arbiter of spiritual progress. Buddhism regarded itself as a rational
spiritual technology, and called its goal 'seeing things as they are'
(Pali: *yathā-bhūta-dassana*). Is Buddhism the first Protestant
movement in recorded history? A modern Christian might find
irony in such a claim when we add that the Buddha invented
organized monasticism. But the Buddha lived in a society which
was either pre-literate or at least overwhelmingly non-literate, with
no extended written texts. I would argue that under such
circumstances a two-tier system (with an 'insufficiency ethic') is
inevitable: if the religion is to survive, it can only be through
specialists who preserve the sacred texts orally—even if they have
no other priestly functions. Indeed, there is evidence that other
radical religious movements of the period failed to survive and that
that failure may have been due to weak organization (Gombrich
1988*a*).

All the traditions and regional variants of Buddhism have
inherited the original dichotomy between the supramundane and
the worldly, and have reflected it in their institutional arrangements.
The Sangha has remained the body of men and women who were
themselves the true salvation-seekers and who preserved Buddhist
doctrine (concretely, the texts) for others. The society at large has
seen 'Buddhism' as the specific concern of the Sangha, and the laity
(often including the rulers) have regarded it as their prime Buddhist
duty just to support the Sangha, not necessarily even trying to
understand what the Sangha was about. For its worldy concerns,
each Buddhist (or partly Buddhist) society has turned to a system of
'interaction with culturally postulated superhuman beings'[4]—a
local religion. In Japan this local religion was given a name—
Shintō, as against Butsudō (Buddhism)[5]—but in other Buddhist
countries it often has no single designation; nowadays anthropologists of Sri Lanka tend to refer to it as 'spirit religion'. As these
local religions are mostly non-literate and have little or no recorded
history, it is tempting to tag them as wholly indigenous. But they
contain elements of diverse origin; in particular, all of them include
features which arrived from India in Buddhism's cultural baggage. I
was struck by the number of Indian deities one encounters in Japan,
and though they seem usually to be referred to there as 'Buddhist
gods', they are, of course, as gods, worldly not salvific.

These local religions in Buddhist countries have considerable
similarity. Bryan Wilson's characterization[6] of Shintō would apply

to all of them: they are largely unorganized, decentralized folk religions with no moral philosophy; they centre on phenomena which penetrate the daily world and are highly particularistic; they provide thaumaturgic services for individuals (giving worldly benefits); and they are also concerned with local communities (they incorporate agricultural and other calendrical festivals and are invoked in common crises such as war and epidemic).[7] Furthermore, in all Buddhist societies, at least until well into this century, the only life-cycle ritual in which Buddhism and its sacralia have played much part is death—the obvious occasion for turning one's mind to ultimate matters. For Buddhists even marriage has been a secular affair—or perhaps one should say *especially* marriage, given that marriage is the central institution for the orderly perpetuation of society and for enjoying life's comforts—in other words, for all that on which the ideal Buddhist turns his back.

Real life, of course, has been less tidy than the norm. Already in the very earliest texts[8] we find the pan-Indian assumption that practised meditators acquire supernormal powers; the Buddha is at pains to deny the importance of such powers, not their existence. The sacredness of Buddhist monks and texts, relics and statues, has been interpreted by the laity as magic power, and harnessed for worldly purposes. Since most translations of Buddhist texts from Indian languages into Chinese are dated, we can trace the history of Buddhist acceptance in China, and see that much of its early attraction was belief in its rain-making and other thaumaturgic powers. Similarly, it was mainly for its superior magic that Buddhism was patronized by the Japanese court from the seventh century onwards. Naturally, the monks and nuns obliged. But the evidence of the texts which they composed and transmitted shows that they rarely lost sight of the distinction between secular and transcendent goals. Texts describing the use of spells (*mantra*) and cosmograms (*maṇḍala*) for secular purposes were translated into Chinese from the third century AD on, but not till the eighth century do we find a text which (clearly under Hindu influence) prescribes such ritual means as a short cut to salvation.[9] Moreover, no Buddhist, so far as I know, has ever thought that a god could save him;[10] if (as in *tantra*) he meditates on a god, it is to realize that god's ultimate lack of essence—to see the god as a projection of his own mind.

3. BUDDHIST SECULARITY IN SRI LANKA AND JAPAN

There is evidently no law that a society has to have a soteriology, let alone that all individuals must believe in or practise one. Though Buddhism flourished in Sri Lanka for well over a thousand years after its introduction, the Sangha there has had some acute crises during the present millennium, and the ordination succession which permits the Sinhala Sangha to perpetuate itself actually died out in the sixteenth, seventeenth, and eighteenth centuries, being renewed on each occasion by missions from the Southeast Asian mainland.[11] The doctrine, meanwhile, was preserved in monastic libraries. Had we academics from a remote and alien culture first discovered Sinhala culture at almost any point in the seventeenth century, we would have found a nominal allegiance to Buddhism but hardly any beliefs or practices in operation but those of the spirit religion. Indeed, it is not necessary to put this hypothetically. Robert Knox, the original of Robinson Crusoe, was a captive near Kandy in central Ceylon from 1660 to 1679, and then wrote a wonderfully lively and informative account of his experiences (Knox 1911). In Buddhist terms, Sinhala society and all its doings at that time, when they had no fully ordained monks[12] or nuns, were entirely secular (*laukika*). The Buddha figures in Knox's account only as 'another great God . . . unto whom the Salvation of Souls belongs' (Knox 1911: 115).[13] Not only then, but in traditional village society even now, people do not believe that they can attain or even make much progress towards *nirvāṇa* until the time of the next Buddha, in the remote future.

The society Knox lived in was small and homogeneous, and had been permeated by Buddhism for more than two thousand years. Many of the attitudes he found were still peculiar to Buddhist civilization (Gombrich 1971: 114, 210, 259, 264–5). Moreover, Ceylon is next to India, and some central elements of its Buddhism are found in Hinduism too: notably the belief in rebirth according to one's deserts. Japan, by contrast, is far from India, and has been heavily influenced by Confucianism. Among the Buddhist laity this has greatly weakened belief in rebirth and in the operation of karma, since that belief is logically incompatible with the idea at the centre of the ancestor cult: that one's dead parents and forebears are available to serve as tutelary deities for the household.[14] The

Sangha in Japan has never died out since its foundation, but its powers and influence have at times been drastically curtailed. In particular, Buddhism was organizationally tightly controlled and ideologically undercut by the state in the period up to 1945. Moreover, as happened in Sri Lanka and elsewhere, the traditional learning of the Sangha lost most of its prestige with the general public after the introduction of Western knowledge and education in the nineteenth century (Gombrich 1988*b*, chs. 7 and 8, esp. p. 197).

Buddhist soteriology, the truly 'Buddhist' half of what outsiders see as the religion of Buddhists, has thus been very weak in Japan for a long time, even though most people identify themselves as Buddhists. Perhaps it has always been weak. Nowadays academic observers, like politicians, count heads and take everyone into account. The voices from the past, however, are those of the élite—the powerful and, above all, the educated. In Japan, as in other Buddhist societies, most of those voices belonged to monks, nuns, or laity educated in Buddhism. But perhaps a social survey of Japan at the time of Robert Knox would not have revealed much more knowledge of Buddhism than what Ronald Dore found in central Tokyo in 1951:

The question: 'What religion are you in your family?' produces in overwhelming proportions the reply 'Buddhism', which refers to the fact that a family has a family temple on whose services it calls if need be. On the other hand, the question: 'Do you personally have any religious belief?' produces eighty-eight noes out of a hundred. (Dore 1958: 329)

Of Dore's respondents, 88 per cent claim *no* religious belief, rather than no specifically *Buddhist* belief. I shall return to this below. First, however, let me remark that I think that my analysis explains the apparently startling fact about new Japanese religions which Bryan Wilson pointed out in his lecture: that the 'salvation' they purvey is not other-worldly. Christian sects, he reminded us, maintain an ascetic moral rigour and a sense of sin, demanding that their adherents separate themselves from the world's wickedness. Salvation will be attained after death, and though it may be experienced by a resurrected body, it will definitely be a non-sensual experience, a purely 'spiritual' joy. Like Christian sects, and new religions everywhere, the Japanese new religions promise a short cut to salvation; but, unlike the Christians, they locate that salvation in this world. For them, salvation does not necessarily exclude hedonism. The founder of Soka Gakkai proclaimed three goals: beauty, goodness, and benefit. (The prominence given to aesthetic pleasure is typically Japanese.) Normal human enjoyments, even golf (by the movement P. L. Kyōdan) are religiously legitimated. Apart from their this-wordly character, the very multiplicity of their goals sets these movements apart from what it seems to me useful to regard as soteriologies.

To a Buddhologist, all this makes perfect sense: these new religious movements are, in Buddhist terms, secular (*laukika*). What else, a Buddhist traditionalist would ask, would one expect of movements headed by laity? It fits this pattern that the religions are not, to my knowledge, anti-clerical: they simply ignore the Sangha and all it stands for. In this they contrast with the recent Sinhala Buddhist sects described in *Buddhism Transformed*; Sri Lanka has come under Protestant influence, Japanese Buddhism has not. In some cases at least, Buddhist sacralia preserve a very traditional position. For example, the Reiyūkai is a large new religion in which the central concern is the prosecution of the usual Japanese cult of ancestors (Hardacre 1984). It is headed by a highly intelligent layman, Mr Tsugunari Kubo, and considers itself Buddhist. A few portions of the *Lotus Sutra* are recited by adherents at their rites, without any regard for their meaning, much as the laity have uncomprehendingly recited Buddhist texts in archaic Chinese for centuries. On the other hand, Mr Kubo, at the helm, has written a doctoral thesis on the *Lotus Sutra*, published it as a large and handsome volume, and uses some of the movement's funds to maintain a magnificent Buddhist research institute for scholars. In other words, he and his followers stand to Buddhism just as most Buddhist monks and their lay supporters and parishioners have stood to Buddhism down the centuries.

4. UN-PROTESTANT SECULARISM IN JAPAN

This may all be secular in traditional Buddhist terms, but how secular is it in the language of sociology? Clearly somewhat. To start with, Mr Kubo has written a book on the *Lotus Sutra* although he is a layman. Moreover, new religious movements such as his, as Bryan Wilson pointed out in the lecture, have many secular features, being styled somewhat like business corporations, with emphases on public relations, bureaucratic competence, and general technical efficiency. However, the adherents of new religions, though influenced no doubt by secular trends in society, are not people in whose lives religion has come to play little part; nor do they seem to live by Protestant-style universalization of the priesthood. What, then, of the 88 per cent of Dore's sample who claimed to have no religious beliefs?

In the same book, Dore shows that many of those he studied continued to perform religious rituals, notably for their ancestors, even though some of them said that the rituals were meaningless or that they did not believe in the existence of the spirits they were 'worshipping'. Dore

is led to wonder whether this can continue for long. In a society in which 'rationality' is increasingly emphasized in all spheres, the view may be expected to spread that to worship non-existent beings—albeit as an expression and demonstration of socially-approved attitudes—is 'like making fishnets when there are no fish'. Moreover, since, ultimately, the social approval accorded to these attitudes—the belief in their absolute intrinsic value—is logically linked to a body of ideas which involve the existence of spirits, scepticism on the latter score cannot fail to affect the absoluteness of the value attached to the attitudes. (Dore 1958: 328)

I agree with Dore that some decline in ritual observance is to be expected, and I believe that it has been found in more recent research. But I would not expect Japanese secularization in this sense to be at all dramatic. I remarked above (following Bryan Wilson) that Shintō, like the other local religions that have complemented Buddhism, has no moral philosophy—one might have said, no ideology—and is highly particularistic and embroiled in the workaday world. Folk religion the world over is much more a matter of doing than of thinking. Bryan Wilson has written that 'No religion can solemnize electronic controls' (Wilson 1976: 103); but not long ago I saw in a Dutch newspaper a photograph of a Japanese priest conducting a funeral ceremony for a huge heap of vandalized telephones.

Protestants have always been hostile to ritual; indeed, in British Christianity the degree of anti-ritualism is the chief index of Protestantism.[15] At the same time, they assume that ritual has a meaning and is normally performed for a purpose beyond itself—instrumentally. Dore asked his respondents for the meaning of their acts of worship at the domestic ancestral shrine; not only were their answers very varied, but many seem to have found the question confusing. Admirably, Dore goes on to report that ancient Chinese scholars in the Confucian tradition

clearly expressed that the spirits 'have neither substance nor shadow', but that rites are performed '*as if* the deceased enjoyed the sacrifice' ... because sacrificial rites represent 'a state of mind in which our thoughts turn with longing (towards Heaven, the Ancestors) ... It is the climax of all those ritual prescriptions we embody in patterned behaviour.' (Dore 1958: 327)

The Confucians thus had a 'conscious "sociological" awareness of the function of rites for society' (ibid.).

Dore doubts whether such a sophisticated attitude could ever be held by most people in a society, and again I agree. But I am not aware that anyone has ever pointed out that a somewhat similar view of ritual was articulated also in ancient India by brahmin ideologues. The school of 'systematic reflection' (*mīmāṃsā*) denied that rituals required any external justification: they held that rites had to be performed simply and solely because they were enjoined (by the Veda); any account of their rationale, whether in terms of their origins or their benefits, was entirely secondary. Even the gods to whom the sacrifices were offered were ultimately to be defined as the names uttered in the ritual, and were thus drained of all independent existence.

The *mīmāṃsaka* theorists agreed with the Confucians that rites were meaningless; but, unlike them, they did not claim that performing rites had a function for society.

The Buddha, in his Protestant spirit, had no use for rituals. He differed from Christian Protestants, however, in regarding them not as noxious but simply as irrelevant to his only concern, salvation. Though Theravada Buddhism is astonishingly meagre in its ritual, certain ritual observances for the laity find their charter as far back as the Pali Canon itself. The Buddha is supposed to have said shortly before his death that if people offered flowers or incense to a stupa or gave it a lick of paint, it would make their thoughts serene and so help them to get to heaven.[16] He thus proposed a functionalist view of ritual which, on the one hand, is entirely consistent with his doctrine that everything essential happens in the mind and, on the other, is not so unlike the Confucian view cited above. (There is no likelihood of influence.) In Sri Lanka I found the same rationale for acts of worship still preserved by the monks in Kandyan villages (Gombrich 1971: 117–8). Dore encountered the same argument when he attended a Shintō shrine in Tokyo to hear a lecture on 'The Inari Faith' (Inari is a Shintō cult). 'The most striking feature of the talk was its apparently sceptical objectiveness . . . The only positive statement of any belief was . . that the object of worshipping at an Inari shrine was to purify one's heart so that one could face the daily task in a true spirit of piety' (Dore 1958: 349–50).

Though, admittedly, one would like more evidence, I think that Dore's data from Japan and mine from Sri Lanka suggest that a sophisticated view of ritual as beneficial in itself, regardless of any magical powers or metaphysical meaning, is quite widespread in Buddhist societies. Moreover, I see no reason to doubt that for many people ritual, even when performed without belief, does meet an affective need—a very familiar tenet of psychoanalysis. If all this is so, there is no reason to expect a sharp decline in ritual practice as society becomes increasingly 'rational'.

5. SINHALA BUDDHISM'S 'DUAL ECONOMY'

Sinhala Buddhism may, I feel, yield to a somewhat more Christo-centric analysis. In ancient India the brahmin pundits, in Japan the Confucian scholars, have been a non-Buddhist class competing with Buddhist monks to supply a detached, non-superstitious view of ritual and theistic observance. In Sri Lanka the only traditional intellectuals have been the monks. When colonial domination, Western education, the spread of literacy, and other factors discussed in *Buddhism Transformed* deprived the Sangha of their cultural leadership (in substance—they retained symbolic trappings), the whole religious sphere came to be seen in the terms set by the Protestant missionaries and familiar to the modern Western world. Buddhism, being atheistic, was defined as a philosophy, an ethical system, a way of life—in fact as anything but a religion, though it had been 'corrupted' into one over the centuries—and the spirit religion was seen as just folk superstition. That Buddhism was not a religion left Sinhala Buddhists rather confused, as I have described elsewhere (Gombrich 1971: 62–3; Gombrich and Obeyesekere

1988: 221–3); but many modernists among them have been happy to consider it as a religion for practical (e.g. political) purposes (Gombrich 1988*b*: 199), but in truth superordinate to other religions—a position strikingly similar to Bultmann's theology of Christianity.

The Sinhala Protestant view of Buddhism came through contact with missionaries, and began among the *haute bourgeoisie*. Anagarika Dharmapala (1864–1933), the most important figure in the movement, came from this class; he was educated in British-run schools, and kept his diary in English. Obeyesekere and I have shown that Dharmapala favoured rationality and poured scorn on folk superstitions—although he believed in astrology, which he (like many others) thought scientific. Our book shows, however, that Dharmapala's successors have come to accept the spirit religion, albeit often with a guilty conscience: 'It is common for contemporary Buddhists to say, "Of course, *as a Buddhist* I don't believe in those things" ' (Gombrich and Obeyesekere 1988: 210). But we go much further: we argue that as Protestant Buddhism has spread through the population, it has led to a new synthesis in which the spirit religion too has profoundly changed in character so as to answer to the affective needs created both by the disruption of traditional communities and by the starkness of a doctrine which was meant not for laymen but for professional monks. Affective needs are intrinsically hard for an outsider to assess, but it could be that the kind of emotional support the Japanese derive from worshipping their ancestors is what so many Sinhala Buddhists now find in communing with their personal guardian deities (*iṣṭa dēvatā*), a category of being new to their cosmology.[17]

Rather than recapitulate published ideas, I wish here to add a new way of looking at what we flirt with calling 'post-Protestant Buddhism'. I posit a cultural analogue to the dual economy, of which Sri Lanka furnishes a striking example: in the nineteenth century and for the first half of the twentieth, the British ran estates which produced cash crops (first coffee, then tea, rubber, and coconuts) for export, with hardly any direct effect on the traditional rice-growing economy of the Sinhala villagers.

Clearly this is not the kind of differentiation which Bryan Wilson had in mind when he wrote: 'Secularization is associated with the structural differentiation of the social system' (Wilson 1976: 40). Western knowledge and the impact of the world economy may create an illusion that Sri Lanka has a modernized, structurally differentiated society which should be secularizing fast. But the dual economy complicates the picture. Let us take medicine as an example, although almost any institution would do as well. Soon after Independence (1948), in the same period of prosperity that legislated for universal free education, free medical treatment at a far-flung network of cottage hospitals was provided for virtually everyone, so that soon every baby could be born in hospital. A generation later, however, most of the imported Western medicines used by such a medical system were in extremely short supply, and were in effect rationed by ability to pay; and as demand for them rose above supply, the same began to happen to doctors' services. Though the government has never given up trying to provide a free health service for all in need, the poor have been increasingly excluded from good care. The population, excepting only a small upper-middle class, has not yet forgotten more traditional methods of health care: traditional Sinhala medicine (*āyur-veda*), divine intervention secured through visits to shrines, and various forms of white magic. As modern medicine becomes scarcer and more expensive, people naturally revert to these less 'rational' remedies. This is most conspicuously true for complaints of psychosomatic origin induced by the stresses of modern life, for which the overburdened hospital system has no time or understanding. Obeyesekere's investigations at modern, mainly urban shrines have revealed a booming trade not only in healing such complaints, but in the solution of all kinds of practical problems, from family quarrels to passing exams to business anxieties. The clientèle is drawn almost exclusively from the modern section of the economy.[18] Similarly, when I write of a 'dual economy of the spirit', I am not talking of traditional villagers (if by now there still are such people) but of the great mass of people who watch American programmes on television (in a shop or neighbour's house if they are too poor to own a set) and have been drawn into 'modern' life.

In his penetrating study of education in Sri Lanka in the 1970s, Dore deftly sketches how this dualism extends from the economy into the very minds of the Sinhalas. 'When colonial Ceylon began to build schools,' he writes, 'it was, as in Japan, a *discontinuous* beginning. Ceylon did gradually develop élite upper-class schools on the British model; but the culture of that upper class was in itself something largely *created* by the schools, not, as in the case of the

British public schools, something already existing in society which the schools simply transmitted' (Dore 1976: 52). At first this simply created a small body of English-educated Sinhalas so estranged from their traditional culture that they usually spoke English even at home and were often illiterate in Sinhala (and the same goes for the Tamil minority). But education came to be perceived, quite rationally, as the gateway to the modern economy and upward social mobility. Universal free education, including university education, was introduced in 1947. A side-effect, which with hindsight appears inevitable,[19] is that the English medium came to be virtually abolished, and the Sinhala population was educated in Sinhala, the Tamil in Tamil. But the essentially modern character of the school curriculum naturally remained. Dore shows where this has led:

Plans were being made . . . to include an introduction to the stars and the solar system. But there was to be no mention of that essential part which the stars *actually play* in village life as the basis of astrology . . . Deliberately to challenge these traditional beliefs, to declare them incompatible with rational science, might be to sharpen the disjunction between home and school . . . But the truth is that the disjunction exists. It is a reflection of the disjunction within the society as a whole between the modern and traditional sectors, between the bridge-head of rationality and salaried employment and high incomes and all mod cons, and the hinterland of superstition and precarious self-employment. (Dore 1976: 130)

Rising population, rising school enrolment, rising expectations, rising frustration. It is Dore's concern to point out the inevitability of this sequence and to suggest an alternative. He is perfectly right about the problem. As he says, Obeyesekere's investigation into the social origins of the insurgents who revolted in 1971 (Obeyesekere 1974) already showed that most of them were high-school graduates frustrated by their lack of opportunity; and it is easy to see that the same frustration has fuelled most of the disastrous turmoil Sri Lanka has been undergoing ever since. The religious movements which Obeyesekere and I document are largely responses of frustration, expressions of personal crisis induced in enormous numbers of young people and their bewildered parents by the failure of the economy to grow with the population and its expectations.

The religiosity of the new-style shrines which are spreading from

Colombo throughout the densely populated and increasingly violent Sinhala countryside is far less 'rational' than that of traditional Sinhala Buddhism (including its spirit religion). It belongs in type rather to what Bryan Wilson calls 'nativistic Third World movements' (Wilson 1976: 46). Secularization needs help from the economy if it is to progress; in a very poor country it may even recede as modernity brings disruption without the compensation of a rising standard of living.

Notes

1. Notably in Obeyesekere 1970.
2. For a reasoned criticism of the term, see Gombrich 1971: 245.
3. The Protestant character of the Buddha's teaching is more fully explored in Gombrich 1988b, esp. pp. 72–81.
4. The allusion is to Spiro's definition of religion as 'an institution consisting of culturally patterned interaction with culturally postulated superhuman beings' (1966: 96).
5. *Shintō* means 'the way of the gods'. 'The word was coined after the introduction of Buddhism, by analogy with the "Way of the Buddha", *Butsudō*' (Heinemann 1984: 213).
6. In the lecture, according to my notes; I am not quoting verbatim.
7. This paper takes no account of the 'state Shintō' cult sponsored by the government till it was banned by the American occupation. That concerned itself with the national community as a whole, and tried to evolve an ideology to match Buddhism. It is now dead.
8. See e.g. Rhys Davids 1899: 87–9, which is *Sāmaññaphala Sutta*, paras. 85–90.
9. I owe this information to Professor Alexis Sanderson.
10. The reader must not be misled: I am referring to what Buddhists call 'gods'. Moreover, the Buddha's teaching that salvation depends on one's own efforts has been preserved by most traditions. However, some early Indian Mahayana texts (such as the *Lotus Sutra*) unambiguously overturn this tenet and introduce a saviour or saviours, who are Buddhas and Bodhisattvas. Japanese Buddhist sects are split between those which preach that salvation comes by one's own efforts (*jiriki*) and those which preach that it is granted by a salvific Buddha (*tariki*, literally 'other power'). But this split is not relevant to my argument.
11. The order of nuns died out in the eleventh or twelfth century, and has

never been revived. Though there are women who lead cloistered lives, strictly speaking there are now no nuns in Sri Lanka.

12. Some monasteries were inhabited and maintained by a class of men, unique to this period, called *ganinnānsē*, who had only the lower ordination (novitiate). They made no pretence of keeping to monastic discipline, but must have provided a modicum of continuity.

13. The only strictly Buddhist activities Knox mentions are to do with sacralia: the making and worship of images, worship of Bo trees, etc.

14. 'In ordinary speech no distinction is made between the spirits of the dead and the Buddhas and Bodhisattvas' (Dore 1958: 313). Very many Japanese Buddhists still keep shrines to their ancestors in their homes and regularly worship their dead parents. The parents are said to have 'become Buddha', and it would be impious to think that one's parents might have been reborn in some lowly condition. But this appears incompatible with Buddhist cosmology, according to which all creatures are reborn according to their moral deserts, in hell, as animals, as ghosts, as humans, or as gods. For Japanese filial piety, the law of karma seems to have been superseded. A doctrinal resolution of this impasse is sometimes found in the interpretation of the ancient (second century AD?) Indian *Sukhāvatī-vyūha Sūtra*, as popularized by the Jōdo and Jōdo Shin sects, according to which the Buddha Amitābha takes the souls of the dead, regardless of their moral record, to a western paradise, where they reside in bliss, cultivating spiritual perfection. Modern researchers, however, have found most Japanese vague about what happens after death. My unsystematic observations on a recent visit were that even highly educated Buddhists—priests and academics—took ancestor worship so much for granted that they were surprised to hear that Theravada Buddhists do not practise it.

15. The centrality of this issue in the British Reformation is beautifully documented by Keith Thomas. Before the Reformation, he says, 'religion was a ritual method of living, not a set of dogmas' (Thomas 1971: 76). Japanologists, please note.

16. Rhys Davids 1910: 156–7, which is *Mahā Parinibbāna Sutta*, V, para. 12.

17. The personal guardian deity is a new category in Sinhala religion, borrowed from Hinduism. See Gombrich and Obeyesekere 1988: 32–3.

18. For a set of case studies drawn from one Colombo shrine, see ibid. 142–58. For evidence of a somewhat more spectacular kind, see Obeyesekere 1975.

19. Inevitable, because the demands of a modern economy tie schooling in a particular language to employment prospects, and this in turn leads to linguistic nationalism, as brilliantly argued by Ernest Gellner (1983; see esp. ch. 3). That Sri Lanka's export-led economy in due course

backfired, so that only those graduates fluent in English became employable, represents a sad footnote to his thesis: so small an economy has to operate in a world language to prosper.

References

Dore, R. P. (1958), *City Life in Japan* (London).
—— (1976), *The Diploma Disease: Education, Qualification and Development* (London).
Gellner, E. (1983), *Nations and Nationalism* (Oxford).
Gombrich, R. (1971), *Precept and Practice: Traditional Buddhism in the Rural Highlands of Ceylon* (Oxford); reprinted as *Buddhist Precept and Practice* (Delhi, 1991).
—— (1988*a*), 'How the Mahāyāna Began', *Journal of Pali and Buddhist Studies*, 1 (Nagoya, March): 29–46.
—— (1988*b*), *Theravada Buddhism: A Social History from Ancient Benares to Modern Colombo* (London).
Gombrich, R., and Obeyesekere, G. (1988), *Buddhism Transformed: Religious Change in Sri Lanka* (Princeton, NJ).
Hardacre, H. (1984), *Lay Buddhism in Contemporary Japan: Reiyūkai Kyōdan* (Princeton, NJ).
Heinemann, R. K. (1984), 'This World and the Other Power: Contrasting Paths to Deliverance in Japan', in H. Bechert and R. Gombrich (eds.), *The World of Buddhism: Buddhist Monks and Nuns in Society and Culture* (London), 212–30.
Knox, R. (1911), *An Historical Relation of the Island of Ceylon* (Glasgow); reprinted as *Ceylon Historical Journal*, 6 (Maharagama, 1958); originally published 1681.
Obeyesekere, G. (1970), 'Religious Symbolism and Political Change in Ceylon', *Modern Ceylon Studies*, 1.
—— (1974), 'Some Comments on the Social Backgrounds of the April 1971 Insurgency in Sri Lanka (Ceylon)', *Journal of Asian Studies*, 33: 367–84.
—— (1975), 'Sorcery, Premeditated Murder and the Canalization of Aggression in Sri Lanka', *Ethnology*, 14: 1–23.
Pithawalla, M. B. (1916), *Steps to Prophet Zoroaster with a Book of Daily Zoroastrian Prayers* (Poona).
Rhys Davids, T. W. (1899) (trans.), *Dialogues of the Buddha, Part I* (London).
Rhys Davids, T. W. and C. A. F. (1910), (trans.), *Dialogues of the Buddha, Part II* (London).

Spiro, M. (1966), 'Religion: Problems of Definition and Explanation', in M. Banton (ed.), *Anthropological Approaches to the Study of Religion* (London), 85–126.

Thomas, K. (1971), *Religion and the Decline of Magic* (London).

Wilson, B. R. (1976), *Contemporary Transformations of Religion* (London, Oxford, and New York).

6

An Africanist Revisits *Magic and the Millennium*

J. D. Y. PEEL

Magic and the Millennium (hereafter MM) is Bryan Wilson's most complex and ambitious book (Wilson 1973). It displays a formidable control over a vast range of heterogeneous and often refractory source materials, as diverse in the perspectives from which they are written as in the societies with which they deal. It was, as it remains, the most sophisticated study of millennial and related movements in the Third World that has been written. From Nigeria, where I was engaged in field-work, I wrote a review that, as I see on rereading MM, should have been more appreciative than it was.[1] The basic perspective from which I write, however, is still that of a sociologist (or social anthropologist or social historian) with one commitment to the understanding of religious change in one region of West Africa, through its fullest contextualization in terms of local culture and history, and another to theory and comparison as necessary corollaries of that task.

Though MM is itself massively indebted to Weber in very particular ways—notably for the master concept of rationalization—its method sometimes seems to imply a disjunction between the projects of the sociologist on the one hand and the historian or ethnographer on the other, which is characteristic of a much more positivist tradition in sociology. Indeed, if an author's metaphors give the best indication of his deep intentions, then Wilson's image of the historian or ethnographer as providing 'bricks' for the theoretical constructions of the sociologist is noteworthy as a throwback to Spencer (1873), when he is at his most forceful in putting down the historians of his day. Wilson is not, of course, dismissive of the work of historians in the manner of Spencer, for he sees the relations between them as 'mutually informative': the sociologist's comparative analysis should 'help the historian and ethnographer to make better bricks' (Wilson 1973: 502). I wonder if the problems of fruitful interaction are not more intransigent yet.

Though Wilson drew very extensively on the literature on African religious movements up to the late 1960s, *MM* does not seem, in its turn, to have engaged the authors of the new wave of studies of religious movements—particularly of western equatorial and southern Africa—of the 1980s.[2] The theoretical preferences of particular disciplines may be partly responsible: social anthropology has always looked to Durkheim and latterly to Marx, rather than to Weber.[3] Africanists have tended to draw their comparisons from within Africa; and neither know or are known by the world outside as much as they should be. But the main reason, I suspect, is the distance between Wilson's objective—to analyse certain ideal types of sectarian response and their transformations—and what has become the objective of recent African studies: namely, to situate religious movements more fully in local cultural patterns and the long-term processes of historical change. These African studies step outside the monographic frame at the very general level of method or the much more concrete level of regional comparison, whereas ideal types of the kind presented in *MM* fall somewhere in between, dealing as they do with empirical variables of a highly general kind. Yet there can be no doubt of the superiority of Wilson's typology of religious movements, grounded in the theories of Weber and Troeltsch, to the untheorized and regionally specific labels, such as Ethiopian and Zionist, which have been repeatedly used in Africanist analysis.

The theoretical sophistication of *MM* is equally evident when we compare it with the only substantial comparative study of millennial movements to have appeared subsequently, that by the historian Michael Adas (1979). Taking as his cases movements against European colonialism in Java, Chota Nagpur, Tanganyika, Burma, and New Zealand, Adas processes the data on each through a single sequence of categories, from the causes of discontent and the failure of other solutions through prophetic visions to mobilization, rebellion, and suppression. It is a highly structural analysis, in which comparison serves less to deepen analysis of the particular cases through getting a purchase on significant differences than to give backing to one of the older general interpretative themes current in the field, Aberle's application of relative deprivation theory. As Wilson (1973: 498) trenchantly remarked in *MM*, this penchant for some single explanatory key merely 'adds to the problems of comparative sociology by reducing the rigour and exact specification of abstract propositions'.

In what follows I shall try to pursue this goal of more exact specification, believing that the touchstone of sociological theory which really tells is whether it enhances our capacity to understand historical particularities. But before coming to the case in question, we have to examine the form and presuppositions of the theory.

The argument of *MM* is concerned with bringing together two main components: empirical data about 'new religious movements arising among less-developed peoples following cultural contact with Westerners' (Wilson 1973: 1) and a set of ideal types, which specify possible supernaturalist responses to the situations in which these people have found themselves. Working on such a broad canvas, Wilson does not exaggerate what he can achieve by way of explanation. 'Some very broad indictors of causal elements are . . . implied' (Wilson 1973: 498) in the correlations which he discerns between types of situation and types of response, but explanation, properly so called, has to be in terms of very specific, local conditions.

Now any human action, individual or collective, is to be understood in relation to both contexts or circumstances and the attributes which actors bring to them. This context/attribute distinction—between what factors are just externally 'there' and what factors are bound up in the histories of the actors, components of their subjectivity—is not absolute, but relative to just what it is whose explanation is being sought. One actor's attributes are part of the context for other actors. What we call 'culture' is an important part of any actor's attributes and at the same time something embedded in, or organizing, much of the context. So this distinction cannot be identified with the vulgar distinction between 'material' and 'ideal' or 'cultural' factors. Nevertheless, culture—*qua* the specific orientations, values, meaningful symbols, and criteria of judgement which mark particular actors—is fundamental to our understanding of how any kind of social action is produced. Yet culture, though thus centrally placed in Wilson's argument, often has a curiously protean—even fugitive—quality to it.

On the one hand, to the extent that it is closely identified with the 'particularly particular' in the data, culture seems to fall below the level at which the broad patterns of response, to which *MM* addresses itself, are determined. So Wilson distinguishes the 'cultural content' of movements from their orientation (i.e. whether they are primarily thaumaturgical, revolutionist, utopian, etc.) (Wilson 1973: 484). 'Differences in the specific cultural elements that are embraced in the new religious movements', he writes, '. . . must not obscure the syndrome of response in which cultural symptoms are organized' (Wilson 1973: 69). The metaphor seems to convey a crossed message here. For if culture is a 'symptom', it is something which reveals the underlying problem to the observer, but is not itself a cause of it. At the same time, it appears, culture in its specificity may 'obscure' the syndrome in which we are essentially interested. The idea that culture needs to be disregarded or eliminated as a variable if social-structural effects are to be clearly discerned is common enough in the achronic, Durkheimian tradition of comparative social anthropology.[4] But Wilson's Weberian interest in the orientations and dynamics of religious movements does not allow him to dispose of culture in this manner.

So there is culture and culture. 'The circumstances of religious movements' emergence and persistence concern us, but the intricacies of their theological arguments do not' (Wilson 1973: 29). This latter is clearly taken to be a trivial form of culture. But the circumstances with which it is here contrasted are not conceived in a purely material fashion, for they too include culture: 'Our purpose is to consider the cultural circumstances in which approximations to each pure type of response arise' (ibid. 130). Important here is something which may variously be treated as part of the circumstances or as an attribute of the actors: the degree of 'cultural socialization' attained by the society in question (ibid. 193). A fundamental condition for many of the ecstatic or millennialist responses which *MM* describes is that among 'less-developed peoples . . . the emotions are subject to much less self-control [*sc.* than in the modern West] and are more easily summoned for collective behaviour' (ibid. 309). The level of emotional self-discipline, explicitly linked to the growth of rationality in thought and organization, is taken as a key indicator of cultural development. The Weberian affinities of this argument are plain. Perhaps less so are the Spencerian ones; but both in concept and in substance, this is all but 'adaptation to the social state', that process by which human character evolves over long stages to be better equipped for perfect social life, in which emotional self-mastery is a crucial element (Spencer 1850).[5] The concept of culture employed here is not the relativist Boasian concept of modern anthropology, but the non-relativist, evolutionary concept used by Tylor.[6] In terms of the contrast with which Norbert Elias (1978) introduced *The Civilizing Process*, it is closer to 'Zivilisation' than to 'Kultur', a universal human progress rather than particular ways of life.

Elias's *The Civilizing Process* differs from *MM* in that it is a commentary on the history of a single society, or rather a group of closely related societies—namely, those of Western Europe—over a specified period. *MM*'s treatment of history is much more complex, since it works at a macro and a micro level, and at each level in forms both concrete and abstract. At the macro level there is the concrete (albeit here only outlined) history of the impact of the West on the world outside Europe. Informing this concrete history is an abstract process of cultural development or rationalization, which can only be realized, and is only partly realized, through it. At the micro level, there are the concrete histories of numerous religious movements, richly contextualized in local experiences of social change. Finally, there are abstract, or ideal-typical, trajectories of sect development, which are defined in terms of movement between one or another of the seven basic orientations to 'the world', or strategies of salvation, which Wilson identifies at the outset of *MM*. The real meat of the book lies in the application of these abstract trajectories to the concrete processes of religious change in Third World societies.

In all four forms of Wilson's history, macro and micro, concrete and abstract, the fulcrum of change is provided by Europe's epochal impact on the rest of world. In Wilson's account, cultural discontinuity—'cultural' here in the Boasian rather than the Tylorian sense—was as much an effect of the impact as societal collapse or social trauma. This view has important analytical consequences, which it is important to spell out. In so far as 'the unprecedented disruption of social circumstances' has led to 'the breakdown and abandonment of previous assumptions and codes of discipline' (Wilson 1973: 501), then it appears that indigenous cultural traditions, in all their variety, can have little relevance for explaining the character of the response of 'less-developed peoples'.

That response has to be explained in terms of 'the logic of the situation', some posited general human motivations, and the level of 'cultural socialization'—'cultural' here in the Tylorian, not the Boasian sense—which the people have attained. The demand for thaumaturgy is a cultural universal in societies at this stage of development, though it may take culturally specific forms (e.g. the Melanesian appetite for 'cargo').

Wilson's extensive use of a non-relativist, Tylorian concept of culture ties in with his unfashionably anti-relativist approach to the question of millennialism's rationality. He staunchly insists that the movements should be seen as the collective acting-out of strong emotions, as wish-fulfilment fantasies, rather than rational attempts to find solutions to problems. This distanced him from many of the anthropologists whose work he drew upon and whose determination to be conceptually charitable he saw as actuated by feelings of guilt at imperialism, by romantic sympathy with alien cultures, and so forth (Wilson 1973: 500). This assessment of motive has a measure of truth; still, there was a real methodological pay-off to some prejudice in favour of actors' rationality. It led to much fuller and subtler accounts of the motivation of millennial-type movements than had previously been given, and had an especially salutary effect on those other adherents of a transcendent rationality, the Marxists.[7] Yet, writing as one who strongly advocated explanation in terms of actors' rationality (Peel 1969), I have to agree with Wilson that major features of the movements—such as the widespread expectation across many cultures that all would be made new with the return of the ancestors or that the white invaders' bullets would be turned to water—are hard to interpret except as the projections of fervent desire.

But where we thus opt against the attribution of rationality, it is important to do so on the right grounds. The bald facts that, as Wilson (1973: 500) put it, 'magic does not work, the millennium will not come', are *not* adequate grounds, since people can rationally arrive at false and fantastic opinions; and, as Elster (1982) has shown, wishful thinking *can* arrive at beliefs both true and well-founded. More fundamentally, where the rationality debate becomes focused on whether and why particular beliefs and actions deserve our epistemological endorsement, it veers away from the main sociological issue. What makes action rational in a sense relevant to sociological analysis is whether it is action aimed at achieving ends in the light of criteria of reality given by the culture.[8] The important question raised by *MM* is how far the beliefs or actions of millennialists are to be explained in terms of values, criteria, and so forth drawn from their cultural backgrounds, and how far they have to be explained otherwise, precisely because of the culture's collapse in the face of unprecedented difficulties. If Wilson is right in supposing the latter, then he is also right in denying the rationality of millennial movements. In that case, what happens in them is that action largely 'shortcircuits' culture; it is generated from the interplay of circumstances and the inherent compulsions and endowments of actors (which for Wilson importantly include the level of emotional self-mastery which a people has developed). If we leave aside this highly questionable notion of emotional underdevelopment, then Wilson has adumbrated a real possibility: that social action is not always cultural to the same extent. Since culture in its dynamic and diachronic form is nothing other than tradition, we must call into question Weber's counterposition of tradition and rationality.[9]

This is an extreme case that we have been considering, albeit one that has pervasive influence in the detailed analysis of *MM*. It underscores the importance of the process by which tradition is created and sustained, and it prompts us to ask how widely and intensely any kind of cultural breakdown in fact occurred among the 'less-developed peoples' under the European impact. Wilson draws a pertinent distinction in terms of potential for development between movements in Africa and Melanesia (including New Guinea) on the one hand and movements elsewhere, such as among the North American Indians and the Maoris (Wilson 1973: 453). The difference rests to a large extent on relative weight of members; the former were not overwhelmed by their colonizers to the point where the only option was to abandon their indigenous culture for the new one: compare a movement like, say, the Religion of Handsome Lake among the western Iroquois with Aladura or Kimbanguist Christianity in western Africa.[10] Wilson rightly sees the latter as 'dynamic responses to changing circumstances . . . which may become a key to the prospects of new nations'. To show how this may be, we have to return from typology to history and explore the integration of old and new in an ongoing religious tradition.

At this point, then, I turn back to West Africa, and particularly to the Aladura movement, which *MM* treated as one of its major cases. Aladura is a movement of independent Christianity whose origins go back to before 1920, which reached a peak in the great revivals of the early 1930s, but which has continued to expand ever since, both within and beyond its Yoruba heartland, to the point where its religious style affects virtually all manifestations of Nigerian Christianity.[11] Though there was the suggestion of a revolutionist orientation in some of the Aladura prophets' utterances in the years around 1930, Aladura falls well within Wilson's category of the thaumaturgical. He advances it as a case in which we may begin to see a process of 'rational mutation', as the thaumaturgical movement focused on charismatic prophet-healers becomes denominationalized. This is a process I discerned myself, arguing along conventionally Weberian lines that literacy (*qua* biblical interpretation) and the emergence of pastoral (as against prophetic) authority mutually facilitated one another, leading to the eventual emergence of pentecostal churches along recognizably European lines, though at the same time well adapted to local religious demand and style.

This trajectory, evident in Aladura's history over three decades since the 1930s, is given a broader significance by Wilson. Like other African religious histories, it is treated as unidirectional, part of the same universal march of rationalization of which Europe's secularization over the past 300-odd years is the paradigm case.[12] Aladura does not just manifest this process, but serves to forward it, through the paradox that the non-rational end of thaumaturgy leads to the adoption of a rational form of organization. 'The disciplining of the emotions in the maintenance of rational structures', Wilson writes of the Church of the Lord (Aladura) 'is itself an important exercise in the diffusion of rational thinking' (Wilson 1973: 193). However that may be in the long term, what is likely to disconcert the historian or the ethnographer here is that an ideally typified process is being used to 'iron out' the specificities, irregularities, and 'detours' of real historical sequences. I am not advancing an argument against the use of historical parallels. Indeed, one way in which the uniqueness of the religious history of modern Africa may be approached is as the synchronization of two epochal processes which in Europe were a millennium apart: the adoption of a world religion and the religious expression of modernization. While both these processes can be seen as involving rationalization of some sort, only the latter entails secularization.

Secularization, as it is discerned in modern societies, involves the interplay of two strands: a decline in the prestige and influence of institutions, personnel, and activities identified as religious; and a change in the overall character of human thought and action, such that it becomes less governed by mystical or transcendental criteria. The first of these processes is predominantly social, the latter predominantly cultural. The latter process might plausibly be represented as an incremental and unidirectional movement from the most primitive forms of culture, as it is in all those evolutionary theories based on the growth of knowledge, technology, 'forces of production', and so forth. But the former process requires the trajectory of history, as it were, to double back on itself. For this strand of secularization cannot happen unless there has been some prior process by which religious institutions have become differentiated and gone on to acquire some hegemonic force in society.

In the traditional cultures of western Africa, 'religion' did not exist as an indigenous category, but was introduced by missionaries and taken up (sometimes reluctantly) by anthropologists to refer to certain cultural and behavioural aspects of the whole community's functioning. It is true that many of those societies were complex enough to have cult groups which yielded distinct identities and were sometimes cross-societal, but, with their specific areas of competence and often voluntary memberships, they did not challenge the absolute priority of ethnic or communal identity. In Africa, people only recognize themselves as having 'a religion' when they adopt Islam or Christianity, religions which not only define themselves as such, but construct 'paganism' as their opposition.[13] Only at this point and in so far as they firmly establish themselves as a basis of identity—that is, of a self-definition of individuals in terms of a valued group membership—can religions manifestly take on that role of 'cultural switchmen' which Weber explored with such penetration. The world religions (and particularly Christianity) have undoubtedly worked to desacralize African life in some spheres, and that is a force for secularization; but against this should be set the novel ways in which they have started to mould social forms according to their own conceptions.

This religious differentiation also raises the question of the relationship between two fundamental aspects of religion, conventionally labelled 'instrumental' and 'expressive'. The first of these figures in *MM* as thaumaturgy and in Weber's *Sociology of Religion* as a this-worldly religious orientation, in both cases aspects salient in primitive religion.[14] 'That it may go well with thee . . . and that thou mayest prolong thy days upon the earth' exactly expresses the orientation of Yoruba religion as the missionaries found it.[15] Horton (1964) points to the same aspect when he stresses the concern of traditional African religions with the 'explanation, prediction and control' of the phenomenal world. 'Thaumaturgy' is an unfortunate designation of the routine character of primitive religion, since it imputes that *miracles*, or extra-ordinary occurrences are being sought. This ignores the routine, prosaic quality of most 'thaumaturgical' action and, as Weber was correct to stress, its continuity with 'the range of everyday purposive conduct' (Weber 1963: 1). It is important not to mistake this if we are to apprehend the peculiar quality of the thought and action manifest in movements like Aladura, which can more properly be called 'thaumaturgical' in Wilson's terms. Here our problem is to explain how people whose traditional 'religion' was importantly concerned with securing health, fertility, prosperity, guidance, and so on responded to unprecedentedly difficult and perplexing circumstances.

The other aspect of religion is again variously labelled with a closely overlapping series of labels. Parsons (1954) sees it as especially marked in modern religion and labels it 'expressive'. With African religion in mind, Horton contrasts 'communion' with explanation/prediction/control, and, significantly, pays more attention to the latter. In Weber it is the ethical, in contrast to the magical; and it bulks large in his account of the cultural breakthrough effected by the prophets who inaugurated the world religions. We see here signs of a familiar danger—of treating the two aspects as the poles of an evolutionary continuum, rather than as interdependent—though Wilson follows Weber in seeing the search for extraordinary interventions as being inherent in all religion. In primitive religions the afflicted individual's treatment typically involves a 'social' diagnosis—in terms of sin, witchcraft, and so forth—and the reaffirmation of social values: the sick body is the token of the threatened community.[16]

In the ethnography of western Africa we find two exemplary forms of this interplay of the therapeutic and the social. On the one hand, there are the kinship groups basically constitutive of society, which are also ritual congregations. Sickness and personal difficulty may be put down to the infraction of kin obligations, and the power to punish and heal attributed to ancestors, who are a sort of greatly enhanced elder.[17] On the other hand, there are groups in which the lines between the therapeutic and the ethical run the other way: cult groups or cults of affliction, which are associational in character (though they may adopt a quasi-kinship idiom) and which attribute healing to a god or 'fetish'. These latter cults are predominantly instrumental in their ethos and, in contrast with lineage congregations, are prone to rise and fall in popular favour. The transience of such cults has been noted among the Akan and in the Lower Congo (McCaskie 1981; Field 1960; de Craemer *et al.* 1976). The much more perduring quality of such cults among the Yoruba and the Aja-Fon is unquestionably related to the way that, there, the cults have become expressively significant for their members, have developed strong membership identities, and have even become socially constitutive (Bascom 1944; Herskovits 1938, vol. 2, esp. ch. 29). It was these associational cult groups, primarily instrumental but capable of developing a more ethical and expressive character, which provided the most common indigenous model in which the world religions were received.

When we look at the impact of the world religions, we are at once struck by the contrast between the missionary and the indigenous views of them. The missionaries conceived themselves to be offering a 'new moral world', and the early congregations do fit neatly into Wilson's 'conversionist' type of movement. The great bulk of the target population, however, was attracted on instrumental grounds, which for the missionaries were subordinate or extraneous. Yet conversions were initially few because, despite the instrumental attractions, people were reluctant to abandon associations and practices bound up with the maintenance of a social and moral order to which they still felt committed. The early converts were mostly individuals of low status, often socially marginal or detached through migration, who had little to lose in embracing the 'new moral world'. It was only after the establishment of colonial rule, with all its political and economic changes, that large-scale conversion started to occur, led by young men, relatively but only temporarily detached from the community's centre, who drew other social categories after them.

We may consider this a shift from an earlier 'egoistic' to an 'anomic' pattern of conversion: the social detachment of individuals yields to the disordered condition of society as the main source of explanation. The first three or four decades of colonial rule were, for the Yoruba, a time of great upheaval in all areas of social life, in which adoption of the world religions ran straight on into independent religious movements.[18] Aladura ran the whole gamut from magic to millennialism, although the latter, while clearly articulated in prophetic utterances in 1918 and again in 1930–1, never became the firm basis of a stable religious orientation. The central explanatory issue here, pointedly but misleadingly addressed in the 'rationality debate', is how far Yoruba religious innovations were a realization of or a departure from the criteria of their culture. Is a model of cultural collapse or abandonment, even in part, applicable?

Clearly many Yoruba came to feel that the means to human satisfaction provided by their culture were insufficient. This, in itself, was no new thing: Yoruba culture had for a century or more been steadily incorporative of new means, but the 'cultural deficit' now seemed to be so great that it demanded more radical measures. These measures were taken especially by individuals—above all, young men making money in new ways, throwing off irksome social controls, and adopting new associations that challenged the integrity of their communities as this had been defined—and all this in a markedly instrumental, not to say often anti-social, spirit.[19] These actions in turn fuelled a general sense of social malaise, of the times being radically out of joint,[20] in which episodes of expansive optimism (e.g. church and educational growth from *c.*1910, the cocoa-led surge of prosperity in the 1920s) alternated with unprecedented terrors and depressions (the dislocations of 1914–18, the epidemics of 1918–19 and 1925–6, and the Great Depression from 1931). Underlying the religious responses to these vicissitudes, all along the spectrum from individual 'magical' responses to collective 'millennial' ones (with the mass thaumaturgy of the revivals of 1930–5 somewhere in the middle), was a major premiss of Yoruba culture: that religion is to do with healing, guidance, and worldly well-being in all its forms. Since this kind of means was already culturally indicated, we are never dealing with a situation which is merely the acting out of desires or pure soteriological demand. Of course it is not action 'prompted . . . by the desire to understand objective truth in a detached way' (Wilson

1973: 500) either, but what a minute proportion of human action that is!

Regional comparison shows that the choice of *which* religious means to employ was not made randomly: the 1918 influenza epidemic, which in sophisticated near-coastal Ijebu aroused a Christian response, in rural up-country Ijesha evoked responses in terms of a 'pagan' anti-witchcraft cult (Peel 1983: 165). We come closest to Wilson's paradigm of unprecedented collapse followed by fantasy response in the case of the utopian expectations of the great revivals (1930–1) and the purer forms of millennialism in general. Here, indeed, popular anticipations went beyond any cultural warrant, beyond what could be rationally specified within the terms of Yoruba culture. But rationality (or lack of it) is hardly the main issue here, since creative innovation by definition goes beyond this warrant. Wilson (1973: 171, 494) does not fail to give credit to the way in which millennialism initiates cultural change, by enlarging social consciousness and creating new forms of social organization. Where reason at once comes in again is in the testing and evaluation of the innovation—a dialectic which is at the heart of any viable cultural tradition. Here the Yoruba showed themselves highly responsive to the realities of their situation: millennial-type expectations were set aside, but thaumaturgy (*qua* divine healing) became institutionalized.

Of course it is true that 'magic does not work' (Wilson 1973: 500), since it follows from what we mean by 'magic'. But thaumaturgical practices, unlike millennial expectations, have continued to flourish among Yoruba of all social classes and educational levels, precisely because they offer real grounds for hope that the practical problems of life can in many cases be mitigated if not solved. Some of their claimed effects are real, even if they do not happen for the stated reasons. But when people say 'the power of the prophet' has healed or helped them, this is less an untruth than a kind of clouded sociological truth. It elliptically acknowledges that the power of the prophet, and hence of his god, is evidenced in, and in a sense made by, the following he has attracted, and that the fellowship of the cult group provides conditions for the 'miracles'.

Wilson (1973: 129–31) presents a model of the mutation of thaumaturgical responses (with explicit reference to West Africa) that offers valuable insights into this process. In 'its pristine form', he argues, the thaumaturgical response is unstable, since it relates to individuals' problems and lacks an effective organization. But where it links up with conversionist social forms, it acquires organizational stability, albeit at the cost of certain changes in its content: a miracle comes to be conceived 'less as an objective event, more as a subjective evaluation', and the fellowship of the cult 'becomes *in itself* the . . . evidence of the deity's operations' (Wilson 1973: 131). All this applies to a great extent to the Yoruba case; but there is more to it yet. The conversionist form is certainly adopted, being continuously available, since it was employed in the early mission congregations, which Aladura groups resemble sociologically more than do the large contemporary congregations of, say, Anglicans or Methodists. At the same time, Aladura groups *re*-unite the instrumental (or thaumaturgical) and the social/ethical functions of religion which tended to part company during those decades when young men led the movement to adopt the world religions. There is nothing 'pristine' about Alatinga, the last significant pagan thaumaturgical movement to sweep Yorubaland (in the early 1950s), which Wilson cites in this connection, for it is essentially a phenomenon of the same epoch. By contrast, the baseline religious form of the Yoruba was quite stable, the cult group devoted to a particular deity; and it is as much to this model, as to the conversionist mission, that the Aladura congregation recalls us. Moreover, as Wilson puts it, 'traditional religious dispositions persist in the entirely new and legitimated contexts of the spiritual churches' (Wilson 1973: 451). I would go further, and say that their thaumaturgy continues to be understood much more as objective 'magical' events than in the subjectivist sense which Wilson's model posits as the logical outcome of their adoption of conversionist organizational forms. The world religions appear to have some way to go in replacing the vigorous this-worldliness of Yoruba attitudes with the other-worldly, transvaluatory, or predominantly ethical concerns which are reckoned to be distinctive of them.

Twenty-five years on from the studies of independent religious movements which Wilson drew on in *MM*, Nigerian religion presents a scene of great vitality and diversity. Several major trends may be distinguished.

(1) Everywhere the world religions have advanced, to the point where only a small and diminishing residuum of Nigerians do not

profess some kind of attachment to one or other of them. Though the initial choice of Christianity or Islam may be contingent and under-motivated, the ensuing commitments are usually stable and consequential.

(2) Prophetist or spiritual churches, whether or not of strictly Aladura origin, have continued to grow and diversify, the most notable perhaps being the Celestial Church of Christ, an Aladura offshoot originating among Yoruba-speakers in Dahomey, and the Brotherhood of the Cross and Star, a Calabar-based movement.[21] Most of these churches combine thaumaturgical with communit-arian concerns, but there is some differentiation of primary focus: Prophet Wobo's Spiritual Healing Church of the Lord (Aladura but outside Yorubaland, based in Port Harcourt), for example, emphasizes its 'medico-counselling' function so strongly as to resemble a clientele more than a congregation.[22] Such pure devotion to solving the problems of clients as they define them means that the wider social framework and its structures and values tend to be taken for granted, if not ratified. Wobo, as a sort of spiritual plumber, is most respectful of the status of his many prosperous clients. It is the more communitarian movements which are most likely to express criticism of the prevailing social order.

(3) A more novel development of this kind has been the Charismatic Movement that has grown vastly since the early 1970s. Though pentecostalism has been present in Nigeria since the early 1930s, well indigenized in Aladura and supplemented from the late 1940s by fresh imports (especially Assemblies of God), this new wave has its seed-bed in the universities and secondary schools (Ojo 1988). Interdenominational campus organizations like the Student Christian Movement and the Christian Union become 'pentecostal-ized', and spread from the campus to the educated youthful urban population, interacting and blending with other evangelistic organ-izations, often of North American provenance. While thaumaturgy is not absent, a new prominence is given to the search for personal holiness and for Christian fellowship within the congregation. This seems to fit with Wilson's model of 'rational mutation', especially in the light of the urban and educated nature of the membership; or it could equally well be seen as a process of 'ethicalization', consonant with the deeper penetration of a world religion. Combined with it is a tendency to social critique—for example of the corruption and incompetence of Nigeria's rulers—perhaps even

an intimation of (in Wilson's terms) a reformist orientation to the world.

(4) Since the late 1970s, there has been a growing polarization of Muslims and Christians throughout Nigeria, a development particularly ominous for the Yoruba, who are more evenly divided between them than any other substantial ethnic group. The roots of this lie in the trajectories of Nigerian and world history, and cannot be further explored here. It is a moot point how far the moves towards the more intense forms of Christian spirituality, as evident in the Charismatic Movement, are due to the challenge of Islamic fundamentalism—whose influence on Nigerian policy the charismatics are very concerned to check—and how far to some dynamic internal to Christianity or, in a manner analogous to Aladura in the 1920s to the 1930s, to the boom-to-bust character of Nigeria's development since 1970. (The occurrence of the same charismatic phenomenon in Ghana, where Islam presents nothing like the same political challenge, would argue against the first of these possibilities) (Hagan 1988). What seems certain, however, is that such political reinforcement of world-religious identities—hitherto, especially for the Yoruba, restrained by the importance of communal and ethnic ones[23]—must put a powerful restraint on any tendencies to secularization.

The most important question which a rereading of *Magic and the Millennium* raises in my mind about the analysis of current religious developments in Nigeria is whether the desacralization of spiritual world-views or the cultural imprinting of the two world religions now contending for hegemony there will be the salient force; or rather, since both are having some significant effect, how they will combine. Only through a concrete history will the matter be resolved. *MM* offers a powerful scheme for the interpretation of history, which, like all such schemes, is selective and partial. Being so social-evolutionary in its character and assumptive of the normative significance of the Western European experience of rationalization, it is bound to be viewed with some reserve by the historian or ethnographer of non-European societies. Even for a critical Africanist, however, *Magic and the Millennium* passes the primary test for a work of theory: it is good to think with.

Notes

1. In the *British Journal of Sociology*, 24 (1974): 255–7.
2. Notably Fernandez 1982; MacGaffey 1983; Comaroff 1985.
3. There are, of course, some striking exceptions; but it is significant that Weber tends to be relevant for them not for the overall character of his sociology, but for what he had to say about particular topics, such as the world religions (cf. Geertz 1968 on Islam; Tambiah 1976 on Buddhism), stratification, and bureaucracy (cf. Smith 1978; Fallers 1956).
4. For example, Lewis, who advocates 'useful typologies which cut across cultural forms' in the study of religion (1971: 12). Compare Fortes and Evans-Pritchard's view that comparison should be 'on an abstract plane where social processes are stripped of their cultural idiom and reduced to functional terms' (1940: 3).
5. The idea that primitive peoples, like the rural lower classes in Europe, are especially prone to be overcome by their passions has a long anterior history in Europe, being clearly expressed in sixteenth-century commentators on the American Indians (Pagden 1982).
6. For a useful discussion, see Ingold 1986, esp. ch. 2.
7. Compare the 2nd, revised edition of Worsley's *The Trumpet Shall Sound* (1968) with the first.
8. This does not presume that all cultures are equally rational. I would accept Jarvie's (1984) argument that only those cultures are 'strongly rational' that have institutionalized the critique of knowledge—i.e. where science is institutionalized. Even in those societies, however, the great bulk of social action is no more rational than in societies which do not have such a 'strongly rational' component in their culture.
9. See Shils 1981, esp. p. 21, on the relations between the 'traditionality of reason' and 'substantive traditionality'.
10. See Wallace's (1969) fine study, not cited in Wilson 1973, although several of Wallace's earlier papers are.
11. Apart from Peel 1968, the major studies of the Aladura movement are Turner 1967 and Omoyajowo 1982.
12. See esp. Wilson 1973: 452: 'A process of secularization occurs . . .', and the argument goes on to itemize all the forces which standardly produce modern secularism.
13. For a detailed study of this in relation to the Yoruba, see Peel, 1993.
14. 'Thaumaturgy is the primal stuff of primitive religion' (Wilson 1973: 70). Cf. Weber: 'The most elementary forms of behaviour motivated by religious or magical factors are oriented to this world' (1963: 1).

15. Deuteronomy 4: 40, quoted by Weber. Cf. the Revd S. A. Crowther on the Yoruba religious search for 'peace, health, children, and money' in CMS Archives, Yoruba Mission (at Birmingham University), CA2 M1, journals for quarters ending 25 Sept. and 25 Dec. 1946.
16. Some exemplary references: Douglas 1970, esp. ch. 5; Bourdieu 1977: 144 ff.; above all, Fernandez 1982, where it is a most pervasive theme.
17. Classically, Fortes 1959.
18. For a synthetic treatment of social and cultural change in one community, see Peel 1983.
19. For examples, see Peel 1983: 104–5.
20. See texts of prayers quoted in Peel 1968: 304–5.
21. See the useful study edited by Hackett (1987), especially the contributions by Hackett herself and J. K. Olupona on the Celestial Church (pp. 161–77, 45–73), by E. A. Offiong on the Brotherhood of the Cross and Star (pp. 179–90). The Brotherhood of the Cross and Star and the Spiritual Healing Church of the Lord have been examined comparatively in Amadi 1982.
22. Amadi 1982, and *idem*, 'Continuities and Adaptations in the Aladura Movement: The Example of Prophet Wobo and his Clientele in S. E. Nigeria', in Hackett 1987.
23. There is no reliable academic study of Muslim–Christian relations in contemporary Nigeria. For a study that argues the increasingly less plausible case that the Yoruba have avoided this polarization, see Laitin 1986.

References

Adas, M. (1979), *Prophets of Rebellion* (Chapel Hill, NC).

Amadi, G. I. S. (1982), 'Power and Purity: A Comparative Study of Two Prophetic Churches in South Eastern Nigeria', Ph.D. thesis, Manchester University.

Bascom, W. R. (1944), 'The Sociological Role of the Yoruba Cult-Group', *American Anthropologist*, 46: 1–75.

Bourdieu, P. (1977), *Outline of a Theory of Practice* (Cambridge).

Comaroff, J. (1985), *Body of Power, Spirit of Resistance* (Chicago).

de Craemer, W., Vansina, J., and Fox, R. C. (1976), 'Religious Movements in Central Africa', *Comparative Studies in Society and History*, 18: 458–75.

Douglas, M. (1970), *Natural Symbols* (London).

Elias, N. (1978), *The Civilizing Process: The History of Manners*, trans. E. Jephcott (Oxford).

Elster, J. (1982), 'Belief, Bias and Ideology', in M. Hollis and S. Lukes (eds.), *Rationality and Relativism* (Oxford), 123–48.

Fallers, L. (1956), *Bantu Beaucracy: A Century of Political Evolution among the Basoga* (Chicago).

Fernandez, J. W. (1982), *Bwiti: An Ethnography of the Religious Imagination in Africa* (Princeton, NJ).

Field, M. J. (1960), *Search for Security* (London).

Fortes, M. (1959), *Oedipus and Job in West African Religion* (Cambridge).

Fortes, M., and Evans-Pritchard, E. E. (1940) (eds.), *African Political Systems* (London).

Geertz, C. (1968), *Islam Observed: Religious Developments in Morocco and Indonesia* (Chicago).

Hackett, R. I. J. (1987) (ed.), *New Religious Movements in Nigeria* (Lewiston, NY).

Hagan, G. P. (1988), 'Divinity and Experience: The Trance and Christianity in Southern Ghana', in W. James and D. H. Johnson (eds.), *Vernacular Christianity: Essays in the Social Anthropology of Religion Presented to Godfrey Lienhardt* (Oxford), 146–56.

Herskovits, M. J. (1938), *Dahomey: An Ancient West African Kingdom* (New York).

Horton, R. (1964), 'Ritual Man in Africa', *Africa*, 34: 85–104.

Ingold, T. (1986), *Evolution and Social Life* (Cambridge).

Jarvie, I. C. (1984), *Rationality and Relativism: In Search of a Philosophy and History of Anthropology*, Part 1 (London).

Laitin, D. D. (1986), *Hegemony and Culture: Politics and Religious Change among the Yoruba* (Chicago).

Lewis, I. (1971), *Ecstatic Religion* (Harmondsworth).

McCaskie, T. C. (1981), 'Anti-Witchcraft Cults in Asante', *History in Africa*, 8: 125–54.

MacGaffey, W. (1983), *Modern Kongo Prophets* (Bloomington, Ind.).

Ojo, M. A. (1988), 'The Contextual Significance of the Charismatic Movements in Independent Nigeria', *Africa*, 58: 175–92.

Omoyajowo, J. A. (1982), *Cherubim and Seraphim* (New York).

Pagden, A. (1982), *The Fall of Natural Man* (London).

Parsons, T. (1954), 'The Theoretical Development of the Sociology of Religion', in *Essays in Sociological Theory* (Glencoe, Ill.).

Peel, J. D. Y. (1968), *Aladura: A Religious Movement among the Yoruba* (London).

—— (1969), 'Understanding Action Belief Systems', *British Journal of Sociology*, 20: 69–84.

—— (1983), *Ijeshas and Nigerians: The Incorporation of a Yoruba Kingdom, 1890s–1970s* (Cambridge).

—— (1993), 'Between Crowther and Ajayi: The Religious Origins of the Modern Yoruba Intelligentsia', in T. Falola (ed.), *African Historiography: Essays in Honour of J. F. Ade Ajayi* (Lagos).

Shils, E. (1981), *Tradition* (London).

100 *J. D. Y. Peel*

Smith, M. G. (1978), *The Affairs of Daura* (Berkeley, Calif.).

Spencer, H. (1850), *Social Statics* (London).

—— (1873), *The Study of Sociology* (London).

Tambiah, S. J. (1976), *World Conqueror and World Renouncer: A Study of Buddhism and Polity in Thailand against a Historical Background* (Cambridge).

Turner, H. W. (1967), *African Independent Church* (2 vols., Oxford).

Wallace, A. F. C. (1969), *The Death and Rebirth of the Seneca* (New York).

Weber, M. (1963), *The Sociology of Religion*, trans. E. Fischoff (London).

Wilson, B. R. (1973), *Magic and the Millennium* (London).

Worsley, P. (1968), *The Trumpet Shall Sound*, 2nd rev. edn. (London).

7

The Evangelical Expansion South of the American Border

DAVID MARTIN

This essay deals with those phenomena of sectarianism and (by implication) secularization which Bryan Wilson has treated with such distinction.[1] The context with which it is concerned is one where the arguments and data of Bryan Wilson's *Magic and the Millennium* are especially relevant. It therefore places itself in the Wilsonian tradition.

It is difficult to recollect now how little was contributed by British sociologists prior to 1960, either to the study of sects and society or, with one or two pioneering exceptions such as John Highet and William Pickering, to the study of religion in Britain. Yet, since 1959, when Bryan Wilson's path-breaking article on types of sects appeared in the *American Sociological Review*, the sociology of religion in Britain has entered on a fruitful phase, in very large measure due to his contribution or following his example. His work was, and is, descriptively rich, logically and coolly articulated, and theoretical without being obscure. These qualities were transmitted to Bryan Wilson's many students on whom he lavished a loyalty and an intellectual care rooted in his sense of the vocation of a teacher. His students and his colleagues in the discipline acknowledge a singular debt to both his intellectual and his personal example.

The growth of a conservative Protestantism in Latin America has been as remarkable as it was unexpected. Up to the 1950s the main Protestant denominations, particularly the Presbyterians and the Baptists, had maintained small footholds in various parts of the continent. Often they had gone there originally under the patronage of liberal governments for whom Protestants were signs of progress and sources of services. Then in the 1960s the Pentecostals and the various evangelical missions began rapidly to overtake the historic denominations, until today more than 70 per cent of the forty million or so Protestants are Pentecostals. Moreover, the historic denominations have tended to grow, though less rapidly, by adopting pentecostal styles; and the Roman Catholic Church has defended itself, in part, by selective imitation.

Within countries and between them the extent of the Pentecostal, or 'evangelical', incursion has been very variable, and this demands careful comparative study. Within Mexico, by way of example, Julian Bridges (1970) has charted a social geography of Protestantism. He shows initially how between 1950 and 1970 Protestant expansion was double the growth in the general population, so that Protestants now account for 5 per cent of the population. But this expansion was very much greater in the south-east (Chiapas, Tabasco, and parts of the Yucatan) and in the industrial suburbs of central Mexico than elsewhere. As will be indicated later, the expansion in central Mexico is different in nature from the expansion in the south-east. To deal with such differences and variations, we need to look both at very broad historical and social preconditions, like the power and influence of the USA and its historic religious pattern, and also at local circumstances, such as Catholic neglect or long-term memories of suppression by alien forces identified with Catholicism.

Apart from the most general element of social change itself, hardly any circumstance is so 'necessary' as to be present in every instance. Pentecostalism grows in conditions $a \ldots n$, where a group of circumstances, b, d and f say, combine together in one instance and another group, d, f, and j, say, in another. A particular combination generates a specific dynamic or Gestalt.

THE LATIN AMERICAN TRAJECTORY

The broadest framework for understanding the appearance of Protestantism on a large scale is the world-historical clash between the Anglo-American and Hispanic worlds over the past several centuries. It is now (at the time of writing in 1988) precisely four centuries since the Spanish Armada sought to return the revolting colony of England to the Roman Catholic imperium. The last stages of that clash were fought out in Texas and Mexico in the mid-nineteenth century and in Cuba, Puerto Rico, and the Philippines in the war which began in 1898. Inevitably there are those who see in the expansion of American Protestantism a continuation of that war by religious colonization.

The clash has been one not only of rival powers but of different trajectories of social change and dramatically different patterns of relationship between Church and State, religion and politics. The Hispanic (and Lusitanian) world is notoriously one in which societies are polarized and have been ruled alternately by a conservative military or by militant radicals, themselves sometimes soldiers. Religion—and more specifically the Church—has been in the centre of this polarization. The overt signs of that have been anti-clericalism and disputes over Church lands, ecclesiastical education, and the extent to which church laws—for example, concerning marriage—should extend to the whole of society. By contrast, in Anglo-American societies there has been much less polarization, and though members of particular religious bodies may be more attracted to one political party than another, religion itself is rarely at issue. The Church has either been eased out of any organic relationship with the state and with the whole social body, as in the USA, or has been much weakened as an independent source of social power by state control and by the existence of large-scale dissent, as in England. It is not identified as a massive rampart of superstition, social passivity, and the forces of the *ancien régime*.

In Latin America (and in the Iberian peninsula) the confrontation of Church and State was ineluctably tangled with other alignments, and persisted for a century and a half. It reached a savage climax in the Mexican (and Spanish) civil wars. The upshot varied from country to country, and that variation is a major local circumstance affecting the viability of Protestant beach-heads. For example, in two countries, Uruguay and Venezuela, the power of the Church was dramatically curtailed and the culture itself widely secularized, though in Venezuela the culture had been barely Christianized in the first place (Maduro 1982). This situation does not assist religious adherence of any kind. Uruguay is a welfare state providing a system of secular education for a population which is in large measure bourgeois—that is, urban and middle class. Pentecostals number some 15,000, and Protestants in general (including some 40,000 Mormons) make up about 2 per cent of the population. In the context of Uruguay, and even of the Argentine, it is worth emphasizing how large-scale migration from Europe in fairly recent times has facilitated secularization.

At the other end of the scale, in Colombia, the church has survived extraordinary internecine violence, and until quite recently has wielded extensive trade union power, as well as insisting that to be Catholic and Colombian are identical. That too has affected the pace of Protestant expansion and its nature. Protestants have suffered martyrdoms in a long, confused civil strife, and they have had to endure inferior civil status in certain respects. Above all, they have had to work within house churches and, as will be shown later, this has channelled the social consequences of their activity into the domestic sphere. Nevertheless, the trials in Colombia assisted their cause more than benign apathy did in Uruguay, and 'evangelicals' there now number some million persons, or about 4 per cent of the population.

The optimum conditions for evangelical expansion are found where the confrontation between Church and State has left the Church paralysed but has not extended to a secularization of culture. In Brazil, for example, the Church was successfully subordinated as early as the time of Pombal in the eighteenth century. Only the final break between Church and State at the turn of the last century allowed a return to an orthodox Catholicism. The Church was Romanized, and this was often carried out by priests brought in from elsewhere. Meanwhile Brazil has retained a common religiosity barely touched by systematic scepticism. This expresses itself in pilgrimages, in syncretistic festivals like the New Year, and in invocations to saints for help and healing, as well as in very influential Afro-Brazilian spirit cults like Umbanda (Fernandes 1985; Fry 1978).[2] There have also been powerful messianic movements, such as the extraordinary regional outbreak associated with Padre Cicero (della Cava 1970), which engendered a version of the Protestant ethic within a deviant Catholicism. Clearly, where the Church is weak and the ground is prepared by cults of the spirit and by the pursuit of spiritual healing, the opportunity for pentecostal conversion may be considerable. However, one must emphasize that the competition from Umbanda has been very keen. There are over twenty million evangelicals in Brazil, making up 15–20 per cent of the adult population. The Assemblies of God alone have a membership of nine million.

Thus the relationship of Church and State needs to have been opened up at least to some degree; but equally the forces of militant secularity need to have come to a halt before the secularization of culture. If one is considering the variable consequences of the conflict of the Church with militant secularity, the optimum outcome with regard to opportunities for evangelical conversion is found in Brazil, not in Uruguay or Colombia.

In general the war between the Church and militant secularity has resulted in something approaching a stand-off, so that both sides recognize the costs of confrontation. Broadly, the Church recognizes three strategies available to restore some measure of power and influence, and the way these work out bears on the opportunities for evangelicals, more especially the Pentecostals.

The first strategy is the oldest, and has by now been largely abandoned. According to this strategy, the Church maintains its alliance with the right, which, in the modern situation means less the old land-owning class than military dictatorships. This alliance was forged to some extent in the early years of the Trujillo dictatorship in the Dominican Republic, in Argentina in the 1970s, and in Guatemala in the years immediately following the military coup of 1954. It was also forged, of course, in Franco's Spain. But such regimes eventually break down, leaving the Church identified with an oppressive system and alienated from the ordinary population. Generally the Church finds the brutality involved intolerable, and begins to put forward some defence of human rights.

Moreover, the military have in recent years evolved into more efficient and bureaucratic stratum, and have created a national security state for which the Church is a useful, but not an absolutely necessary, ally. The military may speak of saving the Church, even from itself, but the Army is not a particularly pious organization (Aman 1987; Smith 1982). The military leadership may look for whatever supports are possible. The Pinochet regime in Chile, for example, managed to elicit a formal *Te Deum* from at least the pastorate of the Methodist Pentecostal Church, and in return awarded some implicit acceptance of the Protestant presence on the part of the state.

Another strategy is to refurbish the supports of the Catholic ghetto through organizations like Catholic Action and the Cursillos. Implicit alliances can then be sought on a pragmatic basis with whatever parties are reasonably democratic and reasonably well disposed to the Church, which usually means Christian Democracy of some kind. However, even these implicit identifications have their dangers when the parties concerned run into problems, as did the government of Frei in Chile. Further, Catholic Action has from time to time developed radical youth organizations which are restive under ecclesiastical discipline and disposed to provide slipways for liberation theology.

The third strategy is that provided by liberation theology, and this offers a chance of regaining some moral hegemony at the cost of undermining the structure of the Church. This is why the Church hovers uneasily between this third solution and the second. The principal vehicle of the third strategy is the base community. These communities are the main rivals to the Pentecostals, leaving aside the spiritist cults and Voodoo. They often appeal to similar sectors of society, though perhaps the pentecostals contain disproportionate numbers of people in service occupations, while the base communities contain at least a good proportion of those in organized labour. Base communities offer the same opportunities for participation and mutual assistance as the Pentecostals, but some of them also tackle social problems by collective action and political advocacy.

However, they are as much a threat as a solution, since they could undermine the Church as well as the national security state. They are lay and democratic in their inspiration, and often sit loose to traditionalist moral norms. The Roman Catholic Church is in the awkward—perhaps contradictory—situation of seeking to recover influence—as well as pursuing justice—through a vehicle which is inherently of the same social nature as the pentecostal groups: voluntaristic, pluralistic, and participatory. Such a vehicle simultaneously threatens hierarchy and unity. This division within the Church softens its competitive edge when faced with the Pentecostals. The Pentecostals, for their part, are in no such difficulty, since participation and fission are together their very life-blood.

THE ANGLO-AMERICAN TRAJECTORY

So far I have traced the special variant of the Catholic pattern of social conflict and change which obtains in Latin America. It is now necessary to trace the Anglo-American pattern, since our concern is with a transfer of elements from that into Latin America. In Anglo-American society, the organic relation of Church to society is not broken up by a contest between militant Catholicism and militant secularity, with one or the other gaining total control in a sequence of revolution and counter-revolution. Obsolescent strata are not so violently ejected that they seek to recover their position by violence. Rather, there is a process of the steady differentiation of religion from government and from other spheres such as education and welfare. The corrosions of established religion initiated by Protestant Nonconformists are part of that differentiation.

The most that then happens by way of religious incursion into the political realm is that different status groups and regional cultures *in part* mobilize in religious form, and to the extent they do, may tend to prefer one party rather than another. Methodists in the artisan class in northern England tended to vote Liberal; Baptists in the American South at one time tended to vote for the ('Southern') Democrats.

It must be added that no party specifically represented a Church or even called itself 'Christian'. Similarly, no Church felt called upon to deliver votes to a particular party or to make pronouncements over the whole range of political issues which might be regarded as *the* Christian view. No issue was so stark that sides had to be taken, for 'good' and against evil, since all programmes contained moral ambiguities. An informed conscience might reasonably choose from almost any of the alternatives.

Moreover, if a group chose to be apolitical, there was no strong compulsion to declare that it had abdicated its public responsibilities and to force it back into the political forum. When Pentecostals are quietistic in Anglo-American culture, it is not usually a matter for much critical comment. If evangelicals are 'conservative' their political stance has usually been, at least until the efflorescence of the New Christian Right, a generalized conservative attitude associated with Americanism, not an active, distinct political commitment. However, it is precisely this which has been transferred to Latin America. There it is regarded as more precisely political, even and especially when it is apolitical. There it is also drawn into the dynamics of polarized systems and stark choices and oppositions based on comprehensively elaborated world-views. In the Guatemalan material briefly sketched below we can see how Protestants are pulled into starkly opposed positions and how their primary opposition to Catholicism feeds into the political stances which they take up.

This is not to say that evangelicals are always or all conservative and quietist. They alternate over time between quietism and activism, conservatism and reform, even between orthodoxy and liberalization; and which way they turn depends on circumstance. In Jamaica in the 1830s and 1860s, evangelical religion was involved in two major revolts of slaves (Martin 1987); in the late nineteenth century it was mixed up in the whole movement of British Nonconformist churches (and the social strata where those churches were strong) to secure full civil rights. In the mid-twentieth century it was evangelical religion which lay behind the movement for black civil rights.

It is especially important to emphasize how, in the context of Latin America, evangelical religion may on occasion simply provide 'free spaces' and avoid any extrapolation into politics. In part, this may be for the same reasons that animated English Methodists during the repressions of the Napoleonic era and that weighed also with southern blacks prior to the mid-twentieth century. It may also be because Pentecostalism in particular recovers a radical dualism, present in early Christianity, which suspects 'the world' as an evil entanglement and simply regards the 'powers that be' as an interim ordinance of God before the final restoration of all things. But, as suggested above, it is also due to the way in which Pentecostalism has emerged from a social system which is so highly differentiated that religion can operate at the level of personal relationships without being pulled into the vortex of powerful and organized political oppositions. The political indifference of Pentecostals is thus very 'advanced' in sociological terms. It was created in American conditions, and it is these same conditions that lend it the capacity to create free democratic spaces. Pentecostalism actually helps to recreate the differentiation of North America in South America, and is therefore before its time, if one may very tentatively use such evolutionary language.

What evangelical religion has provided in Anglo-American culture and now provides in Latin America is an enclosure, a protective box in which novel seeds may grow. It contains mutations at the level of culture, and nurtures them by creating a strong boundary between itself and the outside world. It creates independence within dependence, and nourishes individuality inside the bonds of collective consciousness and solidarity. The dialectic of personal independence and religious dependence, of communal enclosure and individualistic growth, is maintained through the whole history of evangelical religion from the Puritan churches of Boston to the Apostolics of the Yucatan.

Inevitably Pentecostalism reflects some of the psychology of dependence located in the older structures of Latin American society. This clutters up the free space. Some investigators have suggested that it reproduces the authority and the dependence of the hacienda in the religious support group of the favela. All that needs to be argued here is that a movement of rural migrants to the great mega-cities will bring with it relics of its members' social origins: its politics will tend to be those of patron and client; mutual support will work through networks of patronage; there will be occasional instances of corruption; the power of the pastoral charismata will owe something to *caudillismo*; and sometimes the age-old passivity of the peasant will reassert itself. These reflections from an ancient past do not nullify aspirations towards a new future and a new individuality.

The line of agument pursued at this point concerns the trajectory of religious change (and differentiation) found in Anglo-American culture, and by extension it shows how implantations from that culture affect and are affected by the classic Latin American trajectory. We have now to bring out two major aspects of the way in which evangelical religion has related to Anglo-American culture which throw light on the roles it now plays in Latin America.

The first of these is the relation to ethnic or regional consciousness. In spite of carrying forward differentiation from the state, evangelicalism can enter deeply into ethnic consciousness and give it a new resonance. Here the original model is not Methodism in England, but Calvinistic Methodism in Wales. When Methodism burgeoned in Wales, it necessarily broke from its English form, and gradually re-formed a whole national consciousness. This model will become relevant below in relation to the burgeoning of Pentecostalism and evangelicalism among the Mayan people of Guatemala. Pentecostalism, like Methodism, speaks in 'a thousand tongues', and one of the remarkable aspects of evangelical penetration has been the translation of the Bible and of preaching into a thousand vulgar tongues. This both reaches the people and revitalizes the language. A perfect example of this was provided for the author when a Presbyterian pastor proferred his own translation of the Psalms in Mayan and a group of young girl catechists sang 'spiritual songs' in Mayan and in Spanish to a guitar accompaniment. It was the clearest possible reminiscence of a Methodist or Presbyterian choir in Wales singing in Welsh and English.

The second aspect is much more complicated, and concerns the relation of evangelical religion to the mobilization of a status group or a group of adjacent status groups. We can think in terms of three major mobilizations roughly a century apart, each with numerous, overlapping derivatives. They are Puritanism, Methodism, and Pentecostalism. Very roughly, each successive mobilization was further away from the Church–State connection, and reached less far into the upper strata and probed further into the lower strata. Each successive mobilization gave evidence of a reduced intellectual content. In the first two the flow of 'power' ran mainly from England to America; nevertheless, Methodism achieved its major impact in America. With Pentecostalism, by contrast, the flow of power undoubtedly emanated from an American base. Thus the flow chart of religious power imitates the flow chart of political power. *Each mobilization represented an erosion of the organic and comprehensive relation of religion to local community and of Church to State; and each required a breakage in order to achieve a voluntary form of religion and in order to become indigenous in other cultures.*

When Methodism broke from the Church of England in 1784, it followed the logic of the American revolution; that is, it created a *new* and different society, one in which religion was voluntary. From then on Methodism, and later the Baptist Church, eroded the American supports of Anglicanism and the other older Churches, and moved powerfully along the frontier and into the American South. The same necessary double breakage occurs in Latin America today: away from the hegemonic and organic Catholic Church and away from the leading strings of the United States. The Methodist Pentecostal Church in Chile, now a million strong, *had* to break from its Methodist parent.

In their precarious penetration of Latin America, the older denominations remained too high in the social scale and too much in leading strings of the United States to expand with any power; and in any case the organic frame of Catholicism remained too strong. Pentecostalism, however, leapt from the deprived of

America to the much more destitute of Latin America, and was autonomous almost from the start.

That brings us directly to the controversial role of the USA in the transmission of impulses to the Hispanic world. Thousands of US missionaries are active all over Central and South America. Very often the impulses are transmitted by high technology: television, cassette, and film, as well as radio. The effects of high technology on the content and style of mission clearly need to be canvassed, especially after the recent scandals among Pentecostals and others promoting the Electronic Church. Whatever that may show, there is inevitably strong North American influence in the backing, the content, and the style, especially perhaps in the large urban missions. Beyond that, the theories of church growth and organization which are sometimes used come from such places as Fuller Theological Seminary, Pasadena, California, and the Church of the Rock, Dallas, Texas.

It is also true that the growth of Protestantism, especially in a fundamentalist form, is often in US interests. The new 'people of God', especially in Central America, are often orientated to the United States. They have networks which take them to North America and are usually well-disposed towards North America. In Puerto Rico, for example, they prefer political association with the USA; in Haiti, they are often led by North Americans. The psychology they foster is closely allied to the Protestant ethic and therefore to the classical US ideal, the politics they espouse are generally non-revolutionary and usually anti-communist.

These facts do not tell us whether we may interpret the growth of evangelical Christianity as a case of 'dependencey', whereby the United States creates religious colonies in parallel with its political and economic colonies. The evidence is that the existence of the USA is a facilitating factor, but not in itself the main reason why some forty million Latin Americans now call themselves 'evangelicals'. Moreover, the influence of the USA varies. It may be strong in the networks which bind together USA-supported missions to the great cities; it may be almost non-existent in some movement to create a 'free space' in rural Mexico. It may be strong in Haiti and Puerto Rico; it is quite weak in Brazil.

OPENINGS FOR EVANGELICALISM

Up to this juncture I have set out some quite general social and historical circumstances bearing on the appearance in Latin America of religious developments once confined to Anglo-American culture. Now it is necessary to look more closely at the material, asking what fissures and shifts in the social fabric offer openings to the Pentecostals and the various evangelical missions. I shall discuss the vulnerable situation of women, attempts to locate a 'free space' in the countryside, the condition of rural migrants to the cities, the growth of the mega-city, and the position of ethnic subgroups, such as slighted and repressed nations, the various tribes, and migrants from Europe and elsewhere.

Pentecostals and free evangelicals attract considerably more women than men. On the surface, this may appear yet one more instance of the incorporation of female helpmeets into religious organizations run by men. Yet the evidence is that the adherence of women to evangelical groups helps advance their social position, and also that they are assisted by changes in the male personality wrought by conversion. This aspect of the advance of the 'evangelicals' has received more attention recently from female anthropologists. These anthropologists are sensitive to the more intimate mutations of culture, and do not require that all changes conform to the 'macho' model of structural revolution to be accounted 'real'.

Elizabeth Brusco (1986) studied evangelicals in a small town in the mountains of North Boyaca, Colombia. Her thesis concerns the way in which changes in male and female roles help to reintegrate the family and assist social mobility. What is interesting here is that during La Violencia in the 1940s and 1950s evangelicals mostly went underground into house churches. In Brusco's view, this experience accelerated changes in the domestic household. The free space sought and created by evangelicals was in the family, and there they firmly rejected the overarching hegemony of Catholicism.

The town she chose had a liberal tradition, which helps to explain its toleration of an evangelical presence. The earliest missionaries were Lutheran and were the more acceptable because they engaged in small-scale development work—for example, an electrification project. They were not specifically aiming at modernization or social advancement, but this came about all the same, in particular because evangelicals had new priorities in consumption. Brusco's most telling example is that evangelicals wanted first of all to acquire a table, symbolizing the family, whereas Catholics first of all wanted a radio.

Brusco identifies machismo and its female complement 'Marianismo' as major impediments. The one leads to sexual aggression, intransigence, and fighting, the other to an acceptance of sacrifice and suffering as the specifically female lot. Now that the cooperative domestic unit has largely broken down, the husbands are often without steady employment, and begin to maraud. The opportunities for female suffering greatly increase, especially since, in general, women have only one opportunity to marry.

The effect of evangelical conversion is that the men acquire certain feminine attributes, accept family discipline, and cease to beat their wives. (As one may easily imagine, this is a major barrier to conversion anywhere in Latin America, especially as the men encounter their scornful peers (Thornton 1981: 131). The women for their part acquire support groups, go to women's meetings, attend classes on family relationships, and begin that interest in education which is the first step to advancement for their children. The dominant evangelical images are of cleanliness and the smell of good food and of the absence of violence and wasteful drinking. This conforms to the general sociological observation, documented from Rochdale to Texas, that those who are washed in the blood of the Lamb rapidly learn to wash behind their ears.

I want now to turn to a study by Jean-Pierre Bastian (1985) of the way in which evangelicalism in rural areas may create a 'free space', even though it is not politically revolutionary. This capacity is worth emphasis for two reasons. One is that much of the earlier literature leaves the impression that Pentecostalism and even evangelicalism generally are tied to rural migration into the cities. The other reason is that Bastian is concerned elsewhere (1984) to bring out the international and specifically Anglo-American links of the evangelicals and the extent to which they inculcate submission as well as inciting resistance. However, in his study of religious dissent in a Mexican rural setting, he emphasizes both their autonomy and their capacity to innovate and resist (Bastian 1985).

He argues that these particular Protestant groups grow not because of North American colonialism, but because of features of Mexican society today. Mexico he describes as a society permanently in crisis and in debt, one that is becoming urban so rapidly that nowadays 60 per cent of the population lives in the towns. During the period of economic change and urbanization from 1960 to 1980, Protestants—and more particularly Pentecostals—multiplied thirteen times.

As the subsistence economy in the countryside has begun to be pulled into a market economy, Protestant expansion has accelerated there also. The older enclaves of the historic denominations had been more in the north and in the towns, but the new pentecostal communities began to appear in the country as well as in the town. Pentecostals are recruiting not only among the marginal workers of the urban areas in the states of Mexico, Puebla, and San Luis Potosi, but also in the villages of the south and south-east. Of particular interest here, as Patricia Fortuny has shown, is that Pentecostals increase most rapidly in areas where families farm for subsistence and where famine is frequent and seasonal migration normal (Fortuny 1982: 33). They are less well represented in areas of capitalist farming.

It may be, of course, that this suggests a double marginality, to capitalist farming as also to organized labour. That point would require extensive documentaion; but here Bastian's concern is with the difference between the rural evangelicals, autonomous and charismatic, and the urban evangelicals, with international links and bureaucratic organization. More than that, the pentecostal and other evangelical pastors have adopted seasonal practices which are reminiscent of pre-Columbian times. On the one hand, they renew ancient rituals calling for rain; on the other, they replace magic (and idols) with Sanidad Divina. Similarly, their invocation of the Holy Spirit both echoes and replaces the spirit cults of the Maya. This point is important, because there is evidence from many contexts that Pentecostalism brings with it elements of modernity, in part by diffusion from the USA, and also takes fire among the tangled brushwood of innumerable cults of the spirits.

This continuity with magico-religious cults is parallel to a continuity observable in Jamaica with what is known as the native 'revivalist' tradition. These earlier cults and traditions embodied symbols of resistance to established religion and to the wider social system, which Pentecostalism subsequently renews. In rural Mexico the caciques are using a system into which Catholicism is locked to back up their imposts, extorting and exploiting in order to enter the market economy. As the established system exhibits a union of economic, political, and social power, so too does the opposition. The evangelical groups construct an autonomous space within the village. Often their chapel has to be on the edge of the village since the centre is occupied. Something very similar is to be observed in Jamaica, where pentecostal buildings are along the margins and roadsides, while the 'established' Anglican, Methodist, and Baptist churches are in the main streets.

Given that the established system in rural Mexico is bonded together in a unified way, it follows that evangelical conversion often has a familial or communal character. One village may fend off incursions, occasionally by violence, while in another village the majority may convert, and occasionally the whole community may do so, complete with its juridical apparatus. (In Guatemala, whole towns may convert.) Sometimes evangelicals are forced to found entirely new villages, with names like Jerusalem, Jericho, and Bethany, and in this they are assisted by national Protestant organizations.

I visited one village in the Yucatan named Xokenpiche, where the Catholic church was locked and in ruins and where the population of 2,500 was now entirely Presbyterian. It had acquired, with some assistance from the United States, a new centre, housing, and a water supply, and seats were arranged around a neat little green adjoining the Bible school. There was also a dispensary called Bethesda. The dispensary is undoubtedly a powerful aid to conversion all over Latin America.

But the dispensary is not necessary. The Pentecostals, at least in rural Mexico, are less likely to provide clinics than Presbyterians or Seventh Day Adventists. Different denominations have rather different responses as far as social provision is concerned. In one village the local school was so lax that the Seventh Day Adventists simply built a new one. In some cases the majority in a village may become Mormon. This opens up frequent communication with the USA, and offers a chance to utilize new techniques. A study of Mormons in a Mexican village by David Clawson (1984) suggests that they too show the fruits of the 'Protestant' ethic: a bus trip to Salt Lake City greatly increases one's aspirations.

Inevitably evangelicals are pulled into politics. Some in the older denominations take radical positions. Generally the more recent pentecostal converts are pulled into whatever is politically opposed to Catholicism, and therefore may well support the Institutional Revolutionary Party against the (Catholic) Party of National Action. Here we see how an apolitical character, which was shaped in separations of religion and politics characteristic of Anglo-American culture, is pulled into the long established polarizations of Latin America. The power and pull of rival identifications will be illustrated below in the context of Guatemala.

It is now appropriate to look at the most familiar facilitating circumstances for pentecostalism. These are found in rural migration to the cities, and have been well depicted in the best-known books in the field: Emilio Willem's *Followers of the New Faith* (1967) and Christian Lalive D'Epinay's *Haven of the Masses* (1969).

Some of the most dramatic instances of this are to be found in Brazil, which also provides an opportunity to sketch an earlier history of Protestantism found in one form or another in most other Latin American countries. This earlier history is one of the spread of the Protestant ethic, under North American auspices, to subordinate groups seeking freer social spaces and gaining some social mobility in the process. Ronald Frase puts it this way: 'Protestantism, through its institutions of schools, churches, seminaries, hospitals, orphanages, publishing houses and sundry programs created a new complex organization which was not subject to the elite which had monopolized the symbols of power, prestige and wealth of traditional Brazil' (Frase 1975: 431). The parallel with Bastian's analysis of rural Mexico is striking. In particular, Protestantism offered power, patronage, and social mobility to the pastorate, and especially to their children.

The two largest groups were the Presbyterians and the Baptists. The former insisted on education as a criterion of leadership, which prevented them from having much vital contact with the uneducated. The Baptists opened up the ministry to 'unlearned men', however; and they anticipated the approach which gave Pentecostalism genuine access to large numbers of Brazilians.

From the 1930s onwards Brazilian society became industrialized, and Pentecostalism burgeoned. The middle classes gained a new sense of power against the old agrarian interests and aristocratic strata, but they were unable to achieve full control. Moreover, the salaried and professional middle classes were ill protected against rampant inflation. What most assisted Pentecostalism was the emergence of a rural proletariat without a patron, which then began a vast migration to the cities. The progress of urbanization appeared to be independent even of the rise of industry, and took the form of agglomerations of favelas in which newly arrived migrants found at least some mutual support. It was these favelas which provided a base for the populist politics of Vargas. Their influence was destroyed by the military coup of 1964.

During this period Pentecostalism created a Brazilian Protestantism entirely free of American control. From 1930 to 1964 only Pentecostalism achieved a rate of growth greater than that of the general population. By 1970 the Assemblies of God numbered about three-quarters of a million. By 1987 the *New York Times* (25 October) was estimating that twelve million Brazilians were Protestant and that twelve million more were in some way touched by Protestant churches. Most of these millions are pentecostal. As always, Pentecostalism has been fissile as well as fertile. It has split into more than a hundred groups. Some are sectarian, others like Brasil para Cristo more open and socially active (Page 1984). São Paulo, one of the largest of the new mega-cities, has become the Pentecostal capital of the world. The historic denominations have felt the pressure of all this, either through people deserting them or through schism, and many of them have paid Pentecostalism the compliment of emulation.

To what extent Pentecostals are to be found in the ranks of organized labour seems uncertain. Rolim in his *Os Pentecostais no Brasil* (1985: 171) cites data to show that Pentecostals are much more strongly represented in the service sectors than in the commercial and industrial sectors (Rolim 1985; Rolim 1979). Out of 315 male Pentecostals, the largest category comprised 72 servants, gardeners, and porters (Rolim 1985: 179). His approach to Pentecostals has a Marxisant cast, viewing their concern with 'power' as a desire for liberty which has been turned aside and projected upwards into an alienated world of 'the Spirit'.

Certainly it is true that Pentecostals respect the powers that be, whether those powers are the Chilean junta or the Sandinistas. In Brazil, with the partial and disputed exception of members of Brasil para Cristo, they rarely carry political activity beyond voting, and their relationships with deputies are those of clients to patrons. Nevertheless, there is now a sizeable number of Protestant deputies in Brazil at state and National level.

Reference to the mega-city of São Paulo allows a very brief aside on the appearance of mega-churches appropriate to such places as Rio de Janeiro, Bogota, Lima, Mexico City—and Seoul. These are largely an American importation, along with other modern techniques of communication, and are associated with the church growth movement. Such churches give members a feeling of involvement in something truly epoch-making, and also offer intimacy through membership in small cells. At the same time, some churches are specifically geared to middle-class and professional groups. These may offer training in business and in psychological skills, as well as participation in seminars and discussion groups. They resemble the large religious organizations found in most American cities, equipped with trained staff and offering a wide range of activities. The Jotabeche Church in Santiago, Chile, caters for a membership of 80,000 in a building which holds 2,000. It has twenty-three assistant pastors, and a sizeable proportion of those who attend are lower middle class. The question raised by these organizations is how far the classic problems of religion in the large city are solvable by social engineering.

A final element in the expansion of Pentecostalism has been its ability to provide a common ethos to subordinate ethnic groups and tribes without reverting to anything like a single national Church. In general, Pentecostalism is part of the long-term erosion of the unity of the Church and the State and the unity of the Church and *the* community. Clearly it cannot mobilize a suppressed nation within a single religious body, since its success depends, at least in part, on division and on adaptation to all the variable fissures of society. But it can offer a shared ethos to an ethnic group, and this capacity has been analysed by Wedenoja (1978) in Jamaica and Virginia Burnett (1986) in Guatemala.

In the smaller tribes it can, of course, lead to either disintegration or revitalization, depending on circumstances. Amongst several studies there is an excellent monograph on Pentecostalism among the Toba of northern Agentina by Elmer Miller (1967).[3] A study by Henry Aulie (1979) documents a more pluralistic situation, in which Presbyterians were followed by Pentecostals among the Chols of Chiapas in Mexico.

A parallel form of reintegration may come about among local concentrations of migrants from overseas, such as Syrians, Germans, East Indians, Japanese, and Italians. Most ethnic migrants hold to their ancestral faith, as do German Lutherans and Catholic (Maronite) Syrians. Certainly such groups are sufficiently imbued with economic initiative not to need injections of the Protestant ethic. But in some circumstances such groups may undergo sufficient disintegration to seek new religious sources of vitality. In this way the Congregacão Crista was founded among the Italians of São Paulo. It is clear that an ethnic group which is very resistant to conversion on its home ground may become suddenly quite open once transported to a new culture and environment.

Nevertheless, the major instances are provided by subnationalities like the Maya of Guatemala and by nations which have been subordinated, like the Jamaicans and the Koreans. I select Guatemala by way of example, especially as Virginia Burnett's analysis is so comprehensive and clear.

In 1871 the triumphant liberal revolutionaries in Guatemala treated the Church with great severity, depriving it even of legal personality. But as was the case with so many other societies, the culture itself was not secularized. The Mayans, who were in the majority, devised a kind of syncretic religious practice, and used the cofradias (fraternities) as vehicles for conserving some of their pre-Columbian traditions. Though the liberals invited Protestants in as agents of progress and providers of services, they had little success. They were regarded as alien, and in any case the plantation owners (like those in Jamaica at an earlier period) did not want the convenient fatalism of their labour force disturbed.

For a while in the 1920s it looked as if Protestants might be under pressure from nationalistic governments as agents of foreign culture, but the atmosphere eased under the influence of Roosevelt's 'good neighbour' policy. With the advent of a government under Arbenz interested in land reform, the Protestants were divided in their response. Some American missionaries reflected the intensely anti-communist stance engendered in the Cold War; on the other hand, many native Protestants became involved in land reform and in peasant organizations.

Then in 1954 there was a military coup backed by the CIA, which inaugurated intermittent reigns of terror. It also partially restored the position of the Catholic Church, helped by a US government which saw Catholicism as a barrier to communism. Protestants found themselves under suspicion, and were occasionally punished.

At this point more US missionaries arrived. They were of a strongly conservative cast of mind, and certainly helped Protestants lose the dangerous stigma of Communism. Some of the missionaries stressed shared religious feeling rather than divisive dogma, and proceeded to modernize the local religious style, with novel techniques of planning, marketing, and communication. This was quite successful, and provided persuasive Anglo-Americn role models; but it was also resented as a foreign importation. An independent Presbyterian Church emerged in the Mayan highlands and also an independent Nazarene Church. Fragments broke off from the Assemblies of God: for example, the Prince of Peace group. This splitting preceded a rapid indigenous expansion as it did in Brazil and also in Chile. Rapid growth was greatly aided by translations of the Bible into the very numerous dialects of the Mayan language, in particular by members of the Central American Mission (CAM). It is insufficiently realized just how much threatened cultures have been revitalized in Latin America, as also in Africa, by translations of the Bible.

At the same time, very rapid urbanization was proceeding in Guatemala. Nearly one-third of the total population was now living in Guatemala City. Yet there was only one priest there for every 30,000 persons. Then in 1976 there was a major earthquake. Aid and personnel poured in from North America, and a major shift in the social landscape began to come about. The spread of Protestant groups—above all of Pentecostals—pulled people away from alcoholism, petty crime, and corruption. Conversion was also a protest against violence and the disintegration of the family brought about by the male macho personality. The new faith encouraged savings, offered education, and discouraged smoking; and it generally inculcated habits which might make for some modest economic advancement following the slogan 'From the dirt to the sky'. Part of the welfare infrastructure was by now associated with the Protestant churches: above all, clinics. For Mayans the clinics dispensed a magical power; so too did the pentecostal healers. Even some of the middle class were converted to evangelical religion: for example, the church known as Verbo, to which General Rios Montt belonged. Montt's brief and controversial time as President combined a drive against violence and corruption with a ferocious and effective attack on the guerrillas offering beans—or death. However, this temporary association with power did not appear to harm evangelicals very much. Some of them, of course, sided with the opposition, and mostly escaped the country in company with members of the Catholic left. Probably most Protestants supported the regime of Montt. Less than a decade later, Guatemalans elected an evangelical President.

Burnett's overall assessment of this very rapid expansion of Pentecostalism and conservative evangelicalism is that Mayan culture is being re-formed in Protestant terms and that the communal organizations of the Mayans are being renewed in the thousands of chapels to be observed everywhere in Guatemala from the barrios of Guatemala City to the jungles of El Peten. What once more is notable is that the apolitical character of Pentecostalism is being pulled into the polarized identifications of a Latin American society.

CULTURAL MUTATIONS

Thus the role, character, and impact of Pentecostalism in Latin America during the last thirty or more years of rapid development parallel the role, character, and impact of Methodism and the evangelical revival during England's industrial revolution. That being so, it is part of a vast process whereby successive religious mobilizations occur, beginning with the Puritan revolution and moving through the massive expansions of Methodist and Baptist religion in America to contemporary Pentecostalism.

There are three aspects to this process. First, it involves the steady erosion of the organic relation of *the* Church to the whole society and the relation of *the* church to the local community. However widely the new religious forms spread, they represent a voluntary, pluralistic system which cannot reconstitute the old organic unions. These dissolutions were initiated in England and fully achieved in America, and are currently spilling over from the United States into Latin America and, for that matter, South Korea.

The groups splinter from their original traditions for various reasons: to initiate and express the collapse of the old organic order; to achieve the autonomy necessary to become genuinely indigenous in different cultures, whether these be Korean or Hispanic; and to express rival charismata and adjust to all the different social environments that they may encounter.

The latest manifestations may have world-historical significance given that in Latin countries such dissolutions have hitherto been achieved by society splitting into two warring, polarized halves, one organically and dogmatically religious and the other organically and dogmatically secular. In this context liberation theology can be seen as an attempt at recovering hegemony which nevertheless employs the voluntary, pluralistic, and democratic form of the base community.

Secondly, this process proceeds mainly at the level of culture, precisely because it is generated by and further extends a system in which religious bodies are partially disengaged from the central nervous system of social power and are partially separated from its antagonisms. This is not to say that the various Protestant groupings are always apolitical in stance. They represent mobilizations of consciousness and of communal organization within particular strata, and there may come a critical moment when they are associated with the interests and aspirations of those strata, as Methodism was in relation to certain strata in England between 1850 and 1920 and as a black Baptist leadership was in relation to the civil rights of blacks in the USA in the 1960s. But the characteristic mode in which such bodies initiate change, especially when repression inhibits overt action, is by the creation of a free space, in which the old hierarchies are inoperative, as for example in rural Mexico. It is precisely because they derive from and represent a dissolution of the old organic unions that they are 'apolitical', and it is precisely this dissolution which decrees that the mode of change they initiate is cultural—that is, the 'free space'. Given that this is their *modus operandi*, they are more—or less— likely, depending on circumstances, to help prevent violent revolution. They are outside the inner dynamics of social violence, and indeed promote a general peaceability, socially and psychologically. They therefore illustrate the problematic initiated by Halévy to the effect that Methodism helped England avoid violent revolution.

Thirdly, within that free space they protect and nourish a new man and even in some circumstances a new woman, particularly in the subversion of machismo and 'Marianismo'. Bernard Semmel (1974) is therefore correct to write of 'The Methodist Revolution'. The groups with which we are concerned in Latin America and the Caribbean usually have pitifully few resources; nevertheless, they do what they can, which is to reorient themselves in terms of habits, disciplines, and priorities and in terms of seeking to reunite the family. They create networks for personal and pragmatic support. A new personal assurance goes with a communal insurance. People save, and avoid waste. They gain a sense of selfhood and a capacity to participate which is expressed in learning how to take responsibilities and to lead and to speak in 'tongues' or sing. A fresh rhythm supersedes repetitious fatality. Practice in speaking and reading together helps to make possible some modest social mobility, at least for some, and particularly for the pastors, if not in this generation then in the next. The network itself makes possible wider vistas and contacts, many of them in North America, and this helps to transmit new techniques and other intimations of modernity. This culture also spreads beyond the confines which protect it. New faiths are efficacious not only on their own account, but in what they force their rivals to emulate in order to survive.

Notes

1. The material for this essay was collected with the help of substantial funding from the Institute for the Study of Economic Culture (ISEC) at Boston University under the supervision of Peter Berger. I am deeply grateful to ISEC, and also for the opportunities provided by my tenure of the Elizabeth Scurlock Chair of Human Values at Southern Methodist University. The essay, written in 1988, has now been developed into a book (Martin 1990).
2. In his very interesting article, Peter Fry pursues a comparison between English Methodism and Umbanda parallel to the comparison I have pursued between English Methodism and Brazilian Pentecostalism.
3. See also Wilson 1973: 121–3.

References

Aman, K. (1987), 'Chile's Army Seeks its God', *Cross Currents*, 36: 459–66.

Aulie, H. W. (1979), 'The Christian Movement among the Chols of Mexico', Ph.D. thesis, Fuller Theological Seminary, Pasadena.

Bastian, J-P. (1984), 'Protestantismos Latinoamericos entre la Resistencia y la sumisión 1961–1983', *Chistianismo y Sociedad*, 82: 49–68.

124 *David Martin*

—— (1985), 'Dissidence religieuse dans le milieu rural méxicain', *Social Compass*, 32: 245–60.

Bridges, J. C. (1970), *Expansion evangelica en México* (El Paso).

Brusco, E. (1986), 'The Household Basis of Evangelical Religion and the Reformation of Machismo in Colombia', Ph.D. thesis, City University of New York.

Burnett, V. G. (1986), 'A History of Protestantism in Guatemala', Ph.D. thesis, Tulane University.

Clawson, D. L. (1984), 'Religious Allegiance and Development in Rural Latin America', *Journal of Interamerican Studies and World Affairs*, 26: 499–524.

della Cava, R. (1970), *Miracle at Joaseiro* (New York).

D'Epinay, C. L. (1969), *Haven of the Masses: A Study of the Pentecostal Movement in Chile* (London).

Fernandes, R. C. (1985), 'Aparacida, our Queen, Lady and Mother, Sarava!', *Social Science Information*, 24/4.

Fortuny, P. (1982), 'Insercion y diffusion de Sectarismo en el campo Yucateca', *Yucatan: Historia y Economica*, 60/30.

Frase, R. A. (1975), 'A Sociological Analysis of the Development of Brazilian Pentecostalism: A Study in Social Change', Ph.D. thesis, Princeton University.

Fry, P. (1978), 'Two Religious Movements: Protestantism and Umbanda', *Stanford Journal of International Studies*, 13 (Spring).

Maduro, O. (1982), 'Le catholicisme au Venezuela', *Amérique Latine*, 11.

Martin, D. (1987), 'The Growth of Conservative Protestantism in Jamaica and Elsewhere in the Caribbean', unpublished paper; now incorporated as Chapter 7 in Martin 1990.

—— (1990), *Tongues of Fire* (Oxford).

Miller, E. (1967), 'Pentecostalism among the Argentine Toba', Ph.D. thesis, University of Pittsburgh.

Page, J. (1984), 'Brasil para Cristo: The Cultural Construction of Pentecostal Networks in Brazil', Ph.D. thesis, New York University.

Rolim, C. R. (1979), 'Pentecôtisme et Société au Brésil', *Social Compass*, 26: 345–72.

—— (1985), *Os Pentecostais no Brasil* (Vozes).

Semmel, B. (1974), *The Methodist Revolution* (London).

Smith, B. C. (1982), *The Church and Politics in Chile* (Princeton, NJ).

Thornton, W. (1981), 'Protestantism: Profile and Process. A Case Study in Religious Change from Colombia', Ph.D. thesis, Southern Methodist University.

Wedenoja, W. A. (1978), 'Religion and Adaptation in Rural Jamaica', Ph.D. thesis, (University of California, San Diego, 1978).

Willems, E. (1967), *Followers of the New Faith* (Nashville, Tenn.).

Wilson, B. R. (1973), *Magic and the Millennium* (London).

8

States, Governments, and the Management of Controversial New Religious Movements

JAMES A. BECKFORD

Even informed scholars fail to agree on the meaning or value of the new religious movements (NRMs) which have aroused so much controversy in Western countries in the past two decades. On the one hand, some believe that the new movements are important because they herald an Aquarian age of self-fulfilment, sensibility, and tolerance. On the other, the movements are said to be exploitative, amoral, and unimportant because they are irrelevant to the major issues of politics and ethics. These different interpretations of the movements' importance are further complicated by differing opinions about the degree to which the controversies surrounding NRMs are central or marginal to wider problems about the relationship between religion and the State. I shall argue that, whatever the significance of NRMs, the societal responses that they elicit are important indicators of emergent problems in the relationships between modern Western States, governments, and religious organizations of all kinds. In other words, I shall treat the movements as 'trace elements'; for it is my contention that the changing fortunes of NRMs can tell us a lot about the social structures in which they operate. In particular, my argument will be that the controversies surrounding NRMs provide an insight into some of the major difficulties facing advanced industrial societies in the late twentieth century. My aim will be to show that, despite the protections afforded by various constitutional guarantees of religious freedom, religious organizations have been adversely affected by the growing capacity of the State to influence and monitor more and more of the activities of its citizens. The tensions between agencies of the State and various NRMs are but one relatively small aspect of much larger problems concerning the disputed frontier between the public and private spheres of life.

After briefly specifying what is meant here by 'the State', 'government', and 'NRMs', I shall summarize the current state of sociological thinking about the controversies surrounding NRMs and the place of the State and governments in the associated tensions and conflicts in the USA and the UK. I shall then place these controversies in the context of some current ideas about the evolution of the modern State and give my own interpretation of the changing relationships between government, the State, and NRMs.

SPECIFICATION OF TERMS

It is important to clarify the basic terms of my analysis, because many writers on the topic of Church and State or religion and the State have failed to draw some elementary, but vital, distinctions.[1] I want to be especially clear about the distinction between 'the State' and 'government'. The two terms are often used as if they were interchangeable, but the ways in which controversies about religion have recently occurred in advanced industrial societies show that it is analytically helpful to distinguish between State and government.

The meaning of the term 'State' is hotly contested. My own preference is for Max Weber's idea that the State is a

system of order [which] claims binding authority, not only over the members of the state, the citizens, most of whom have obtained membership by birth, but also to a very large extent over all action taking place in the area of its jurisdiction. It is thus a compulsory organization with a territorial base. Furthermore, today, the use of force is regarded as legitimate only so far as it is either permitted by the state or prescribed by it. . . . The claim of the modern state to monopolize the use of force is as essential to it as its character of compulsory jurisdiction and of continuous operation. (Weber 1978: 56)

An important advantage of Weber's conceptualization is that it introduces the notion of *legitimacy* into the discussion of the State. This will have a direct bearing on my discussion of the State's response to NRMs.

If the State is an apparatus of social administration and control, backed by a monopoly over the legitimate exercise of force in its territory, any given *government* tries to direct the apparatus to its own ends. But in democratic regimes the electoral process, the separation of powers, and in some cases the existence of provincial assemblies all help to loosen a government's hold over the State. There can be tension between them.

Finally, the term 'new religious movement' has the advantage of being relatively free from the evaluative and outdated theoretical connotations of labels such as 'sect', 'cult', or 'minority religion'. But it suffers from the disadvantage of being too inclusive. It refers indiscriminately to phenomena as diverse as the Charismatic Renewal, the movement for social justice in the Roman Catholic Church (Neal 1985), the (itself variegated) Human Potential Movement, the bewildering plethora of movements based on Asian spiritualities, and the Jesus People movement—to name only a few of the movements to which the term has been applied. In an attempt to avoid the worst problems of the exceedingly wide scope of 'NRM', I shall confine my analysis to those movements which have become *controversial* in a number of countries. These movements are often designated as 'cults' in everyday parlance. They are, by definition, the movements which have most clearly attracted attempts by State agencies and governments to control their activities.

The controversies arise from a wide range of accusations, grievances, and recriminations on the part of NRMs and their opponents. The movements have been accused of, for example, deception, fraud, exploitation, psychological manipulation, profiteering, political chicanery, and violence. In return, they have charged their opponents with kidnapping, misuse of scientific evidence, prejudice against religion, and intolerance. I have argued elsewhere (Beckford 1985) that the changing character of these 'cult controversies' can be understood in terms of the ways in which NRMs are typically 'inserted' into their host societies. That is, the pattern of relations that NRMs sustain with the wider society governs the kind of controversies in which they tend to become embroiled.

THE AMERICAN PROBLEMATIC

Most controversial NRMs or 'cults' either originated or 'took off' in the USA. Americans have probably constituted the largest single national category of NRM members, participants, and sympathizers. It is not surprising, then, that American accounts of cult controversies have tended to dominate the sociological and historical literature on the topic. This has had the effect of colouring the presentation of the sociological issues involved in cult controversies in a very particular way. I am not suggesting that the American accounts are wrong or seriously inadequate. My point is, rather, that the special, if not unique, position of religion in the history, constitutional law, and public life of the USA has encouraged American commentators to construe the problems arising from State and governmental attempts to manage NRM-related controversies in a one-sided fashion. The discussion is dominated by a preoccupation with a perceived threat to the constitutional injunction against the federal State's 'entanglement' in religion (see Demerath and Williams 1987; Pfeffer 1987; Shepherd 1985).

Authoritative accounts of relations between NRMs and the State or government in the USA have taken four basic forms.[2]

(1) The earliest formulation of the official responses to NRMs in the USA proposed that the State *inevitably* became involved in attempts to resolve disputes between NRMs and other groups and institutions (Robbins 1981). This official involvement in arbitration was expected to lead to the creation of public policy relating to controversial NRMs, but the wider implications were left unexplored. It was simply suggested that more overt conflicts between the State and NRMs would be likely to ensue from the latter's reluctance to accept such official arbitration. The State's role is implicitly construed here as one of neutral arbitration between disputants, with no special significance attaching to the fact that one of them claims religious status.

(2) But as the intensity of cult/anti-cult conflicts and controversies increased, there was a growing awareness that they were inseparable from wider issues concerning 'the role of "new religions" in modern America, the needs to which these movements respond, the cultural and social conditions in which they are flourishing, and the psychological processes which operate within them' (Robbins 1985b: 7). More important for my purposes, the controversies were said to be 'closely related to an emerging general crisis of church and state relations' (ibid.). This was allegedly because, as the State came to monitor more and more aspects of

life, the privileges and exemptions enjoyed by NRMs (and other religious organizations) elicited resentment from non-religious sectors of society. Indeed, the special exemptions were particularly provocative in the case of NRMs which provided all manner of 'secular' services to their members. Resentment was therefore said to be increasingly directed at 'cults' because, in addition to being 'unfamiliar' and lacking grass-roots support, they were 'particularly *diversified and multifunctional* enclaves lying outside the web of regulation which increasingly enmeshed "secular" organizations' (Robbins 1985*b*: 9). The resentment was also said to be focused on the belief that the more 'totalistic' NRMs deprived their followers of personal autonomy and dignity.

(3) An even stronger formulation of the grounds for NRM controversies in the USA cast them as merely a subset of more general problems concerning 'Church autonomy'. The process of secularization and the declining prosperity of mainline denominations in the USA had allegedly combined to put virtually all religious organizations in a marginal position, where their tax exemptions and other privileges were supposedly in jeopardy. Thus, NRMs which fell foul of State monitoring agencies were believed to serve as ' "point men" for respectable churches' (Robbins 1985*a*: 239). It followed that 'Controversial movements such as Scientology, Rajneesh and the Unification Church are situated at the cutting edge of church/state boundary disputes involving questions of church autonomy' (Robbins 1985*a*: 243).

(4) At the time of writing, assertions about State and government control of NRMs in the USA have reached the point of claiming that the 'traditional flexibility and freedoms usually afforded religious groups in the US' (Richardson 1988: 4) were being abandoned by governmental officials and courts of law. This claim is supported in part by evidence of attempts by the Internal Revenue Service (IRS) to equate religious organizations with charitable organizations for taxation purposes, in order to require the former to adhere to public policy as a condition of retaining their tax-exempt status. The implication may be that the increasingly intrusive and restrictive monitoring of the finances of NRMs by tax officials is the thin end of a wedge which could eventually mean that *all* religious groups would forfeit their special constitutional privileges unless they make their teachings and practices conform closely with the prevailing criteria of charity. In other

words, it may no longer be enough for an organization to be religious: it may also have to be charitable in law if it is to benefit from fiscal and other privileges.

The argument about the decline of the flexibility and freedom characteristic of relations between the State and religious organizations in the USA is also supported by evidence that appellate courts, including the US Supreme Court, have handed down decisions in the 1980s which virtually overturn some of the earlier 'landmark' decisions concerning the religion clauses of the First Amendment. It is as if the ground gained by unpopular and minority religions earlier this century were being denied to today's controversial NRMs. This has been interpreted as a sign that American courts nowadays favour more traditional expressions of religion and that the US is 'in the process of "establishing" a more bland, less exciting type of religion that is nonthreatening to the dominant culture and power structure' (Richardson 1988: 8). The IRS and the Immigration and Naturalization Service (INS) are allegedly the main agents of this new policy to constrain non-traditional religious groups to be more conformist. If successful, this policy could, according to Richardson, redefine and restrict the place of religion in the American social order. This would clearly represent a drastic disturbance of the pattern of Church–State relations, and would have a harmful effect on all religious groups—not just the controversial NRMs.

It may be an exaggeration to describe the current condition of religion/State relations as a 'crisis'; but it is certainly true that a number of legal cases involving religious organizations has recently illustrated the *continuing* tension, at least in American law, between the freedom customarily accorded to religion and the rights reserved by the State to investigate allegations of wrongdoing in its territory (see e.g. Robbins *et al.* 1985: 95–110). Prominent cases have concerned exemption from taxation, conditions of employment, the definition of charitable status, the responsibilities of public trustees, the disclosure of financial records, public support for parochial schools, enforced conformity with 'public policy', involvement in the Sanctuary movement, and prayers in public schools.

In my view, one of the most significant aspects of the ways in which sociologists have framed the attempts of agents of the American State to monitor and control NRMs is the assumption that, normally and historically, religious organizations have been beyond the reach of official surveillance except in cases where there is an overwhelming justification for intervention to punish or prevent criminal activity. The assumption makes sense in the context of US history and constitutional law; but it means that questions about the control of NRMs have been dominated by a concern for preserving certain taken-for-granted freedoms and privileges. The discussion understandably centres on legal and normative, rather than sociological, issues. As a result, questions about the changing nature of the State and the conditions which shape its legitimacy and power tend to have lower priority on the research agenda of most sociologists of religion in the USA.

Nevertheless, attempts have been made to understand the significance of Church–State problems in the USA without confining them to a legal and normative framework. This involves trying to situate these problems in the context of social pressures which constrain agencies of the State to adopt strategies the effect of which is, probably unintentionally, to limit some of the freedoms previously enjoyed by religious organizations. For example, Roland Robertson (1981) has observed that the recent history of religion in the USA is marked by a growing contradiction between, on the one hand, the long-standing assumption that acceptable forms of denominational religion are functional for *national* identity or integration and, on the other, the emerging idea that religion is best understood and practised as a matter of *private* conviction. It is as if religion is tolerated only on condition that it is civic-minded *and* confined to private spirituality. If NRMs and other religious groups put their religious convictions into political, social, or economic practice, they allegedly leave themselves open to the charge of breaching the dubious but widely taken-for-granted wall of separation between Church and State (or, better, religion and politics). In other words, now that it can no longer be assumed that religious organizations will all preach and practise a shared set of common values, the definition of what is acceptably religious has shifted in the direction of private belief or even beliefs that 'certainly occupy in the life of [individuals] "a place parallel to that filled by God" in traditional religious persons' (*Welsh* v. *US* [1970] 398 US 340). Collective expressions of religion, below the level of some overarching civil religion, have allegedly become problematic. NRMs, lacking long-established credibility and deep roots in communities, are therefore the first victims of the increasingly restrictive definition of religion for legal purposes.

Current controversies surrounding NRMs reflect a further aspect of the relation between religion and the State which has been examined by both Robertson (1981) and myself (Beckford 1979, 1985). I am referring to the argument that modern Western governments, in their attempts to promote the interests of national capital and in the search for legitimation of their promotional activities, have increasingly used State agencies in order to intervene in matters which were previously of private concern. Jürgen Habermas (1979) has dubbed this tendency 'the colonization of the life-world'. Similarly, Claus Offe (1984) has interpreted the State's penetration of what was formerly the private sphere as a strategy for mitigating the contradictions of the capitalist welfare state in a time of recession. These arguments are clearly based on debatable assumptions about the dynamics of late or disorganized capitalist societies; but there is unlikely to be major disagreement with the observation that the State, via accredited agencies, has come to play an increasingly intrusive role in the lives of individuals and communities. It is only to be expected, therefore, that those NRMs which offer their own, distinctive, and frequently dissident forms of the 'good life' or 'good society' will attempt to resist what they consider to be illicit State incursions into matters of ultimate significance. The likelihood of conflicts with State agencies is thereby increased.

Another implication of NRMs' resistance to the State's intrusion into the 'privileged' domain of religion is that they are often forced to have recourse to law. That is to say, they try to defend themselves by reference to specific laws; but, ironically, this aggravates their already precarious, unpopular position. This is because the importation of legal arguments into a sphere of life which is usually characterized by strong loyalties and relatively personalistic relationships may make the original problem even more intractable by placing it on an inappropriately formal basis. As Offe (1984: 281) has remarked about the application of legal statutes to conflicts concerning marital relationships, 'The very recourse to legal regulations violates principles of mutual recognition, encourages cynicism between actors, and may even encourage them to retaliate by "escaping" the consequences of the law.' In short, some problems may simply not be amenable to 'legalization', and may actually be aggravated by it. An illustration of this irony is the resentment that some NRMs have generated in public opinion by their recourse to law for the purpose of defending their interests. In the eyes of their critics, this only confirms that they are not authentically religious, and probably have something to hide.

Yet another consideration that deserves more attention than it has so far received in American accounts of official control of NRMs is the fact that the number, scope, and effectiveness of *anti-cult* groups have increased in parallel with the growth of controversial NRMs. Some of these have been able to put pressure on State agencies at all levels to intervene on behalf of the supposed victims of 'cults'. They have often taken the initiative in alerting State officials to what they claimed to be the abuses of all kinds perpetrated by NRMs. In fact, the monitoring actions of State agencies have usually been reactions to the demands of 'concerned citizens'.

This *mediating* activity of anti-cult groups is important, because it feeds into the pattern of attempts by States to derive some legitimacy from their *consumer protection* work (Richardson 1986). Enactment and implementation of laws designed to protect individuals from anticipated harm or fraud are prime means for creating or sustaining the idea that the State merely pursues its citizens' freedom of action and best interests by defending their rights as individuals. This is the State's 'watchdog' role, and it creates a convenient link between the notion of citizens as individual *consumers* and that of the State as the neutral *regulator* of various markets. The role is easily defensible in conditions of religious pluralism, in which the metaphor of the 'spiritual supermarket' rings true. The State can therefore try to justify its intervention on the grounds of merely averting abuses and excesses in a 'normally' harmonious area of life. *Caveat vendor* is the warning to religious entrepreneurs. But the advocates of a strict separation between religion and the State in the USA regard the operation of consumer protection as unconstitutional in relation to religious matters. This is also one of the reasons why opponents of controversial NRMs are at pains to deny that such movements are 'really' religious.

If the State's attempts to control NRMs have been largely reactive and couched in terms of the rationale of consumer protection, the supposed site of religion/State conflicts has to be rethought. It seems to me inadvisable to consider the conflict as a *direct* struggle between religion and the State; rather, the struggle is primarily between groups competing for the ability to define the religion/State relationship in particular ways. In other words, the main actors are identifiable groups within civil society. They struggle against each other at least as much as they do against agencies of the State. The latter, of course, have their own interests as well; but these interests lie less with controlling religion directly than with achieving a solution to conflicts within civil society which will enhance, and be consonant with, the State's legitimacy.

I can summarize my qualifications of, and expansions upon, the dominant American interpretations of the place of 'cult controversies' in the pattern of unquiet relationships between religion and the State in the USA as follows:

(a) The State is undeniably extending its capacity for monitoring and controlling many previously 'privileged' spheres of social life; this is evinced by the increasing frequency of disputes between the State and religious organizations. But this has relatively little to do *directly* with the multifunctionality of NRMs, the resentment generated by the regulatory gap between secular and religious organizations, the perceived attack on Church autonomy, or the relegation of religion to the status of charitable activity.

(b) The growth of the State's monitoring activities is better understood as a response to an increasing and wider problem of legitimation. Strengthening their role as consumer watchdogs is the preferred strategy of many governments for legitimating their increasingly corporatist stance towards competition in the capitalist world order.

(c) The State has very few reasons to take the initiative in controlling today's NRMs, but is content to respond to the agitation of anti-cult lobbies in line with its consumer protection role.

THE MONITORING OF CONTROVERSIAL NRMS IN THE UK

Most of the NRMs which have aroused controversy in the USA have been exported to Western Europe. They are no less controversial in Europe; but the grounds for the controversies are different in ways which reflect, among other things, different relations between religion and the State (Beckford 1981). There are some similarities with the controversies in the USA, but, more important, the different patterns of historical development have guided religion/State problems into some strikingly dissimilar channels in European countries (Beckford 1985; Shupe *et al.* 1983).

The two main continuities with the American pattern of controversy can be sketched quite briefly. First, most West European governments, like their American counterpart, have repeatedly denied that they have any special prejudice against NRMs; and they constantly affirm the freedom of individuals to choose their own religion. They claim that they take sanctions against NRMs only if there is clear evidence of wrongdoing or danger.[3] No special legislation to deal specifically with NRMs has been enacted, although proposals for such laws have been debated in some places. Second, European anti-cult lobbies have been just as energetic as their American counterparts in bringing pressure to bear on governments to check the abuses allegedly perpetrated by certain NRMs, and they have tirelessly supported legislative action against 'destructive cultism'.

The West European contexts of 'cult controversies' differ from the American in many particulars, but the more significant differences include the following. First, the numerical and financial strength of NRMs in Europe is much less. Second, the extent of religious indifference and anti-religious sentiment is much greater in Europe. Third, the degree of constitutional and/or customary protection for the *absolute* freedom of religion is weaker than in the USA.

Relations between the State and NRMs in the UK illustrate the significance of these differences. Cult controversies in the UK, as in the USA, have been dominated by the grievances of NRM members' relatives, by the scandals and scare stories put out by journalists, and by some famous legal actions. Neither the State nor any particular government has been centrally implicated in these basically private activities. On the other hand, certain NRMs have encountered difficulties created by government and State officials.

The UK lacks a written constitution; the British people are as much 'subjects' as 'citizens'; and there are established Churches in England and Scotland. In these circumstances, there is neither separation of religion and State nor even-handedness towards religious organizations (Barker 1987). No less important in my view is the fact that the fiscal and other exemptions enjoyed by most religious groups are not granted to them for being religious, but only for being deemed charitable in law—that is, for the public benefit, by virtue of their supernaturalist teachings. In the absence of a constitutional guarantee of religious freedom, opportunities exist for the exercise of official discrimination against NRMs. For example, the Minister of Health and the Home Secretary jointly issued an order in 1968 banning foreigners from entering the country for the purpose of studying Scientology. The Ministers claimed that Scientology was suspected of damaging the mental health of certain people, and the ban remained in force until it was equally mysteriously lifted by the Home Secretary in 1980. Scientology was also singled out by the British government as the object of an official inquiry conducted by Sir John Foster, QC, and published by Parliament in 1971 (Foster 1971). A much more secretive inquiry into the affairs of the Exclusive Brethren was conducted in 1975 (see Wilson 1983).

A more recent attempt by the British government to act against a particular NRM was less successful. When the High Court found that the *Daily Mail* had not been guilty of defaming leading members of the Unification Church in 1981, the jury recommended that the charitable status of two sections of this NRM should be revoked because it was really a political organization and did not, therefore, qualify for the privileges of a charity. The Charity Commissioners came under pressure from the government's chief law officers to comply with the jury's wishes, but they refused to do so on the grounds that, 'as a matter of law, the teaching and practice of [the Unification Church's] divine principle . . . do not go beyond the very wide bounds which have been applied by the court for the purpose of ascertaining whether or not the propagation and practice of any particular religious creed is charitable in law' (*The Guardian*, 18 March 1983).

This is an intriguing case of tension between a government and part of the State apparatus, and it illustrates the need to distinguish analytically between 'State' and 'government'. In May 1989 the government outlined its plans for tightening up the criteria of charitable status partly in order to make it more difficult for religious organizations to obtain registration as charities if their activities are not deemed to be for the public benefit. The proposed changes in the surveillance of charities were intended to provide the

Charity Commissioners with more exacting criteria by which to assess the *bona fides* of candidates for charitable status in law.[4]

The British State is constituted in such a way as to permit governments to exercise these kinds of powers with relative impunity (Barker 1987). Only the Church of England and the Church of Scotland enjoy substantial immunity, but the price for it is high: the Anglican church must be, at least nominally, led by the Head of State; the appointment of bishops is partly in the Prime Minister's gift; and Parliament ultimately has the power of veto over major changes in Church policy. Government ministers do not shrink from publicly criticizing the established Church if it appears to advocate a departure from their policies, as was seen in the hostile response to the report of the Archbishop of Canterbury's Commission on Urban Priority Areas (1985), which was highly critical of the government's inner-city policy. Other religions are tolerated; but freedom of religion is not enshrined as a right in English or Scottish law. This makes it difficult, but not impossible, for religious minorities to obtain special exemptions from the laws governing, for example, the compulsory wearing of crash helmets by motor cyclists (a problem for male Sikhs), the permissible slaughter of animals (a problem for some Muslims), or military service (formerly a problem for Jehovah's Witnesses).

No agency of the British State monitors religious affairs specifically, and, aside from the sectarian dimension of the conflict in Northern Ireland, major crises in the relationship between religion and the State are relatively rare. When problems do arise, they are handled piecemeal and on an *ad hoc* basis, usually by the police or the Home Office, as questions of public order. Thus, Home Secretaries have decreed that it would not have been in the country's best interests for the Revd Moon, the late L. Ron Hubbard, or the late Bhagwan Shree Rajneesh to stay in the UK.

In so far as this kind of discrimination is ever rationalized in public, the stated reasons usually refer to the protection of mental health and family relationships. This represents an extension of the 'medicalization of deviant religion' (Robbins and Anthony 1982) and the 'therapeutic state' (Robbins 1979). But the State provides no effective means by which such administrative *fiat* can be made publicly accountable—except through Parliament (see Robilliard 1984). Moreover, official agents of social control are virtually all salaried servants of the State, not elected officials. They are relatively less susceptible, therefore, than are their American counterparts to organized attempts to influence their actions (Wallis 1988; Beckford and Cole 1988). This renders them less accountable to the public.

Finally, the secretive and relatively unaccountable workings of government in the UK make it very difficult for voluntary associations such as NRMs or anti-cult groups to exercise a direct influence over official policies or practices. The lobby system operates in the context of Parliament, but does not really extend to government departments. Moreover, these departments remain as detached as possible from voluntary associations, thus reducing the scope for most forms of direct patronage and interest-group politics. As a result, cult controversies have only rarely been officially recognized as any kind of social problem. Instead, they are treated as if they raised no particular problems for the religion/State relationship and are normally confined to the private sphere. The State's argument is that it intervenes only in cases where government ministers perceive a well-founded threat to the health or general well-being of the population.

Successive British governments have therefore claimed that, although many people may be suspicious of self-professed and wealthy gurus, 'it is one of the principles of a free society that people may propagate ideas which the majority of us do not share and do not like' (Under Secretary for the Home Office, *Hansard*, House of Commons, 23 Feb. 1977). The government has used this principle of non-intervention in all but cases of perceived threat to well-being or of proven criminality as a justification for refusing to subsidize Family Action Information and Rescue (FAIR), the main anti-cult organization in the UK. On the other hand, the government considers this principle to be compatible with its decision to subsidize Information Network Focus on Religious Movements (INFORM), because this organization's main objective is to disseminate reliable information about NRMs. A government spokesperson defended the subsidy to INFORM on the grounds that 'The public exposure of the true nature and activities of cults will help people to reflect more carefully before being involved. Such an approach, adopting a non-judgmental stance seems from the Government's point of view to be the most desirable' (*Hansard*, House of Lords, 10 Feb. 1988, cols. 271–2).

But it would be wrong to confuse the low visibility of State interference in NRMs with an absence of control. Agents of the British State intrude arbitrarily and secretively into the affairs of some religious movements[5] (and many other organizations), but it is difficult for the victims to challenge or gain immunity from this intrusiveness. By contrast, the attempts made by agencies of the American State, such as the IRS or the INS, to intervene in the affairs of NRMs usually meet with strong and effective legal resistance. This has misled some observers into believing that confrontations between NRMs and the State are necessarily more heated in America than in the UK. In fact, the sound and the fury generated in these confrontations appear to be so great only because it is rare for agencies of the American State to get away with such close monitoring of any religious group. The potential for serious intrusions into religious groups in the UK is much greater, but the reaction is muted both by the secrecy veiling all operations by agents of the State and by the knowledge that this secrecy is sanctioned by law.

The constitutional framework within which officers of the State and government ministers operate in the UK does not regard the freedom to practise religion as an entitlement or a right. Nor is there any constitutional prohibition against official 'entanglement' in the affairs of religious groups. Consequently, the privileges and exemptions that certain religious groups enjoy in the UK are categorically different from absolute entitlements. They are, in fact, *concessions* granted by Parliament on condition that the groups in question meet certain criteria. The groups must be able to prove that they serve religious purposes, that they are not subversive of religion and morality, and that they are in the public interest. The fact that concessionary privileges and exemptions may be removed if it can be shown that these criteria are not being met places the entire issue of religious freedom in a context which is vastly different from that in which it arises in the USA. The issue is far from being crucial to any of the constitutional problems facing the UK, and, consequently, the question of State control over NRMs is unlikely to become linked with broader concerns about, for example, the erosion of personal liberties or the aggrandizement of State power.

CONCLUSION

NRMs may be relatively small and weak, but there are several reasons for thinking that their treatment at the hands of official agencies of control is a symptom of problems that increasingly face all religious bodies in the advanced industrial societies outside the State Socialist countries. In the first place, NRMs may simply be the first to fall victim to intensified programmes for monitoring all social phenomena which do not fit easily into any government's model of the State's consumer-protection role and therapeutic responsibilities. Large, diversified religious organizations may have sufficient resources to be able to divert or resist the surveillance. But NRMs are likely to be more vulnerable in this respect. The controversies surrounding them may therefore herald increasing difficulties for all 'ideological groups' in the future (Jones 1984).

In the second place, increasingly centralized and would-be omnicompetent States appear to be arrogating to themselves various tasks which were previously in the care of religious bodies. Explicit concern for the quality of life, the direction of social development, and the definition of health, illness, life, and death is prominent in public policy debates and governmental programmes. It is not surprising, then, that NRMs which promulgate ideas at odds with those of the dominant culture in any country will be especially subject to close surveillance and control. Mainstream religious groups may also come into conflict eventually with the quasi-religious State on issues such as tax exemption, foreign policy, and immigration control.

In the third place, there is evidence to suggest that officials of some States have made use of the increasingly close and co-operative relationships among many Western countries in order to monitor and/or control the activities of NRMs. Exchanges of information about some controversial NRMs are believed to have taken place between various governments and police forces; representatives from member states of the European Community have debated the problems allegedly caused by NRMs; and cross-national co-operation has been recommended by several official inquiries. In short, as the distinctive religious profile of Western countries has become blurred by the forces of secularization and pluralism, there are fewer obstructions to inter-governmental co-operation in the monitoring of multinational religions. NRMs, as the weakest such organizations, have therefore been among the first targets; but there are good reasons for expecting that other religious groups may eventually be subject to similar cross-national controls.

In these three respects, the management of controversial NRMs discloses broader issues of contention between religion and States. The significance of NRM-related controversies is potentially very wide indeed, and goes to the very heart of debates about the protection or expansion of autonomy for all regional and minority cultures, voluntary associations, and social movements in Western States. The various modes of exercising control over controversial NRMs may be the first stirrings of a breeze that could develop into a storm for relations between religion, the State, and governments.

Notes

1. e.g. none of the papers published in the special edition *Annals of the American Academy of Political and Social Science* on 'Religion and the State' in January 1986 made any attempt to conceptualize the State clearly.
2. See e.g. Robbins 1979, 1980, 1981, 1985*a*, 1985*b*, 1988; Robbins *et al.* 1985; Richardson 1985, 1986, 1988; contributions to *Annals of the American Academy of Political and Social Science*, no. 446 (1979); and Kelley 1982.
3. e.g. Earl Ferrers, replying for the Conservative government to a debate on 'Pseudo-religious cults' in the House of Lords on 10 February 1988, acknowledged that 'We are all aware of the consequences which involvement with cults can have for people, particularly the young, and of the distress and alienation caused to parents.' But this was counterbalanced by the need to recognize that 'order has to be balanced against liberty' and that 'the cure can sometimes be even more harmful than the evil it seeks to remedy'. Consequently, 'where there is no breach of the law, we cannot take action against an organization just because some people regard its activities as socially undesirable. . . . It is not for the Government to adopt an anti-cultist approach. In fact they must scrupulously attempt to avoid being partisan' (*Hansard*, House of Lords, 10 Feb. 1988, cols. 270–1).
4. *Charities: A Framework for the Future*, presented to Parliament by the Secretary of State for the Home Department, May 1989; Cm 694.

5. In the course of a masterly discussion of the legal and moral issues arising from a failed attempt by the British attorney-general to deny the status of a charitable trust to certain sections of the Exclusive Brethren sect, Bryan Wilson (1983: 81–2) observed that 'action affecting religious movements may be taken at official, but subpolitical, levels to which neither the public at large, nor the victim in particular, have much access, and in the counsels of which they can exert virtually no influence'.

References

Archbishop of Canterbury's Commission on Urban Priority Areas (1985), *Faith in the City* (London).

Barker, E. V. (1987), 'The British Right to Discriminate', in T. Robbins and R. Robertson (eds.), *Church–State Relations* (New Brunswick, NJ), 269–80.

Beckford, J. A. (1979), 'Politics and the Anti-Cult Movement', *Annual Review of the Social Sciences of Religion*, 3: 169–90.

—— (1981), 'Cults, Controversy and Control: A Comparative Analysis of the Problems Posed by New Religious Movements in the Federal Republic of Germany and France', *Sociological Analysis*, 42: 249–64.

—— (1985), *Cult Controversies: The Societal Response to New Religious Movements* (London).

—— and Cole, M. A. (1988), 'British and American Responses to New Religious Movements', *Bulletin of the John Rylands University Library of Manchester*, 70: 209–25.

Demerath, N. J., and Williams, R. H. (1987), 'A Mythical Past and an Uncertain Future', in T. Robbins and R. Robertson (eds.), *Church–State Relations* (New Brunswick, NJ), 77–90.

Foster, J. (1971), *Enquiry into the Practice and Effects of Scientology* (London).

Habermas, J. (1979), *Communication and the Evolution of Society* (Boston).

Jones, R. K. (1984), *Ideological Groups: Similarities of Structure and Organisation* (London).

Kelley, D. M. (1982), (ed.), *Government Intervention in Religious Affairs* (New York).

Neal, M. A. (1985), 'Social Justice and the Sacred', in P. E. Hammond (ed.), *The Sacred in a Secular Society* (Berkeley, Calif.), 333–46.

Offe, C. (1984), *The Contradictions of Capitalism* (London).

Pfeffer, L. (1987), 'Religious Exemptions', in T. Robbins and R.

Robertson (eds.), *Church–State Relations* (New Brunswick, NJ), 103–14.

Richardson, J. T. (1985), 'The "Deformation" of New Religions: Impacts of Societal and Organizational Factors', in Robbins *et al.* (1985), 163–75.

—— (1986), 'Consumer Protection and Deviant Religion: A Case Study', *Review of Religious Research*, 28: 168–79.

—— (1988), 'Changing Times: Religion, Economics, and the Law in Contemporary America', *Sociological Analysis*, 49: 1–14.

Robbins, T. (1979), 'Cults and the Therapeutic State', *Social Policy*, 2: 42–6.

—— (1980), 'Religious Movements, the State and the Law', *New York University Review of Law and Social Change*, 9: 33–49.

—— (1981), 'Church, State and Cult', *Sociological Analysis*, 42: 209–25.

—— (1985*a*), 'Government Regulatory Powers and Church Autonomy: Deviant Groups as Test Cases', *Journal for the Scientific Study of Religion*, 24: 237–52.

—— (1985*b*), 'New Religious Movements on the Frontier of Church and State', in Robbins *et al.* (1985), 7–27.

—— (1988), *Cults, Converts, and Charisma* (London).

—— and Anthony, D. (1982), 'The Medicalization of New Religions', *Social Problems*, 29: 283–97.

—— Shepherd, W. C., and McBride, J. (1985) (eds.), *Cults, Culture, and the Law* (Chico, Calif.).

Robertson, R. (1981), 'Considerations from within the American Context on the Significance of Church–State Tension', *Sociological Analysis*, 42: 193–208.

Robilliard, St John A. (1984), *Religion and the Law: Religious Liberty in Modern Law* (Manchester).

Shepherd, W. C. (1985), *To Secure the Blessings of Liberty: American Constitutional Law and the New Religious Movements* (New York).

Shupe, A. D., Hardin, B., and Bromley, D. G. (1983), 'A Comparison of Anti-Cult Movements in the United States and West Germany', in E. Barker (ed.), *Of Gods and Men* (Macon, Ga.), 177–91.

Wallis, R. (1988), 'Paradoxes of Freedom and Regulation: The Case of New Religious Movements in Britain and America', *Sociological Analysis*, 48: 355–71.

Weber, M. (1978), *Economy and Society* (Berkeley, Calif.).

Wilson, B. R. (1983), 'A Sect at Law: The Case of the Exclusive Brethren', *Encounter*, 60: 81–7.

9

Ennobled Savages: New Zealand's Manipulationist Milieu

MICHAEL HILL

While the qualities of Rousseau's Noble Savage are celebrated in modern pop therapy, he did not act in the way his modern admirers do. The Noble Savage did not 'let' himself feel good about his garden. He did not 'get in touch with' or 'into' his resentment. He had no therapist working on this throat to open up a 'voice block'. ... In fact, the utter absence of calculation and will as they have become associated with feeling is what nowadays makes the Noble Savage seem so savage. But it is also—and this is my point—what makes him seem so noble.

(Hochschild 1983: 193–4)

This paper falls into three parts. In the first I critically assess a recent debate among sociologists of religion about the extent to which New Zealand, along with Australia and Canada, provides a fertile environment for the growth of sectarian and cultic groups. The assessment revolves principally around the related concepts of pluralism and secularization. Then I examine three motifs which indicate the *style* of minority religious participation in a New Zealand context: the weakness of mainstream Christianity and the selective dynamics of minority religious groups; the cultural emphasis on therapeutic goals; and the strength of an ethic of consumerism. Finally, I suggest an interpretation of the human potential aspect of manipulationism which derives from Hochschild's concept of 'emotional labour' and the psychological consequences of its commercialization. Her work has important implications for the study of contemporary therapeutic groups, and furthers an understanding of their growing popularity. It is to an assessment of their alleged growth in New Zealand that we turn first.

I

Contemporary forms of religion in New Zealand have recently attracted scrutiny in a comparative sociological context, albeit in a somewhat oblique way. The initial source of interest can be found in a paper originally published by Rodney Stark in 1985 and reprinted in *The Future of Religion* the same year (Stark and Bainbridge 1985). In the course of a discussion on 'Europe's Receptivity to Cults and Sects', data on Canada, Australia, and New Zealand are introduced under the category of 'other English-speaking democracies' (ibid. 483). Such an approach is not unfamiliar to New Zealanders, who are accustomed to world maps on which their country is either perched on the right-hand extremity of an interrupted world projection or—in unique double projection—appears on both right and left borders (to avoid truncating superpower geographies!). Its inclusion in the Stark and Bainbridge discussion has both empirical and conceptual relevance.

Their argument, in brief, maintains the distinction between sectarian groups as schismatic offshoots and cultic groups as innovative imports, and suggests 'a tendency for cults to do best where the conventional faiths are weakest but for sects to do best where these faiths are somewhat stronger. In effect, we argue that cults reflect efforts by the unchurched to become churched and sects reflect efforts by the churched to remain churched' (ibid. 491). Using 'a hodgepodge of sources, many of indifferent quality' (ibid. 477), Stark and Bainbridge provide the following assessment of the New Zealand religious economy. A calculation of Indian and Eastern cult centres and communities per million population ranks New Zealand (with 5.2) alongside Australia (5.3), and both far ahead of Europe (1.8) and the USA (1.3). The calculation for Scientology churches (0.32) and staff (17.7) per million population sees New Zealand ranked comparatively high, though considerably lower than Denmark. New Zealand has the highest proportion of Hare Krishna temples per million population (0.65), much higher than Europe (0.08) and the USA (0.15), and surpasses even the USA in the number of Mormons per million population, with 11,725 as against 11,001. Australia and New Zealand together have the highest number of Seventh-Day Adventist congregations per million population (24.43) of any country listed, and New Zealand also ranks among societies with the greatest number of Jehovah's Witness congregations per million population (38.39).

The suggestion that Australia and New Zealand may have an over-supply of Indian and Eastern cult centres because of their proximity to Asia is rejected on the grounds that these two countries also score high on American-based (sectarian) movements. The apparent proliferation in New Zealand of religious movements appealing to both the churched and the unchurched appears to be the sociological equivalent of double projection; indeed, Stark and Bainbridge claim that their findings 'suggest that some nations have religious economies very receptive to religious novelty and innovation and that the spectrum of their receptivity is broad' (ibid. 490–1). In their view, religious change is best understood by examining whole religious economies rather than a few 'firms' in those economies. In situations in which conventional religious 'firms' do not hold a monopoly and lack vigour, sectarian and cultic imports—as well as indigenous innovation—are likely to be common. From this perspective, New Zealand finds itself prominently situated on the chart of sectarian and cultic geography.

The methodology on which this conclusion is based, however, has been severely criticized. Bibby and Weaver point to glaring weaknesses in the failure of Stark and Bainbridge to compare cult movement rates, which are relatively minute, with those of conventional churches. Furthermore, comparisons between countries 'lead to claims that a rate for the Hare Krishna cult in Australia, for example, is "very high"—when there are only six temples in the entire country; New Zealand—with two temples—is described as having "the highest rate of all" ' (Bibby and Weaver 1985: 449).

An assessment of cult activity, based on centres per million population and disregarding overall population size and numbers of adherents, is largely meaningless in a country like New Zealand. New religious movements operate on a smaller scale than their counterparts in North America and Europe, and like many other organizations in New Zealand their administrative structure is likely to be dispersed through the main population centres. Furthermore, there are particular cultural features in the population's ethnic pluralism which account for some of the more striking features. The high Mormon figure, for example, is substantially attributable to the success of missionary activity among the Maori, especially during their post-Second World War migration to the cities. Maori comprised 60 per cent of total Mormon numbers in 1971, and still accounted for around 50 per cent in the early 1980s (Hill and Zwaga 1989: 77).

A variety of evaluations of the Stark and Bainbridge thesis have been put forward by Wallis (1986). He concludes on the basis of his own calculations that receptivity to cults is higher in Canada, Australia, and New Zealand than in the USA, and that this receptivity compares with the receptivity rates of Scandinavian countries. I suspect that his calculations are sometimes invalidated by inflated claims on the part of the groups themselves; the figure for New Zealand Scientology membership as of June 1977 of 42,000, which is quoted by Wallis (ibid. 498), contrasts dramatically with their stated adherence in the nearest census (March 1976) of 309 (New Zealand Census 1976: 14). Given the availability of five-yearly census data on religious adherence in Canada, Australia, and New Zealand, at least for groups of reasonable size, it is remarkable that the Stark/Bainbridge debate should have consistently ignored it.

Wallis further notes that although Canada, Australia, and New Zealand have high cult rates, often exceeding those of the USA, 'their church attendance rates are not appreciably lower than for the US' (Wallis 1986: 499). He then quotes a figure of overall attendance rates, from various New Zealand studies, of between 35 and 42 per cent. These studies, it should be noted, include local studies conducted in the 1960s, and refer to reported monthly attendance. With the availability of national survey data collected in the 1980s it is now possible to make more precise statements about attendance rates and to incorporate these in a comparative framework which includes not only the three Commonwealth countries but also the USA, the UK, and Scandinavia.[1] In this way the two patterns of cult activity identified by Wallis—an increase with declining church attendance *and* a particularly high rate in 'Anglo-Saxon, Protestant-dominated, immigrant-based societies, despite continuing high rates of church attendance' (ibid. 499)—can be scrutinized.

The comparative framework is provided by David Martin's general theory of secularization, which links religious participation with pluralism in societies with a predominantly Protestant culture in the following way: 'If you take participation and pluralism they run in a direct positively correlated line from the USA to Canada and Australia, to England, to Scandinavia. Indeed figures are respectively about 40+ per cent, 25+ per cent, 10+ per cent and 5 per cent (or less) per Sunday' (Martin 1978: 35). Data from a number of surveys in the early 1980s which have been cited elsewhere (Hill and Zwaga 1989: 80–1) allow us to differentiate more precisely the attendance patterns in different countries. On the criterion of weekly church attendance as a percentage of the population aged 15 and above, the rates are Canada, 36 per cent; Australia, 20 per cent; and New Zealand, 16 per cent. Furthermore, there would appear to be a relationship between overall attendance rates and the proportion in the total population claiming Roman Catholic adherence, with the latter contributing to higher participation. In 1981, census Catholics comprised 47 per cent of the population in Canada, 26 per cent in Australia, and 14 per cent in New Zealand. The absence of a simple linear relationship between attendance rates and Catholic proportions may in part be explained by ethnicity, since a significant proportion of post-war Catholic immigrants to Australia have been Italian, and this feature, in the USA as well as Australia, has been associated with a low level of religious participation (Lewins 1976: 126–7; Greeley 1979: 119).

Leaving open the question of Canada, where the high ratio of Catholics (47 per cent in 1981) to Protestants (41 per cent) (Mori 1987: 13) produces a distinctive religious situation (Westhues 1978), New Zealand and Australia can certainly be assigned to the third of Martin's monopoly–pluralism categories, representing a more pluralistic environment than England (Martin 1978: 20). If anything, New Zealand could, on a variety of indicators, be placed at a more pluralistic point on the monopoly–pluralism continuum than Australia, once again suggesting that the Catholic factor is crucial to an understanding of attendance rate. Thus, whereas in Australia one can speak almost of 'two cultures', an Irish Catholic working-class culture and a British Protestant middle-class culture (Ely 1980–1: 563)—or, even more, an English Anglican élite—the religious history of New Zealand has been characterized by a marked absence of such cleavages, and consequently an absence of pressure to adopt a religious identity. Jackson, for instance, thinks that the Anglican–Nonconformist divide which was so sharply drawn in England had 'only a vestigial existence' in New Zealand from the early days of settlement (Jackson 1983: 55). A somewhat different interpretation, though one which nevertheless emphasizes the heightened pluralism of religion in New Zealand, is given by Geering; he suggests that the throwing together of Christian denominations which had to some extent been geographically segregated in Britain created a more pluralistic situation (Geering 1985: 217). Early attempts by the Church of England to reproduce in New Zealand the established position it held in England were firmly resisted (Wood 1975).

That the religious indentity of the population of New Zealand was from the nineteenth century onward both pluralistic and relatively weak is demonstrated by two further pieces of evidence: nominalism and irreligion. Nominalism can be gauged from a comparison of those claiming adherence to a particular religious denomination in the New Zealand Census (which has included a question on religion since the mid-nineteenth century) and estimates of 'usual attenders' made by census enumerators. In 1889–91, for instance, 'usual attenders' comprised only 15 per cent of census Anglicans, 35 per cent of Roman Catholics, and 56 per cent of Methodists. In 1981, some three-quarters of the New Zealand population had a census religion label, and at the same time, as has been shown, the adult weekly attendance rate was about 16 per cent.

Irreligion has always been accorded a respectable status in New Zealand, and as early as 1880 the country was considered a Mecca of secularity by a group of English free-thinkers, who noted that 'there is so much greater freedom for opinions in New Zealand than [in England], that what are called heterodox, do not stand as an insuperable obstacle to high office in the Chief Council of the Country' (quoted in Lineham 1985: 62–3)—a reference to the Premier, Robert Stout, and John Ballance, Minister of Defence and of Lands. And while the prosaic volumes of the New Zealand Census have long recorded every nuance of irreligion (free-thinker, agnostic, humanist, and more), it is noteworthy that before 1971 the Canadian and Australian censuses did not take 'No' for an answer (Veevers and Cousineau 1980: 199; Wilson 1983: 24). The overall impression that religion has always had a low social profile in New Zealand is confirmed by a leading New Zealand historian:

It would also be misleading to imply that the New Zealanders are a very religious people—some of them go to church when they are christened, many when they marry and more when they die. The prevailing religion is a simple materialism. The pursuit of health and possessions fills more minds than thoughts of salvation. The most respected personage in the community is the doctor, who is often regarded as both aristocrat and priest. The New Zealanders surpass all Europeans and rival the Americans in their love of motor-cars and washing machines. Acquisitiveness, like Puritanism, provides a strong incentive to work. (Sinclair 1969: 288)

It will be the task of the second part of this paper to examine the three motifs contained in this quotation: weakness in traditional religion (the Stark/Bainbridge 'cultic vacuum'); a concern for health (the therapeutic search); and acquisitiveness (the ethic of consumerism).

II

An examination of the broad trends in religious adherence in contemporary New Zealand, based on census data, reveals a clear pattern. Since the Second World War, and at an accelerating rate, the major non-Catholic denominations have shown persistent decline: Anglican adherence dropped from 38 per cent of the population in 1951 to 26 per cent in 1981, and the corresponding drops for other groups are 23 to 17 per cent for Presbyterians, and 8 to 5 per cent for Methodists. Until 1966, Roman Catholic adherence had slowly increased to 16 per cent, but by 1981 had fallen away to 14 per cent. There is a statistical 'wobble' in the 1986 census figures because the actual question was changed from a write-in to a pre-coded response, with the result that some denominations experienced slight increases in adherence (it might be cynical to hint that the greatest beneficiary of the change, 'Presbyterian', had previously been a potential source of spelling difficulties). The percentage of those stating 'no religion' rose from 5 per cent in 1981 to 16 per cent in 1986, but the decline in the percentage responding 'object to state' from 15 to 8 per cent suggests that this category had contained many non-adherents until the questionnaire change (New Zealand Census—1986).

While adherence to traditional Christian groups has been declining, there has been a minor and selective increase in both sectarian and cultic adherence. 'Pentecostal' adherents increased from 6,369 to 15,717 between 1981 and 1986, and there were increases, though less spectacular, in other forms of conservative evangelical adherence, such as the Baptists. The only other increases of comparable proportions occurred in groups influenced by immigration from South-East Asia and the Pacific Islands (Buddhist, Hindu, Islam, and Samoan Congregational, for example). Sectarian groups such as the Jehovah's Witnesses and Mormons, which experienced rapid growth in the 1960s and 1970s, have recently grown more slowly, and the Mormons reached a plateau between 1981 and 1986. Within the 'cultic milieu' (Campbell 1972)—where, it must be emphasized, numbers of adherents are very small by comparison with traditional groups—there is evidence of a recycling process similar to the 'circulation of the saints' which has been suggested in the case of conservative evangelical Christianity (Bibby and Brinkerhoff 1983). Between 1976 and 1986, both Christian Science and Scientology lost adherents, while entirely new categories appeared for the first time in the 1986 census: Sufi, Satanist, and Centrepoint (see below). Christian Scientists numbered 369 in 1986 and in none of the other named groups was membership higher than 200. Since the census only records categories of adherence numbering 100 or more, there is a residual category of 'all other religious professions': between 1981 and 1986 this declined from around 20,000 to 16,000, or 0.5 per cent of the total population. One may conclude from these figures that, however dynamic, visible, and influential the minority sector of New Zealand religion might be, its numerical strength is nowhere near as impressive as the Stark/Bainbridge thesis would have us believe.

Though the crude criterion of numerical strength is not especially useful in interpreting sectarian and cultic activity in a New Zealand context, it seems plausible in the light of Sinclair's therapeutic motif to suggest that there might at least be a tendency among successful groups towards the type which Wilson labels 'manipulationist' (Wilson 1970, ch. 8). His depiction of such groups as emphasizing 'the ability to realize the good things of the world, and particularly long life, health, happiness and a sense of superiority or even of triumph' (ibid. 141) implies that they might find particular resonance with the secularized, materialistic, *and* therapeutic value system of a society like New Zealand.[2] Manipulationists have often been characterized as syncretistic, combining the insights of modern science with their own special *gnosis* to produce a novel amalgam, so that in their therapeutic mode they should be evident on the fringes of orthodox medicine. Is there any evidence for such activity in New Zealand?

Indeed, there is. The growth of and interest in 'alternative' therapies has been such that in 1987 the New Zealand Health Department published a special report on its research in this area under the title *In Search of Well-Being: Exploratory Research into Complementary Therapies* (Leibrich *et al.* 1987).[3] The research identified a substantial number of therapist practitioners, with particular concentrations in the major urban centres and in areas of the country that are popular with those seeking 'alternative life-styles'. A number of conferences with a focus on complementary therapies were reported to have been held, in addition to a major exhibition of 'alternative medicine' in Auckland. The clienteles of these complementary therapies tended to come from better educated social backgrounds, echoing Troeltsch's epigram, 'the secret religion of the educated classes' (Campbell 1978). Another theme in the self-presentation of therapies was that of idealized human personality—in such phrases as 'inner peace, sustained happiness', and 'deepen self-understanding in life purpose'. This too has been a key feature of the form of contemporary religion which Durkheim referred to as 'the cult of man' (Westley 1978; Hill 1987). The patients studied placed great importance on the goals of taking responsibility for oneself, gaining control over one's life and future, and taking an active role in improving health (in terms of which the word 'patient' is perhaps an infelicitous usage!). Their prevailing emphasis in evaluating therapies was on a holistic world-imagery (Beckford 1985*b*: 85–6).[4]

Manipulationist groups have usually been seen to have a loose-knit, fluid form of organization; indeed, the word 'organization' has sometimes seemed inappropriate for the amorphous, individual-istic environment in which they operate. A similar unstructured approach could be seen among the New Zealand complementary therapies, where a wide variety of group activities was evident. The services provided were given titles such as 'class', 'course', 'workshop', 'retreat', 'experience', 'celebration', and 'fair', with an emphasis on the 'empowering' function of group activity. Also characteristic of manipulationist syncretism is the tendency of therapies to appear in clusters, as the following catalogue of one practitioner's offerings demonstrates: 'Nutrition, Iridology, Ortho-bionomy, Massage, Tissue Salts Therapy, Bach Flower Remedies,

Homeopathy, Herbalism' (Leibrich *et al.* 1987: 99). In this milieu, the client's approach is the typical 'mix and match' or 'shopping around' pursuit of 'seekership' (Campbell 1972: 172).

Another manipulationist movement in the therapeutic mode which has had some success in New Zealand is Transcendental Meditation. The claims of TM clearly exemplify the 'superiority and triumph' themes identified by Wilson, with their emphasis on 'invincibility', 'creativity', and 'infallibility' (MERU 1978: 9). In 1975 the movement's recruitment curve reached its peak (Bainbridge and Jackson 1981: 135), and that year was claimed as the Dawn of the Age of Enlightenment (Posner 1985: 99); but, as recruitment began to decline, the claimed benefits of TM's meditation technique underwent a process of amplification. In 1977, the *siddha* (superman) programme was launched, and in the following year the World Government of the Age of Enlightenment announced a 'Global Research Project' which included Wellington, New Zealand's capital city. Its intention was to demonstrate the 'Maharishi Effect'—the belief that 'only about one per cent of the population of a community practising the Transcendental Meditation technique is needed to improve the quality of life as a whole' (WGAE 1978: 1). The 'Ideal Wellington Campaign' was part of a project involving 102 countries in which one city or province had been chosen to participate: Wellington was included because a claimed 0.98 per cent of its population in 1978 were TM meditators, as against 0.51 per cent in New Zealand as a whole and 0.24 per cent in Auckland (where a rival meditation technique was popular). On this basis, it was claimed, Wellington was close to triggering the 'Maharishi Effect'.

The campaign's literature cited a variety of research on crime indices in the USA to show that cities with one per cent of TM meditators had lower crime rates; but the benefits claimed for Wellington over Auckland went considerably further. They included a reduction in sickness beneficiaries, fewer paternity orders for extramarital children, fewer welfare beneficiaries, less divorce and separation, lower prices, lower growth in unemployment, reduction in road deaths and in hospital admissions, fewer civil court cases, and more cargo moved in the port. (In a private discussion with one of the campaign leaders, the claim was further extended to include fewer days lost through strikes and a lower incidence of venereal disease.) In a society in which acquisitiveness is combined with a strong ethic of welfarism, the inventory of TM's social benefits could not fail to achieve considerable resonance: the movement's utopianism has been noted elsewhere (Posner 1985). It is further indicative of the movement's market orientation that when the Ideal Wellington Campaign began to lose momentum, attention was directed to the then relatively affluent farming community. This market segment was targeted because, it was claimed, farmers, given their long working day, would benefit from a period of meditation, and also because the agricultural working environment was close to 'the ground state of natural law'.

One of the most noteworthy, and at times highly controversial, groups within the manipulationist milieu in New Zealand is Centrepoint. The focus of Centrepoint is a community of around 200 members based in countryside to the north of Auckland City: it had its origins in the early 1970s. The founder of Centrepoint was Bert Potter, who started his career as a businessman employing Dale Carnegie techniques, but rapidly became a sales motivator supported by a successful business base. His first encounter with the Human Potential movement came when he read a 1969 *Playboy* article which described Esalen, the growth centre in California where a group of innovative therapists were working. Potter visited Esalen for three months in 1971, and this experience was a decisive influence on his subsequent career. On his return he began to associate with sympathetic mental health professionals and counsellors, and together they ran experimental therapy groups. Further therapeutic input came from a psychiatrist who had visited Cold Mountain Institute, another American growth centre, and from Potter's own visit to the Bhagwan Rajneesh's ashram in Poona. This last encounter led to the idea of founding a community, and the Auckland property was bought at the end of 1977 (Oakes 1986: 26). As backgrond to this communal venture, it should be pointed out that in the 1960s and 1970s a range of alternative communities had been founded in New Zealand, and that in 1973 the Labour Government had adopted the idea of a 'Kibbutz system in New Zealand' to be known by the Maori word 'ohu', 'a voluntary work party' (Jones and Baker 1975: 20–1).

Two striking features of Centrepoint which can be located within the broader sociological discussion of the Human Potential movement are its means of securing enlightenment (Wallis 1984: 3) and its pattern of multiple participation and eclectic borrowing

(Stone 1976: 94; Wallis 1985: 134–5). For a number of years, leadership in Centrepoint was, according to numerous accounts by members, principally *charismatic*. Bert Potter's central role as spiritual guide has been compared to that of an Eastern guru, and in the one substantial study of the community, by a member, he is referred to as 'this man who calls himself God' (Oakes 1986: 214). Since 1987, however, the community—by now containing members with a range of professional and therapeutic skills—seems to have been taking on a more *technical* emphasis: in the literature published by the community advertising its workshops, for instance, a special announcement is included which states: 'The August/September [1987] 7-Day Intensive with Bert . . . will be his final workshop. Bert has devoted many years to the training and development of our team of leaders, who will now be responsible for the Centrepoint Workshop Programme' (Centrepoint 1987). More recently, Potter has moved out of the community to a house which overlooks it, and currently plays a less prominent role in decision making, though he still refers to himself as a guru, and—in a comment which suggests that technical as well as charismatic legitimation may be precarious—one observer notes that 'Potter is aware of his influence, and has perhaps increased it by his move' (Mannion 1988).

Multiple participation and eclectic borrowing have been a feature of Centrepoint that can be traced back to Potter's early career in Dale Carnegie courses. It is valuable to trace the interconnections not only within Centrepoint's belief system but also between complementary therapies discussed in the previously cited Health Department Report. Wallis's 'map' of the Growth movement (Wallis 1985: 135) shows links between the following therapies which are part of the Centrepoint synthesis: psychodrama, group dynamics and sensitivity training, Schutz, Encounter, Gestalt psychology, Rogers, Gestalt therapy, Jung, Reich (orgonomy), bio-energetics, primal therapy, psychoanalysis, transactional analysis, and hypnotherapy. Further co-ordinates which have been charted in Centrepoint's progress include Dale Carnegie, Rajneesh, Buddhism, Hinduism, Taoism, Perls, and neuro-linguistic programming. One function of this range of inputs is to allow for a broad integration of the community around the diffuse goal of personal growth; a second function is to encourage members in the pursuit of their own specialized therapeutic skills. The latter are then marketed to the community's clients in the form of weekends and workshops.[5]

The marketing orientation of the manipulationist milieu, an orientation which has strong resonance with Sinclair's cultural motif of acquisitiveness, has often been noted in sociologists' accounts (Wilson 1970: 165; Wallis 1985: 138–9; Robbins 1988: 121–33). An involvement in economic exchange has long been a significant feature of religious organizations, and has often been an essential element in the survival of smaller religious groups lacking inherited or state financial support. The *type* of exchange engaged in reveals some fascinating contrasts. In an earlier period of industrialization, the nineteenth-century new religious movements sometimes marketed a *product*; thus the Seventh-Day Adventists perfected the cornflake; the Oneida Community, silverware; and the Shakers, furniture. In modern complex societies, new religious movements market therapeutic *services*, from Scientology's E-meter to the scientifically promoted benefits of Transcendental Meditation (TM). To these could be added a long list of -punctures, -pressures and -bustions, and a vast range of psychological and holistic theories. Those new religious movements which continue to market products rather than services tend to originate in societies which are still experiencing industrialization, such as ISKCON in India and the Unification Church in Korea.

As Campbell has pointed out, an ethic of consumerism, resting on an attitude of continued desire coupled with the treatment of consumption as an end in itself, is as important for the maintenance of capitalism as was the Protestant ethic of disciplined austerity for its initial growth (Campbell 1983, 1987). Sinclair's succinct equation of acquisitiveness and Puritanism in the New Zealand cultural context is a sharp insight which suggests that the consumer ethic might well be found in the area of beliefs. Within this area, manipulationist groups have been shown to be particularly well attuned to consumer demand and market strategies and responsive to the fact that demand for services is consumer-led. As consumer tastes change and new services are marketed, such groups respond by employing strategies of market segmentation and product differentiation (Wallis 1985: 147). TM's siddhi yoga and, in New Zealand, marketing approach to farmers are examples of responses to a receding market. Bibby and Weaver adopt a consumerist model when they describe groups operating on the boundaries of science as offering 'a-science' explanations which are drawn upon either because scientific explanations are unavailable or because the questions for which clients are seeking answers are not amenable to scientific response (Bibby and Weaver 1985). Because people tend to supplement scientific explanations, a market for 'a-science' is created, and although no 'a-science' offering is guaranteed success, 'a-science advocates who can read and create consumer demand, as well as publicize and deliver their products, stand to know market gains' (ibid. 451). In the three examples considered here—complementary therapies, TM, and Centrepoint—New Zealand's 'a-science' market appears to operate in very much the way Bibby describes.

III

In this chapter the general features of New Zealand's manipulationist milieu have been mapped out: in the concluding section I will attempt to locate these within a framework of interpretation. A review of several recent discussions reveals not only a variety of emphases, but also an underlying consensus about those aspects of modern Western society which provide a responsive environment for the growth of new religious movements offering spiritual fulfilment and personal authenticity. The search for authenticity is not a novel preoccupation; as Gellner points out, doctrines of the 'Hidden Prince' are permanent favourites in philosophy (Gellner 1964: 86). But it is a search that has been embarked on with increasing solicitude since the eighteenth century and the onset of industrialization. Rousseau's 'noble savage' served as a contrast to the growing commodification of human personality in eighteenth-century Paris (Hochschild 1983: 185); Weber noted the rationalization, intellectualization, and 'disenchantment' of the modern world, in reaction to which, genuine creativity had retreated to the private sphere (Gerth and Mills 1970: 155); and the countercultural movement of the 1960s had as its goal the recovery of a 'true authentic real self' which the established authorities were seen to have stolen or concealed (Foss and Larkin 1986: 102). In their different ways, all these accounts point to the severance of authentic human personality from its public sphere of engagement and to the consequences of this in a more inward-turning culture.

Among those who have examined this broad historical movement in Western society is Sennett (1976), who argues that an earlier balance between public and private life has been eroded, so that human personality has become a major preoccupation in social relationships. As the boundary between public and private life is increasingly threatened, it is also more actively contested (Robertson 1979: 309): on the one hand, as Sennett shows, the 'private' sphere of personality tends to invade the 'public' spheres of work and political life; on the other, the 'public' agencies of the State attempt to extend their surveillance over the 'private' areas of family and religious participation (Beckford 1985*a*: 283–8). Located on the boundary itself, mediating structures such as the family, the community, and traditional religious groups, are rendered increasingly precarious by, on the one hand, a narcissistic retreat on the part of individuals from broader social concerns and, on the other, the increasing invasion of technical-bureaucratic control by the public sphere (Robbins 1988: 36–43; Redfoot 1986). The outcome is a situation of disjunction between the secular, rational environment of the broader society and the pursuit of non-rational, spiritual goals in a distinct cultural milieu. In a social system which is increasingly governed by the criteria of certification and specialization, religion becomes 'the only place where social experimentation is possible' (Zaretsky and Leone 1974: xxxvi).

Though new religious movements of a manipulationist kind have often been seen as responses *to* the differentiated environment of a modern society, it has also been pointed out that they have considerable resonance *with* such an environment. To the perceptive predictions of Durkheim and Troeltsch may be adduced the observation that some religio-therapeutic groups recruit affiliates heavily from 'autonomous' professionals (Wallis and Bruce 1986); and Beckford has pointed to the homology between the modes of participation in holistic movements and the educational and occupational experiences of the participants, especially the common pattern of 'serial careers' (Beckford 1985*b*: 87).

It is in the area of occupational experience and cultic resonance that Hochschild's concept of 'emotional labour' offers a particularly insightful contribution to the interpretation of the public/private disjunction in modern societies (Hochschild 1983). Basing her analysis on the Marxian concept of alienation, and even more directly on C. Wright Mills's work on the personality dimensions of

certain forms of occupation, she distinguishes the human consequences of physical labour from those of 'emotional' labour, by
which she means work in which the management of feelings is a key
component in the provision of a service. She estimates that one-
third of American workers' jobs include a high component of
emotional labour, and because of women's concentration in the
service sector, this is especially true of women's occupations: an
estimated one-half of all working women have jobs that call for
emotional labour, compared with one-quarter of men (Hochschild
1983: 11, 171). Because emotional labour involves a redefinition of
'self' within the work environment (suppressing 'inappropriate'
feelings and channelling them into organizationally approved
responses), the result is a feeling of estrangement. An important
indicator of this disorder can be found in the way that the high
regard for *natural* feeling in modern societies coincides with an
instrumental stance towards feeling typical in an occupational
context (ibid. 22). In other words, we place a premium on
unmanaged feeling because it is becoming scarce. And the cultural
emphasis on 'natural' spontaneous feelings engenders an unprecedented 'search for authenticity'. It is precisely at this point that
movements of the Human Potential type make available their
therapeutic services.

There is irony in the statement that 'The more the heart is
managed, the more we value the unmanaged heart' (ibid. 192),
because the therapeutic contexts in which such authenticity is
sought offer different varieties of *structured* spontaneity. While the
image of the spontaneous 'noble savage' pervades the Human
Potential movement, as Hochschild demonstrates, the movement
offers techniques for accessing spontaneity rather than the lack of
'feeling rules' which characterized Rousseau's creation; to this
extent, nineteenth-century books on etiquette have been replaced
by books on therapy. Furthermore, the range of therapies included
in Hochschild's inventory (ibid.) closely parallels Wallis's 'map' of
the Growth movement discussed above in the context of Centrepoint.

Against a background of the combined resonances of, first, a
weakness in traditional forms of Christianity as part of a broader
process of social legitimation; second, an emphasis on the pursuit
of therapeutic goals; and third, a strong ethic of consumerism, the
manipulationist movement—mostly in the form of exotic imports,

but also incorporating local syncretistic variants—has found a fertile environment in New Zealand. While their numerical significance is not as great as some comparative treatments would claim, the visibility of such groups is enhanced by a steady flow of information both in the media and through what Campbell terms the 'institutions of the cultic milieu' (Campbell 1972: 126): courses, lectures, and advertisements. The clientele within this milieu is overwhelmingly drawn from those of white, middle-class, professional backgrounds—this is the conclusion of the Health Department study as well as that of Centrepoint—and the possibility of further continuities between clients' educational/occupational experiences and the therapeutic services offered within this milieu is a fascinating area for further research which Hochschild's analysis opens up. Just as she sees the manipulationist response as a mid-course between managed feelings and their protean expression, so Weber too looked to a more privatized context for the expression of those ultimate values which had retreated from the public sphere: they were finally to be found, he thought, in 'direct and personal human relations .... in *pianissimo*' (Gerth and Mills 1970: 155).[6]

Notes

1. It is interesting to note that parallels with Scandinavia have been found elsewhere. Comparisons between New Zealand and the Scandinavian countries have most often been made on a popular level—for instance, New Zealand has been called 'the Sweden of the South Pacific'—but there have been some academic comparisons, such as those between New Zealand and Denmark in the area of economic development (see Sutch 1966: 428, 433, 476).

   More recently, political scientists have made comparative analyses of political processes in New Zealand and Scandinavia. In the case of Denmark, Norway, and Sweden, Aimer (1979) has studied parliamentary organization and Roberts (1979), proportional representation. Denmark and Norway have provided parallels in discussions of parliamentary structures (Roberts 1977) and the growth of neo-liberalism and right-wing protest parties (Aimer 1988).

2. To the evidence that movements of a manipulationist type find resonance in contemporary New Zealand can be added the claim that

such movements have historically shown rapid growth in this as in other nineteenth-century settler societies. Ellwood has drawn attention to New Zealand's receptivity to Spiritualism and Theosophy and to the absence of pressure for ethno-religious solidarity, as a result of which the 'spiritually liberating-for-experimentation capacity of immigration was instead permitted full play' (Ellwood 1988: 104).

3. A clear justification for incorporating alternative/complementary therapies in the category of new religions has been advanced by McGuire, who notes: 'They do appear to function as religions for many adherents—providing cosmologies, rituals, a language for the interpretation of believers' worlds, a social context for belief and practice and a group of fellow believers' (McGuire 1985: 275).

4. While the distinction between alternative/complementary therapies and orthodox medicine is usually portrayed as a marked contrast between holistic and mechanistic approaches, it should be noted that by the mid-twentieth century there had been a substantial incorporation of 'socio-moral discourse' into 'medical discourse' in such a way as to enhance the plausibility of holistic approaches: 'The new rules of medical inquiry were organized not around the taxonomic logic and anatomical perspective of the nineteenth and early twentieth century but around a systems-theoretic logic and an ecological perspective' (Arney and Bergen 1984: 60). Beckford attributes the growth of new religious movements which show an overriding preoccupation with healing in part to their affinity with the increasingly important world-image of holism (Beckford 1985b: 75).

5. The combination of a strong communal membership base with tangential involvement by those partaking of the group's services is a key feature of 'client cults' (Stark and Bainbridge 1983: 15).

6. For their generous assistance in reading and commenting on earlier drafts of this paper I wish to thank 'Tricia Blombery of the Christian Research Association, Sydney, and my colleagues Allison Kirkman and Dr Kwen Fee Lian.

References

Aimer, P. (1979), 'Scandinavian Parliaments: Models for New Zealand', in J. S. Hoadley (ed.), *Improving New Zealand's Democracy* (Auckland), 29–41.

—— (1988), 'The Rise of Neo-Liberalism and Right Wing Protest Parties in Scandinavia and New Zealand: The Progress Parties and the New Zealand Party', *Political Science*, 40/2: 1–15.

Arney, W. R., and Bergen, B. J. (1984), *Medicine and the Management of Living. Taming the Last Great Beast* (Chicago).

Bainbridge, W. S., and Jackson, D. H. (1981), 'The Rise and Decline of Transcendental Meditation', in B. R. Wilson (ed.), *The Social Impact of New Religious Movements* (New York), 135–58.

Beckford, J. A. (1985a), *Cult Controversies: The Societal Response to the New Religious Movements* (London).

—— (1985b), 'The World Images of New Religious and Healing Movements', in R. K. Jones (ed.), *Sickness and Sectarianism* (Andover), 72–93.

Bibby, J. A., and Brinkerhoff, M. B. (1983), 'Circulation of the Saints Revisited: A Longitudinal Look at Conservative Church Growth', *Journal for the Scientific Study of Religion*, 22: 253–62.

Bibby, R. W., and Weaver, H. R. (1985) 'Cult Consumption in Canada: A Further Critique of Stark and Bainbridge', *Sociological Analysis*, 46: 445–60.

Campbell, C. (1972), 'The Cult, the Cultic Milieu and Secularization', in M. Hill (ed.), *A Sociological Yearbook of Religion in Britain—5* (London), 119–36.

—— (1978), 'The Secret Religion of the Educated Classes', *Sociological Analysis*, 39: 146–56.

—— (1983), 'Romanticism and the Consumer Ethic: Intimations of a Weber-style Thesis', *Sociological Analysis*, 44: 279–96.

—— (1987), *The Romantic Ethic and the Spirit of Modern Consumerism* (Oxford).

Centrepoint (1987), *The Centrepoint Personal Development Calendar, August 1987–January 1988* (Albany).

Ellwood, R. S. (1988), 'Research note', *Turnbull Library Record*, 21: 104–5.

Ely, R. (1980–1), 'Secularization and the Sacred in Australian History', *Historical Studies*, 19: 553–66.

Foss, D. A., and Larkin, R. (1986), *Beyond Revolution: A New Theory of Social Movements* (South Hadley, Mass.).

Geering, L. (1985), 'The Pluralist Tendency: Pluralism and the Future of Religion in New Zealand', B. Colless and P. Donovan (eds.), *Religion in New Zealand Society*, 2nd edn. (Palmerston North), 214–27.

Gellner, E. (1964), *Thought and Change* (London).

Gerth, H. A., and Mills, C. W. (eds.) (1970), *From Max Weber: Essays in Sociology* (London).

Greeley, A. M. (1979), 'Ethnic Variations in Religious Commitment', in R. Wuthnow (ed.), *The Religious Dimension: New Dimensions in Quantitative Research* (New York), 113–34.

Hill, M. (1987), 'The Cult of Humanity and the Secret Religion of the Educated Classes', *New Zealand Sociology*, 2: 112–27.

Hill, M. and Zwaga, W. (1989), 'Religion in New Zealand: Change and Comparison', in J. A. Beckford and T. Luckmann (eds.), *The Changing Face of Religion* (London), 64–87.

Hochschild, A. R. (1983), *The Managed Heart: Commercialization of Human Feeling* (Berkeley, Calif.).

Jackson, H. (1983), 'Churchgoing in Nineteenth-Century New Zealand', *New Zealand Journal of History*, 17: 43–59.

Jones, T., and Baker, I. (1975), *A Hard-Won Freedom: Alternative Communities in New Zealand* (Auckland).

Leibrich, J., *et al.* (1987) (eds.), *In Search of Well-Being: Exploratory Research into Complementary Therapies* (Wellington).

Lewins, F. (1976), 'Ethnic Diversity within Australian Catholicism: A Comparative and Theoretical Analysis', *Australian and New Zealand Journal of Sociology*, 12: 126–35.

Lineham, P. J. (1985), 'Freethinkers in Nineteenth-Century New Zealand', *New Zealand Journal of History*, 19: 61–81.

McGuire, M. B. (1985), 'Religion and Healing', in P. E. Hammond (ed.), *The Sacred in a Secular Age* (Berkeley, Calif.), 268–84.

Mannion, R. (1988), 'Potter Finds Centre at New Point', *Dominion Sunday Times*, Wellington, 17 July, p. 17.

Martin, D. A. (1978), *A General Theory of Secularization* (New York).

MERU (Maharishi European Research University) (1978), *Global Research Programme* (Seelisberg).

Mori, G. A. (1987), 'Religious Affiliation in Canada', *Canadian Social Trends* (Fall), 12–16.

New Zealand Census of Population and Dwellings (1986), Series C, Report 14 *Religious Professions* (Christchurch).

Oakes, L. (1986), *Inside Centrepoint: The Story of a New Zealand Community* (Auckland).

Posner, T. (1985), 'Transcendental Meditation, Perfect Health and the Millennium', in R. K. Jones (ed.), *Sickness and Sectarianism* (Andover), 94–112.

Redfoot, D. L. (1986), 'Excursus: The Problem of Freedom', in J. D. Hunter and S. C. Ainley (eds.), *Making Sense of Modern Times: Peter L. Berger and the Vision of Interpretive Sociology* (London), 101–18.

Robbins, T. (1988), *Cults, Converts and Charisma: The Sociology of New Religious Movements*, Special edition of *Current Sociology*, 36/1, also published in Beverley Hills, Calif., 1988.

Roberts, N. S. (1977), 'New Models for New Zealand: Three Small Democracies Compared', *New Zealand International Review*, 2/2: 14–17.

—— (1979), 'Proportional Representation: Lessons from Abroad', in J. S. Hoadley (ed.), *Improving New Zealand's Democracy* (Auckland), 73–83.

Robertson, R. (1979), 'Religious Movements and Modern Societies: Toward a Progressive Problem Shift', *Sociological Analysis*, 40: 297–314.

Sennett, R. (1976), *The Fall of Public Man* (Cambridge).

Sinclair, K. (1969), *A History of New Zealand* (Harmondsworth).

Stark, R. (1985) (ed.), *Religious Movements: Genesis, Exodus, and Numbers* (New York).

—— and Bainbridge, W. S. (1983), 'Concepts for a Theory of Religious Movements', in J. Fichter (ed.), *Alternatives to American Mainline Churches* (Barrytown, NY).

—— (1985), *The Future of Religion: Secularization, Revival and Cult Formation* (Berkeley, Calif.).

Stone, D. (1976), 'The Human Potential Movement', in C. Glock and R. N. Bellah (eds.), *The New Religious Consciousness* (Berkeley, Calif.), 93–115.

Sutch, W. B. (1966), *The Quest for Security in New Zealand, 1840–1966* (Wellington).

Veevers, J. E., and Cousineau, D. F. (1980), 'The Heathen Canadians: Demographic Correlates of Nonbelief', *Pacific Sociological Review*, 23: 139–216.

Wallis, R. (1984), *The Elementary Forms of the New Religious Life* (London).

—— (1985), 'The Dynamics of Change in the Human Potential Movement', in Stark (1985), 129–56.

—— (1986), 'Figuring Out Cult Receptivity', *Journal for the Scientific Study of Religion*, 25: 494–503.

—— and Bruce, S. (1986), *Sociological Theory, Religion and Collective Action* (Belfast).

Westhues, K. (1978), 'Stars and Stripes, the Maple Leaf and the Papal Coat of Arms', *Canadian Journal of Sociology*, 3: 245–61.

Westley, F. (1978), ' "The Cult of Man": Durkheim's Predictions and New Religious Movements', *Sociological Analysis*, 39: 135–45.

WGAE (World Government of the Age of Enlightenment) (1978), *Ideal Wellington Campaign: A Global Research Project* (Wellington).

Wilson, B. (1983), *Can God Survive in Australia?* (Sutherland, New South Wales).

Wilson, B. R. (1970), *Religious Sects* (London).

Wood, G. A. (1975), 'Church and State in New Zealand in the 1850s', *Journal of Religious History*, 8: 255–70.

Zaretsky, I. I., and Leone, M. P. (1974), *Religious Movements in Contemporary America* (Princeton, NJ).

10

Charisma and Explanation

ROY WALLIS

Charisma remains an evocative and controversial concept. Sociologists have not been alone in using the term or in generating the confusions which surround it. Weber himself cannot escape some of the blame for that confusion. His partial and fragmented discussions of the concept have been taken up in widely differing ways by sociologists persuaded that different themes or criteria from his accounts were, in fact, the canonical ones. Yet, in exploring the literature on charisma, one is struck by the fact that little has been done with a concept so frequently and laboriously redefined. The typical discussion selects the characteristics held to be constitutive of charisma, and applies these to some chosen leader to show that he or she does, indeed, fall under the definition.

Now this is not an entirely worthless activity. We often feel that we understand some phenomenon better when we know that it is an instance of a general class. Being informed that a mysterious object is an olive may permit the formulation of an appropriate activity in connection with it—such as putting it in a Martini. However, in the case of phenomena designated charismatic, we are little helped in this way, because until we know precisely how charisma is being defined on each occasion, we do not know whether to put it in our Martini or hang it on the wall.

Beyond merely identifying phenomena as falling within a general class, the point of formulating a concept is surely either to explain something *about it* or to explain something *by it*. It is, I suggest, only of any importance what charisma is, if we think that by designating it one way rather than another, we can explain its occurrence, variation, composition, and so forth, *or* if we think that designating it in this way will help us to explain something else. I do not think that we have got terribly far in either of these enterprises.

EXPLAINING CHARISMA

The attempt to explain charisma is clearly hampered by variation in the range of meaning attached to the term. Is charisma compatible with the modern world? On the most inclusive forms of definition employed by functionalists such as Shils (1965, 1968), charisma is not only compatible with the modern world, but an essential feature of every form of society. Wilson (1975), on the other hand, with a conception of charisma which appears to exclude anything but alleged supernatural powers as a basis of legitimation, finds charisma most uncharacteristic of the modern world except in very diffused and attenuated forms. Others, who adopt an exclusive definition, but not quite as exclusive perhaps as Wilson, find significant signs of charisma in advanced industrial societies.

Now there may be perfectly legitimate differences of opinion as to the extension of the term; but it is less clear that this is so for Shils and those who follow his (and perhaps more accurately Parsons's) lead. Shils employs a definition of charisma so vague and nebulous as to exclude very little with any certainty:

The charismatic quality of an individual . . . lies in what is thought to be his connection with . . . some *very central* feature of man's existence and the cosmos in which he lives. (Shils 1965: 201)

The charismatic leader is one who creates order (or disorder). 'The . . . author of order arouses the charismatic responsiveness;' and 'whatever embodies, expresses or symbolises the essence of an ordered cosmos or any significant sector thereof awakens the disposition of awe and reverence, the charismatic disposition' (1965: 203). Now this, of course, is extremely vague. What these 'very central features' of our existence are and what it is to be connected with them are difficult enough to determine, but the problem is further compounded by Shils's obliteration of the distinction between charismatic and other forms of authority in his claim that 'Every legitimation of effective large-scale power contains a charismatic element' (1965: 204). It is scarcely surprising that so amorphous a phenomenon can find no explanation beyond the claim that it is 'rooted in the neural constitution of the human organism' (1968: 386).

Such treatments of charisma lend themselves to the pursuit of distinctive features or characteristics of charismatic leaders, the particular 'quality of an individual personality by virtue of which he is considered extraordinary' to quote one of Weber's less helpful formulations of the problem (Weber 1968: 241). Thus, ability to inspire awe or to display 'mastery of fate' and 'world-ordering capacities' (Spencer 1973) or the exhibition of 'self-confidence' (Tucker 1968) are held to be significant, the latter despite the frequent evidence of periodic self-doubt in the reflections of a number of charismatic leaders. One of the bolder adaptations of the Shilsian neurophysiological theory is that of Liah Greenfield, who argues that:

Genuine charisma thus means the ability to internally generate and externally express extreme excitement, an ability which makes one the object of intense attention and unreflective imitation by others. (Greenfield 1985: 122)

This advances the youthful popular entertainer (or worse) to paradigmatic status as exemplar of the charismatic. The effort to determine the common characteristics even of those upon whom *all* serious commentators would confer charismatic status—and I discount the absurd elevations by Spencer (1973) and Toth (1981) of Richard Nixon and Spiro Agnew—has proved fruitless in the face of the highly diverse personalities, behaviour patterns, and leadership styles of the clearest cases. The Shilsian approach, then, lends itself to a form of trait psychology which, so far, has been thoroughly defeated by empirical variety.

Beyond this neurophysiological theory of charisma, it seems to me that we have explanations stressing primarily sociological, psychoanalytic, or interactional factors. We cannot here review all the contenders at length. Sociological theories have focused on contextual factors—such as social and cultural crisis—which appear to be particularly conducive to the acceptance of charismatic claims. Weber (1947: 363) himself located in circumstances of 'suffering, conflicts or enthusiasm' the conditions giving rise to charismatic leaders. Bryan Wilson develops this concern in *The Noble Savages* (1975), in a persuasive discussion of the way in which charisma may vary in its incidence and form in different social contexts.

This *macro-sociological/contextual* approach eschews the search for distinctive attributes of personality possessed by charismatic leaders, and identifies the phenomenon as essentially *relational*, resting upon recognition of a claim:

Charisma denotes a quality not of the individual, but of a relationship between believers (or followers) and the man in whom they believed. His claim, or theirs on his behalf, was that he had authority because of his supernatural competences. Charisma is not a personality attribute, but a successful claim to power by virtue of supernatural ordination. (Wilson 1975: 7)

Wilson views charisma as a response to social disruption. The prophet embodies the wish for dramatic change in the face of present evil. The qualities of personal trust upon which the charismatic relationship depends, the disposition to see the world and events in mythical terms, to view social relationships and organization in personal terms, and to construe all present evils as susceptible to messianic transformation are more characteristic of simple societies than of developed, complex societies. In the latter, reliance upon instrumental expertise, technology, role performance, and rational procedures subverts reliance upon personal trust. The scale of the problems of complex societies and the historical awareness of a literate culture similarly undermine the likelihood that faith will be vested in any single figure viewed as uniquely capable of effecting the immediate resolution of major social and economic problems. Social change and current dissatisfaction will, therefore, be more likely to issue in the rise of charismatic figures in the former than in the latter.

Weber was particularly interested in the manner in which and conditions under which charisma may be transformed and decline, developing this theme in his seminal discussions of institutionaliza-tion and routinization. Wilson has extended this analysis in terms of his argument that charisma most typically occurs in modern society in diffused and attenuated forms.

In contrast to this *macro-sociological/contextual* approach to the explanation of charisma, there is a *psychoanalytic* approach to account for the advancement of charismatic claims and their acceptance by a following. The psychoanalytic approach improves substantially upon trait psychology in locating charisma as essen-tially a *relational* phenomenon, but it advances upon the macro-sociological approach in seeking to specify why conditions of social disruption evoke this form of relationship. One school of thought argues that social change produces anxiety, guilt, insecurity, and ambivalence, which generate conflicts between id, ego, and superego. The individual seeks a resolution of these conflicts and anxieties through submission to the dictates of an idealized object figure. Personal perfection, unachievable on the basis of one's own resources, is projected on to another, a surrogate parent figure. The relationship is thus essentially *narcissistic*, the followers receiving approval and confirmation of their worth through the charismatic leader who instantiates their idealization (Schiffer 1973; Downton 1973).

Charles Camic (1980: 7) has developed the idea that charisma involves 'attributions of specialness or extraordinary power to certain persons or objects'. Again, following Weber, he argues that 'extraordinary human needs [are] preconditions for imputations of specialness to need-gratifying persons' (1980: 8). Camic identifies four types of extraordinary needs: dependency needs, id needs, superego needs, and ego-ideal needs, which he relates to different forms of charisma. 'When the Ego is passive with respect to certain dependency, or ego-ideal, or superego, or id needs, those who gratify the ungratified needs in question are considered to be special' (Camic 1980: 13). Ego passivity may be an outcome of socialization or 'the loss of an emotionally significant object'. In times of social change and disruption, 'individuals lose . . . meaningful leaders, institutions, roles, identities, and so on' (ibid.).

There are, of course, major problems with this approach, not least of which is the dubious theoretical baggage of the extended and sometimes conflicting metaphors of psychoanalysis. The more significant problem, however, is the lack of any substantial evidential basis for any of the claims advanced. While occasional biographical accounts of charismatic followers may lend themselves to analytical interpretation, this is—like most psychoanalytic evidence—typically *post hoc* anecdotal reconstruction.

No evidence yet exists which demonstrates that the followers of charismatic leaders display more evidence of the 'extraordinary needs' described than those who do not become followers. No evidence exists that the followers of charismatic leaders display greater 'Ego passivity' than non-followers or that they have been subjected to different socialization processes or that they have suffered greater 'loss of an emotionally significant object'. The theory has a certain narrative plausibility, but entirely lacks empirical foundation.

None the less, the approach does point the way towards one fruitful avenue of enquiry: namely that the charismatic relationship involves—indeed, is built upon—an exchange between leader and follower.

Along with *psychoanalytic* and the *macro-sociological/contextual* explanations for the emergence and change of charisma, a more *micro-sociological/interactional* approach is developing. This is concerned with the interpersonal processes of negotiation of the charismatic claim. As yet in its infancy, this approach seems promising, as evidenced in studies by Balch (1982) and Wallis (1982) among others.

Balch (1982) and Wallis (1982) have explored the emergence and stabilization of a charismatic self-conception in the case of two leaders of new religious movements. Contrary to the personality trait approach which hypothesizes 'self-confidence' as a necessary characteristic of charismatic leaders, both these studies locate evidence of considerable insecurity and self-doubt in the biographies of the individuals concerned. They point to the crucial role played by a companion who provided support and encouragement to the leader to view himself as someone specially endowed with a mission and who assisted in the definition of his utterances as revelatory.

Wallis (1986c: 150–1) takes this mode of analysis further in demonstrating how, in the case of Moses David, leader of the Children of God, charisma was constructed in the process of social interaction:

It emerges out of a particular structure of social relationships in which an exchange takes place of mutual attribution of status and worth. The putative charismatic leader emboldened by this flattering recognition of the status and identity to which he aspires, then seeks to realise in his behaviour the powers and status with which he has been credited: to live up to the image with which he has been endowed. In the process others are elevated with him as intimates or lieutenants. Their significance derives from him. Having been raised up, and recognized as special by him, they add to the recognition of the leader, endowing him with still further significance as author of the movement and their own fortunate condition, leading him to take ever more seriously the conception of himself as someone out-of-the-ordinary.

Such a conception is exported outwards from the inner circle, intimates securing recognition for themselves as they secure recognition for their leader, protecting the leader from damaging or discrediting intrusion, and excluding those who disturb the pattern of reciprocity.

This approach assumes no prior 'extraordinary needs'. Rather, until evidence to the contrary is forthcoming, it assumes the motivations of those who become followers of charismatic leaders to be initially diverse. Motivations are shaped in the process of interaction, and the rewards that constitute the follower's side of the exchange may come to be defined and valued only in the course of that interaction.

CHARISMA AS EXPLANATION

But there is also the other side of the coin: namely, *charisma as explanation*. Here, the debate has been, if anything, still more fierce. While much commentary—the journalistic even more than the sociological—has 'explained' all manner of things by reference to charisma, Peter Worsley and Bryan Wilson have taken quite the contrary view. 'Charisma', Worsley (1968: xviii) says, 'is not an *explanation* of behaviour.' And Wilson expands this position:

Charisma is a sociological, and not a psychological, concept. But precisely for this reason—because it expresses a social relationship and is a mode of legitimizing leadership, it does not serve us well as a causal category . . . *charisma* expresses the balance of claim and acceptance—it is not a dynamic, causally explanatory, concept; it relates to an established state of affairs, when the leader is already accepted, not to the power of one man to cause events to move in a particular direction. (Wilson 1973: 499)

This argument has much force in respect of both a great deal of journalistic usage and probably even a significant quantity of sociological work. As Claude Ake (1966) has argued, those theorists, such as Shils, Wallerstein, Apter, Runciman, and others, who seek to explain the often temporary integration of new states by reference to the supposed charisma of leaders such as Nkrumah, Houphouet-Boigny, Ben Bella, and the like typically assume what is to be explained. If charismatic leadership crucially entails recognition of the leader's gift of grace and unreserved commitment to his cause, then the explanation of cohesion and integration becomes a tautology. In short, since the support he enjoys is *evidence* of his charisma, a leader's charisma cannot be the explanation of the support he enjoys.

This is equally a problem in more circumscribed contexts than an entire society. Dekmejian and Wyszomirski (1972) make a very plausible case for the charismatic status of the Mahdi of Sudan in terms of the continuing loyalty of many of his lieutenants despite military defeat. But we clearly cannot *explain* their continuing commitment—and Dekmejian and Wyszomirski do not seek to do so—as a consequence of the Mahdi's charisma without falling into tautology. The test is whether we would regard the hypothesis as falsified if these lieutenants had not remained loyal or whether—as seems more likely—we would simply have regarded the Mahdi as not, or as no longer, charismatic.

Robin Theobald, who is acutely aware of such difficulties, none the less believes that charismatic authority can have explanatory value in relation to social movements. Theobald suggests that Mrs Ellen White came to be accepted 'by a small community of believers as the embodiment of the spirit of prophecy and that the visions and instructions conveyed in them served to bind together this small community enabling it to achieve consensus on the fundamental beliefs of Sabbatarean Adventism' (Theobald 1980: 95), and hence that Mrs White's charisma enabled this Adventist group to overcome 'pronounced fissiparous tendencies'. But even here it is not entirely clear that tautology can be avoided. If we cannot identify Mrs White as a charismatic leader *independently* of the recognition and commitment of the 'small community of believers', then their recognition and commitment, and by extension their cohesion, cannot be *explained* by Mrs White's charisma without circularity.

All attempts to explain cohesion and related phenomena by means of charisma seem to face such difficulties. A similar case is Nyomarkay's (1967) account of factionalism in the Nazi Party, which argues that an ideological leader is merely first among equals, and competing factions may make persuasive claims to legitimation through alternative interpretations of the ideology. In consequence, factions may develop into schisms with whole factional groups leaving together. A charismatic leader, however, is the final arbiter of message, policy, and practice, and the faction that fails to secure his or her approval therefore lacks legitimation, and cannot justify continued advocacy of a divergent programme. Factional leaders may leave the movement, but lacking legitimacy, they do so virtually alone.

On the face of it, this argument seems compelling. Moreover, it seems to meet the test of the hypothetical counterfactual: namely, if a charismatically led movement experienced schism, would this hypothesis be falsified or would we cease to regard it as charismatically led? The answer this time must be, I think, that we can perfectly well envisage a charismatically led movement suffering schism. Thus the hypothesis is a viable one: charisma *may* be employed to explain a difference in the rate of occurrence of another phenomenon or its non-occurrence. The fact is, however, that there are examples of charismatically led movements in which schisms *have* occurred. Laurence Oliphant was the cause of a schism in the Brotherhood of the New Life, despite the charismatic leadership of Thomas Lake Harris, who was considered a second incarnation of Christ (Wallis 1975: 44; Schneider and Lawton 1942). The charismatic claim of the founder of the Mormons, Joseph Smith Jr., seems undeniable, yet William Law led away a group of dissenters (O'Dea 1957: 164). Wycam Clark also broke away from Smith in 1831 to found the Pure Church of Christ, although it is said that 'The sect disintegrated after a few months' (Arrington and Bitton 1979: 66; for other cases, see also p. 67).

What seems crucial for the avoidance of schism in a charismatically led movement is the effective *containment* of charisma and of alternative sources of legitimate claims to authority. Particularly in the early stages of a charismatic movement, there is a tendency for other members to advance claims to charismatic legitimacy, which can issue in conflict with the original leader (see e.g. O'Dea 1957: 157–60) and schism unless successfully managed. Thus it is not merely charismatic leadership that explains the absence of schism in such movements; it is charismatic leadership *plus* the effective efforts of such leaders to secure a monopoly over access to the source of charismatic legitimation or alternative sources of authority. But this is once again to present a tautology rather than an explanation.

The schism in the Oneida Community between Noyesites and Townerites which led to the Community's dissolution is also instructive. Noyes was clearly a charismatic leader for many Oneidans, but Towner and his followers, coming later into the movement, were unwilling to subject themselves completely to that authority. They advanced a more rational-legal model of government. Clearly for the Townerite faction, Noyes was less than fully charismatic, and their challenge to his authority led Noyes himself to question his continuing gift of grace; but as Theobald (n.d.) has argued more generally and as Olin (1980) has argued in this particular case, the charismatic leadership of a movement may entail a charismatic relationship with only a minority of members at any time. Others may be involved for all manner of different reasons and may subject themselves to the leader's authority only conditionally, and without a shared conception of legitimate authority. Thus, the basis of schism exists even in a charismatically led movement.

However, this does suggest another way in which charisma can have an explanatory role. Charismatic leadership is a fundamentally precarious status and relationship. The claim rests purely on subjective factors. The 'gift of grace' may evaporate in the eyes of the claimant or of his followers in the face of failure. Others may make competing claims based on access to the same alleged source of legitimation. Charisma may become routinized and subject to the constraint of emerging institutional patterns or bureaucratic expertise. Thus it poses a wide variety of problems arising from its precariousness. On the other hand, it offers, in its innovative potential, a very wide range of opportunities. Thus charisma provides a context both of problems with which an appropriately motivated leader must deal and of opportunities which an appropriately motivated leader may exploit, along with certain facilities whereby these things may be done. In this way, charisma may provide an explanation of resulting actions—particularly the actions of the leader himself—and of their consequences.

For example, Thomas O'Dea, discussing the origins of the Mormons, points out that, having been founded upon the basis of revelation, it was possible that others besides Joseph Smith would claim prophetic gifts, thereby threatening his uniqueness and authority. His associate Oliver Cowdery flirted with the idea of a prophetic calling of his own (O'Dea 1957: 157). Hiram Page claimed to have received revelations through a stone, and at different times others displayed prophetic gifts, sometimes directly challenging Joseph Smith's authority. The precariousness of charisma permitted such challenges, creating a problem which Smith was forced to face and which he dealt with by strategies aimed to constrain the diffusion of charisma. Through prophecy he reasserted his priority, and 'he concentrated the right to receive revelation in his own person' (O'Dea 1957: 159). In addition, he arrogated to himself other sources of authority to buttress his charisma. He had himself made president of the High Priesthood and later of the Church, as well as 'sole Trustee in Trust' for Church property. These actions were clearly consequences of the precariousness of charisma, and of Smith's efforts to cope with it.

Doyle Paul Johnson (1979) has developed a very similar argument in relation to the People's Temple. Through the pursuit of organizational growth, delegating authority to trusted close associates, moving to an isolated environment, and so on, a leader may attempt to cope with the problems posed by the precariousness of charisma. Wallis (1982) has argued that developments within the Children of God in terms of rapid changes in organizational structure, the elevation and subordination of regional leaders, constant changes in ideology and practice, and so forth were a consequence of its leader, Moses David's, efforts to cope with the threat to unrestrained exercise of his charisma from the process of institutionalization.

Elsewhere, Wallis (1986b) has sought to show how charisma can provide opportunities for charismatic leaders to indulge the darker desires of their subconscious. Through effective resistance to the threat of institutionalization, charismatic leaders may be able to render followers exclusively dependent upon them, eliminating constraints or inhibitions upon their whims, leading to the possible emergence of unconventional sexual practices and violence. Wallis (1986b) argues that, construed in this way, charisma provides an *explanation* for developments in the Manson Family, the People's Temple, Synanon, and the Children of God. The argument can clearly also be deployed in relation to the Rajneesh movement (see Wallis 1986a).

These cases, then, illustrate the possibility of salvaging an explanatory role for charisma in terms of the problems, opportunities, and resources it provides within which a leader must formulate his strategy and conduct his activities. It suggests that charisma has a greater role as an explanation of a *leader's* actions and their consequences than—as it is usually employed—as an attempted explanation of the behaviour of his *followers*.

References

Ake, C. (1966), 'Charismatic Legitimacy and Political Integration', *Comparative Studies in Society and History*, 9: 1–13.

Arrington, L., and Bitton, D. (1979), *The Mormon Experience* (London).

Balch, R. L. (1982), 'Bo and Peep: A Case Study of the Origins of Messianic Leadership', in R. Wallis (ed.), *Millennialism and Charisma* (Belfast), 13–72.

Camic, C. (1980), 'Charisma: Its Varieties, Preconditions, and Consequences', *Sociological Inquiry*, 50: 5–23.

Dekmejian, R., and Wyszomirski, M. J. (1972), 'Charismatic Leadership in Islam: The Mahdi of the Sudan', *Comparative Studies in Society and History*, 14: 193–214.

Downton, J. (1973), *Rebel Leadership* (London).

Greenfield, L. (1985), 'Reflections on Two Charismas', *British Journal of Sociology*, 36: 117–32.

Johnson, D. P. (1979), 'Dilemmas of Charismatic Leadership: The Case of the People's Temple', *Sociological Analysis*, 40: 315–23.

Nyomarkay, J. (1967), *Charisma and Factionalism in the Nazi Party* (Minneapolis).

O'Dea, T. (1957), *The Mormons* (Chicago).

Olin, S. C., Jr. (1980), 'The Oneida Community and the Instability of Charismatic Authority', *Journal of American History*, 67: 285–300.

Schiffer, I. (1973), *Charisma: A Psychoanalytic Look at Mass Society* (Toronto).

Schneider, H. H., and Lawton, G. (1942), *A Prophet and a Pilgrim* (New York).

Shils, E. (1965), 'Charisma, Order and Status', *American Sociological Review*, 30: 199–213.

—— (1968), 'Charisma', in D. Sills (ed.), *International Encyclopedia of the Social Sciences* (New York), vol. 2, 386–90.

Spencer, M. E. (1973), 'What is Charisma?', *British Journal of Sociology*, 24: 341–54.

Theobald, R. (1980), 'The Role of Charisma in the Development of Social Movements', *Archives de sciences sociales des religions*, 49: 83–100.

—— (n.d.), *Charisma: A Critical Review* (London).

Toth, M. A. (1981), *The Theory of the Two Charismas* (Washington, DC).

Tucker, R. T. (1968), 'The Theory of Charismatic Leadership', *Daedalus*, 97: 731–56.

Wallis, R. (1975), 'The Cult and its Transformation', in R. Wallis (ed.), *Sectarianism* (London), 35–49.

—— (1982), 'Charisma, Commitment and Control in a New Religious

Movement', in R. Wallis (ed.), *Millennialism and Charisma* (Belfast), 73–140.

—— (1986*a*), 'Religion as fun? The Rajneesh Movement', in R. Wallis and S. Bruce, *Sociological Theory, Religion and Collective Action* (Belfast), 191–224.

—— (1986*b*), 'Sex, violence and religion', in R. Wallis and S. Bruce, *Sociological Theory, Religion and Collective Action* (Belfast), 115–27.

—— (1986*c*), 'The Social Construction of Charisma', in R. Wallis and S. Bruce, *Sociological Theory, Religion and Collective Action* (Belfast), 129–54.

Weber, M. (1947), *Theory of Social and Economic Organization* (New York).

—— (1968), *Economy and Society*, ed. G. Roth and C. Wittich (New York).

Wilson, B. (1973), *Magic and the Millennium* (London).

—— (1975), *The Noble Savages: The Primitive Origins of Charisma* (Berkeley, Calif.).

Worsley, P. (1968), *The Trumpet Shall Sound* (London).

11

Charismatization: The Social Production of 'an Ethos Propitious to the Mobilisation of Sentiments'

EILEEN BARKER

The story is told of the summer camp organizer who asked parents whether their child was a leader or a follower. One mother answered, 'Oh, my son is quite definitely a leader—the trouble is, no one will follow him.'

Charisma as a term expresses less a quality of person than of relationship; it contains the acceptability of a leader by a following, the endorsement of his personality and the social endowment of power. . . . *Society, or at least a section of it, endows a leader.* On his part, he must have some grounds on which a claim to exceptional competence can rest: on theirs, there must already be *an ethos propitious to the mobilisation of sentiments.* But charisma expresses the balance of claim and acceptance—*it is not a dynamic, causally explanatory, concept; it relates to an established state of affairs,* not to the power of one man to cause events to move in a particular direction. (Wilson 1973: 499; *emphases added*)

In advanced Western Society, it appears that claims to real charisma, if they are to succeed, must be supported by exotic provenance. . . . If God is alive he must come from a society that is still traditional, unplanned, unprogrammed, and in which arcane mystery, and occult philosophy may still flourish. . . . Yet it is clear that however dependent are modern societies on bureaucracy, technology, and conscious planning, the appeal of the charismatic does not entirely die. (Wilson 1975: 114–5)

This paper was first conceived in response to an invitation from Bryan Wilson to contribute to a series of seminars that he was organizing on the subject of charisma.[1] It addresses a question that is expressed implicitly by Wilson in the above quotations, but which has, on the whole, been ignored by sociologists of religion—notable exceptions being Wilson himself and Roy Wallis (1982).

The question is: How is it that people in the West come to accord a leader charismatic authority over them? While agreeing with Wilson that charisma cannot function as an explanatory concept in and by itself, I would argue that the *process* whereby the state of affairs becomes established and is maintained *does* entail a dynamic which *can* contribute to the explanation of a particular genre of social behaviour.

Given that the sociological concept of charisma describes a relationship, it follows that at least part of the explanation for 'events to move in a particular direction' must be traceable to the genesis and, just as important, the perpetuation of that relationship, rather than to the characteristics or personality of the 'one man'. Thus, using Wilson's words, the question can be stated as: How does one arrive at a 'state of affairs' in which 'a section of [Western] society' will 'endow a leader' with charismatic authority?

I

Power is the ability to get others to do what one wants them to do. Authority is legitimate power; it is exercised when someone is believed by others to have the right to tell them what to do and the right to expect that they will do it. No guns are needed to wield authority. Charismatic authority is accorded to a person whom his (or, occasionally, her) followers see as having special grace from God and/or personal characteristics that make him or her extraordinarily special.

Following Max Weber (1947: 324–92), whereas the claim to traditional authority typically rests on a hereditary right to obedience or some immemorial precedent that ought to be followed (the Japanese Emperor was revered as the Prince of Heaven; the Church of Rome claims the authority of apostolic succession), the claim to charismatic authority typically demands a break from tradition; it permits, it inspires, and it encourages innovation. Whereas legal/rational authority is typically circumscribed in that limits are set on the range of commands that can be legitimately issued (the bureaucrat will not have the authority to tell you what you should eat for breakfast), charismatic authority is typically unrestricted in scope, and may be applied to all areas of a person's life. The charismatic leader may be accorded the right to decide whom you may marry, with whom you may sleep, by whom you may have children, how you may cut your hair, what clothes you should wear, what work you should do, where, under what conditions, and perhaps even whether, you should live. And all this may be changed at a moment's notice—even without a moment's notice.

To a non-follower, the authority wielded by a charismatic leader may seem capricious, irrational, and totally incomprehensible. Those who are accorded traditional or rational/legal authority have to fulfil certain criteria of eligibility (such as hereditary rights or democratic election), and they, like those over whom they hold authority, are expected to abide by a set of impersonal rules. Charismatic leaders are unfettered by rules; no one can anticipate where they are going or, perhaps, tell where they are coming from; rules and traditions are made only to be broken by those with charisma; reinterpretations or complete changes of doctrine can be revealed and contrary orders issued. No one else can grasp and interpret the way, the truth, and the light with certainty; the word of the charismatic leader is both unpredictable and unquestionable.

Although sociologists will insist that charismatic authority is not a 'big man theory' depending merely upon a particular personality type, they have pointed to the fact that the charismatic leader tends to be accorded authority only under certain social conditions, typically when the members of the society have been subjected to certain *external* pressures such as economic unrest, foreign invasion, or the disruption or exposure of an established cultural milieu (Wilson 1975). I do not wish to deny that such external features can play an important—perhaps even a necessary—role in the development of a charismatic relationship, but I would wish to argue that these are not sufficient for our understanding. We may need also to be aware of the *internal* processes at work.

In line with his general theory of secularization, Wilson concluded from his study of 'the primitive origins of charisma and its contemporary survival' that, although one may find elements of 'derived charisma' and 'diffused charisma', the charismatic leader is unlikely to be accepted in modern society—except when 'his power lies only within the circumscribed arena of his own voluntary movement' (Wilson 1975: 111). By looking at a particular group of followers, members of the Unification Church, and the development of their relationship with one man, the Reverend Sun Myung

Moon, I shall attempt to demonstrate that, as far as Unificationism is concerned, not only can charismatic authority not be reduced to the psychological characteristics of the leader, but also that it is not a consequence of merely external features of the society or a particular social situation from which the followers have sought refuge.

The argument is that charismatic authority can result, at least in part, from social processes that take place within the group which is headed by the person who is accorded the authority. While it is possible that external events and previous experiences may need to be invoked to explain why someone joins the Unification Church, neither these nor a direct encounter with Sun Myung Moon can explain why his followers come to accord him charismatic authority. It is not until they are in the movement that the followers *learn* to recognize the charisma of their leader and thereby come to accept that he should have a virtually unlimited say in how they live. The process of socialization by which this learning takes place is one that I call charismatization.

Perhaps if I were to recount two experiences that I had during the course of my study of the Unification Church, it would help to highlight the reasons why the question of charismatization came to present me with a challenge. Taken together, these two experiences persuaded me that something not all that obvious was taking place which needed to be explained. While Moon's charismatic authority undoubtedly 'worked', it seemed to work only for those who had been subjected to life in the Unification Church for some time. Others, outside the movement, have granted Moon respect, and may even be in the employ of one of the many Unification-associated organizations, but such people do not grant Moon charismatic (as opposed to rational/legal) authority over their lives.

The first incident occurred early in my acquaintance with the movement, before my study had officially begun. It was during a banquet at the conclusion of a conference in New York in 1975 to which academics had been invited by the Unification Church to discuss problems related to 'the Unification of Science and Absolute Values'. The after-dinner entertainment was pleasant enough, but the room was becoming uncomfortably hot, so I slipped out for a breath of fresh air. When I returned, the way back to my table was blocked by an influx of Unificationists who had been let in to hear the climax of the event, an address by Moon himself. I crept in among them. Moon was speaking in Korean, in what sounded to me like a bellicose tone and with decidedly ferocious gesticulation; the translation seemed ponderous and uninspiring. After a while, shuffles and murmurs from the main body of the hall suggested boredom and embarrassment. Some of my academic colleagues got up and left, one or two in evident distress. Had I not been a sociologist of religion, I might have followed them, but I had become engrossed in observing the Unificationists around me. They were rapt; eyes were aglow, bodies rigid with attention. There could be no doubt whatsoever that the message which was being heard by Moon's followers was not the one that was being heard by his guests. After the speech was over and Moon had been escorted out by his bodyguards, I found myself surrounded by ecstatic enthusiasm and adoration. 'Wasn't he wonderful?' I was asked in tones of hushed awe. Like my academic colleagues, I couldn't see it. But I could see that they saw it.

The second incident occurred four or five years later. By that time, I had spent a considerable amount of time doing participant observation within the movement.[2] I was listening to a lecture at which I was the only non-member, and in front of the audience was a large picture—perhaps 10ft by 6ft in size—which showed Moon sitting on the grass with his wife and two of his children. He was looking out of the picture with a benevolent smile. The lecturer was telling us about the role of the messiah and the suffering that Moon had endured for our sakes. I was not paying much attention to the words, but I was familiar enough with their general import. Outside, the sun was shining, and through the open windows I could smell fresh mown grass and hear the buzzing of the bees and the chirping of the birds. Suddenly I became aware that, engulfed in a pleasant, warm glow, I was smiling back at the picture.

Here was I, an 'objective social scientist' who certainly did not accept Unification theology and had no intention whatsoever of ever becoming a Moonie; yet I had caught myself responding with what I suspected might be an utterly inane smile to the picture of a man whom I had considered totally unattractive and anything but charismatic. Pulling myself together with a start, I scribbled a note reminding myself to reread the final paragraph of *Nineteen Eighty-Four*, when Winston realizes that Big Brother loves him and that he loves Big Brother.[3]

Needless to say, I did not join the Unification Church, nor did I accord Moon any charismatic authority over my life. But I had been offered a glimpse of something that made me ask what I might have been experiencing during the course of my participant observation of the Unification Church that could have led me, in a state of semi-conscious awareness, to feel such warmth towards a man towards whom I had previously had only negative feelings. It was rather like the sudden realization that the psychologist's picture of an ugly witch, if perceived in a slightly different way, can be seen as a pretty young woman. How was the shift in perception accomplished? After some reflection and further study, I came to the conclusion that there were a number of factors which could contribute to the relatively vulnerable new recruit in a relatively authoritarian organization embracing Moon's charismatic authority.

II

The foundations for the Unification Church were laid by Sun Myung Moon in Korea in the 1940s. Its beliefs, as written down in the *Divine Principle* (Kwak 1980), are based on a special interpretation of the New and Old Testaments. These are said to have been revealed over a period of several years, after Jesus had appeared to the sixteen-year-old Moon on Easter Day, 1936, saying 'I couldn't complete the mission I came to do. You have come to complete what has been left undone' (Abe 1977: 187).

The early days of the Church in Korea were fraught with controversy. Moon became a contentious figure, and was imprisoned on a number of occasions; but he gradually built up a following, and by the late 1950s missionaries were sent out to communicate the message to the rest of the world. The Holy Spirit Association for the Unification of Christianity (to give the movement its full title) became visible in the West in the early 1970s when Moon moved to the Unites States. Clean-cut young 'Moonies' were to be seen on the streets of North American and European cities, selling flowers, literature, and candy and attempting to persuade other young people to attend a public rally or visit one of the movement's residential centres in order to learn more about the Divine Principle. Although in those days it was not always easy to find out much about the beliefs and practices of the movement, the vast majority of Unificationists do, in fact, believe not only that there was, born in Korea between 1917 and 1930, a Christ, born as a man in the flesh, who can succeed where generations of humans (from Adam and Eve to Jesus and from Jesus to the present day) have failed (Kwak 1980: 199–214), but also that Moon is this messiah who can lead those who will follow him to establish the Kingdom of Heaven on earth.[4]

There have been numerous accusations levelled against the Unification Church: brainwashing, the breaking up of families, deceptive practices, heretical beliefs, political intrigue, financial skulduggery, and exploitation of the rank and file membership by a corrupt leadership. Moon has frequently been portrayed as a Svengali-like character with hypnotic powers who is capable of turning decent, well-educated young Westerners into mindless zombies prepared to die for their leader. Much of what has been written about both the Unification Church and its leader is sensation-mongering rubbish: some of it is untrue, and some of it is distortion or exaggeration.

It is clear, however, that most Unificationists are willing—indeed, eager—to submit to many of the demands put upon them in Moon's name. They consider he has a legitimate right to tell them where and at what to work and how to live; and most of them accept that his special powers are such that he is capable of choosing the right marriage partner for them—a partner whom they may never have met and who may come from a completely different culture, unable to speak their language. When, in a speech, Moon (1973c: 5) declares, 'When I matched 235 couples out of the Japanese family, it took me only 8 hours and some minutes. Can you imagine? How could I do this? To other's eyes I looked as though I was drawing lots or something like that . . . You don't know who will suit you best. Isn't that so?', there is a resounding 'Yes!' from his audience—and this is not merely an empty response to rhetoric: several thousands of his followers have married the person with whom Moon has matched them in one or other of the Unification mass weddings, known as 'blessings'.

Moreover, Moon's followers, despite the fundamental importance assigned to the concept of the family in Unification theology, have been prepared to leave their children at his behest:

In 1969, Father [Moon is called and calls himself Father] sent out all the blessed couples on a totally sacrificial path. The blessed children were put into orphanages and their parents went off to unknown places, devoting themselves for 3 years to do the will of God. (Moon 1987: 4)[5]

Similar instructions have been given to mothers to leave their young children on other occasions, and the mothers have usually (although by no means always) obeyed.

On several occasions, Moon has declared that he expects, were he to deem it necessary, that Unificationists should become martyrs for the cause. For example, in one of his speeches he asks, 'Are you ready to be martyred, kill yourself, for the sake of Master [Moon]? . . . If at the command of our Master you would have to die fighting against communism in a Communist country, would you do that? I would not like this to happen, but you must be prepared for that' (Moon 1973*a*: 12). However, it should be stressed that, first, many leaders (and nations) frequently employ the language of self-sacrifice to the point of death and, second, there is no evidence of Moon ever having made a life-threatening demand on any of his followers.

A generalization that is frequently invoked to explain why people join a new religious movement is that they are 'spell-bound' or 'lured' by a charismatic leader. Leaving aside for the moment whether this could ever contribute to an adequate explanation of conversion, it must be clearly underlined that, as far as the Unification Church is concerned, such a reason is a complete non-starter. People do not join the Unification Church as the result of their going to a revivalist rally and coming forward to dedicate their life to God after being inspired by Moon's preaching in the style of a Charles Wesley, a Charles Finney, or a Billy Graham—or a Bhagwan Rajneesh or a Maharaji.

On the contrary, although a handful of the 400 or so members to whom I administered a questionnaire in the late 1970s had heard Moon give a public lecture, 95 per cent of the membership had not set eyes on him before joining the movement. Most had not seen him until they had been in the movement for at least several months. About a third of the British membership still had not been in the same room as him after a year or more in the movement, and those who had seen him were unlikely to have had any personal interaction with him. Ten per cent (15 per cent of the British membership) had never seen him, and over half the American and British respondents had seen him only by attending a talk he had given. About a quarter had spent a few minutes in personal or near-personal contact with him, but only one in ten of the entire sample had ever spent more than a few minutes with him.

It is true that when Moon addresses his followers (rather than the general public) there *is* a revivalist atmosphere. Mass responses to his questions are forthcoming; hands are raised in eager salutation; and the general feeling is one of excitement and enthusiastic commitment to God and to the cause, and, probably especially, to the leader to whom unquestioning obedience is sworn. But this is on 'internal' occasions. Hundreds of thousands of non-members who have seen Sun Myung Moon on more public occasions are not drawn by his charismatic powers. The reactions of the academics at the conference was by no means atypical. The majority of those who have attended rallies and other gatherings at which Moon has spoken tend to react with, at best, polite indifference; for others, the feelings aroused are repugnance or even revulsion. The 'untutored' Westerner is more likely to interpret the guttural tones of the unfamiliar Korean and the extravagant gesticulations with which Moon tends to accompany his words as evidence of something unpleasant, threatening or dangerous; they are more likely to believe that they are in the presence of a man who is out to get what he can in the way of money and power from others who are fool enough to follow him than they are to believe that this is a man sent from God who can legitimately tell them what to do. Yet, as I have already said, those who are in the movement watch and listen to Moon with rapture, their eyes shining as, it appears, they hang on his every word. Why?

Not all new converts are aware of the crucial centrality of Moon's role in the Unification movement at the time of their joining, but the majority are. Over half the European converts in my sample had accepted that Moon was the messiah as soon as they had heard the conclusion of the *Divine Principle*, which proclaims that the Lord of the Second Advent is on the earth at the present time; and well over 80 per cent had accepted him as the messiah by the time they joined the movement. Over half my American sample had accepted that he was the messiah before they joined; the Japanese were not allowed to join the movement until they had accepted his messiahship.

But, as intimated earlier, people do not join the Unification Church because they have perceived Moon as the possessor of charisma.[6] It is not altogether surprising, therefore, that the emotions that these converts felt towards Moon were not those typical of the followers of a charismatic leader. There were feelings of gratitude and of respect; but if recent converts expressed feelings of love, this was love of an abstract nature, not of a kind that focused on Moon's personal qualities so much as on a leader who filled a messianic position. Indeed, according to Unification theology, messiahship is an office, and the person in that office may fail to fulfil the mission he was sent to perform. This, it is believed, is what happened when Jesus was murdered before he had the chance to marry—a prerequisite to his fulfilling his mission of restoring the Kingdom of Heaven on earth (Kwak 1980, ch. 3 and 13).

But new converts are in a particularly vulnerable position. This is the time when they are most likely to leave the movement; but it is also a period during which they are particularly 'open', in the sense that they are still adjusting to the new set of glasses through which they are now perceiving the world. They will have a number of gaps in their new world-view. They will also, to some extent at least, have abandoned their previous set of values; and, in so far as they have abandoned these, they will no longer have them as an independent benchmark against which to test and evaluate the new ideas and demands to which they are exposed (Barker 1989: 33ff.).

We have, then, as the 'raw material' for the process of charismatization, new recruits who are particularly susceptible to new ideas and who, although they have as yet no recognition of Moon as a charismatic personality, have been taught to accept the importance and specialness of what Moon has done through his revelation of the *Divine Principle* and his messianic mission. It is Moon's divine task to see that God's kingdom is restored, and everyone is dependent upon him to achieve this awesome goal. What are some of the factors that contribute towards a further, more exalted perception of Moon?

The Unification Church is a relatively closed environment in which outside influences are kept to a minimum. Contact with outsiders has been mainly for the purposes of 'witnessing' or fund raising.[7] Although reading newspapers or watching television may not be forbidden, there is little time for such activities. Members might keep up contact with relatives and old friends, but the importance to their lives of these outsiders is often diminished in the face of the perceived urgency of establishing God's Kingdom on earth (Barker 1983; 1989: 87–9).

The Unification Church is also a relatively authoritarian environment, in which the convert (and, indeed, all the members) are subject to constant pressure both from their leaders (immediate and further removed) and from their peers. There is a clear line of hierarchy with Moon at the head. In any particular situation each person knows whom he or she is expected to obey, and every member is responsible to a 'central figure' to whom respect must always be shown: 'Whenever we serve our central figures, we symbolically minister to God and True Parents [i.e. Reverend and Mrs Moon]' (Kwak 1985: 1). Compliance with the leaders' demands is expected, as is conformity to the general ethos and strict moral standards of the movement.

None of this is to suggest that new converts are 'brainwashed' (Barker 1984); but it is to suggest that they are under the sorts of pressure to obey and to conform that one might find in a convent or in the Armed Services. As with the novice or the fresh recruit, the power which is wielded by the organization tends quickly to be accepted as necessary and legitimate. Converts to the Unification Church have embraced the teachings, or at least declared that they want to belong to the movement, and part of the price—or challenge—or reward—is to be numbered among those who have heard and are prepared to follow God's Divine Principles, whatever personal sacrifice may be entailed.

Partly as a consequence of these two factors—the relatively closed and the relatively authoritarian nature of the movement—new converts will have their attention focused inward towards the movement and its goals and, of course, towards the person who is at the apex of the authority structure: the Reverend Sun Myung Moon. Indeed, the whole atmosphere in a Unification centre is permeated with reminders of Moon and his role. There are photographs of him everywhere (although not always in the rooms open to the public). Members prize their own personal photo of him—often with his wife. In the prayer room, there is a simple table covered by a cloth with perhaps a candle and a vase of flowers, but always with a picture of Moon and his wife. Notices that are to be found in the kitchen, the bathroom, and other places and, indeed, all correspondence between members, will end with the initials ITN—In Their Name, or In True Parents' Name, True Parents being, of course, Father and Mother, that is, the Reverend and Mrs Sun Myung Moon.

While the teachings to be found in the *Divine Principle* are relatively easy for outsiders, especially potential recruits, to discover, the Unification Church has a further set of beliefs that is not normally accessible to outsiders. Some time before I became interested in the process of charismatization, I had decided to call this internal theology 'Moonology' because of the degree to which it centres on the person of Moon,[8] with explanations of the dates concerned with the establishment of the Kingdom of Heaven on earth all being related to his accomplishments—in particular to his marriage to his present wife in 1960 when, 'for the first time in human history, the True Parents set the standard of love centred on God' (Moon 1973c: 2). The marriage, Moon has claimed, 'was equivalent in significance to the very moment of the crucifixion of Jesus'.

There is no space here even to begin to explain the complicated numerology and use of time periods connecting the life of Moon and his family to historical events, but perhaps a few excerpts, taken almost at random from just one of Moon's many speeches, will give an indication of the flavour, if not the import, of 'Moonology'.

Just as Jesus was supposed to come on the foundation of Israel and Judaism, Father was to be received upon the foundation of Korea and Christianity. . . . The reason that Father returned to satanic communist North Korea voluntarily is that He [*sic*] had set the conditions for North Korea to be able to return to God's side in the future. . . . Whilst Father was laying His victorious foundation on the national level, He was also working for the international level through His first tour in 1965, the first international blessing and the blessing of Holy Grounds in many nations. . . . In 1971, Heavenly Father [God] asked Father to go to America. . . . The big scandal of Watergate was at its height and no-one except Father knew how to solve it. . . . You can see from this that the destiny of America and of the world lays [*sic*] in Father's hands. . . . [In 1983] Father mobilized the entire [Korean] nation through his rallies of Victory over Communism and brought a final show down between God and Satan. . . . Satan could not invade Father Himself so he turned to Father's family. . . . At that time there was still tremendous opposition from the Korean government, christian churches and other organisations and God had to allow Satan to take away the precious son of true Parents as a ransom and sacrifice to pay off this debt. . . .[9] During the time of Hueng Jin Nim's ascension to the spirit world, Father was working to open this gate to the spirit world. This had to be accomplished before three days were over. . . . Father indemnified in 40 years, 4000 years of Judaeo-Christianity. . . . You must remember this formula, 1945 + 43 years = 1988. These 43 years are equivalent to the 430 years the Israelites spent in Egypt. (Moon 1987)

As might be gleaned from the above quotations, the internal theology would seem to endow Moon with certain near-miraculous powers. He is, furthermore, believed to be in constant touch with God, 'negotiating' the way forward in the light of events as they happen in both this and the spirit world in order to ensure that Satan's attempts to thwart God's plans are themselves thwarted, despite the incomprehension and/or obstructions of world leaders and religious, political, economic, and other secular organizations.

Moon, is, moreover, endowed with the power to forgive—and in a movement with such high expectations of its membership, a great deal of forgiveness may be needed. After the 'matching' at which Moon selects partners for his followers, but before the actual wedding ceremony, the engaged couples go through a special ritual, not usually known to outsiders. This is the Holy Wine Ceremony during which Moon officiates and, it is believed, the blood lineage of the participants is purified. It is believed, furthermore, that children born to the blessed couples will be born without fallen nature—the Unification equivalent of original sin. 'The immediate children of the True Parents and those who follow them as their spiritual children have nothing in common with the people of the fallen world' (Moon 1973c: 2).

Moon is presented as the perfect example whom his followers should emulate. He is said to epitomize the ideal of the perfect father, the perfect husband, and the perfect son. Curiously enough, the fact that, according to the movement's own standards, Moon would seem to have been anything but perfect in these roles is taken to prove not how he has fallen short of the ideal, but rather that he has made the supreme sacrifice for us by sacrificing his family in the pursuit of establishing the Kingdom of Heaven on an as yet unprepared earth (Barker 1983).

Although the members would deny that they pray *to* Moon, they certainly pray *through* him in their prayers to God (who is referred to as Heavenly Father). Before reciting the weekly Pledge that each member makes at 5 a.m. on Sunday mornings and other special occasions, the worshippers make three full bows. They are instructed that 'Our attendance to God is offered through the True Parents, who are Heavenly Father's representatives, and in this sense we can imagine that the first bow is dedicated to God, the second to True Father, and the third to True Mother' (Kwak 1985: 29). During the course of the recitation of the Pledge, Moon's followers declare themselves 'proud of becoming the child of the One True Parent'.

Both in Moon's internal speeches and in the general 'folk culture' of the movement, one can learn about the numerous myths surrounding Moon's life. The term 'myth' is being used here in the technical sense, not to imply that the stories are untrue, although some of them might test the credibility of the non-member—such as the tale that I have heard from several members about how Father was once praying in an upstairs room and was so saddened by the suffering that God was experiencing that he started to weep, and wept so much that the tears which fell on the floor came through the ceiling of the room below.

Other stories are circulated about Moon's childhood and about the times in prison when he 'amazed' his fellow prisoners by the hours he spent in prayer and the way in which he would give up his meagre rations for others. It is also told how, after a severe beating, he was once thrown out and left for dead; but his disciples found his smashed and naked body and, giving up all hope, 'started to make funeral arrangements, but after one week, a miracle happened! Father breathed again' (Abe 1977: 189). Such stories, frequently related by early Korean members, may take the form of small homilies; not only do they serve to illustrate Moon's amazing powers, they also incorporate interpretations of the wider meaning of a particular action, so that they are, in this respect, reminiscent of sacred writings. One of the favourite stories is of how, after he had been released by the Allies from a labour camp at the end of the Korean War, he and two of his followers fled south to Pusan and how, instead of abandoning one of the followers, Mr Pak, who had a broken leg, Father pushed him on a bicycle and, when necessary, carried him on his back. The other disciple, Won Pil Kim, recounts:

As I was telling this story one time, Father commented, 'If I could not have made it, carrying Mr Pak across the island, then I could not be responsible for the restoration of the universe.' This is typical of Father's attitude; whatever he does is not just for the person immediately involved, but because that person represents many other people, and ultimately the world. Father regarded Mr Pak as a representative of mankind. North Korea was a symbol of hell, or the satanic world, and South Korea symbolized Canaan, or heaven (Kim 1983: 14).

Members vie with each other to bear witness to their personal experience of Moon's extraordinary powers—how, for example, they stood by as Moon passed in a corridor and how they immediately knew that 'he could see right through me—deep into my innermost being'. Those who have not had the privilege of being in Moon's presence may, none the less, tell of a dream in which he appeared to them and imparted some amazing information which was borne out by subsequent events, or they will tell of some deep insight or feeling of love that has changed their lives. Artefacts that Moon has used (a cup he has drunk from, a chair he has sat on, a garment he may have worn) become treasured items—almost, it sometimes seems, like the holy relics to be found in Catholic churches.

Stories are also told about how human Moon is: how he sings with the members in a far from perfect voice, then bursts into laughter at his musical incompetence; how he wears underclothes that have been darned; how he loves to fish or to play with his children. Yet somehow the very fact that these stories are told seems to suggest that Moon is *not* quite human. The stories are, in paradoxical fashion, proof that he is more than human because he sometimes does ordinary, human things. And there is no doubt that not only in his speeches, but in the common lore of the movement, Moon is considered far more than human. It is not altogether surprising to find him referred to with a capital 'H' for 'He' and 'Him', as in the transcript quoted above.

Moon's not inconsiderable achievements are continually rehearsed. Who, thirty years ago, could have imagined that he would have established a daily newspaper such as the *Washington Times*, that he would have bought valuable properties such as the New Yorker hotel in Manhattan, that he would have control over a vast empire of businesses in most of the developed and many underdeveloped countries around the world, including the People's Republic of China, that he would be masterminding the building of an international highway, that he would be on intimate terms (as thousands of photographs can testify) with many of the world's most influential politicians, academics, commentators, clergy, and businessmen, or that he would have an audience with President Gorbachev, the last great leader of the Communist world? Moon is, indeed, believed by his followers to have played a key role in the recent collapse of Communism, this being a crucial part of his battle against Satan.

Even when external events seem to be going in the wrong direction, these are interpreted in a manner that can enhance rather than diminish Moon's specialness. They are taken to indicate that Satan has become really worried by Moon's success. It may be that Moon had given those in a key position the opportunity to do the right thing, but that they had failed him (and therefore God): 'If Pres. Nixon had listened to Father's advice, he would not have been thrown out of the White House and the world situation would have been different' (Moon 1987: 6). Despite the claim that 'through Father's support of Ronald Reagan, he could become the next president of America . . . Pres. Reagan's administration had not enough courage, strayed from its principles and allowed Father to go to Danbury' (ibid.).[10] Moon was, however, prepared to sacrifice himself to make up for these presidential failures: 'In reality, Father went to Danbury to indemnify the failure of America and especially that of Nixon and Carter' (ibid.). 'Father chose to return to America and go to Danbury because He wants to save the nation of America and the world. Father allowed Heung Jin Nim's death in order to indemnify the failure of Christianity' (ibid. 8). Moon so loves the world that he was willing to sacrifice his own son.

If Unificationists ever feel doubts about Moon or the legitimacy of his demands, they are unlikely to voice them. Even the underground magazines that flourished for a while in the mid-1980s, although they criticized second-level leaders on numerous counts, seldom, if ever, voiced any criticism of Moon.[11] Apparent mistakes or failures by Moon are nearly always explained within the movement as the mistakes of those under him or, when this might be counter-productive, as when he 'matched' a brother and sister for marriage, the apparent slip is interpreted as proof of his incredible insight—how else could he have recognized the close spiritual (if not the close genetic) bond between the two? When, very occasionally, mistakes are admitted, these are taken as illustrations of 'how human [that is, 'special'] he is'.

And, of course, in so far as charismatic authority is accorded to Moon, his employment of it—and the unpredictability that it brings in its wake—helps to reinforce the feeling that he is indeed someone special and unquestionable *because* he is so unpredictable. Furthermore, as time passes, his followers reinforce their beliefs through their own actions in daily compliance with those mores of the movement which celebrate the charismatic authority of the messianic leader. And then they, in turn, transmit the belief in Moon's charismatic personality to others, thereby reinforcing yet further the spiral of the legitimation process.

It is possible that the very fact that Moon is not directly in touch with the majority of his followers enhances their perception of him as a charismatic personality. While not going so far as to say that the social and physical distance allows him to be all things to all people, it does allow individuals a certain degree of freedom in which to construct an image of Moon that will fit or resonate with their own values and ideals. One can, indeed, learn of numerous different 'Moons' from Unificationists. On the other hand, the reliance on mediators for the charismatization process is fraught with the dangers attendant upon the routinization of charisma.[12] The mediators, not themselves being endowed with a charismatic aura,[13] may do or say things that are unacceptable to the follower; and in so far as their words and actions need a certain credibility for the charismatization process, Moon's image may suffer.

The process of charismatization certainly should not be viewed as either inevitable or irreversible. By no means everyone who joins the Unification Church becomes permanently, or even temporarily, convinced that Moon has the right to rule their lives. A few members have decidedly ambivalent feelings towards him; one or two have been prepared to tell me of their deep dislike for and distrust of the man, yet they have stayed in the movement (at least for a while) for other reasons, such as the friendship, the security, or the opportunity to be engaged in interesting and challenging work. Some Unificationists refuse to marry the partner whom Moon chooses for them; some refuse to go on the mission they are told to go on; some insist that they will go and see their parents despite the fact that there is a special 'condition' or task that needs to be fulfilled within a given time and to which, they have been told, priority must be given. Yet others—in fact, the vast majority—have left the movement, sometimes disillusioned and bitter at having been 'taken for a ride', sometimes feeling simply that, although they found the experience rewarding in a number of ways, they are no longer convinced that Moon and/or his movement is really capable of fulfilling the Unification promise. While some of these leavers continue to accept that Moon may be the messiah, they are no longer willing to accept that he or the lieutenants to whom he has delegated authority have the right to control the detail of their lives.

III

In attempting to understand the existence of charismatic authority in any particular instance, there are several variables that need to be taken into account. To start with, there is the general social environment. Weber (1947) and Wilson (e.g. 1973, 1975, 1990) are among those who have noted that it is at times of rapid change or unrest, which could be due to economic, political, social, or military upheavals, that the charismatic leader is most likely to be heard. Then, obviously enough, there is the person him or herself. Not everyone has the potential to offer a new message; and not everyone who offers a new message is heard. It is necessary, but not sufficient, for the leader to possess some (possibly indefinable) characteristics that enable him or her to be, minimally, capable of taking advantage of a situation in which the message might be heard. Within the context of new religions in the contemporary West, Wallis (1982) has given us an excellent case study with his description of how David 'Moses' Berg, the founder of the Children of God, originally became a charismatic leader, and how he maintained his authority through his interaction with those who were close to him in the movement.

The aim of this chapter has been to complement the approaches of Weber, Wilson, and Wallis by focusing on a further factor—on the internal structure and culture within which converts and grass-roots members find themselves—rather than on the wider social situation, on the leader himself, or even on those who enjoy a direct relationship with him. I have argued that there are situations in which charisma clearly does not 'work' simply as a consequence of a one-to-one or face-to-face experience during which followers-to-be recognize something special in the individual, but that, once they have become part of the movement, the followers may be taught by others to recognize the charisma.

Social scientists always need to be wary of falling into the tautological trap of confusing 'naming with explaining'; that is, they must not believe that because they use a concept, such as 'charisma', to describe the fact that followers accord their leader a special kind of authority, they have thereby explained *why* the leader is accorded the authority. It is possible, however, that the concept can help to sensitize us to certain processes that contribute to this state of affairs; it can lead us to recognize that there are questions to be asked that might not otherwise be asked, and it may alert us to noticing the cumulative effect of a number of factors that might not otherwise be noticed in such a context.

Moreover, the fact that followers accord charisma to their leader can provide a partial explanation in the sense that it makes more understandable what was otherwise incomprehensible and/or unexpected behaviour, such as when, at the suggestion of a Korean who speaks practically no English, well-educated, middle-class Westerners accept a marriage partner whom they have never met. The granting of the charismatic authority may thus provide the critical link in a 'dynamic, causal explanation'. Or, to put it in a slightly different way, having analysed the social production of 'an ethos propitious to the mobilisation of sentiments', it can be argued that, just as illuminating as the traditional explanation 'I do this because it has always been done this way', or the rational/legal explanation 'I do this because it is the reasonable/lawful thing to do in the circumstances', is the charismatic explanation 'I do this because He asks it of me'.

Notes

1. The research on which this paper is based was conducted with help from the then Social Science Research Council of Great Britain and from the Nuffield Foundation, to both of whom I would like to express my gratitude.
2. I was well into the second, the 'interactive', phase of the three stages of participant observation that I describe in Barker 1987: 144.
3. 'He gazed up at the enormous face. Forty years it had taken him to learn what kind of smile was hidden beneath the dark moustache. O cruel, needless misunderstanding! Two gin-scented tears trickled down the sides of his nose. But it was all right, everything was all right, the struggle was finished. He had won the victory over himself. He loved Big Brother' (Orwell 1954: 239).

4. For further details about Unification beliefs and history, see Barker 1984.

5. This quotation is taken from the original transcript of a talk by Moon as translated by Dr Bo Hi Pak and circulated among the membership; an edited summary of the talk was published in *Today's World*, Mar. 1987, pp. 12–17.

6. For an analysis of why people do join the movement, see Barker 1984.

7. This is less obviously the case now that members are older, often have young children, and work more frequently in an 'outside' environment (Barker 1989: 12).

8. The talks of Moon are each typed up and distributed to members under titles beginning 'Master Speaks' and, more recently, 'Reverend Sun Myung Moon Speaks On. . . .'. Many of these talks appear, usually in a somewhat edited version, in the monthly magazine *Today's World*.

9. The second son of the Reverend and Mrs Moon, Heung Jin Nim, was involved in a car accident in the United States. He died nearly two weeks later. See *Today's World*, Jan./Feb. 1984 for an account of the accident, the Reverend and Mrs Moon's interpretation of what happened, and the rituals that took place in the movement following the tragedy.

10. Danbury was the prison in which Moon served the sentence he was given for tax evasion.

11. One of these, *The Round Table*, was edited from New York; another, *Our Network*, from the West Coast of the USA.

12. Weber's (1947) concept of the routinization of charisma—a process whereby there is a 'return to the every-day' with the authority becoming institutionalized—could be of relevance in understanding some of the tensions that arise to prevent unfettered charismatization from continuing indefinitely. Indeed, this can be observed as a cause of 'decharismatization'. There is no space to explore such a possibility here, however.

13. There have, in fact, been a few cases where others within the Unification movement have become endowed with at least a modicum of charismatic authority. However, their authority has crumbled in the face of Moon's superior position when, perhaps inevitably, it has come to the crunch.

References

Abe, M. (1977), *Church Leader's Manual* (Tokyo).

Barker, E. V. (1983), 'Doing Love: Tensions in the Ideal Family', in

G. James (ed.), *The Family and the Unification Church* (New York), 35–52.

—— (1984), *The Making of a Moonie: Brainwashing or Choice?* (Oxford).

—— (1987), 'Brahmins Don't Eat Mushrooms: Participant Observation and the New Religions', *LSE Quarterly*, 1: 127–52.

—— (1989), *New Religious Movements: A Practical Introduction* (London).

Kim, W. P. (1983), 'From Pyongyang to Pusan', *Today's World* (April), 9–21.

Kwak, C. H. (1980), *Outline of the Principle: Level 4* (New York).

—— (1985), *The Tradition: Book One* (New York).

Moon, S. M. (1973*a*), 'Master Speaks: Change of Blood Lineage III', First International Training Session, HSA-UWC, 21 Jan.

—— (1973*b*), 'Master Speaks: Relationship between Male and Female', Second 100-Day Training Session, HSA-UWC, 20 May.

—— (1973*c*), 'Master Speaks: World Day', HSA-UWC, 1 June.

—— (1987), 'Day of Victory of Love', HSA-UWC, 2 Jan.

Orwell, G. (1954), *Nineteen Eighty-Four* (Harmondsworth).

Wallis, R. (1982), 'The Social Construction of Charisma', *Social Compass*, 29: 25–39.

Weber, M. (1947), *The Theory of Social and Economic Organization* (Oxford).

Wilson, B. R. (1973), *Magic and the Millennium* (London).

—— (1975), *The Noble Savages: The Primitive Origins of Charisma and its Contemporary Survival* (Berkeley, Calif.).

—— (1990), *The Social Dimensions of Sectarianism: Sects and New Religious Movements in Contemporary Society* (Oxford).

12

The Apocalyptic Theme in Religious Orders

JEAN SÉGUY

According to Ernst Troeltsch, the religious Order[1] institutionalizes certain features of the sect type inside the Church. Yet, as regards the eschatological—especially the apocalyptic—theme frequently found in Christian sectarianism, Troeltsch claims that it tends to be neglected in religious Orders. With them, he stresses, asceticism soon takes the place of eschatological expectations. His argument is that such expectations show up as exceptions in a few medieval cases only, in connection with the Franciscan movement (Troeltsch 1960: 113).

In this chapter I raise two questions about these convictions of Troeltsch. First, is the German author's opinion on the exceptional presence of the apocalyptic theme in religious Orders and its exclusive location in the Middle Ages still acceptable in view of the historical evidence today? Second, what type of historical situation is it that favours particularly the development of a special affinity between certain Orders and certain forms of apocalyptics, and what social functions do such apocalyptics fulfil?

ADVENTIST RELIGIOUS ORDERS

The affinity that has existed at times between the religious life—in its technical Catholic sense—and certain forms of apocalyptics is most clearly evident in certain so-called institutes of perfection. In this chapter and for convenience, I have decided to call all these institutes '(religious) orders', whatever their respective canonical status. I have also elected to label them 'Adventist', simply because they longed ardently for the *advent* of the Last Days.

As early as the fourteenth century, a famous Dominican preacher, St Vincent Ferrer, tells in one of his works entitled *De Vita Spirituali* of a 'certain impatient desire for the *advent* (*adventus*) of those days'. This was characteristic in his opinion of certain groups of particularly religious-minded people in his own time. In fact, he was one of them. I have thought it expedient to keep here to the vocabulary of a man who was both a participant in and a theorist of the hopes and expectations at work in the orders singled out for consideration.

THE MEDIEVAL PERIOD

The Adventist theme, as understood here, enters into history in the twelfth century with the foundation of the Order of Fiore by Joachim of Fiore.[2] This was an offshoot of the Cistercian Order, but it never played an important part in Church or monastic history. It was eventually reunited with its parent body in 1570.

Joachim's fame does not rest, however, on this modestly illustrious foundation, but on his philosophy of history. More will be said about this later. For the moment it is sufficient to stress that some of the significant elements of the Joachimist system—in particular, its threefold division of history and its conception of an Order of the Last Days—are to be found in all Adventist Religious Orders, whether medieval or modern.

For a time at least and in their infant days, the Dominicans, founded in 1215, cherished apocalyptic motives; they even claimed a leading role for themselves in the End of Times. But this eschatological mood did not last long with them. It persisted longer and had deeper consequences among the Franciscans, founded in 1226.[3] In fact, the very hierarchy of the Franciscan Order favoured a mild form of apocalypticism in the decades immediately following Francis's death.

On the whole, the Franciscan Spirituals exhibited more radical leanings. They were not an Order or a fully organized party; they formed a current of thought, as well as an informal network of influence. Their members—or perhaps, better, their sympathizers—stood for the Rule *ad litteram*, against official Church interpretation and what was going to be more and more the practice of the Order as a whole. They backed their protest by recourse to apocalyptic themes, stressing particularly the leading role that, according to them, the Seraphic Order was to play in the Last Days.

The late-thirteenth century Clarenists, named after their leader, Angelo Clareno, could be said to belong to the Spiritualist movement (von Auw 1979). They shared its vigorous literalism and eschatological expectations. They formed an autonomous wing of the Franciscan Order; yet some of them showed decidedly unorthodox tendencies, to the point of joining the ranks of the doctrinally ill-famed Fraticelli.

The fourteenth-century Observant Franciscans and the fifteenth-century Amadeites were both fully orthodox, literal followers of Francis's Rule. They inherited some of the apocalyptic concerns of their Spiritual predecessors; like them, they held firm convictions about the leading role that they believed the Seraphic Order, and more especially the literalist friars, would be called to play in the Last Days.

The Hermits of St Augustine, who were founded in the thirteenth century, showed only occasional and individual interest in the Joachimist view of history until a number of them took enthusiastically to Joachim of Fiore in the sixteenth century. They were then instrumental in having Joachimist and post-Joachimist literature printed and circulated. Moreover, they cherished the notion that their order was the one predestined to preside over the last period of history. By an irony of fate, Egidio of Viterbo, the general of the Augustinian friars at the time of Luther, headed the Venetian group of Joachimist Augustinians who held such exalted views about the future of their Order. As a reformer, Luther, who had been a Hermit of St Augustine himself in his monastic days, also held rather precise eschatological expectations; but he did not expect his former brethren to play any privileged role in the Last Days.

It is not without interest to note here that, Troeltsch's opinion to the contrary notwithstanding, the medieval Orders which claimed to be the End of Times Order did not all belong to the Franciscan family. At least three of them did not. Such was the case with Joachim's Order of Fiore, to begin with; although the Dominicans had shared Franciscan eschatological enthusiasm briefly, they had, like the Augustinian hermits, other roots and references. However, one cannot but notice that these three groups were mendicant Orders like the Franciscans themselves. In other words, they had left behind the monastic pattern of the religious life, together with its heavy implications in terms of power and property. They stressed poverty not only as a motto and a way of life, but also as an expression of protest against a more and more commercialized society and a rich and powerful Church. In all this, as well as in their apostolic zeal, they displayed strong similarities with the Franciscans. This seems to be as much as can be conceded to Troeltsch on this point. Recourse to Joachimist imagery on the part of these non-Franciscan groups seems connected in one case—the Order of Fiore—with close personal proximity to Joachim himself. In all the other cases the motivating factor seems to have resided in a strong awareness of the newness of the mendicant life in relation to the ideal of Church Reform in those days and its eschatological meaning (Ladner 1959).

THE MODERN PERIOD

The Joachimist system of thought was typically medieval in more than one sense.[4] Yet, it did not pass away with the waning of the Middle Ages; nor did it prove obsolete in the light of sixteenth-century modernity. Protestant polemicists saved it from oblivion by having recourse to it in their anti-Catholic polemics. This did not enhance Joachim's reputation in the Catholic Church. But the Cistercian's fame had weathered other earlier storms, and proved able to withstand the new one. In spite of some suspicion about it in various quarters, the Joachimist philosophy of history—at least in some of its aspects—did not lose its appeal altogether with the creators and members of modern religious Orders.

From its very foundation in the sixteenth century, the Society of Jesus (the Jesuits), a most rationally organized mendicant Order, seems to have nourished a discontinuous, fragile, and at times half-underground tradition of eschatology in the Joachimist perspective. In this regard it is significant that the seventeenth-century scholar Paperbrock, who did more than anyone to contribute to a theological reappraisal of Joachim, was a Jesuit.[5]

The Austrian and South German Bartholomeites, named after their seventeenth-century founder, Bartholomew Holzhauser, were an institute of secular priests who took three religious vows. They did not directly claim the privilege of being the Order of the Last Days; in fact, they admitted that the role of the *Viri apostolici* was reserved for a group of priests leading a life much like their own.[6] St Vincent de Paul held a more or less similar opinion concerning his own Congregation of the Mission (Lazarists) (Séguy 1983*a*).

The conviction that he was forming a crack regiment destined to fight the Lord's battles in the Last Days and introduce an era of peace and triumph for the Church under Mary's aegis was an explicit part of Louis-Marie Grignion de Montfort's outlook regarding his Company of the Missionaries of Mary (Montfortians, eighteenth century) (Séguy 1982).

The same outlook can be seen at work very explicitly in the Society of the Heart of Jesus, a group of priests and laymen (with a feminine counterpart, The Daughters of the Heart of Mary (Rameri 1976; Rayez 1966; Genos 1985)) founded in the revolutionary atmosphere of 1791 Paris.[7]

The contemporary and short-lived (1792–6) Society of Mary, which was recruited from among French *émigré* clergy in Spain (and for that reason often styled the 'Society of Mary of Spain'), also adopted the same perspective, inherited from the Joachimists (Séguy 1984*a*). Such was the case, too, with the two Societies of Mary, the Marianists of Bordeaux and the Marists of Lyons. Like the ones already cited, these two French Restoration groups claimed for themselves, respectively, the privilege of introducing the last Age of history and of leading it to its triumphant close.[8]

A few other cases from the second part of the nineteenth century deserve mention. Mélanie Calvat, one of the two visionaries of La Salette (1846), wrote a plan of an 'Order of the Apostles of the Last Days'. In spite of an attempt to make the plan materialize, it failed to take shape.[9] Although the Virgins of the Expectation, founded in 1903 by a Sicilian canon, Antonio Catiglione, were approved at first, they were soon disbanded by order of the relevant authorities. It is not certain, however, that their eschatological perspectives had anything to do with the Joachimist heritage (Desroche 1969: 84, 253). The Society of women gathered by Claire Ferchaud, from 1917, near Cholet (Maine-et-Loire, France) never received full ecclesiastical approval or an official name. It has been refused permission to accept new members for a long time, and is presently on the verge of extinction. Its founder's perspectives were clearly post-Joachimist; it did not fail to claim a privileged role for itself in the Last Days (Mouton 1978; Ferchaud 1974).

JOACHIMISM AND THE END OF TIMES ORDER

Joachim of Fiore (*c*.1125–1202), mentioned earlier in this chapter as the founder of the first Adventist Order was a Cistercian monk.[10] He spent most of his life meditating on the prophetic pages of the Bible and unravelling their mysteries. His system of interpretation soon became popular. This was probably because it managed to identify and articulate a positive and necessary way of expressing the feelings of uncertainty and expectancy which pervaded the Christian world at a time when the failure of the Crusades was slowly becoming obvious to many.

Joachim's popularity led to a multiplication of the manuscripts of his works. It also gave rise to the abundant literature now known as post- or pseudo-Joachimist. In both its forms, genuine and not so genuine, this literary heritage has become a treasure, on which commentators and preachers have often drawn without restraint. A schematic reminder of its basic configuration will show why it was particularly successful in attracting the attention of certain founders and members of religious Orders.

Joachim's system divides history into three *Status* (improperly but commonly called 'Ages'), each of them named after one of the persons of the Trinity, and each with its own characteristic institutions and typical leaders. From this point of view, history becomes the place in which God's gracious purpose unfolds itself in three successive dispensations, from Creation to Judgement Day. Nothing needs to be said here about the Age of the Father, except

Fig. 1. *Joachim's breakdown of history*

First Status (Age of the Father)	Second Status (Age of the Son)	Third Status (Age of the Spirit)	CELESTIAL	JERUSALEM
From Creation to the time of John the Baptist's father	From John the Baptist to Joachim's own days	From the defeat of Antichrist to Armageddon and Judgement		
{ Law { Marriage { Patriarchs	{ Grace { Clerical celibacy { Priests	{ Spiritual Illumination { Universal celibacy { Monks		

that it coincides with the Old Testament period. The New Testament times run through the Second and Third Ages; but the transition from the one to the other signals a qualitative jump similar in some respects to that between the First and Second *Status*—that is, between the Old and New Testaments. It seems that in Joachim's mind the break between the Ages does not entirely eliminate the kind of continuity that makes for the coherence of the whole. However, it remains difficult to account satisfactorily for the qualitative jump implied in the passage from the Second to the Third *Status*. This is a theological difficulty that—together with a few others—Joachim's opponents soon detected and exposed.

According to Joachim, the Age of the Son will end in much turmoil and bloodshed. At the end of it, Antichrist is to reveal himself and persecute the Just with great cruelty. The Church will emerge purified and free from this trial before Antichrist is destroyed by Christ's own power.

Joachim prophesies that in the last days of the Second Age, before Christ's victory takes place, a religious Order of *Viri spirituales* (or *Evangelici*) will appear. Whether it will be one Order only, with both a contemplative and an active branch, or two distinct Orders working hand in hand, one contemplative, the other active, remains uncertain. It is important to notice, however, that the Abbot of Fiore's conception identifies the union—still considered problematic or an exception in his own days—of contemplation and action as the distinctive mark of the End of Times Order. Once in existence, the mendicants did not take long to discover that this *ante eventum* description fitted their case admirably. Joachim's prediction placed heavy duties on the shoulders of the *Viri apostolici*: they were to lead the faithful in their struggle against Antichrist, to bring the Church into the Third Age, and to set the tone for that period. Awesome as these responsibilities were, they did not deter some of the mendicant Orders from claiming the role for themselves. Some of the apostolic Orders were to follow in their wake later.

Joachim sees the transition from the Second to the Third Age and this last *Status* itself as a time extremely rich in exceptional events. First of all, and in connection with the appearance of the *Viri spirituales*, a Spiritual Pope is to ascend to Peter's throne. Then the Jews will be converted to Christ, as will the Muslims and most of the pagans; finally, all the heretics and the schismatics will return to the Church. Still according to the Abbot of Fiore, a period of universal peace will follow the defeat of Antichrist. But it is not to last for ever. Two small marginal peoples, Gog and Magog, enticed by Satan, then unfettered, will reject the spiritual consensus of the period and will wage war against the Just. Having returned to earth, Christ will defeat these rebels. The general Judgement will then bring history to its close, with the Just eternally rewarded in the Celestial Jerusalem and the wicked forever tormented in Hell.

Joachim has little to say about life in the Third Age. His view is that men and women will be taught and illuminated by the Spirit directly: they will lead a life of perfect poverty and chastity under the *Viri spirituales* as their counsellors. The Church will also be spiritual at that point, and so will the Pope, the Papacy, and the sacraments. However, Joachim offers no clue as to what a spiritual Papacy and spiritual sacraments might be. Nor does he give a detailed explanation of the relationship that will prevail in the Third Age between the Pope and the *Viri spirituales*. They are supposed to work under the Pope and, at the same time, to set the tone for all men and women in that Age, including the Pope and the hierarchy as a whole. With the exception of Gog and Magog, all the peoples of the earth and their leaders will then be united under Peter's successor. Yet, for Joachim, the Papacy will be glorified only in so far as it is reformed and adopts the virtues and mores of monasticism. The Third Age is to see the triumph of the monastic ideal and the glorification of a Church built in its image.

It is a far cry, however, from Joachim's position to the position that some radical Joachimists took later, when they denounced the Papacy as Antichrist occupying Peter's See. The Cistercian abbot's intention seems better reflected in the interpretation of his thought given by some sixteenth-century Hermits of St Augustine, who imagined the Spiritual Pope who would reign in the Third Age as one of their own. They depicted him wearing the habit and the girdle of their Order; at the same time they identified themselves in the role of the *Viri spirituales* (Reeves 1969: 266, 376; *idem* 1976: 55).

For various reasons (Baraut 1974), Joachim's posthumous reputation has not always been good in the Church. Yet his own works and the literature appearing falsely under his name long remained popular in certain quarters. Themes such as the Third Age of history, the End of Times Order, the Spiritual (or Angelic)

Pope, and so forth became widely popular in medieval religious culture. They soon took on an autonomous life, dissociated from Joachim's name and system. This is precisely how they appeared in the works of a number of medieval representatives of Marian devotion and forerunners of the cult of the Heart of Jesus: Hildegard of Bingen (in fact, a predecessor of Joachim), Mechtilde of Magdeburg, Gertrude the Great, Brigid of Sweden, and others fell into this category. The writings of these canonized saints circulated widely in religious houses and among priests and educated laity. They were still very popular in the same quarters long after the end of the Middle Ages, both in their original languages (Latin in most cases) and in vernacular translations. The circulation of these works kept alive in the pious public a number of originally Joachimist themes. They also maintained among the same audience an aspiration to a moment of universal triumph for Christianity, as well as a desire for a purified Church, ultimately led by the Spirit, and an Order of Spiritual Men.

St Vincent Ferrer's *De Vita spirituali* played an important, though not exclusive, part in the phenomenon under discussion. Its paragraph on the *Viri apostolici* was still well known in seventeenth-century France, where the *De Vita spirituali* circulated in its original Latin as well as in a French translation; both of them were to be republished in the nineteenth century (Morell 1866). It must also be remarked that certain sixteenth-, seventeenth-, and eighteenth-century annotated Bibles and biblical commentaries played a part in preserving some traits of the Joachimist heritage. In so far as they expounded the general features of the Cistercian's philosophy of history in order—more often than not—to dispute its validity, they contributed to its transmission.

The eighteenth century saw the emergence, especially in the French—and to a certain extent in the English—lower classes of a minimal, diluted, autonomous form of Joachimism (Garrett 1975: 10–11; de Lubac 1981: 330, 335; Reeves and Gould 1987: 3–5, 31, 40–2). Impoverished and unsystematic as it was, this set of originally Joachimist images and themes, completely disconnected from their literary sources, helped a number of people—of various social origins—to make sense for themselves of the Revolutionary upheaval and its consequences. Both partisans and opponents of the French Revolution had recourse to it in their attempts to interpret religiously the exceptional events through which they were living.[11] In the English-speaking world this autonomous form of Joachimism made its own restricted contribution to the Prophetic Revival. This, as is well known, accompanied, followed, and interpreted the developments of Revolutionary and Napoleonic times (Garrett 1975).

The nineteenth century gave autonomous Joachimism a further chance. Many of the social, political, cultural, and religious utopias of the period took their general frame of reference from odds and ends of the Joachimist heritage, eventually secularizing it in part.[12]

The restitution of Joachim of Fiore and Joachimism to history by a number of nineteenth-century historians of repute (Ernest Renan, to begin with) marked an important milestone in the posthumous career of the Cistercian monk. Yet, this scientifically clear version of 'what had once been' proved to be devoid of utopian appeal for a long time. Post-Joachimism showed itself more productive, at least in the beginning. The Adventist Orders contemplated by Mélanie Calvat and Claire Ferchaud apparently took their inspiration from Grignion de Montfort's own interpretation of the post-Joachimist heritage (Séguy 1982). Yet, in our own age, when the time came for a revival of interest in eschatology and utopia, the historical Joachim and his scientifically canonized work were at the centre of the discussion. But no End of Times Order came out of the political theologies that emerged in the late 1960s and the 1970s.

SOCIAL CAUSES AND FUNCTIONS OF THE APOCALYPTIC THEME IN RELIGIOUS ORDERS

Two facts emerge from the discussion at this point. On the one hand, Troeltsch did not realize the full extent of the apocalyptic Joachimist current in religious Orders; nor, apparently, did he have any idea of its modern manifestations. On the other hand, one has to admit that, except for a relatively short period of time and in connection with the Franciscan movement in the first decades following the death of St Francis, this current has never had strong social effects in Church or society. Yet, throughout the centuries and practically down to our own times, a small but not negligible number of new Orders have claimed for themselves the role of the *Viri apostolici* of the Joachimist tradition.

Meticulous discussion of the detailed causes of this long-term phenomenon which has evaded analysis thus far would be out of place here. But even a bird's eye view of their history reveals rather clearly that Adventist Orders tend to appear—like Joachim's own Order of Fiore—in moments of uncertainty. This is particularly true when, for whatever reasons, groups of people feel trapped by the course of history regardless of their social origins. Periods of political, social, and cultural unrest, as well as times of revolutionary upheaval, are just such moments.

In these periods of uncertainty, the desire to make sense religiously of an everyday life experienced as full of menace and fraught with still more dangers in the future can lead individuals or groups who are especially affected to have recourse to the language of apocalyptics.[13] In some extreme situations this language is seen by certain people as providing the only possibility of expressing the exceptional nature of the danger that they perceive to be lurking in their daily lives. In the process of applying a specific tradition of apocalyptics to the times in which they live and of predicting their future, the same individuals or groups eventually come to identify themselves with certain paradigmatic individuals, groups, or events pertaining to that tradition.

In this respect, the Joachimist Third Age of history, with its stress on the monastic virtues as virtues fit for all Christians, its End of Times Order, its emphasis on the marriage of contemplation and action, its insistence on the Spirit and spirituality as the ultimate reference for action, was bound to attract the attention of reformers of the religious life—like Joachim himself—and of Church reformers more generally. From the twelfth century onwards, Joachimism, rather like millenarianism, has offered certain groups of people longing for a different Church and a different world an ideological opportunity to make sense of their era and to envisage the future with confidence.

Yet, the interpretation of history devised by Joachim was not absolutely unequivocal. The Third Age could be—and has been—understood as an age of entire freedom from all man-made rules and authorities, with the Spirit as the only sufficient guide and the ultimate source of legitimation. The issue at stake in this extreme perspective was one of authority and power. Not surprisingly, its upholders have always met with determined opposition from the Church. The groups that professed Joachimist or post-Joachimist convictions and wished to remain within the Church had to be very wary of failing to make a clear enough confession that the institutional Church was their ultimate instance of legitimation.

The founders of religious Orders all have a message, and some of them a charisma of their own, around which their followers gather. At the same time, a group can be called a religious Order only in so far as it belongs to a Church and is subordinate to its hierarchy. Hence, a twofold source of legitimation can be observed in any religious Order: its founder's charisma and message on the one hand and the charisma of the Church office on the other. Obviously the former must be subordinated to the latter, the grace offered by the individual claiming an extraordinary experience to 'the state of grace of the institution' (Weber 1968: iii. 1140). Inside an Order— at least, theoretically—reference to the founder and his or her message and charisma can be sufficient to induce members to commit themselves to the ends of the institute and to comply with orders from legitimate superiors. Yet, these Orders are only legitimate in the eyes of the Church in so far as they draw their ultimate legitimation from her and exercise their authority in accordance with her own interpretation of the founder's experience and within her own definition of the finality of the Order.

In ordinary circumstances and after an eventual phase of more or less difficult negotiations and mutual adjustment, the two sources of legitimation usually work smoothly together. When this fails to happen, however, the incipient group and its founder (and his or her successor[s]) can be ordered to disband or else find itself, wittingly or unwittingly, outside the Church; then and there it evolves into a sect or a mystical *réseau*, or network. At this point the apocalyptic motive may enter into the picture in order to account for the situation of the newly independent body and to legitimate it. In such a case, the new body identifies itself with the apocalyptic forces of good; it sees itself as the elect remnant destined to govern the earth in the Last Age of the world. Conversely it looks upon its opponents, especially the Church, as constituting the Lord's enemies, identifying them—and her, rather specifically—with Antichrist. Medieval movements with a post-Joachimist perspective, like the Fraticelli, the Segarellists, the Manfredists, and others, fell into that category. Ultimately they found their legitimation in their leaders' supposedly extraordinary experiences or charisma and in Scriptures as they themselves interpreted them in the light of the Joachimist heritage and of their leaders' convictions. With them the apocalyptic motive fulfilled a legitimating function in so far as it justified their dissent and sacralized it.[14] At the same time, it identified the beliefs that were to be held orthodox in those groups, clearly marked their limits, and integrated them.

The same integrative and legitimating function can be seen at work in Adventist Orders. But in this case integration is first of all with the Church, and legitimation concerns the role that the Order claims for itself *within the Church*. Two cases can be considered here. The first occurs when the Order meets with serious difficulties in its fight for recognition within the Church of what it considers to be its own vocation. In this case the apocalyptic motive serves to legitimate the protest—explicit or implicit (Séguy 1979)—that the Order tries to convince the Church authorities to accept and support. The struggle of certain medieval Franciscan groups to have their own interpretation of the Rule of St Francis and its reforming overtones accepted in the Church found its legitimation in the apocalyptic vocation that the same Franciscans claimed for themselves and that confirmed the charismatic claim already made on behalf of the founder. In that case the apocalyptic perspective in its Joachimist garb helped the Seraphic Order to assert its own conception of itself within the Church in so far as the Church could tolerate an Order claiming its own sources of legitimation and advocating reform along its own lines. It is well known that it took some time before the Franciscan heritage was fully integrated and accepted in the Church, a process in which it lost some of its supporters and much of its reforming potential.

A second ideal type of possible relations between the apocalyptic perspective and legitimate authority can also be discerned. In this case integration and subordination to the Church are much more easily achieved. The protest which is either explicit or implicit in the apocalyptic discourse of the Orders in question tends to be directed against the world rather than against the Church. In so far as some dissatisfaction with the Church is shown, however, it is likely to be with tendencies, parties, or groups in conflict with the Papacy and the bishops or with priests and lay people who follow the Church's lead more willingly.

In this case the apocalyptic motive supports legitimate authority, advocating reform along its own lines. This was true in the Middle Ages of the Observantines, the Amadeites, and the Hermits of St

Augustine, when sections of these Orders took to the Joachimist line. The modern Adventist Orders all correspond to this, so to say, easy-going type. Even so, there is a lingering degree of ambivalence and implicit protest against legitimate authority. This emerges clearly in the case of the Hermits of St Augustine, which was discussed earlier. The fact that they portrayed the Spiritual Pope as one of them implied dissatisfaction with the authority of the Church as it was operative in those days and their desire, expressed graphically, to exercise that authority themselves. However, they took no practical step in that direction, a fitting stance in a case of implicit protest. A similar observation could be made about the Society of the Heart of Jesus, founded by an ex-Jesuit, Fr Pierre de Clorivière, at the time of the French Revolution, and about the Marists.

The important thing to notice in these and similar cases is that the (extra) legitimation derived from the claim that the Order has received an extraordinary call to exercise a specific leading role in the End of Times is put—expressly—at the disposal of the Church hierarchy. It must also be remarked that all the modern Adventist Orders have been particularly well integrated into the post-Tridentine tradition of Marian devotion. Grignion de Montfort is paradigmatic in this respect (Laurentin 1984). In his view and in subsequent Adventist perspectives, the last *Status* of history was to be the Age of Mary as well as the Age of the Holy Spirit. This characteristically post-Reformation conception went together with an exceptional attachment to the Papacy.

In a time when, from the Reformation and especially the Revolution onwards, Catholicism had lost much of its grip on Western society and more and more of its social plausibility, the new Adventist Orders came to its rescue in their own specific way (Séguy 1986). They did not claim the (extra) charismatic legitimacy which they might have felt entitled to claim for themselves. They offered it to a distressed Church and, more precisely, to a battered Papacy. The fact that this was not devoid of all ambiguity did not matter very much. Clorivière could envisage—and perhaps in a sense anticipate—that all the bishops and eventually all the clergy would become members of his Society. Fr Colin could also claim that the Spiritual Pope would be a Marist. The effective integration of their respective Orders into the Church and their strict subordination to the ecclesiastical hierarchy soon became more important than any claim they could make to fulfilling a reforming role in the End of Times.

For various reasons, however, the apocalyptic perspective seems to have played very little—if any—part in the full development of modern Adventist Orders. This negative phenomenon was not simply one of the expected effects of routinization and institutional-ization. It had more to do with the increasingly uncertain status of apocalyptics in modern society and the modern Church, from the second part of the seventeenth century onwards. Yet, three things remained characteristic of the Adventist Orders even after they were deprived of their eschatological perspectives: their conspicuous devotion to Mary, their special attachment to the Papacy, and their will to serve the Church in difficult times. That was enough to ensure them a successful future in the modern world.

CONCLUSION

Proper answers can now be offered to the questions raised at the beginning of the chapter. In particular, it can be safely asserted that the apocalyptic theme is not as exceptional in religious Orders as Troeltsch assumed. Nor is it typically medieval. Yet, at the end of our inquiry, it also has to be admitted that Adventist Orders, numerically speaking, form a very minor category in the history of the Church. They are, none the less, interesting in the eyes of the social scientist.

In this chapter I have stressed both the legitimating and the integrating functions of the apocalyptic theme, and have established that this can work in two directions, informing dissent both within and without the Church. Claims to a privileged role in the events at the End of Times on the part of religious Orders do not necessarily remove them from the Church. In certain circumstances, some forms of post-Joachimism appear compatible with integration into the Church and with subordination to its hierarchy, the two sociological marks of the religious Order. Yet, the Adventist perspective is not devoid of a certain—generally transitory—amount of at least implicit protest. This too can be integrated in favourable circumstances.

The interest of the category of Adventist Orders is to draw the attention of sociologists necessarily to the concept of *implicit protest.* I consider this to be a discreet invitation to try to apprehend the religious Order from the point of view of a sociology of conflict (Séguy 1984*b*).

Notes

1. See the section below on 'Adventist Religious Orders' for the use of the term 'religious order' in this chapter.
2. See Reeves 1969, 1976.
3. See the joint letter of John of Parma, OFM, and Hubert of Romans, OP, the leaders of their respective Orders, in de Romans 1889: 494–500.
4. See Séguy 1983*b* for a short general overview of the modern period.
5. See Reeves 1976: 117–19, 121, 132–5, 166–7; Haubert 1969: 119–33; Vaucher 1941; and Vallin 1987: 65–9.
6. See Berdonces 1974 and Holzhauser 1856, esp. i, 195–8, the passage on the *Viri apostolici*. The latter work was translated from the Latin and continued by Canon de Wuilleret.
7. Morlot 1988: 13–26, 91–170; Rayez and Fevre 1971–3. See Séguy 1986 for a further discussion of the problem discussed in this chapter.
8. On the Society of Mary (of Lyons) see Coste 1982 and Zind 1969: 118–20, 123. For the Bordeaux Society of Mary, see Zind 1969: 128–34. On the possible dependence of the two Restoration Societies of Mary on the Society of Mary of Spain, see Zind 1969: 65–6.
9. The text of the plan is in Guilhot 1973. See Stern 1979 for the historical problems raised by this plan. See also Jaouen 1946.
10. See Reeves 1969, 1976; Baraut 1974; and the two excellent contributions by Dupuy 1967*a*, *b*.
11. See Garrett 1975 for the French and English cases. Caffiero has recently studied the Italian case; see Caffiero 1988.
12. See Garrett 1975 and especially de Lubac 1981 and the excellent research of Reeves and Gould 1987.
13. See Oliver 1978; Léger and Hervieu 1983; and Tedeschi 1989. In addition to providing information on their particular subjects, these three books all have a very interesting discussion of the much disputed question of millenarianism and social class. See also Sandeen 1980. In the case of Joachimism and post-Joachimism there seems to be no necessary link between this body of doctrine and any particular social class.
14. See Manteuffel 1970, ch. 5, on these movements.

References

Auw, L. von (1979), *Angelo Clareno et les Spirituels italiens* (Rome, Edizioni di Storia e Letteratura).

Baraut, C. (1974), 'Joachim de Fiore', in *Dictionnaire de spiritualité*, vol. 8 (Paris, Beauchesne), cols. 1179–1201.

Berdonces, J. (1974), 'Bartolomitti' in G. Pellicia and G. Rocca (eds.), *Dizionari degli Istituti di Perfezione*, vol. 1 (Rome, Edizioni Paoline), cols. 1070–3).

Broutin, P. (1958), 'L'Oeuvre pastorale et spirituelle de B. Holzhauser', *Nouvelle revue de théologie*, 90: 510–25.

Caffiero, M. (1988), 'Prophétie, millénium et révolution; pour une étude du millénarisme en Italie à l'époque de la Révolution française', *Archives de sciences sociales des religions*, 66: 187–99.

Coste, J. (1982), 'Maristes et eschatologie', *Recherches et documents du Centre Thomas More*, 36: 25–6.

Desroche, H. (1969), *Dieux d'hommes* (Paris, Mouton).

Dupuy, B.-D. (1967*a*), 'Joachim de Flore', in *Catholicisme*, vol. 6 (Paris, Letouzey et Ané), cols. 848–87.

—— (1967*b*), 'Joachimisme', in *Catholicisme*, vol. 6 (Paris, Letouzey et Ané) cols. 887–95.

Ferchaud, C. (1974), *Notes autobiographiques* (2 vols, Paris, Téqui).

Garrett, C. (1975), *Respectable Folly* (Baltimore, Johns Hopkins University Press).

Genos, A. (1985), 'La Société du Coeur de Marie', in F. Morlot and E. Genos (eds.), *Fondations nouvelles: Pierre de Clorivière* (Paris, Desclée de Brouwer and Bellarmin).

Guilhot, H. (1973), *La vraie Mélanie de La Salette* (Sainte-Cénéré, Éditions S. Michel).

Haubert, M. (1969), 'Indiens et Jésuites au Paraguay: Recontre de deux messianismes', *Archives de sociologie des religions*, 2: 119–33.

Holzhauser, B. (1856), *Interprétation de l'Apocalypse*, trans. de Wuilleret (2 vols, Paris, Louis Vivès). 1st Latin edition, 1699.

Jaouen, J. (1946), *La Grâce de La Salette* (Paris, Cerf).

Ladner, G. B. (1959), *The Idea of Reform* (Cambridge, Mass., Harvard University Press).

Laurentin, R. (1984), *Dieu seul est ma tendresse: R. L. présente L. M. Grignion de Montfort* (Paris, O.E.I.L.).

Léger, D., and Hervieu, B. (1983), *Des communautés pour les temps difficiles: Néo-ruraux ou nouveaux moines* (Paris, Le Centurion).

Lubac, H. de (1981), *La Postérité spirituelle de Joachim de Flore*, vol. 2: *De Saint-Simon à nos jours* (Paris, P. Lethielleux).

Manteuffel, T. (1970), *Naissance d'une hérésie: Les adeptes de la pauvreté volontaire au Moyen-Age* (Paris, Mouton).

Morell, M. (1866), *Traité de la vie spirituelle par s. Vincent Ferrier . . . avec des commentaires sur chaque chapitre par la Mère Julienne Morell* (Poitier, J. Oudin).

Morlot, F. (1988), 'Società dei Sacerdoti del Cuore di Gesù', in *Dizionari degli Istituti di Perfezione* vol. 8 (Rome, Edizioni Paoline), cols. 1672–8.

Mouton, C. (1978), *Au plus fort de la Tourmente: Claire Ferchaud* (Montsurs, Éditions Résiac).

Oliver, W. H. (1978), *Prophets and Millennialists: The Uses of Biblical Prophecy in England from the 1790s to the 1840s* (Auckland, Auckland University Press).

Rameri, M. L. (1976), 'Figlie del Cuore di Maria', in G. Pellicia and G. Rocca (eds.), *Dizionari degli Istituti di Perfezione*, vol. 3 (Rome, Edizioni Paoline), cols. 1570–2.

Rayez, A. (1966), *Formes modernes de vie consacrée: Ad. de Cicé et Clorivière* (Paris, Beauchesne).

—— and Fevre, L. (1971–3), *Foi chrétienne et vie consacrée; Clorivière aujourd'hui* (Paris, Beauchesne).

Reeves, M. (1969), *The Influence of Prophecy in the Later Middle Ages* (Oxford, Clarendon).

—— (1976), *Joachim of Fiore and the Prophetic Future* (London, SPCK).

—— and Gould, W. (1987), *Joachim of Fiore and the Myth of the Eternal Evangel in the Nineteenth Century* (Oxford, Clarendon).

Romans, H. de (1889), *Opera de Vita Regulari* (Rome, Befani).

Sandeen, E. (1980), 'The "Little Tradition" and the Form of Modern Millenarianism', *Annual Review of the Social Sciences of Religion*, 4: 165–81.

Séguy, J. (1979), 'La Protestation implicite', *Archives de sciences sociales des religions*, 48: 187–212.

—— (1982), 'Millénarismes et "ordres adventistes": Grignion de Montfort et les Apôtres des Derniers Temps', *Archives de sciences sociales des religions*, 53: 23–48.

—— (1983*a*), 'Monsieur Vincent, la Congrégation de la Mission et les Derniers Temps', in L. Mezzadri (ed.), *Vincent de Paul: Actes du colloque international d'études Vincentiennes* (Rome, Edizioni Vincenziane), 217–38.

—— (1983*b*) 'Profetismo. Sec. XVII–XIX', in G. Pellicia and G. Rocca (eds.), *Dizionari degli Istituti di Perfezione*, vol. 7 (Rome, Edizione Paoline), cols. 983–6.

—— (1984*a*), 'La Société de Marie "dite d'Espagne": Mariologie, apocalyptique et contre-révolution', *Revue d'histoire des religions*, 201: 37–58.

—— (1984*b*), 'Pour une sociologie de l'ordre religieux', *Archives de sciences sociales des religions*, 57: 55–68.

—— (1985), 'Charisma in the Modern World' in *Actes de la 18th Conférence Internationale de Sociologie des Religions* (Lausanne, Éditions de la CISR), 51–64.

—— (1986), 'Des sociétés pour les temps de la fin: Le P. de Clorivière et l'Apocalypse', in *Un fondateur dans la tourmente révolutionnaire; Pierre de Clorivière (1735–1820)* (Paris, Colloque du Centre Sèvres), 111–33.

Stern, J. (1979), 'Mélanie Calvat', in *Catholicisme*, vol. 8 (Paris, Letouzey et Ané), cols. 1110–11.

Tedeschi, E. (1989), *Per una sociologia del Millennio: David Lazzaretti: Carisma e mutamento sociale* (Venice, Marsilio).

Troeltsch, E. (1960), *The Social Teaching of the Christian Churches* (New York, Harper Torchbooks).

Vallin, P. (1987), 'Ramière (Henri), jésuite, 1821–1884', in *Dictionnaire de spiritualité*, vol. 13 (Paris, Beauchesne), cols. 65–9.

Vaucher, A. F. (1941), *Une célébrité oubliée: Le P. Manual de Lacunza y Diaz (1731–1801)* (Coullonges-sous-Salève, impr. Adventiste).

Weber, M. (1968), *Economy and Society* (3 vols, New York, Bedminster Press).

Zind, P. (1969), *Les Nouvelles Congrégations de Frères enseignants en France de 1800 à 1830* (Le Montet, Saint-Genis-Laval, privately printed).

13

From Religion to Psychotherapy: Yoshimoto Ishin's *Naikan* or 'Method of Inner Observation'

SUSUMU SHIMAZONO

THE CONCEPT OF PSYCHOTHERAPEUTIC RELIGION

Although Bryan Wilson's theory of sectarian movements was first established on the basis of examples taken from Western Christianity in the modern period, he has further expanded and applied it beyond these limits to the non-Western and non-Christian world. His book *Magic and the Millennium* (1973) is the fruit of this endeavour. He deals with religious movements in various parts of the world, but his main attention seems focused on movements in relatively simple societies which have experienced external pressures. Japan is not mentioned. This does not mean, however, that Wilson is not interested in the new religious movements of that country. Indeed, in *Religious Sects* (1970), a slightly older work, he devotes quite a few pages to a description of Japan's new religions. As a student of Japan's new religions, I would like to offer a few comments on Wilson's view of sects. It is not my intention, however, to argue about the extent to which his attempts at theorization have succeeded as a whole. I shall deal with only one part of his typology, and, focusing on one specific Japanese example, try to develop Wilson's insights a little further into a more universally applicable theory.

In *Religious Sects* Wilson states that many of Japan's new religions belong either to the thaumaturgical or to the manipulationist type of sect.[1] Although he presents their founders and successors as thaumaturges, these sects are typically closer to the manipulationist type in his opinion. As a preliminary step in my discussion, I shall try to apply his typology of sects to Japan's new religions. According to Wilson, both the manipulationist and the thaumaturgical types of sect are principally concerned with problems of health and other kinds of this worldly benefits.[2] Admittedly, millenarianism, social reform, and utopian community are also objects of attention in Japan's new religions, but healing and other this-worldly benefits constitute the main point of interest. Wilson's view that the majority of Japan's new religions belong to the manipulationist or thaumaturgical types is therefore basically correct. But the problem remains of deciding under which of the two—manipulationist or thaumaturgical—it is appropriate to classify them. I will focus particularly on the concept of manipulationist sects in this chapter; but in order to arrive at a correct understanding of the situation in Japan, I must give some thought to the question of how to modify this concept.

According to Wilson, sects of the manipulationist type seek salvation in the here and now. Salvation is not something to be attained in another world after death, in an afterlife. It does not consist in a transcendental state completely separated from this world's environment and from the present state of body and mind. Ongoing happiness in this world in the form of, for example, good health, prosperity, and success is believed to pass for salvation. Therefore, unlike many other types of sects, manipulationist sects do not think that the present world is essentially evil. Of course, they believe in the existence of evil; but in their view, it is perfectly possible to eliminate evil from this world. The cosmos is intrinsically harmonious, and human beings are expected to live happily in harmony with the cosmos.

Evil derives from people's false thoughts. It is therefore possible to do away with evil and unhappiness by changing people's way of thinking. Indeed, manipulationist sects teach what false thoughts are and how to change them. They offer people not objective moral norms but new modes of thought. They do not want to change the world, but to change the way in which people relate to the world. Although this change, which comes about through faith, is subjective, it is thought that the individual's objective situation also changes for the better as a result. The label 'manipulationist' is given to this type of sect precisely because it wants to change people's fate by means of subjective changes.

Many sects develop in metropolitan centres, where relationships are impersonal and dominated by role performance. Right thinking constitutes a sophisticated mode of thought in manipulationist sects, involving abstract ideas and methods of intellectual analysis considered appropriate for coping with complicated human relationships in modern city life. The adherents of such sects are, characteristically, city dwellers and individualistic. They detest restraints on their freedom, and are not too keen to establish communities of believers.

A typical example of older manipulationst sects is Christian Science, which drew heavily on the Christian tradition. Later on, however, sects of this type became increasingly syncretistic. For example, there were many deviations from orthodox Christianity in New Thought and Positive Thinking, and groups like the Theosophical Society and the Vedanta Society found much of their inspiration in Asian religion. More recently established manipulationist sects include Scientology, which has adopted much from depth psychology, and groups which show a strong interest in UFOs.

The distinction between the manipulationist and thaumaturgical types depends on whether the emphasis is on intellectual refinement or on an unsophisticated faith in miracles. Thaumaturgical religion is most evident in less developed societies, and is said to be devoid of complicated teachings. Spiritualism is included in the thaumaturgical type, but Christian Science and the Theosophical Society, which developed their respective teachings under the influence of Spiritualism, are considered to be manipulationist.

A number of Japan's new religions fit into Wilson's manipulationist type as summarized above; or at least, they resemble it closely. Such religions include Seichō-no-Ie and Hito-no-Michi Kyōdan (which subsequently became PL Kyōdan). However, there are others which differ somewhat from this type, such as Tenrikyō, Ōmoto, and Sōka Gakkai. The question therefore arises of the respects in which Japanese new religions which resemble the manipulationist type differ from the other groups.

A further examination shows that in Japan's new religions some of the characteristics of manipulationist sects are widespread, while others are not so all-pervasive. Generally present are the notion and affirmation of salvation in this world, together with the idea that the cosmos and the relationship between the cosmos and human beings is basically harmonious (Tsushima *et al.* 1979). If these aspects of the characteristics of such sects are emphasized, we have to admit that almost all of Japan's new religions belong to the manipulationist type. Religions which correspond closely to the movements characterized by Wilson as manipulationist sects are called 'harmonial religions' by Ahlstrom (1972), and most of Japan's new religions qualify as such.

On the other hand, there are some characteristics of the manipulationist type which are conspicuous in Seichō-no-Ie and Hito-no-Michi Kyōdan but are not so frequently seen in other religious groups, such as changing one's way of thinking, or 'thought switching'.[3] Evil and unhappiness originate from false thinking, according to these groups, and the core of their teaching is that by changing one's thinking, one's fate is also changed and happiness is achieved. Most of Japan's new religions pay considerable attention to changing people's fate in the present world. As a means to this end, some offer magical practices, prayers, and rituals. Others stress ethical behaviour in life, missionary work, or public service. However, in Seichō-no-Ie and Hito-no-Michi Kyōdan, the emphasis is on changing one's ideas, rather than on other things. Of course, since 'changing one's ideas' is closely connected in many cases with deepening one's faith and with carrying out various practices, it is also to some extent a feature of types of religious groups that differ from Seichō-no-Ie and Hito-no-Michi. Yet, the most important feature of these two new religions is their insistence that changing one's ideas *itself* brings about a change of fate.

The belief that changing one's ideas can improve one's fate has replaced the traditional religious belief that improvement can come about only through the intervention of a transcendental power. Whereas formerly one prayed for healing through the power of the divine, healing is now to be achieved through thought-switching. This change has come about partly because in the present situation belief in the divine has become increasingly difficult, and partly because the credibility of the claim that changing one's ideas really does have a beneficial impact on life also seems to play a role in this. In the complex relationships that characterize modern society there is a great danger that psychic instability, caused by anxiety and fear of unknown people, will prevent adjustment. In such circumstances, a change of ideas can adroitly regulate the human psyche and thereby change social life for the better. A rationalistic way of thinking and a pragmatic conception of mental processes are widely found in this type of religion. Wilson's argument that manipulationist sects develop in urban society, in which human relationships are complex and impersonal, can be more easily understood when we take into account that this is so because complex and impersonal human relationships require the objectivization and technical manipulation of the mind.

A variety of Japan's new religions display these kinds of characteristics, but the concept of manipulationist sects does not adequately account for this aspect. We could call the missing aspect 'psychotherapeutic', since, as mentioned above, religions which aim at changing one's ideas try to cope with the problems of the heart in a pragmatic, technical way and have many features of secular psychotherapy. We could say that, with the spread of psychotherapy and psychological thinking, elements of psychotherapy have gradually been adopted by religion as well. It has become difficult to accept a divine, transcendental commander, so to speak, and absolute ethical norms in modern society. Instead, an ethical attitude which puts a high value on peace of mind and on adjustment to the environment has become predominant. Philip Rieff (1966) and Robert Bellah and associates (1985) have described this attitude as 'therapeutic'.[4] In their view, the modern era reveals an ongoing process whereby the symbol system that solves ethical problems shifts from religion to psychotherapy. Some sects of the manipulationist type manifest this kind of therapeutic attitude to such a degree that it is justifiable to refer to them as 'psychotherapeutic religions'. It may be possible to acquire a deeper insight into some of the phenomena that have occurred in Japan's recent religious history if we use this concept of psychotherapeutic religion instead of that of a manipulationist sect.

In the next section I will introduce a system of thought and practice which was established in Japan around the middle of the twentieth century and which can be located somewhere between religion and psychotherapy. Although it is not generally considered to be a new religious movement, it has close resemblances to such, and is therefore a fitting focus for a study of the relationship between religion and psychotherapy in Japan. By investigating this concrete example, I hope to unearth clues regarding the extent to which various phenomena which we can call 'psychotherapeutic religions' have developed.

YOSHIMOTO NAIKAN

The psychotherapeutic method called 'Yoshimoto Naikan' which is operative in present-day Japan has attracted the attention of psychologists and psychiatrists as a practice rooted in Japanese culture. The creator of this method, Yoshimoto Ishin, simply called it *naikan*, or 'method of inner observation'. But since this term is also used to designate other things, the practice in question is now called Yoshimoto Naikan, after the name of its creator, in order to avoid confusion.[5]

This practical method of therapy consists mainly of being confined for a week in a small space of about one square metre, screened off from others by a folding partition, so that one can reflect deeply on one's past relationships with other people. The Naikan client is supposed to sit all day from 5 a.m. until 9 p.m. in this secluded corner, except for meals and visits to the toilet. He or she is engaged in intensive meditation (naikan), and has contact only with the *shidōsha*, or 'counsellor', who pays regular visits. No special sitting posture is prescribed, so one is permitted to perform the self-reflection in a relaxed way. One is asked to reflect on three questions: 'What care have I received?', 'What have I done to repay it?', and 'What troubles have I caused in my relations with particular people?' On average, the first two questions each occupy 20 per cent of the time, while 60 per cent is devoted to the third one. In most cases, reflection starts with the relationship with one's mother. Beginning with the first years of elementary school, one gradually moves on, in periods of three years, to the present time. Once reflection on the relationship with one's mother is complete, one proceeds to the relationship with one's father, and then to that with one's brothers and sisters, superiors, teachers, and friends. Sometimes one is also told to reflect on lies told in the past or thefts committed and to calculate the expenses incurred by one's parents for one's education, or even the total amount of money one has spent on drinking.

The counsellor visits every hour and a half or two hours, and asks the client what he or she has recalled during that reflection period. If reflection has not proceeded well, the counsellor does not stay, but simply recommends that the client continue further with serious introspection. Otherwise, he acknowledges the client's confession and announces the theme for the next Naikan period. The length of the interview is usually no longer than three to five minutes. During meals and at the hours of rising and going to bed, clients listen to audio tapes on which model clients record their reflections. Moreover, since in a typical situation, several clients are meditating in the same room, separated only by folding screens, the general tone if not the details of the confession made by each client to the counsellor can be heard by others. When the Naikan proceeds well, the client becomes aware of 'how much care he or she has received', 'how little he or she has paid in return', and 'how much more he or she has caused trouble'. The client becomes filled, not only with deep feelings of guilt, but also with a sense of gratitude towards other people and starts weeping. On the last day of the session the clients come together, and participate in a colloquium for about an hour.

As of 1983, there were about twenty special places in Japan where Yoshimoto Naikan therapeutic sessions were held. At the Naikan Centre in Yamato-Kōriyama in Nara Prefecture, where the creator of the Naikan method, Yoshimoto Ishin, conducted interviews as a counsellor, about 1,300 people underwent treatment in 1982 alone. There are also many hospitals, prisons, reformatories, high schools, and other institutions all over the country where Naikan practices have been adopted. However, if Naikan is practised only at the special sessions and in groups, the effects quickly evaporate. In order to maintain the benefit, clients ideally have to engage in Naikan every day in their own homes, a practice called 'daily' or 'diffused' Naikan, as distinct from the 'concentrated' Naikan at the sessions. If 'daily Naikan' constitutes the real goal, then 'concentrated Naikan' is but a process of initiation into this psychotherapeutic method. In reality, however, it seems to be quite difficult to keep up the practice of 'daily Naikan'.

Yoshimoto Ishin's books contain some letters from a woman client who sent him a weekly report on her daily Naikan for twenty-three years without a break. As an example of the self-introspection performed in Naikan, I quote here from one of her letters:

I have been investigating the attitude I have towards my mother. Among the things I received from her I should first mention that my older brother and sister, after leaving school, went to live and work elsewhere. Also my mother, leaving my younger brother and sister in the care of our grandmother, went out to work. But selfish as I am, I did not like to be with my grandmother and I followed my mother. She did the cooking for many craftsmen, but I think she took me with her while caring very much about people's feelings. I have done nothing to repay her. I caused her many troubles. Also at the place where my mother worked I often wandered far away to amuse myself and did not come back until late. I do not know how much I was a source of anxiety to her. Really, I have no excuse for this (Yoshimoto 1983: 99–100)

Yoshimoto Naikan has become a matter of interest to many psychologists and psychiatrists. Many scientific papers dealing with it as a psychotherapeutic method have been published, and in 1978 an Academic Association for Naikan was established. There are many people who consider Yoshimoto Naikan to be a therapy or cure for neuroses, mental diseases, and social deviance. Yoshimoto died in 1988, but his Naikan will certainly be kept in existence, not only by his personal followers but primarily by psychologists and psychiatrists.

THE DEVELOPMENT OF YOSHIMOTO NAIKAN AS PSYCHOTHERAPY

The creator of Yoshimoto Naikan, Yoshimoto Ishin, was born in 1916, the third son of a wealthy family which ran a large farm and sold fertilizers in Yamato-Kōriyama in Nara Prefecture. His 4-year-old sister died from illness in the second year of elementary school. This led his mother to become a fervent member of a temple of the Shin sect (True Pure Land Buddhism), and the young boy often accompanied her to listen to Buddhist sermons and the chanting of sutras. After graduating from the horticultural school of Kōriyama at age 17, Ishin started working as a calligraphy teacher and, through his frequent visits to temples, he also became an enthusiastic student of the teachings of the Shin sect. Two years later he was introduced to Morikawa Kinuko, who was to become his wife. Many members of the Morikawa family were ardent supporters of a group of believers, known in the Shin sect for their special brand of faith, who were centred on the Taikan hermitage in Fuse, Osaka Prefecture. Under their influence, Yoshimoto was led to a religious experience which gave direction to the rest of his life.

The Shin sect is the largest sect of Japanese Buddhism. It follows the tradition of the Pure Land school, which believes in salvation after death through the power of Amida Buddha by rebirth in the Western Paradise. The sect was founded by Shinran (1173–1262), who gave a new orientation to this faith in salvation after death. According to the teachings of Pure Land Buddhism, ordinary people do not possess the capacity for being saved. But Amida Buddha vowed to save these weak beings. In Amida's all-encompassing mercy, he ordained that whoever performs the simple act of reciting the *nenbutsu*, or sacred formula 'Namu Amida Butsu', will be saved and reborn in the Pure Land—that is, the ideal world of the Buddhas. In other words, the Pure Land school teaches that human beings cannot be saved by seeking wisdom or by performing ascetic practices through their own efforts (*jiriki*), but only by relying on the saving power of Amida Buddha (*tariki*). Mahayana Buddhism, especially the Pure Land school, stresses salvation from an external source. It was the most powerful tradition in Japanese Buddhism, and Shinran became one of its most famous leaders. By the sixteenth century, Shinran's Jodo-Shin sect had become the largest group not only within Japanese Pure Land Buddhism but also within Japanese Buddhism in general. He gave new depth to the idea of salvation by faith and to the teaching that human beings cannot perform any good deeds by themselves. Even reciting the *nenbutsu* or believing in Amida Buddha does not stem from one's own initiative, but are possible only through the power of Amida Buddha. As such, human beings are immersed in evil, and it is not in their nature to be saved. Only when this has been sufficiently recognized, does faith spring up from the bottom of one's heart that Amida Buddha will grant his salvific power so that, even in life, one may enter the state of being reborn into the Pure Land Paradise.

In the movement's early years, Pure Land believers often had doubts about rebirth in the Pure Land after death. This was also the case in the Shin sect. As a result, groups appeared at various times which, in addition to nurturing a thorough awareness of human sinfulness, performed esoteric ascetic practices in order to confirm by means of mystical experiences that they had been saved by Amida Buddha. In the Edo period, many of these groups were called *kakure nenbutsu*, or 'hidden nenbutsu believers', and were suppressed as heretics. But since the Meiji period, they have to a certain extent acquired the right to exist as subgroups within the recognized sects. In any case, the group around the Taikan hermitage in Fuse, a temple founded by Nishimoto Taikan, was one of those which retained a deep faith that esoteric practices would lead to salvation. A practice called *mishirabe*, or 'self-inspection', was cultivated in the group around the Taikan hermitage. In this practice, believers were confined in a small room and required to look back intensively upon their sins, ponder the inescapability of death, and become aware of the fearfulness of hell. Contact with outsiders was forbidden during this practice. Those who were undergoing it, called *byōnin*, or 'patients', were placed in extreme circumstances, deprived of food, water, and sleep. Believers who had already attained the consciousness of being saved, called *kaigonin*, or 'enlightened ones', took turns to visit them and urge them on to deeper self-awareness. Thereby, the patients could also achieve the mystical experience of being convinced of their salvation by Amida Buddha. Through this 'experiencing a concentrated mind' (*ichinen ni au*), the patients were saved, and convinced that they would be reborn in Paradise after death (called *shukuzen-kaihotsu*, or 'development of the goodness stored in past lives').

Yoshimoto had apparently seen himself as a respectable believer of the Shin sect, and had taught Buddhism to many people. When he met the believers of the Taikan hermitage, however, he lost his self-confidence, and began to think that he was no more than a believer who had acquired some knowledge of Buddhism, but who still lacked a real religious experience. In 1936, at the age of twenty, he therefore took part in the *mishirabe* for the first time. But, haunted by strong doubts about himself, he was not able to gain the conviction of salvation. Concealing this from his father, who opposed the kind of special faith that puts emphasis on secret practices, and after experiencing a similar frustration two or three times, he married Kinuko whose relatives were associated with Taikan, and finally came to the enlightenment of salvation more than a year after his first *mishirabe*.

From 1938 on, Yoshimoto, who had opened a wholesale leather clothes business in Osaka, used his free evenings for visiting people and propagating the faith of the Taikan hermitage. Taking care of his shop during the day, he succeeded in making his business very prosperous. Within a few years he had established twelve branch stores, and was employing many staff. He continued as president of his company after contracting tuberculosis in 1949, but finally stopped working in 1953, claiming that business was not his real task but had only been a temporary means of building up the capital necessary for the propagation of faith. He then opened the Naikan Centre in Yamato-Kōriyama, living off the income from his capital, and devoted all his energy to the diffusion of Naikan therapy.

In the meantime Yoshimoto had initiated various reforms in the faith of the Taikan hermitage. Opposition had been growing since about 1940 between those believers who took the stance that only one salvation experience was necessary and those who took a position which stressed the substantial depth of self-introspection of *mishirabe* as such. The former invited people to an ecstatic experience, and were successful for a while in attracting many participants. But their faith tended not to last for long. The latter, on the other hand, acknowledged that the experience of real salvation was for only a few, but that their faith was of a more lasting nature. Yoshimoto took the later position, and strove to reform the *mishirabe* practice still further. After 1943 he made the employees of his company undergo the experience of Naikan, and, from then on, the aspect of ecstatic, esoteric religiosity declined in importance even more. This development subsequently led to psychologists, psychiatrists, and other intellectuals evaluating the Naikan experience positively.

BETWEEN RELIGION AND PSYCHOTHERAPY

Between 1940 and 1953 the practice of *mishirabe*, which had been based on the faith of the Shin sect of Pure Land Buddhism, gradually developed into a form of self-introspection almost equivalent to present-day Naikan and, consequently, of a strongly psychotherapeutic nature. The reforms that were made in this meditation practice at that time can be summarized as follows (Yoshimoto 1983: 47–62):

(1) Emphasis was placed not on a one-off experience of salvation but on the continuity of reflection. Whereas in the beginning one was to continue reflection in an unhurried way while undergoing the experience of *ichinen ni au*, this experience of salvation soon ceased to be the goal. In other words, it was not so much the experience following from reflection as the process of

reflection itself which acquired more and more value. Concretely speaking, concentrated meditation no longer concluded with an experience of salvation, but simply ended after a period of one week. Moreover, whereas previously, there was no requirement of systematic meditation after undergoing the experience, daily meditation was now to be continued after the concentrated meditation.

(2) Esoteric elements, ascetic practices, and special religious terms were eliminated from the process of meditation. Meals and adequate sleep were now allowed, and contacts with outside people also became acceptable. Moreover, the meaning of terms became secularized, as *mishirabe* was changed to *naikan*, and *kaigonin* to *shidōsha*, or 'counsellor'.

(3) In practical terms, this meant that questions about the identity of the people on whom one should reflect, the duration of the reflection, and the kind of things about which one should feel guilty were specified. The process of reflection was systematically ordered, and made more comprehensible. Moreover, the practice of several *kaigonin* taking turns visiting was replaced by having a single counsellor visiting on a regular basis.

(4) There was a shift of emphasis from a sense of transiency to a sense of sin. Formerly, one tried to heighten the hope for salvation by instilling fear of death and hell (by thinking about *mujō* or the transiency of all things). Instead, one is now mainly urged to deepen one's awareness of debts towards others. This has had the practical effect of stressing the guilt one feels towards certain persons as a specific topic of reflection.

It is a moot question what Yoshimoto Ishin thought about the relationship between Naikan and religion. It is certain that he himself firmly believed in rebirth in Paradise after death through the power of Amida Buddha. He also thought that someone who had attained religious faith was an ideal Naikan client. Around 1950 he qualified as a Buddhist priest and, in 1955, registered his home in Yamato-Kōriyama, the site of his Naikan practice, as a religious body in law, called the Naikan Temple. The Naikan Centre became a separate institution attached to the temple. On the other hand, he stressed that Naikan was not a religion. This might be related to the fact that he wanted to disseminate Naikan as a meditation practice in detention houses, juvenile reformatories, and high schools, and the Japanese constitution forbids religious groups from propagating their message in prisons and other public institutions. However, when it comes to psychotherapy, prison employees can easily apply it to their daily duties.

The fact that Yoshimoto did not lay too much emphasis on a belief in salvation by Amida Buddha and rebirth in Paradise after death may be due to the experience he gained as a manager whose employees were practising Naikan. The female employees who practised *mishirabe* (or Naikan) under instructions from their company president became happier than before. They were more grateful to others and stopped making complaints, and human relationships became very smooth. Judging from these practical effects, Yoshimoto apparently came to realize that there was no specific need to stress faith in salvation through Amida Buddha and rebirth in Paradise. He was strongly convinced, furthermore, that Naikan should not be confined to a limited number of selected people, but should be widely propagated throughout the world. He thought that it was therefore much better for Naikan not to take the form of religion. In fact, in so far as Naikan has become widely known, this has mainly been through the contribution of psychologists and psychiatrists who look upon it as a form of psychotherapy. Whereas academics and the mass media have generally been critical of new religious movements, they have been very positive about Yoshimoto Naikan.[6]

On the other hand, the claim that Yoshimoto Ishin himself considered Naikan to be a form of purely secular psychotherapy is less certain. He called it 'seeing into oneself', or 'method of inner observation'. As it was a method of coming to one's deepest reality, he seems to have thought of it as something which transcends the traditional conflicts between religious schools and which universalizes the truths that they contain on another, higher level.[7] Perhaps it is correct to see it as a new type of religion for intellectuals familiar with scientific thinking, one that is respectful of the authority of science. Moreover, I have to add that Naikan has been adopted in various new religious groups.

YOSHIMOTO NAIKAN AS A PSYCHOTHERAPEUTIC RELIGION

When we compare Yoshimoto Naikan with new religious groups, we see that there are considerable differences in organization and practices. Taking into account that Naikan does not claim to offer physical healing or to manifest mystical powers, it might be better to refrain from calling it a new religion. It is also difficult to classify it under the head of 'manipulationist sects' in Bryan Wilson's typology. However, I believe that it can be called a 'psycho-therapeutic religion', in the sense used at the beginning of this chapter.

There are also a number of differences between Yoshimoto Naikan and Seichō-no-Ie and Hito-no-Michi, which can lay similar claim to the title of 'therapeutic religion'. Nevertheless, there are reasons for calling it a 'religion' in the broad sense because of the following features: (a) the practice of deep inner reflection, (b) concentration on the fundamental religious problem of awareness of sin, (c) the view that gratitude is essential not only towards other people but also towards something that transcends people, (d) the emphasis on a feeling of emotional liberation very close to an experience of religious conversion, and (e) the implanting of a thought pattern in accordance with a specific practice concerning a person's way of life and ethical conduct. With regard to organiza-tion, it is true that people who have experienced concentrated Naikan do not remain in touch with each other afterwards, so in that regard it does indeed bear more resemblance to psychotherapy than to religion. But the number of contemporary new religions which do not emphasize organizations of believers is certainly on the increase. It may be possible, then, to understand it as something close to what Thomas Luckman (1967) called 'invisible religion'.

By contrast with Seichō-no-Ie and Hito-no-Michi, Naikan does not promise physical healing or any manifestation of mystical powers. Another big difference is that, whereas the former religious groups display a strong tendency towards a kind of positive thinking which denies worry and fear and urges people to adopt a cheerful state of mind, Yoshimoto Naikan encourages participants to become deeply conscious of their sins. In other words, Yoshimoto Naikan adopts a pessimistic view of human nature. In fact, it is said that care must always be taken because not a few clients contemplate suicide. The attitude of emphasizing a person's goodness could be said to be the polar opposite of emphasizing their badness.

The difference might be explained as follows. In the case of Seichō-no-Ie and Hito-no-Michi, attention is directed towards the impersonal human relationships in urban society, and efforts are made to eliminate and liberate people from the overloaded interpersonal conflicts entailed by stressful city life. By contrast, attention is given in Yoshimoto Naikan to the close human relationships which still exist even in urban society, and this is the model on which attempts are made to re-establish attitudes towards other people. Yoshimoto Naikan has this stance in common with many new religions. For example, in the various groups of the Reiyūkai tradition, people are strongly urged to repent of their sins. Similarly, in Seichō-no-Ie and Hito-no-Michi, reflection on one's sins and repentance are stressed to some extent. Both consciousness of sin and positive thinking are adopted in many new religions. But it is interesting to note how in Seichō-no-Ie and Hito-no-Michi on the one hand and Yoshimoto Naikan on the other, all of which are typical psychotherapeutic religions, there tends to be a strong emphasis on one or other of these two orientations.

The concept of psychotherapeutic religion is based on the assumption that in urbanized society a shift in thinking has occurred on a broad front, away from religion towards psychotherapy. If this presupposition is correct, the advance of urbanization makes the development of therapeutic religions possible in various cultural traditions. Wilson's concept of manipulationist sects was established on the basis of concrete examples from the particular cultural traditions of the West. By contrast, I believe that the concept of psychotherapeutic religion possesses a more universal applicability.[8]

Notes

1. The other types are the conversionist, revolutionist, introversionist, reformist, and utopian sects.
2. My description of the concept of manipulationist sects is based on Wilson 1970 and 1973. An earlier work (Wilson 1967) lists only four types, among which the one then called 'gnostic' corresponds to the manipulationist type.
3. I have dealt with this point in two (Japanese-language) essays: Shimazono 1988 and 1989.
4. Before adopting the term 'therapeutic', Rieff spoke of 'psychological man'. See Rieff 1959 and Homans 1979.

5. My main sources on Yoshimoto Ishin include Miki 1976; Yoshimoto 1977, 1983; and Takemoto 1984. The contents of Yoshimoto 1977 are almost the same as those of Yoshimoto 1965.
6. Yoshimoto 1980 contains articles and descriptions taken from newspapers, magazines, dictionaries, and other general publications which speak positively about Yoshimoto Naikan.
7. Yoshimoto 1983 refers to Naikan as 'a way which corresponds to all religions'. Moreover, the idea that Seichō-no-Ie and Hito-no-Michi Kyōdan are not 'religions' or that they are 'ways corresponding to all religions' has been proposed from time to time.
8. Translated from the Japanese by Jan Swyngedouw.

References

Ahlstrom, S. E. (1972), *A Religious History of the American People* (2 vols.; New Haven, Conn.).

Bellah, R., *et al.* (1985), *Habits of the Heart* (Berkeley).

Homans, P. (1979), *Jung in Context: Modernity and the Making of Psychology* (Chicago).

Luckmann, T. (1967), *The Invisible Religion* (New York).

Miki, Y. (1976), *Naikan ryōhō nyūmon: nihonteki jiko-tankyū no sekai* (*Introduction to Yoshimoto Naikan, The World of the Japanese Search for the Self*) (Tokyo).

Rieff, P. (1959), *Freud: The Mind of the Moralist* (Garden City, NY).

—— (1966), *The Triumph of the Therapeutic* (New York).

Shimazono, S. (1988), 'Seichō-no-Ie to shinri ryōhōteki sukui no shiso-: Taniguchi Masaharu no shisō-keisei-katei o megutte' ('Seichō-no-Ie and the Idea of Psychotherapeutic Salvation: The Formation of Taniguchi Masaharu's Thought'), in T. Sakurai (ed.), *Nihon Shūkyō no seitō to itan* (*Orthodoxy and Heresy in Japanese Religion*) (Tokyo).

—— (1989), 'Toshigata shinshūkyō no kokoronaoshi: Hito-no-Michi Kyōdan no shinriryōhōteki kyūsai-shinkō' ('Healing of the Mind in New Urban Religions: The Psychotherapeutic Salvation Beliefs in Hito-no-Michi Kyōdan'), in Y. Yuasa (ed.), *Taikei Bukkyō to Nipponjin 3- Mitsugi to shugyō* (*An Outline of Buddhism and the Japanese: Secret Teachings and Ascetic Practices*) (Tokyo).

Takemoto, T. (1984) (ed.), *Gendai no espuri 202, Meisō no seishin ryōhō: Naikan ryōhō no riron to jissen* (*Contemporary Spirit 202, Mental Therapy of Meditation: The Theory and Practice of Naikan Therapy*) (Tokyo).

Tsushima, M., *et al.* (1979), 'The Vitalistic Conception of Salvation in

Japanese New Religions', *Japanese Journal of Religious Studies*, 6/1–2: 139–61.

Wilson, B. R. (1967) (ed.), *Patterns of Sectarianism* (London).

—— (1970), *Religious Sects* (London).

—— (1973), *Magic and the Millennium* (London).

Yoshimoto, I. (1965), *Naikan yonjūnen* (*Forty Years of Naikan*) (Tokyo).

—— (1977), *Naikan no michi* (*The Way of Naikan*) (Yamatokōriyama, Naikan Kenkyusho).

—— (1980), *Naikan nijūgonen no ayumi* (*Twenty-five Years of Naikan*) (Yamatokōriyama, Naikan Kenkyusho).

—— (1983), *Naikan e no shōtai* (*Invitation to Naikan*) (Tokyo).

14

Worlds at War: Illustrations of an Aesthetics in Authority; or, Numbered Notes Towards a Trilogy, of which the General Title is 'Sacred Order/Social Order' ©

PHILIP RIEFF

A. A violent order is disorder; and
B. A great disorder is an order. These
Two things are one. (Pages of illustrations.)

(Wallace Stevens, 'Connoisseur of Chaos')

(1) *Let there be fight? And there was.*[1] And there is. James Joyce's (1975: 90) pun on the seven first words of Jewish world creation (Genesis 1: 3) is more than mildly amusing; it gives the reader the most exact and concise account I know of the sociological form of culture. Culture is the form of fighting before the firing actually begins. Every victorious firing force of social order, including those of imperial Rome and the democratic West after World War II, aims to declare peace on its own political terms. Thus the Roman imperial standard in the ruined temple of defeated Israel. Thus General Douglas MacArthur as the ruler of the defeated military monarchy of Japan after the Second World War. Thus the resurrection of the German Catholic Centre Party, Adenauer the true Allied-sponsored successor to Hitler in the mid-twentieth century, as Windthorst, founder-leader of the Catholic centre in the late nineteenth century, unsponsored, even in political moments crucial to the Church, by the Vatican, never succeeded Bismarck. Thus President Bush's error in not taking the open road to Baghdad to put on trial those in corrupt power, and to install a democratic regime in Iraq. Mosaists on one side of her internecine

battle line; Freudo-Marxists on the other; can Israel continue to survive her own founding centrality in our worlds at war? As Israel goes, so will go the world creations derived from it.

(2) *The politics of culture.* Unless a culture is defeated culturally, as Jewish culture was not, from the Roman conquest to the refounding of the Jewish state in 1948, it will reassert itself politically, later if not sooner. The fights and firings between Islam and Israel, cultural as they are political, are complicated if not paralleled by the fights within Israel between worlds at war the world over. The shattering of once distant world spaces into sharply edged and closely contending life-worlds fighting for their lives can be heard, however muted and unseen its furies behind even the kinder and gentler battle cry of those I shall soon number among our *third* worldlings: *Live and let live!* But tolerance is not respect, which is what our third worldlings want and cannot be given. A world culture of respect for contraries, as for truth and transgression, could not endure its own universalization. A world culture, if it could come to be, would not be; it would be an anti-culture, unprecedented in being so without mediating references to predicative sacred order in correlative social.

(3) *Anti-cultures.* By *anti-culture* I mean one that does not—because it cannot—mediate between sacred order and social; not least because there is nothing to mediate. For the virtuoso artists of anti-culture, as I define them here and now against the teaching authorities[2] of culture properly so-called, social orders are themselves mediate institutional expressions of fighting group interest; those interests, however shifting, engaged in a primordial life necessarily deadly at times: the permanent struggle for the power to support materially an endlessly deficient sense of well-being. Thus doth relative deprivation make bourgeois bravos of us all.

(4) *The common historical task of cultures, uncommon otherwise.* The historical task of all cultures is the creation of a world apart from other, opposing worlds. Cultural work is the subtler fighting matter and manner of disarming competing cultures, not least by partially incorporating them. If its disarming manner of invasion is successful, a culture may not need to employ the definitively political means of enforcement: force of arms. None the less, every culture may maintain, as its last resort of defence in the mediation of its predicative sacred order, the right of arms. It is the historical case that rigidly armoured world creations, in defence of themselves,

as in ancient Egypt, may not function generously enough in their partial incorporations of opposing worlds, to survive those worlds. Cultural barriers open only to close. They bend in order not to break. A broken order becomes so great a disorder that its guiding élites may be seen fighting for their death even as they act out their proleptic membership in its common fancy of a new world order. But retreats, made strategically enough, do not lead to ruin; only demoralizations of order lead to their ruin. Retreats in depth cannot be so deep that touch is lost with those stable intuitions of right and wrong by which the character in culture is graven as the sacred self of everyone from the moment of their conception in it.

As new world denials of sacred order, unprecedented in the history of culture, invade, more and more deeply, the institutions of teaching authority representing some reading praxis of sacred order, the interdicts at the head of all sacred orders since Sinai are under attacks even more relentless than their essentially different parallels in pagan world creations, the taboos. The most telling of these new world denials of all sacred orders is that deathwork of the sacred self, the abortionist movement. In the culture of commanding truths, whatever their other internecine contentions, every human is, from the moment of conception, created a sacred self, after the image of the Creator.

To be is to be chosen, once and never before or after. Sacred history no more repeats itself than does genetic history. In every act of procreation, there is not merely the male and female. Every man born of woman, even at the first moment of being and for nine months unborn, is endowed equally by his or her Creator, with the sacred self by which his or her identity is as it is in its god-relation. The most familiar of all self-references in the English language is less familiar in its god-relation and familiar least in the rebel questioning of that relation. Hamlet's question, as if to no One, answers itself more precisely in the double meaning of its German translation.

(5) *Zu zein oder nicht zu zein.* In German, the parent question of humanity—*Am I thy Master or art thou Mine?*—gives its own answer. *To be, zein, is to be His, zein.* I have made this the fifth note to illustrate the pivotal commanding truth in the Decalogue at Sinai. To honour thy father and mother is to recognize, and honour, the presiding presence in every moment of procreation. To

be is to be His. To be is to be chosen. 'Pro-choice' represents the thinnest transparency of the *world-woman* as a third culture anti-godterm. Women are no more rightly private in their identities as sacred selves than men, nor more than fetuses.

(6) *This word is your life (Deuteronomy 32: 47)*. Being female, no woman is entitled by right to disobey the commanding truth of world creation: *choose life* (Deuteronomy 30: 20). From the true command, *choose life*, there may be remissions. But any such excusing reason cannot, except at the cost of true world decreation, do other than subserve the interdict against the taking of a life so innocent as that of the sacred self, even as the biological body of that identity begins its cycle of life in the life-space that is its first home.[3] In that uncanny life-space, there can be no remission from the nurture of the life in that space, nor the transgression of a deathwork against the *body/sacred-self* in that space. The cost of the abortionist movement is the entire lifeworkword of the traditions, in their commanding truths, out of Jerusalem. The officer class of the abortionist movement must be made to understand that they are also the officers of an abolitionist movement; the object of that movement is the entire world, in all its contending varieties, out of Israel.

(7) *The remissive mode in moral demand systems*.[4] All cultures accent, more or less sharply, certain sights and sounds that may express the vast body of experience within which a certain indifference, calculated as Iago's or apparently uncalculated as Rousseau's, to any right way prevails. I call this life-space of humane indifference the *remissive mode*, where what is otherwise not to be done may be done, pardonably. Remissions subserve the interdicts above them; or, if they expand unpardonably, subvert the interdicts, and thus become transgressions masked as rationalities or enlightenments. Life is led mainly in a remissive muddle. Middling in the mercy granted it (Psalm 51), the human condition consists in shuffling and sidling between commanding truths in the interdictory mode and their transgressions in the repressive mode inseparable from revelation. In this complex stability, cultures have been moral demand systems in which prohibitions are the predicate of permissions. As remissive motifs, rock hymns, definitely not for singing and dancing by the aged, are one form that may illustrate remissive Christianity's retreat in order to lure back the supernation of the young from their noisy exodus. More often than not, cultural

warfare has its sound of music. *The voice of them that sing do I hear* (Exodus 32: 18).

Yet even the most sophisticated strategies of retreat and exodus shed their symmetries at the other and superordinate metamorphic sign of culture complicit in its fighting form: *world creation/rule*.[5] In the act of transferring its culture of creation, no teaching authority—no rabbinate, no magisterium, none of the school marms who brought me up at the Franklin Pierce or Joyce Kilmer grammar schools in the city of Chicago—can compromise that fundamental form, continuous world *creation/rule*, without compromising itself out of existence as a class of remembrancers conveying their legitimating doctrine of debt yet to be paid to the *sovereign/world Creator*. Those who suffer from myopia may have their perspectives lengthened, horribly as von Kleist imagined in his review article on the showing of Caspar David Friedrich's great painting of teaching authority of the Word all but overwhelmed by primacies of possibility represented by Friedrich as encroachments of land, sea, and air, images of world decreation. That world picture, titled *Monk by the Sea*, gave von Kleist his proleptic sense of the horror and pleasure, his eschatological expectation, that would overtake the world—his world and ours, still—when the Word yielded to some primordiality or other. To see Friedrich's picture was, to von Kleist, seeing it then and there, 10 October 1810, in Berlin, to see as if one's eyelids were sheered away. The horror did eventually give itself a place name: *Auschwitz*, the deathwork against the Jews. This is the world decreation to which the contemporary German painter Anselm Kiefer alludes in *Das Buch*, his world picture in response to both Friedrich and Auschwitz.

(8) *Living in truth*. Sacred orders of life are carried by words of creation inseparable from the doings of everyday life. God is truth. Living in their truth, observant Jews at morning prayer thank God for renewing their world, i.e. their truth. The *Our Father* in the Roman liturgy concludes with its announcement of the *world without end* presiding even over death. Any other kind of news of worlds ending is the bad news that a culture hears the moment it no longer lives in its truth. 'Pluralism' and 'multiculturalism' are embodied mendacities, doctrines of death that a culture may sign against itself, as if to signal its own fated sense of fragmentation so fine that it becomes disembodied: alive abstractly, fictively, and

therefore dead. 'Pluralism' and multiculturalism': these are polite names for hard cultural wars gone soft. Pluralists represent shrewd enemy élites of third culture more often than merely tolerant allies of and in second. All cultures, in their truths, are agonist, even as in the unintended outcomes of the *agon* they may be compromised as pluralist. But even soft wars are agonizing, however good-humoured, between those knowing enough in their true lives to fight for them.

(9) *The historical task of culture*. Intensely alive in their own endlessly received and repeated truths, unending there and only there, true world creations comprise the historical task of cultures. To transliterate otherwise invisible predicative sacred orders into their visible modalities of institutional expression in social orders, there is the spiritual sociology of culture in its embodied life sentences. Truth hovers in the sphere between sacred order and social, transparently obvious only when the ineluctable modalities of the invisible made visible are made so by those who enact truths they may well otherwise doubt.

(10) *The historical sociology of truth*. A truth will always appear as something else in social order: something in the range of enactable truths inseparable from their occasions of address by I to Thou. Truths are never abstract. They live in their moments and between those who embody those moments. As transliterations of otherwise unspeakable languages of sacred order into social, illustrated here by the *Our father, our king* formula in the democracy of Jewish prayer, cultures were and ever shall be what they represent: symbolic worlds. The bloodiest world wars are fought over symbols and their embodiments. Cultures are the *habitus* of human beings, universal only in their particularities symbolically inhabited; only in so being, an inhabited symbolic, does a culture become, in its *is-ness*, what it represents. *Is-ness* is the deep down thing that is what it represents. By culture, as a self-representational symbolic, I mean to suggest the contrast of a culture as symptomatic. A symptom represents what it is not. As symptoms, 'life-styles', alternatives to world-inhabiting symbolics of truth, may lead to even bloodier wars, which then will be fought, as they were in the 1940s, by fanatical sceptics impressed most by their disbelief in anything except their own self-inventions. That way totalitarianism lives again: the fateful symptom of true worlds suffering a temporary death sentence. To be embodied symptom is

to represent what one is not. The world fight for the turf of truth is always between embodied symbols, i.e. truths, and symptoms, i.e. lies, which represent what they are not. False worlds are false in their cultus. The living world of faith is as it seems. Only dying worlds, like Don Quixote's or Hamlet's or Kafka's, seem to be what they are not. That *seeming, seeming,* as Isabella says of Angelo, represents the systemic mendacity of desire, as it pretends to the very virtue against which it contends.

(11) *The number of world types.* To generalize the present welter of symbolic *is-ness* and symptomatic particularities of what is and yet is not into three world types may, or may not, reveal more than it conceals of our present worlds at war. So far as they are sightings of real warring truths and lies, back to back, my illustrations divide into three cultures that I number, for reasons typological as well as chronological: *first, second, third.* In their present synchronicities, our three worlds carry the weight of war by other than armed means. A purely political culture is a contradiction in terms. No man is so political that he lives a purely public life. Rather, every public man lives privately as well, within his own irreducibly personal vision of the highest—the highest being our shared, normative *habitus.* Like every other, my theory is blinkered by the truth of my *habitus,* more or less embodied and weighted within myself as the second world remembered. In my case, my world is a stubborn truth, refusing to yield its weight to the lightness of a systemically mendacious, and therefore incredulous, third. Fighting for clarity in my confused world, as I must if I am to write of it, I see third worlds recycling their fantasy versions of otherwise dead firsts against retreating seconds in a war of worlds without any foreseeable victory in sight for either.

(12) *Fertile void/primary imagination.* Third-world movements cannot be called, rightly, 'neo-pagan', precisely because this neologism tantalizes in its near-deadly accuracy. So far as my mind's eye can see into a world so remote, so dead, as pagan firsts, those worlds can be only remotely reconceivable as supremely imaginary, their colour green, even Kendal green, only when spun by that fat original fiction of all true white homeboys, Falstaff. There are big fat liars, counterfactuals masterly as Falstaff, framed Masterpiece Theatres of first-world rebellions against relatively— and correlatively new, even still—new second-world orders. Poussin's *Dance Round the Golden Calf* (c.1635, London,

National Gallery) and Schoenberg's *Moses und Aron* (1932) are two among many counterfactual masterpieces representing what they are not: the ever archaic first world, its power past, in revolt against the ever present second world, its authority presiding even over imagined primacies of possibility, the revolutionary third world. In historic reality, those green worlds were dark as death.

There is death, and there are deaths. The primordiality of death, as Heraclitus hails it in what we, here and now, can read of his symbolics, there and then, is only remotely like the primordiality, death the instinct of which life is a brief disturbance, conjured by Freud. Freud's primordial is without order. A believing fatalist is only remotely like an unbelieving fatalist. *Et in Arcadia ego* may have suited Poussin's mind's eye, but it did not suit Freud's. Rather, the plain English of Freud's unbelief would read: *in the midst of death there is life*. Like Samuel Taylor Coleridge's *irremissive* gentlings of interdictory truth in his strategic masterpiece of a literary wargame against the second-world literality, *Biographia Literaria*,[6] Freud's remissive therapy has led to precisely the defeat he dreaded and anticipated, the triumph of post-Freudian man. *Irremissive* is to *remissive* as *primary imagination* is to *commanding truth*, fusions triumphant over distinctions, the war of the animal over the human won, as Franz Marc prophesied in his world picture *Tierschicksal* (Basle, Kunst Museum). Paul Klee finished Marc's deathwork after Marc's death in 1916. In their different ways, Coleridge's masterpiece and Marc's remains are both exemplary counterfactuals: primary imagination where soul once was, fighting animals smart as they are empty, sensualists without spirit, sectaries without that sense of shame in sacred order without which the true sense of guilt in social order cannot be cultivated. Third-world arts and sciences, values and other decreations of truths, make pervasive nothings of both sacred orders and their socialized selves. Each and every body, from womb to grave, from moment of conception to memory of their beings, each spiritual in their own identity, personality, and incommunicability, can never be outside their god-relations. Only in our god-relations are we in the godly world, our own, and unalienated in its objective correlatives, truth itself subjective as it is objectively commanded. Hamlet's trouble is more accurately diagnosable now. He suffered from that severe repression-of-revelation syndrome suffered later by Freud. Both denied the fact that subjectivity is truth.

Deathworks imply workers. The genius of such work implies equalities between the images of god and their Maker proclaimed in the primacy of Coleridgean *imagination*: *the soul that is everywhere, and in each* (Coleridge 1979: ii. 13) as if this could supersede as counterfactual the artifactuals of Genesis 1: 26–7, Genesis 2: 7, 18–25, Galatians 2: 20, none of which can be taught mindfully often enough as, if nothing more, here and now, counterfactuals of creation. Surely this counterfactual meets the factitious standard of third-world works of decreation: that nothing is but what is not.

In the repressive mode, imagination remains undeceived by its own supreme fictions, however painfully impoverished the consequent reality. Poets of our third world are definitive. In their highest visions, they see nothing.[7] In this nothing, everything is possible, every fusion permitted. *Myriad-minded* Shakespeare, as Coleridge calls that genius, foresaw the transsexual possibility in that song of songs sung by Falstaff, antic womanizer, unmannerist of his manly self. *He/she* sings: *my womb, my womb, my womb, undoes me* (*2 Henry IV*, iv. iii. 24–5). A war song do I hear: against the eternally drawn distinction of Genesis 1: 27; against the eternally promised fusion of Genesis 2: 24, that fusion for family as the social form of forms.[8]

Against these distinctions and fusions, that discipline of decreation, sociology, post-French Revolutionary in origin, continues to deal its deathworks, the more prosaically the more to its original purpose, to the sacred self, at once atomized and collectivized—*le jé pulvérisé* as the Durkheimian in its unselfconscious self-parodies. After all, Durkheim's sociology was his suicide. Sociology is the afterlife of theology, sociologists the negative cadre of rabbinate, magisterium, ministry.

That there are brilliant parodies in the marked genius of the third-world nothing that is not and the nothing that is, is clear enough in the intention of Joyce's learned assault upon the Word that is second-world life. *In the buginning is the woid* (Joyce 1975: 378) is far too self-conceited an assault on the Creator of our second worlds to be 'neo-pagan'. The death of that one *Creator/god* is the death of all pagan gods. No first world constituted space without sacrality, *habitus* without its habitual gods, however few or many there may have been presiding in or contending over a sacred space. No space is sacred to the measure of third-world space. Taoist first-world fertile voids really did invite Zen painters'

marks, few as they were. Those marks refined the emptiness of raw
silk unmarked then marked. By contast, in paintings by one of our
third world's most *celebrated/pricey* painters, Cy Twombly, the
marks are not defining occupations. Rather, Twombly's marks site
the sterilities of their surroundings, sterilizations of vacuity prized
for their safe inanitions, by the smart empty revolutionary rich in
their calculated collecting panics. The fertile void of Zen Taoist
pictures invites the disciplined peace of entry. Twombly's pictures
guarantee the prestigious smartness of emptiness, inanitions to be
read reverently as if they were profundities.

(13) *World peace.* Like any achieved in the deeply personal
interior of a *habitus*, peace between our second and third worlds
would require perfectly congruent public and private abidings in
both one world and the other, without a trace of conflict or
confusion. Only such an impossibly logical and rational culture
could be the predicate of a peaceful world. The alternative to such a
fantasy, of a world at one with itself and with everyone in it, is
limited word war between our second worlds and third: *Kulturkampf* to keep away *Daseinskampf.* That distancing requires
distortions of truth so to ease the disorders between sacred order
and social as they interpenetrate in a way represented most clearly
in Matthew 18: 18.

(14) *On being made alone in the second world: the accused god.*
Within my second world of limited wars, there remain those
irreducible incommunicabilities and almost unreadable transliterations by which even those many still at home in that same—but
never self-same—world, our second, find themselves with their
equally lonely Maker. There is true identity: the specially burdensome sense of being alone in a world which was, is, and ever shall
be accompanied by a saving sense of another being who is there, the
coexistent Creatorself, in both private life and public. In Galatians
2: 20, that *I* is addressed as the *Not I. Sacred self, imago Dei, Not I:*
these seem to me objective godterms of subjective truths not two
the self-same of the common faith I call *culture.*

(15) *The second world Godof.* Call that godterm the God of
Abraham, the God of Isaac, the God of Jacob. The subjectivity of
commanding truth is inseparable from the objectivity of truth.
Every pious Tom, Dick, and Francis addresses the god that is
personal to him and cannot be abstracted in any way that destroys
personality. Even as fools see not the same tree, the wisest men

know they never see the same god; or, at the most terribly private of times, any god. Doubt is the ineliminable predicate of faith. There, in that agonistical relation, is the entire social psychology of the sociology of religion. It follows, as night follows day, that the limiting term of second cultures, each personal god, is there mainly, in the traditions out of Jerusalem at least since Job, to be accused of not being there: his revelations fictive and his laws inoperable.

(16) *On dogs obeyed in office.* The god making accusations has been from the first an accused god. Even a dog is obeyed in office, if office rather than truth-in-person is the godterm of authority. So a bureaucrat may pray: *Godof* bureaucrats, save us from *dogs*—that four-letter word for charismatics spelt backwards. From the authority forged in that power of images identified after, but never identical with, the image-creator—authorizing identity—no second-world creature can escape. There is no alternative to this uniqueness of personal existence; nor to the martyrdom it risks to resist the first and final worlds of resolution into primordials that are always tantamount to the death of the sacred self. Alas, that subjectivity is truth. Existence is itself authorized by our relation to the Other—call him Uncle Tom or Uncle Claudius, by whatever quasi-paternal name—of which God is the final term. Without that outwardness, inwardness or subjectivity, as Kierkegaard called the god-relation, becomes impossible.

(17) *On the outwardness of sociology.* Sociology is impossible without theology: the inwardness of truth even in its most awkward, if not god-awful, language. From the perspective of a sacred sociology, the present world fight is explicable largely as a flight from authorizing identities, into our third world as a vast defaulting second, itself self-accused, under the new consummately accusative rubric *repression. Knowing yet not knowing* is the shortest and unsurpassed Freudian definition of repression. What Freud knew, even as he knew not, is that the basic repression being exercised by Freud himself was and remains as the most cunning intelligence of third-world indirections, the repression of revelation: knowing and, at the same time, not knowing those directive truths presented in the culture of commands at every moment that may be grasped as their own by their agents. By contrast, according to third-world teachings, all crimes derive from the repressions second-world traditions of revelation superimpose upon a possibility largely sexual in its primacy.

(18) *Moses/Freud: the reading of second worlds by thirds incarnate as yet another infidel Jew.* Where Moses was, there let Freud be. Third-world doxologies of address to the primacy of possibility represent the coming culture as the oldest, most archaic, sheerest eroticism of possibility made new, specially in the amorality of its intimate relation to two other representations of what a culture is not: murder and false cultus. Freud's Moses was murdered twice: first by the Jews even before they had lived as Jews in truth and then again by Freud in his deathwork. Freud's *Moses* essays, in inanition of historic Jewish life in truths, were published in his death month and year, September 1939. These essays represent his final inversive efforts to distance the time of the primal crime with which cultures end, as in Freud's present. He assigned the primal crime to the remotest past, as if then, with that crime, cultures and their moralities began by élite reaction formation, however slow. But in historical reality, the primal crime occurred before Freud's eyes. Even as he retreated to England from the sight of the primal crime in Vienna and throughout Europe, the truth of that crime retreated, in his defensive mind's eye, to the most remote and fictive past.

(19) *A third world does not exist as such.*[9] More precisely, third worlds exist in oppositional mixtures of fact and fiction that may be called *faction*: so to name the fighting élites—Freudian, Marxist, or otherwise nameable—within our second worlds. Third-world fighters against the inhabitants of seconds invent themselves as they would be: liberationists of all *man/womankind* from everything and everyone they consider to be censors of desire. *Liberation* is the current entitling cant name for the primacy of possibility transliterated into propaganda for consuming *life-styles* that represent third cultures in their negational essences: as oppositional lies to second cultures of commanding truths. The culture of commanding truths is to the culture of life-styles as Sacred Scripture is to literature.

(20) *Third-world literature.* The literary genius of our third world at its most articulate prepolitical and supranatural may be illustrated by James Joyce's *Finnegans Wake.* In that fiction for all anti-second world factions, the primacy of possibility, the sometime surnamed *Finn,* wakes again to fight again against all other godterms that are represented as other than figments of themselves: desire in some emergence that is bound to test itself against all

godterms of limits—i.e. against the structure of culture itself. That structure has been always and everywhere constituted as sacred order, of which social order is its agency institutionalized. On the sites of sacred orders, third-world élites fight their wordwars. In this stipulation, third worlds are self-acknowledged as fictive creations. Like Moriarty and Holmes, the last of third worlds will go down with the last of seconds. But then both will be revived for a public that will demand the return of both together. The *show/ war* must go on. Fictions cannot live without their factions.

(21) *The seven last words.* As secular is inseparable from sacred, so third-world fighters for a world that can never be, except negationally, have been given their own seven last words. *Foght. On the site of the Angel's* (Joyce 1975: 90). This brilliantly comic displacement follows immediately his seven first, as he attempts to write a new testament of his own fictive creation as an oppositional world to the older habitable second. Artist that he is, Joyce is no more representative of third-world fiction than Nietzsche. The representative third-world fiction embodied is that faction which passes itself off as *Black*.

(22) *The colour of our third world.* Blackness embodied is the crucial cultural invention of white second-world élites in revolt against all sacred orders. There is no racial reality in the *third world* as *a euphemism . . . for . . . ideological Blackness* (Naipaul 1988: 40). This euphemism is now more colonizer than colonized. Our fantasy world is a rerun of an old movie, *The Sheik*, remade in Technicolor to represent the political demography of an erotically freer world once somewhere east of Suez and now somewhere south of the Sahara—where Africa dances. The question was once asked: *Why are Methodists against fornication?* Answer: *Because it might lead to dancing*, as around the Golden Calf. The pseudo-pagan *African-American* of racialist fiction, once *black*, *coloured*, and *Negro* and most recently and yet differently again *Black*, represents what it is: culture as symptom.

(23) *A synchronic of three cultures.* Until our third, every oppositional world has constituted a form of address to some sacred order from somewhere within one or another socialization of that order. At least from Sinai and its oppositional Golden Calf onward, second-world orders have opposed all varieties of firsts. What now remains of those firsts? None remain except as recyclings of third-world aesthetics in the present war against

seconds. Different as philosophical Athens and aboriginal Australia, pagan worlds had something essential in common: mythic primacies of possibility from which derived all agencies of authority, the godterms of which I shall call, for its illuminations of this historic present, the subject of sociology as an historical discipline: *pop*.[10] Whether Greek essences or aboriginal dreamtimes, an all-inclusive *pop* once characterized highest authority. From this primordial, all worlds and everything in them derived. Those *pop* first worlds have been recycled by third worlds in a variety of disarming assaults not only upon the exclusivist and intolerant aesthetics of authority by which our seconds have continuously reconstituted their embattled identities, but, more important, upon all authority. According to third-world doxa, not even a dog is to be obeyed in office. Third worlds translate no sacred order into social order. As negations of all sacred orders, in second or first worlds, our third constitutes a culture without historical precedent: an anti-culture.

(24) *The self-consuming anti-culture.* Unprecedented, these *pop* inventions of pagan worlds refer to readings of themselves alone, toward some supreme fiction, at which not even virtuoso readers can arrive in life so far as it is not led in literature. Third worlds are more dangerous in their comic inventions of themselves than any tragic text in first- or second-world literature. Being of the comedy that is existence, that comedy now becomes hypercritically conscious of itself. Third worlds propose new poetics without moralities and religions (Nietzsche 1974: 74; see also Kierkegaard 1962).

(25) *A transparency through which to read our new world fight.* In his most *vivid transparence*, 'Notes toward a Supreme Fiction', Wallace Stevens made poetic the untruth that the most enlivening belief of the present age is an *updated paganism* which confirms in fact the common third-world fiction that *loss of faith is growth*.[11] So supreme a fiction requires, Stevens proclaims, a hopeful new trinity: Hope *Must Be Abstract. It Must Change. It Must Give Pleasure.* Else, no third world can supersede life in truth with a *theatre of trope*. As a theatrical trope, third-world heralds, from Nietzsche to Stevens and many more following after, have claimed the death of the one *Godof* second worlds *as the death of all.* This death of all gods is continuously reinvented by imaginations tired of the commanding particulars of second-world truth. Some militant fiction or other becomes the one thing possible, some *absolute*

angel of consuming desire—the merely *possible, possible, possible*[12]—as stand-in for the sheerly *invisible/actual* of second-world sacred orders that must be taken on faith and at its word; or not be taken in any but naïve or sophisticated senses. Absolute angels of consuming desire *must be possible* in order to prosecute the war between *mind and sky*, of which Stevens was such a constructive illustrator.

(26) *The deconstructionist strategy*. Jacques Derrida illustrates the latest literary sophistication in the strategy of exodus from second-world truths. That strategy implies something sinister in the policing character of second-world truths. *Everything comes down to one of those reading exercises with magnifying glass which calmly claim to lay down the law, in police fashion indeed* (Derrida 1987: 326). Derrida's reading of second-world readers is correct. Second-world professionals of the reading discipline are, as they have been since Sinai at least, the real police. But such a police must fail whenever they abandon their relentlessly calm manner of laying down the law. The real police are reading élites who must teach the truth of their readings against all competing readings in the agonistic institutions that now, if not always, are the training grounds of therapeutic truths—schools, theatres, television studios, hospitals, and political parties.

(27) *The old reading élites and the new*. The real police in second worlds were once called *Rabbi* or *Father* or by whatever title of *teaching/policing* office these ministers of sacred order were known. Whatever the magisterium was called, a thought police-man's lot has never been a particularly happy one. In their original second worlds, *Rabbi* and *Father* were titles of *teaching authority*, derived from truth once revealed and ever to be repeated, not least in the unprecedented particularities of the private lives led by the police themselves. Second-world authority is never abstract, always embodied: exemplary rather than juridical. Living in truth is not often a visibly privileged claim. Nor are those lives part of the fashion worlds of successful and beautiful people. There is a force of respectful admiration, rather than ignorant opposition in Stevens (1976: 389) asking *What rabbi, grown furious with human wish does not look for what was, where it used to be?* Second-world teaching élites carry teaching authority that is rarely at one with the power or glamour of the establishments and counter-establishments in the social order. Third-world counter-establishments have their

own set of privileges. Their affirmative action therapies, for example, are to morally demanding theonomies as *hospital/theatres* are to *synagogue/churches*. Third-world teaching authority is historically unique, even if it is classically Greco-Roman in inspiration.[13] It casts roles where identities were,[14] so to invent a third-world order relentlessly negational in its recognitions of any predicative sacrality.

(28) *Second-world priorities of prohibition over permission, illustrated from Matthew.* No world has ever existed before our third except as societal readings of sacred orders. The readings were made, most often aloud, from somewhere within sacred order. Of second-world readers, the Jew Jesus spoke most precisely of the priority of prohibitions over permissions. Prohibitions always precede permissions, as sacred orders precede social. Transliterated into present second-world terms, Matthew 18: 18 reads as follows: *Whatever you prohibit in social order will be prohibited in sacred order. And whatever you permit in social order will be permitted in sacred order.* The priority of sacred order over social, and the inseparability of one from the other, has never before been subjected to such fierce fighting words as in the last century or so. What second cultures bring near, in their reasonably good faiths of world creation, third cultures keep far apart, in the bad faith of rights and privacy, upheld against the commanding truth of the sacred self not yet born into the public world.

(29) *Kulturkampf.* The Germans had a compound word for the fighting. *Kulturkampf* first appeared in common German use in the early 1870s during the struggle of the National Liberal political party to disarm by law the *moral/educational* authority and political pulpitry of a renewedly triumphalist Roman Catholic hierarchy. Élites of the *Kulturstaat*, both Catholic and Protestant, then learned a lesson deadly to souls even as it was protective to bodies: never to oppose a *Machstaat* that signed *concordats* with them. A prudent *adiaphora*, operating in a range from clerical indifference to conformity, meant that there was no second-world teaching authority to protect the Jews from the war of extermination, the final solution of primal force, launched against them in 1939 when *Kulturkampf* became *Daseinskampf*, a life and death struggle.

(30) *The culture of prudence.* Prudence is a natural virtue. No more than the Jews are a natural nation is the Church a natural

institution. As the supersessive Israel, the Church maintained its silence in the face of that most peculiar institution of our emergent third world: the death camps. The most imprudent draft of an imprudent encyclical, prepared on orders of Pius XI, *Humani Generis Unitas*, directing Catholics to stand fast against persecution of Jews, was never published by his successor, Pius XII, who ascended the throne of Saint Peter in 1939.

(31) *Again, war and yet more war against the Jews.* The old war against Israel has not ended. Its embodiment in the Jewish *Machstaat* remains unrecognized by Rome. Even so, the old war unended, a new war against the Jews has been launched, one even more difficult for the Jews, specially in the diaspora, to recognize. Rome, after all, is Jerusalem's oldest internecine foe. The new foe wears a camouflage of colour far nearer the truth of a war in which Rome itself appears an outpost of a Jerusalem besieged by yet another third-world power recycling variations of first.

(32) *The colour of primal force.* As a voice of the third-world white, aspiring to a racial condition of the primordial long embedded in the white imagination, Lou Reed's third world lyric *I Wanna Be Black* expresses clearly the comic yet implacable character of our third world's war against the Jews.

(33) *The comedy of release from sacred order.* Comedy is to tragedy as faith to fleeing life. Cultural repression is to cultures of revelation as internal flight is to religious memory. As one of the flightiest of third-world artists, the post-Jewish Reed sings yet another declaration of war, by yet another warring, though fictive, nation. Whether they like it or not—and many do not—the Jews are what they are represented to be in the libretto below: the founding national embodiment of our second-world sacred order. This is what it means to be chosen. It is not as if the Jews could choose not to be what they are chosen to be. Reed's libretto, ironical as it is, recognizes the Jews and remythologizes the blacks into a primal power figure: the Black.

(34) *Typologically perfect words of some scarcely musical noise of war music.*

> I wanna be Black
> I wanna have some natural rhythm
> Shoot twenty feet of jism too
> And fuck up the Jews

I wanna be Black
I wanna be a panther
Have a girlfriend named Samantha
And a stable full of foxy whores
I wanna be Black

I don't wanna be no fucked-up, middle class
College student any more
I just wanna have a stable
Of foxy whores
Yeah, Yeah, I wanna be Black

I wanna be Black
I wanna be like Martin Luther King
And get shot in the Spring
And lead a whole generation too
And fuck up the Jews

Yeah, Yeah, I wanna be Black
Yeah, Yeah, I wanna be Black
(Reed 1977)

(35) *A truth: Reed's black is a white pop fiction.* Twenty feet of shot semen is a considerable distance, however mythic the measure of that rhythm. Long before it turned racialist Black, *panther* was the ancient Greek animal of sexual predation, its body odour luring victims near enough for the pounce. Kafka recycled the image of the panther, power streaming from its jaws, as the successor to the Jewish hunger artist, who is too fastidious to accept any of the commanding truths, i.e. his nourishments; he dies of inanition. *Anorexia*, we psychiatrists now say. *Black* becomes the colour of primal sexual force, so coloured primarily by white *pop* artists.[15] Post-Christian and post-Jewish whites need their fix of primal force fiercely as they need their contempt for the real police, of whom the police in uniform are street surrogates. Hatred, and laughter at the very possibility of sacred fear, without which no society can survive, is the latest and yet oldest fashion of totemic mind-sets. This totemic mind-set is not for real, everyday blacks. It is a racialist aesthetic, brutal in its primitivism, that appeals at once to demoralized poor blacks and to affluent young whites of a culture

in which the real police, the mediating élites, mediating between sacred order and social, have traded truths for therapies.

(36) *The world/woman in love and hatred.* Reed's four-letter word for the therapeutic answer to the Jewish Question may be read illuminatively in the context of Don Giovanni's war hymn *Viva la libertà*. But Mozart's Don does sound two centuries and light-years of musical grace away from Reed's Black. Reed's figure sounds more like a reprise of Norman Mailer's 'White Negro' of the late 1950s (Mailer 1957).[16] Yet Mozart's aristocratic Don of primal force and Reed's jism-shooting Black are synchronic soul brothers. To that fictive character, the truth of the world is a woman. Leporello begins his scorecard aria as a foretelling of the third-world *overclass/underclass* life-style: the *truth/world* as a woman to be had and as swiftly abandoned.

(37) *By the numbers.* In whatever size, shape, age, and number, the world of sacred order is there as an object of fun profanations.[17] At the time of Leporello's famous reading, the latest score made by the primal force figure amounts to 2,065, each a profanation of love into sheer sex.

(38) *Black underclass as parody magisterium.* It is as a corporate embodiment of sheer sex and violence, with the ecstasy of drugs added, that the black underclass has become the most influential carrier class in contemporary American—and, therefore, world—culture.

(39) *The Glitz Madonna of our third world.* Freudo-Marxism has been joined without wedlock to motifs of release, comic as they are racist, from all interdictory modalities of life. The current third-world Madonna, born innocently enough before her rebirth in fictive Blackness[18] as Madonna Louise Veronica Ciccone, is reborn in every video release immaculately reconceived for *pop* culture, as a negation of our second-world Madonna.

(40) *From the top down.* Low culture takes its cues from our trashed high culture. Remember Rieff's second law of social and moral change: the rot starts at the top, always. The pathologies of the black underclass ape the privileges of the white overclass. Cultural revolutions make their way from the top down, not from the bottom up. Within each warring nation, there are teaching élites at war over the bonding of the embodied worlds that constitute the nations. It is that internecine war, fought from within to dissolve the second world and its bondings, in identities, personalities, and

incommunicabilities, that is the special subject of sociology of religion in and for our time, and, probably, for a long, hard time to come.

Notes

1. These notes are taken from the first volume of the trilogy to which I refer in the title. The subtitle of that volume is: *My Life Among the Deathworks*. Michael Scott Alexander, my senior research assistant at the University of Pennsylvania, has put into print and sent directly on to Professor Beckford at the University of Warwick, his own readings of my unreadable scribbles traversing the edited copy arrived yesterday, here in Bellagio, from London. [*Philip Rieff. Villa Serbelloni, Bellagio (Lago d'Como) Italy. 28th May, 1992.*] Of course, now that he has ascended to his Fellowship at Yale and I have descended again to Philadelphia, I assume responsibility for Mr. Alexander's responsibilities. Without his successors, Rachel Greene, L. Dana Jackson, and Michael Unglo, this paper would not have been edited in one fell swoop.

2. These are the rabbis, the magisterium, the ministers who were never scourges of the there and then, being the authority of the past represented by those guiding élites, more often than not contending against each other, all seeking to direct power in the service of commanding truths.

3. In his great essay 'The "Uncanny"' (Freud 1955: 245), Freud discusses the meaning of home: 'It often happens that neurotic men declare that they feel there is something uncanny about the female genital organs. This *unheimlich* place, however, is the entrance to the former *Heim* [home] of all human beings, to the place where each one of us lived once upon a time and in the beginning. . . . [U]nheimlich is what was once *heimisch*, familiar; the prefix 'un' [*un-*] is the token of repression.'

4. On culture as a moral demand system, see Rieff 1987: 237.

5. Cf. Nietzsche 1974: 4: 'A church is above all a structure for ruling.' The metamorphic mark/stands as the sign of a change in the constitution of culture.

6. 'The poet, described in *ideal* perfection, brings the whole soul of man into activity, with the subordination of its faculties to each other, according to their relative worth and dignity. He diffuses a tone and spirit of unity, that blends, and (as it were) *fuses*, each into each, by that synthetic and magical power, to which we have exclusively

appropriated the name of imagination. This power, first put in action
by the will and understanding, and retained under their irremissive,
though gentle and unnoticed, control (*laxis effertur habenis*) reveals
itself in the balance or reconciliation of opposite or discordant
qualities: of sameness, with difference; of the general, with the
concrete; the idea, with the image; the individual, with the representative; the sense of novelty and freshness, with old and familiar objects;
an order; judgement ever awake and steady self-possession, with
enthusiasm and feeling profound or vehement; and while it blends and
harmonizes the natural and the artificial, still subordinates art to
nature; the manner to the matter; and our admiration of the poet to
our sympathy with the poetry' (Coleridge 1979: ii. 12).

7. See Philip Larkin's 'High Windows':

> When I see a couple of kids
> And guess he's fucking her and she's
> Taking pills or wearing a diaphragm,
> I know this is paradise
>
> . . . .
>
> And immediately
>
> Rather than words comes the thought of high windows:
> The sun-comprehending glass,
> And beyond it, the deep blue air, that shows
> Nothing, and is nowhere, and is endless.
>
> (Larkin 1988: 165).

8. That Falstaff is an unfamilied comic figure of deformation, a figure of
profanation and joyful release from the interdictory commanding
truths of the foundationally Jewish wordworld, is his instinctual
nature: as we may read it in his boast of being a coward by nature, in
the helter-skelter of his wit, and in his satirical conceit of himself as the
world, sweet, kind, true, valiant, being itself godless as it is old in its
primordiality. To banish this 'plump Jack' is to 'banish all the world'.
But the adoptive son of this anti-godterm, remembrancer of authority
in the highest, even in his deliberate acts of folly, Crown Prince Hal,
will not be fooled. He knows the demonic is there in the comic,
transgressive as it is irremissive. Falstaff, smartly self-emptied of the
Not I, recognizes the grace in Hal's deadly accurate judgement of him:
'reverend vice . . . grey iniquity . . . father ruffian . . . cunning but in
craft . . . crafty but in villainy . . . villainous but in all things . . .
worthy but in nothing' (*1 Henry IV*, II. iv. 418–56). The inversions are
revealing and relentless. Old Falstaff becomes 'ungracious boy', the
young Prince his true judgemental father.

   Irremissive is to *transgressive* as *comic* is to *demonic*. Like the
knocking at the gate in *Macbeth*, the knocking of Falstaff's Pistol, at

the gate of Master Shallow's 'house/garden', speaks the demonic hidden in Falstaff's comic. Commanded by his master, Falstaff, to deliver, like a man who belongs to nothing other than 'this [profane and only] world', Pistol pronounces the death of highest authority in its office. Pistol delivers the shot at the sacred order of authority in and over the world and, then immediately, celebrates the continual artifactual of the counterfactual: 'I speak of Africa and golden joys.' Then and there the demonic supersedes the comic. Falstaff darkens triumphantly. He says that highest authority is 'sick for me. Let us take any man's horses.' Now and here, crime becomes sovereign: 'The laws of England are at my commandment . . . and woe to my Lord Chief Justice!' (*2 Henry IV*, v. iii. 72–135). Symbolic truth is not less true for being symbolic. Kurtz, and the darkness of his Africa, shows nothing and everything, untrue as it is true, in it. The comic yet systemic mendacity of Falstaff's negational description of his sacred self as 'a Jew' . . . an 'Ebrew Jew' may be irremissively comic. But in this near here and now, the demonic shows nothing comic—as Charles Chaplin learned to his sorrow when he tried to play Hitler for laughs. The decreation that is art, reinventing sacred order as if it were nothing, becomes a deathwork. Coleridge's misprision, in *Biographia Literaria* (1979: ii. 12), of the deadly irremissive in life, as if it were a gentling manner of control—in Freud's word, *sublimation*, in Coleridge's Latin parenthesis italicized by him (*laxis effertur habenis*)—conceals the demonic in every irremissive, however comic be its fiction of release from the commanding truths of sacred order. From the vertical in authority, there is no escape, either in apotheosis or apostasy. Obedience, however deferred, will be exacted.

 9. See Shiva Naipaul, 'The Illusion of the Third World', in Naipaul 1988: 37. .

10. As an acronym for *primacy of possibility*.

11. Richardson 1988: 290. On fiction in the meaning of Wallace Stevens, see his letter to Henry Church dated 8 Dec. 1942, in Ehrenpreis 1972: 119. The nature of poetry, and all art, has changed, because we have 'reached a point at which we could no longer really believe in anything unless we recognized that it was a fiction. . . . [W]e are doing this all the time. There are things with respect to which we willingly suspend disbelief; if there is instinctive in us a will to believe, or if there is a will to believe, whether or not it is instinctive, it seems to me that we can suspend disbelief with reference to a fiction as easily as we can suspend it with reference to anything else. There are fictions that are extensions of reality. There are plenty of people who believe in Heaven as definitely as your New England and my Dutch ancestors believed in it. But Heaven is an extension of reality.' Stevens here asserts, as if dogma of third worlds, aesthetics in authority. For all art and science,

notwithstanding their effects and affects, refer entirely to themselves as realities. The third-world godterm for the reality of sacred order becomes *supreme fiction*.

12. Stevens, 'Notes toward a Supreme Fiction', in Stevens 1976: 380–408. I read Stevens as the most admirable of third-world poets. Stevens is the most lyrically precise in his neo-Arnoldian compassion for all those who live in our third world. All those have found that, having abandoned their belief in God, poetry—art generally—can take its place as the style of redemption. All wars are wars about what are now called *life-styles*.

13. On first-world Greco-Roman inspiration for third-world role playing, see Nietzsche 1974: 302–4.

14. Ibid. What is 'dying out', writes Nietzsche, is 'fundamental faith'.

15. And, indeed, by black rap groups such as Public Enemy and N.W.A., to name but a few from the vast field of *transgression/entertainment*. Cf. the recently celebrated 'Fuck tha Police' by N.W.A. 1988; further see *Village Voice* 1989: 33. The data rise to meet the truth of the theory.

16. The anti-Jewish Jew Mailer, from a nation that has almost lost its sense of being at war, attributes that sense of nationality to blacks. They know, as whites know no longer, down to the 'cells of [their] existence' that life is war, 'nothing but war'. Blacks can 'rarely afford the sophisticated inhibitions of civilization' and 'kept for [their] survival the art of the primitive'. Black life is in the 'enormous present'. Black music is 'orgasm'. White and black in America are destined to marry. The black brings the only 'cultural dowry' available in the twentieth century: a 'morality of the bottom', with its 'emphasis upon "Ass" as the soul and "shit" as the circumstance'. The dowry has as its capital the orgasm, the impulse of Reed's 'jism'. However differently titled by whites—It, *id*, *prana*, orgone, blood, feeling good, life-force—the 'perpetual climax of the present' is some wordiness for the primacy of possibility. Mailer wondered if the 'last war of them all will be between the blacks and the whites'. With blacks, Mailer coupled women, the beautiful, the pillagers, and the rebels. With whites, he coupled men, the ugly, the managers, and the regulators.

Mailer fuses 'cool' with sensual over-excitement. Though, in his essay, the fusion is out of control—rather, it controls his essay—that fusion may be, in its manner at once of distance and sexual excitement, the key to understanding the fictive power of *pop* assigned the black. The same key unlocks other mythic primacies of erotic possibility. In *Don Giovanni* the fusion of impersonality and sexual excitement is assigned to the Don's treatment of women as the world to be had and then abandoned. The Don is the classiest model of a model underclass man.

17. *Don Giovanni*, Act I, scene v, Recitative and Aria 4: 'Madama . . . veramente . . . in questo mondo . . . Madamina, il catalago e questo.' Cf. Nietzsche 1966: 2: 'Suppose truth is a woman—what then?' Cf. also Nietzsche 1974, preface to 2nd edn., p. 38: ' "Is it true that God is present everywhere?" a little girl asked her mother; "I think that's indecent"—a hint for philosophers! One should have more respect for the bashfulness with which nature has hidden behind riddles and iridescent uncertainties. Perhaps truth is a woman who has reasons for not letting us see her reasons? Perhaps her name is—to speak Greek— *Baubo*?' The Virgin Mother is never shown naked. Third-world women, even as they oppose pornography, assault second-world standards of modesty in dress—so the topless sunbather beside the European swimming pool and the braless jogger of contemporary America. Cf. Rieff 1984: 183 on dress and undress.

18. *Rolling Stone 1989*: 'Do you ever feel black? Oh yes, all the time. . . . if being black is synonymous with having soul, then, yes, I feel that I am.' This Madonna of third world *pop* is to the Madonna of second-world sacred order as the largely American polemicists of *pop* have made black to white.

References

Coleridge, Samuel Taylor (1979), *Biographia Literaria*, vols. 1 and 2, ed. J. Shawcross (London).

Derrida, Jacques (1987), *The Truth in Painting* (Chicago).

Ehrenpreis, Irvin (1972) (ed.), *Wallace Stevens* (Harmondsworth).

Freud, Sigmund (1955), *The Complete Psychological Works of Sigmund Freud*, vol. 17, ed. James Strachey (London).

Joyce, James (1975), *Finnegans Wake* (New York).

Kafka, Franz (1971), 'A Hunger Artist', in *The Complete Stories*, ed. Nahum Glazer (New York), 268–77.

Kierkegaard, Søren (1962), *The Present Age*, trans. Alexander Dru (New York).

Larkin, Philip (1988), *Collected Poems*, ed. Anthony Thwaite (Boston).

Mailer, Norman (1957), 'The White Negro', *Dissent*, 4/3: 276–93.

Naipaul, Shiva (1988), *An Unfinished Journey* (New York).

Nietzsche, Friedrich (1966), *Beyond Good and Evil*, trans. Walter Kaufmann (New York).

—— (1974), *The Gay Science*, trans. Walter Kaufmann (New York).

N.W.A. (1988), 'Fuck tha Police' (Priority Records).

Reed, Lou (1977), 'I Wanna be Black', Metal Machine Music, from the album *Street Hassle* (Arista Records).

Richardson, Joan (1988), *Wallace Stevens—The Later Years 1923–1955* (New York).

Rieff, Philip (1984), *Fellow Teachers: Of Culture and its Second Death* (Chicago).

—— (1987), *The Triumph of the Therapeutic* (Chicago).

—— (1990), 'Aesthetics of Authority: Images in Sacred Order' (unpublished draft for the trilogy titled, 'Sacred Order/Social Order').

Rolling Stone (1989), interview with Madonna, 23 Mar. p. 58.

Stevens, Wallace (1976), *The Collected Poems* (New York).

Village Voice (1989), 34/41.

15

Christ and the Media: Secularization, Rationalism, and Sectarianism in the History of British Broadcasting, 1922–1976

ASA BRIGGS

The influence of the mass media on twentieth-century society and culture has often been described as 'continuous, insistent and pervasive', to quote the Revd John Stott who wrote a preface to a series of London lectures given by Malcolm Muggeridge in All Souls Church, Langham Place, in 1976 under the title *Christ and the Media*. Stott was repeating what Muggeridge in the first sentence of his first lecture had already called a 'truism'. 'The media in general and TV, in particular, and BBC Television especially, are incomparably the greatest single influence in our society today, exerted at all social, economic and cultural levels' (Muggeridge 1977: 1).

Muggeridge's subsequent thesis was comprehensive and highly polemical. 'This influence,' he immediately added, 'is largely exercised irresponsibly, arbitrarily and without reference to any moral or intellectual, still less spiritual, guidelines whatsoever' (ibid. 23). 'Standards' had slipped. No one was strong enough to defend them. In his polemic, Muggeridge had little to say about religious broadcasting as such. He focused on the way in which, as he saw it, the media—and television in particular—had created and belonged to 'a world of fantasy'. 'We, the legatees of Christendom, are . . . succumbing to fantasy, of which the media are an outward and visible manifestation . . . The effect of the media at all levels is to draw people away from reality, which means away from Christ' (ibid. 60).

One of Muggeridge's questioners after his second lecture was the Revd John Lang, then Head of Religious Broadcasting at the BBC, who directly challenged the very little that Muggeridge had had to say about religious broadcasting. Muggeridge's response was inadequate. His reputation as a 'personality' had been built up entirely through the media, and he had been and was to be directly concerned with several specifically religious programmes,[1] but he chose to add nothing to the little that he had already said. In reply to a further questioner who asked him 'Could you say a word as to why we do not have on television or radio minority groups like Jehovah's Witnesses, Mormons, Seventh-Day Adventists and other people of that nature?'—not a new question—he replied, 'I'm afraid you really have to direct that question to Mr Lang or Sir Charles [Curran, the first Roman Catholic Director-General of the BBC]. I have no hand in such matters at all' (ibid. 93). In the course of his lectures Muggeridge had refused to distinguish between sects, saying: 'Roman Catholics or Anglicans or Jehovah's Witnesses . . . there is but one category: one Common Fellowship in Christ. This, it seems to me, is a true image of Christian brotherhood' (ibid. 72).

Whether or not it was Muggeridge's business to be less general and more discriminating in these much publicized lectures—John Stott treated him as 'a true prophet of the twentieth century' (ibid. 121)—no historian or sociologist of broadcasting—or of religion—could rest content with such statements. 'Methodological essentialism; spurious holism; the tendency to confuse typological formulations with historical reality' have all been rightly condemned in relation to the sociology of religion (Wilson 1967: 2), as have comprehensive theories of impact in relation to the sociology of the media (Klapper 1949; Adler 1981). Relatively little attention has been paid by either historians or sociologists, however, to the specific experience of British religious broadcasting except in my four-volume history of broadcasting (Briggs 1961, 1965, 1970, 1979) and in the Revd Kenneth Wolfe's (1984) invaluable monograph on the Churches and the BBC, covering the years from 1922 to 1956. Fortunately Wolfe is now planning a second volume on the more recent and perhaps more critical period since 1956.

It was in 1956 that three talks on broadcast religion given to the St Paul's Lecture Society were published, the first of them by R. J. E. Silver, then Head of the BBC Audience Research Department, whose approach broke new ground. In his talk 'The Audiences for Religious Broadcasts', Silver drew some of his conclusions from a series of interviews carried out in 1954 with some 2,000 persons on their attitude to religious broadcasting, which showed that it was not true that non-church-goers did not listen to religious broadcasts. Nearly a quarter of them listened to religious broadcasts frequently, and a further quarter listened occasionally. That, Silver suggested, meant that 'religious broadcasting is a means whereby the influence of Christian teaching and Christian worship is brought to bear in some degree upon half the people who are outside the Churches' (Silver *et al.*, n.d.: 7).[2]

As far as the specific history of religious broadcasting is concerned, no two countries have ever evolved quite the same pattern in sound or on the television screen, and this is a major point of historical and sociological interest in itself. The differences were already there before the advent of television. The basic technology of broadcasting has been the same everywhere. So too have been several of the cultural and social tendencies common to 'advanced societies', and influencing, particularly through market economics, the ways in which people think and behave. Indeed, there is a substantial literature, never far from controversy, both on 'secularization' and 'consumerism'; and Wilson (1966: 41) has pointed out that, 'compared to the amount of entertainment, music, news, drama, secular education and all the other types of item carried by television, radio, Press and cinema, religious information has become a very tiny part indeed'.

None the less, whatever these common tendencies may have been and however 'marginal' the use of mass communication by religious sects may be said to have been,[3] there are, in fact—and have been—sharp contrasts between different societies and cultures, if now less sharp than they once were, in the amount, the context, and the style of broadcasting output. Indeed, there has been just as great a contrast between religious broadcasting in Britain and the USA as there has been in political broadcasting. The criticisms too have been different. In Britain they have focused not only on the exclusion of 'certain kinds of religion' but on the limitations of the particular kind of religion being presented.[4]

It is interesting to note that in 1962, in the report of the Pilkington Committee on Broadcasting (1962, ch. 9), religious broadcasting and party political broadcasting in England were treated together in the same chapter under the revealing heading 'Some particular kinds of programme'.[5] In fact, religious broadcasting was never treated like political broadcasting except that mainstream Churches, like major political parties, were able to influence who did not broadcast. Competition between religious groups within the religious spectrum invited to broadcast was firmly ruled out.

In 1957, an experienced broadcaster, the Roman Catholic priest Illtyd Evans, discussing the differences between religious broadcasting in sound and on television, drew his parallel not from politics but from music. In pre-war years, before the introduction of television, Evans claimed,

The religion that was approved had, in musical terms, the cadences of the voice and ideals of perhaps the more popular broadcaster—Sir Walford Davies. Listening to his setting of 'God be in my head and in my understanding' you have an accurate record of high-minded, doctrinal, neutral and ethically optimistic inspiration: the very pattern for the civic service and the Empire messages on Christmas afternoon (Evans 1957).

Across the Atlantic, by contrast, a very different Roman Catholic broadcaster, Bishop Fulton J. Sheen, was scheduled on the television screens in the early years of television in 1952 in a weekly series *Life is Worth Living* in such a way as to put him in direct competition with Milton Berle and his Texaco series, a 'showbiz' placing which led Berle to quip 'We both work for the same boss, Sky Chief.'[6] Having quoted this quip, Eric Barnouw (1975: 145), historian of American broadcasting, had virtually nothing to say of religious broadcasting in his *Tube of Plenty*, published in 1975. His only reference, for example, to the evangelist Billy Graham, whose appeal spans the Atlantic, is to one appearance by Graham in Edward R. Murrow's *Person to Person* series, which also featured among many other 'personalities' Liberace and the Duchess of Windsor (Barnouw 1975: 208). More recent detailed studies have filled in the gaps and brought the story, a still changing story, up to date. Some of the studies are the most sophisticated sociological studies of religious broadcasting that we have for any country—far more sophisticated than the BBC inquiry of the 1950s, when sound was still the dominant medium—although there is little of a comparative dimension in them (Hadden and Swann 1981; Gerbner *et al.* 1984; Horsfield 1984; Fore 1987).

In the later years of television, American-type broadcast evangelism of the 1970s and 1980s, with its gallery of controversial and financially involved presenters, has scarcely been 'marginal'. Nor has it depended solely or even mainly on 'the nexus of pulpit and pew'. It has been a major topic in the Press. It has also been of sufficient significance socially and culturally for it to have been deliberately kept off British television screens, just as party political programmes based on paid advertising have never been allowed a place in the programming of British commercial television companies. Satellite broadcasting, however, now promises to change the pattern under the influence of another Sky Chief, and the specific subject of its possible global use for distinctively American-type religious broadcasting has already been raised in Parliament, notably in the House of Lords in May 1990, when one speaker not surprisingly stressed not the obnoxious character of what would be broadcast but the 'complexity' of the matter.[7]

This is the time, therefore, to look back and try to explain the striking differences between British and American religious broadcasting. To what extent have they been simply a matter of programme policy and presentation? To what extent have they reflected more general broadcasting policy, dismissed in its later phases by Malcolm Muggeridge as 'irresponsible, arbitrary and without reference to any moral or intellectual, still less spiritual, guidelines'. To what extent have they reflected social and cultural differences that were there before the age of broadcasting? After all, the United States lacked the religious and political establishments that Britain in varying degrees took for granted. To what extent have they reflected more recent changes in the approach to the claims of religion within an increasingly secularized society? One speaker in the brief House of Lords debate of May 1990, Earl Ferrers, talked of a 'long tradition' in British broadcasting 'which applies the concept of religious broadcasting in a way which reflects the range of religious views which exist in this country while giving proper weight to the tradition of Christian belief'. Ferrers admitted that it was not easy 'to put it into a specific formula'.[8]

A debate in the General Synod of the Church of England in 1973 had said little of such a 'tradition', however, and had concentrated less on such basic questions than on the differences in the impact of 'sound' and of 'vision' on religion, for long a favourite topic inside the BBC and one which had inhibited the development of religious television (Briggs 1979: 781 ff.). It had touched also on the relationship between the BBC and the Independent Broadcasting Authority, with some critics blaming competition for a perceived decline in the standards of religious broadcasting. Yet, there was one brief reference in the discussion paper prepared for the Synod to a very different and very important question relating to social and cultural change. Should Christianity retain 'a social position in the field of religious broadcasting at a time when Britain is becoming a plural society embracing people of many different faiths'? And in this context the word 'tradition' was applied not to a tradition of religious broadcasting but to the Christian religion itself:

Christians are likely to answer 'Yes' to this question for one or more of three reasons. First, because they believe that the Christian faith, founded in Jesus Christ, is the unique truth about God, man and social relationships. ... Secondly, because the majority of British people still claim to be Christians, however tenuous their links with the Churches may be. And thirdly, because Britain's culture and the ethics of public life are derived from Christian tradition, which can neither be ignored nor forgotten.

An addendum reads somewhat lamely: 'At the same time, the belief in Christianity's spiritual claim should not prevent us from considering the needs of other faiths in our society' (Church of England 1973). That was not to be the last word.

The Report of the Annan Committee, published in the same year as Muggeridge delivered his London lectures, was more forthright. Faced with evidence about religion from all quarters, it concluded that it was 'easier to draw plans for a new Tower of Babel than for a new Jerusalem' (Annan Committee: 318). Not surprisingly, perhaps, it concluded that a new, fourth channel, supplemented by local broadcasting, would be a 'particularly suitable place for programmes designed for the smaller religious groups' (ibid. 319).

Recent trends in religious broadcasting are difficult to evaluate. Nor is all the evidence about policy-making yet available. This brief, highly selective and basically non-comparative study focuses on Britain, not on the United States. It begins with the formation of the British Broadcasting Company in 1922, and ends with the Report of the Annan Committee on Broadcasting in 1977.

Near the end of this long period, an official BBC statement on religious broadcasting emphasized the distinctiveness of the British situation, drawing neither on politics nor on music for its parallels, but ending with a not uncharacteristic note of self-praise:

Like the House of Lords, cricket, and the Church of England, religious broadcasting in the BBC is a peculiarly British phenomenon: slightly odd, hard to explain and yet remarkably resilient and effective. Its form and organisation were not planned. But in the process of development it evolved a structure which combined freedom and control in a way which has been the envy of other broadcasting organisations. (British Broadcasting Corporation 1975: 1)[9]

Was the slight oddness really as hard to explain as this summary suggested?

The statement of 1975 was in four parts, and should be compared with the BBC's evidence to the Annan Committee, prepared, like the statement, while Lang was Head of Religious Broadcasting. The first part, 'early arguments', had little to say about the Reithian years before the War, when the first policies were forged, or about the difficult but challenging years between 1963 and 1967, when Kenneth Lamb, a layman, was Head of Religious Broadcasting and the Reithian years faded into the distant past.[10] Nor was there much in the statement about CRAC, the Central Religious Advisory Committee, a key institution to understand in any attempt at explanation not only of the BBC's role in religious broadcasting but that of the IBA also. 'This Committee, which still exists,' the statement noted correctly but incompletely, 'was to be the BBC's link with the Churches—along with parallel Committees in Scotland, Wales and Northern Ireland—and its primary source of advice about religious programmes.' But very clearly the Committee's role was, and is, advisory. What went on the air was the BBC's responsibility (ibid. 1–2).

Taking the experience of the long period from 1922 to 1976 as a whole, six distinctive features of religious broadcasting in Britain stand out. First, it operated within an institutional framework that survived the introduction of competitive television in 1955. Second, it concentrated throughout—and the statement of 1975 omitted this also—on what from time to time was called 'the religious mainstream'. Much 'religion' was excluded. Third, there were always controversial issues relating not only to exclusion but to bias, and there were always other controversial issues, some bound up, like 'closed hours' for religious broadcasts (see below), not with sectarianism but with secularization. Fourth, religious broadcasters felt a strong urge to explain what they were seeking and what they believed they were achieving, both through definition, always difficult, and, equally important, through debate, internal to the BBC but also on many occasions public. Fifth, whatever the debate, acts of religious worship were regularly broadcast, such broadcasts reflecting continuity and change in the approach of the Churches themselves to their own services, and there was always a place for other religious programmes, the character of which reflected changes less in the Churches than in the arts, techniques, and motivations of the broadcasters. Sixth, as the BBC's evidence to the Annan Committee put it, one object of religious broadcasting was to speak to the religious interests, concerns, and needs of those 'on the fringe of, or outside, the organised life of the Churches' (1977: 319).

The development of an institutional framework began early in the history of broadcasting, and was related to the BBC's own emergence not just as a provider of programmes but as a national institution. The Director-General established a special relationship with the Archbishop of Canterbury to devise what Reith called vaguely, but significantly, 'some sort of control for the religious side' (Stuart 1975: 131). Reith's practical demonstration to Archbishop Davidson in March 1923 of the wonders of wireless was of lasting importance: it drew the Establishment into broadcasting (Briggs 1961: 241; Wolfe 1984: 6). Before that, there had been a brief but lively and now largely forgotten non-institutionalized phase in the history of British broadcasting, inaugurated, pre-Reith, by the Revd Dr J. Boon broadcasting from the Burndept Aerial works in South Peckham (Wolfe 1984: 3). It was Boon's simple but firm belief that 'the Church should strike out now and at once' to carry 'the gospel into the very homes of the people'. There should be no 'squabbling' about it: it (and at this point it was the Church of England only that was referred to) had 'to remain united'.[11] The first radio preachers to estalish their reputation after Reith were strong popular evangelists; they included the Revd P. B. Clayton of Toc H, Prebendary Carlisle, the Revd Stoddart Kennedy, 'Dick' Sheppard, and Gipsy Smith, preachers who had something at least in common with a later generation of American evangelists (Briggs 1961: 273).

Reith, while he greatly approved of the tenor of Sheppard's preaching, took a somewhat different line when he talked of 'some sort of control'. 'Christianity', he observed in his fascinating book *Broadcast over Britain*, which greatly appealed to Davidson, 'happens to be the stated and official religion of the country. . . . This is a fact that those who have criticised our right to broadcast the Christian religion [and they had included more clergymen than 'rationalists'] would do well to bear in mind' (Reith 1924: 200). They had to bear it in mind constantly, for Reith was more successful in his mission than Dr Boon. He maintained from the start that 'attendance at Church, while excellent and desirable, is not necessarily of any religious or spiritual value', and with the full support of the Archbishop of Canterbury set out to protect a special place for BBC religion. Even before the BBC received its Royal Charter and became a public corporation in January 1927, the Archbishop of Canterbury stressed the 'establishment' of broadcasting, which he called 'a well-assured factor in our national life—a uniquely widespread influence'. Thereby one Establishment formally acknowledged another.[12] Within a decade, another bishop, Dr C. S. Woodward, bishop of Bristol, was to claim that the BBC's attitude to religion was 'entirely due to the faith of one man'.[13]

The Central Religious Advisory Committee was brought into existence in June 1926, also before the Royal Charter, the successor to an earlier Sunday Committee which had drawn in Nonconformists and one Roman Catholic layman. It was chaired by a future archbishop of York, Dr Garbett, then bishop of Southwark, and it included from the start representatives of a number of churches. By 1931, with Garbett still in the chair, it consisted of five Anglicans, five Free Churchmen, two Roman Catholics, and Dick Sheppard as 'supernumerary'. CRAC was the first and by far the most influential of a cluster of BBC advisory committees, and it was to prove the most longstanding and distinctive. When the Independent Television Authority came into existence in 1955,[14] following long and contentious Parliamentary debates, it was to be the only body common to both BBC and ITA.

The 'sort of control' it exerted continued within a broader notion of the Establishment: thus, for example, the General Secretary of the British Council of Churches was a member from 1958 to 1962.[15] Criticized by a number of people who advised the Pilkington Committee, on the grounds that it did not adequately represent 'consumers' (Pilkington Committee 1962: 133), CRAC survived intact, although its membership was widened, and after 1962 its members met the BBC and the ITA separately, thereby allowing a rather greater—and often contentious—degree of innovatory competition.[16] The Revd Robert Runcie, future arch-bishop of Canterbury, was to be its chairman from 1973 to 1979. By 1976 CRAC included five laymen, there having been demands for their representation for many years.

The notion of a 'mainstream', the second main feature of British religious broadcasting, goes back to the beginnings of CRAC, and was to be reiterated in the BBC's evidence to the Pilkington Committee. An early definition of the term 'mainstream' of the 'Christian tradition' was that of the then Director of Religious Broadcasting, the Revd F. A. Ironmonger, a former editor of a Church of England newspaper, the *Guardian*, and, like Lang, a future dean of Lichfield. He had been in his BBC post for two years when he declared that 'facilities for broadcasting' were given by the BBC to 'ministers of all important denominations that can be said to be in the mainstream of the Christian tradition'.[17] What he said then was echoed a generation later. 'The first aim' of religious broadcasting, the Revd Roy McKay, Head of Religious Broadcasting since 1955, told the Pilkington Committee (1962: 88) 'is that it should reflect the worship, thought and action of those Churches which represent the main stream of the Christian tradition in this country'.

The denominational range of early sound broadcasting had been wide enough to include at least one Unitarian and one Moravian service, but there had been no broadcasts from Christian Scientists or Christadelphians, and membership of the Free Church Council became something of a test of Nonconformist claims for representa-tion on CRAC. Roman Catholic pre-war broadcasts, attacked by militant Protestants, never included the Mass, although some continental stations then broadcast Mass regularly (Briggs 1965: 236); and when, after the War, the Mass was televised—for the first time in 1954 from Leeds Cathedral—there were further protests.[18] There were protests of a different kind when an Anglican Folk Mass was televised three years later.[19]

The lack of open access for all led to complaints both from sects and from rationalists before and after 1929—and from inside as well as outside the BBC[20]—but Garbett stood firm, as did most of his successors. If the door were thrown open to Christian Scientists, he wrote in 1927, 'it would be impossible to avoid throwing it open to Theosophists, Buddhists and other similar bodies' (Wolfe 1984:

11). It was not until 1976 that the first non-Christian member of CRAC was appointed—Rabbi Hugo Gryn.

By then, CRAC had changed its approach, and was seeking new guidelines. The first object of religious broadcasting, it now maintained, was 'to seek to reflect the worship, thought and action of the principal religious traditions represented in Britain, recognising that those traditions were mainly, though not exclusively, Christian' (Annan Committee 1977: 319). 'Surely it would be the sound democratic method in a country which is officially Christian', one student of broadcasting wrote in 1937, 'to yield space generously from time to time to the reasoned expression of opposing arguments, and to allow free thinkers and adherents of the less populated sects at any rate a hearing now and again?' (Thomson 1937: 105). And the point was made far more bitterly in a wartime pamphlet by 'Clericus', published by the Thinkers' Forum. In radio days it anticipated Muggeridge's post-television 'truism' about the power of the medium: 'The potency of religion for good or evil is matched by the potency of the BBC as an instrument of religious propaganda,'[21] but it carried an opposite message. 'The voice of the BBC', 'Clericus' maintained, 'is regarded by people as the voice of authority, delivering the truth and nothing but the truth'—a remark that would have been treated more sceptically in the days of Muggeridge (ibid. 5). Changing the imagery, 'Clericus' added that 'the BBC could hardly do more in the way of plugging religion if the Director of Religious Broadcasting were the Director-General himself. The refusal to allow any dissentient voice to be heard is a flat denial of the democratic principle and of the right of freedom of discussion embodied in the Atlantic Charter. The policy underlying this refusal is essentially the same as that adopted by the Nazis' (ibid. 47).

It was the main thesis of 'Clericus' that 'listeners want argument', a thesis that in time came to appeal to the religious broadcasters themselves. There was something of a turning-point in BBC policy in this connection when in 1952 Dr Kathleen Bliss suggested not so much argument as dialogue: 'The object was not to promote controversy between "Christians" and "non-Christians", but to foster conversations over barriers which were very high indeed.'[22] The first result was a series *Encounters of Belief* broadcast in 1953.

There was no support inside the BBC for setting up a committee parallel to CRAC on which would be represented 'those religious

sects too unorthodox to be represented or accepted by CRAC and
ethical and humanist organisations'. The idea, which was put
forward in 1951 by a group which included Lord Dowding, a
Spiritualist, and Bertrand Russell, a rationalist, was no more
acceptable than the idea of humanist contributions to *Lift up your
Hearts* (Briggs 1979: 788–9). None the less, a Spiritualist was to
appear on Tyne Tees Television screens in 1961, 'a red letter day
for psychic history'[23] six years after Mrs Margaret Knight had been
allowed to present three programmes on the BBC's Home Service
from 'a Humanist point of view' (Briggs 1979: 800). On the earlier
occasion the Press had been more hostile than the Churches. The
Daily Express saw Mrs Knight's account of 'Morals without
Religion' as 'an explosive attack on Christianity'.[24] The *Daily
Telegraph* warned the BBC that it was behaving recklessly when the
ITA had 'just been charged by Statute to see that programmes do
not include anything likely to be "offensive to public feeling" ',[25]
yet the ITA was to prove more adventurous in its religious
broadcasting than the BBC had been, and took both the BBC and
the Churches by surprise when a year later, on 8 January 1956, it
launched its own controversial programme *About Religion* (Wolfe
1984: 529).

Attacks on any opening up of religious television remained
common, revealing depths of prejudice that had their origins long
before the creation of the BBC. There were, however, other
controversial issues—the third distinctive feature in the history of
religious broadcasting in Britain—most of them centring first on
the question of 'the closed period' on Sunday, which was restricted
to religious broadcasting, and, second, on how to present religion
on the television screen. Inevitably these features brought in to
question also the relationship between the BBC and ITA.

There had certainly been far more than a 'sort of control' in the
idea of a special period reserved for religious broadcasting on
Sundays from 6.15 p.m. to 7.25 p.m., an idea that, according to the
American historian of British broadcasting, Burton Paulu, revealed
not only the influence of the Churches but 'the paternalistic attitude
of the government towards broadcasting (Paulu 1981: 280). It was
a major turning-point, therefore, when in 1972, after some strange
alliances had opposed the moves, the government decided to
suspend all controls over television broadcasting hours; and
although both the BBC and the IBA (Independent Broadcasting

Authority, as the ITA had now become) responded by saying that they would stick to the 'closed period' for religious broadcasting, 'a measure of flexibility' was introduced (with the approval of CRAC) in 1976.[26] The time now allotted was reduced to 35 minutes, between 6.40 p.m. and 7.15 p.m.

There was even more argument about what to broadcast during the 'closed period' than there had been during the 1930s about the BBC's policy concerning Sunday as a whole. In a wartime atmosphere it had not proved difficult to erode the protective broadcasting of which Reith had been so proud, and this had led to the successful invasion of pre-war British 'closed' hours each Sunday by commercial companies operating from Europe and offering non-restricted popular fare. The Revd J. W. Welch, then the BBC's Director of Religious Broadcasting, had tried to hold back the tide, but the Director-General, F. W. Ogilvie, had argued that change had to take place 'out of a sense of duty to the Forces in their special circumstances'.[27]

The popular fare provided on post-war television during the years of the 'closed period', in the 1950s and 1960s, particularly in the case of the commercial companies, was far more popular than wartime radio fare. It was strongly attacked, however, in religious and other circles, and one programme in particular, *Stars on Sunday*, produced by Yorkshire Television, generated unprecedented hostility even though—or perhaps because—it was the first religious series to enter the Top Twenty popularity charts. Its peak audience was 15 million, and its producers received 5,000 viewers' letters each week.[28] Singled out by the Annan Committee for special attention, it was bitterly criticized by several of the smaller religious sects and by some influential members of the Church of England. The Independent Methodist Church claimed that it could not be defined as religious broadcasting at all (Annan Committee 1977: 318). It was no asset as far as the Methodists were concerned that the Archbishop of Canterbury and Cardinal Heenan had both appeared on it and that, according to an audience survey, the cross-section of viewers, measured by age, sex, and class, was almost identical for *Stars on Sunday*, *Coronation Street*, and *Crossroads* (Church of England 1973: 50).

The fourth distinctive feature of British religious broadcasting has been the willingness—anxiety, even—of religious broadcasters and those in charge of the general direction of broadcasting to try to explain what they are doing, why, and with what effects. This can be treated only briefly. One key source is an appendix by Professor Basil Mitchell to the Report of the Broadcasting Commission of the General Synod of the Church of England in 1973, which had included several references to *Stars on Sunday*. As early as 1948, Sir William Haley (1949), then Director-General of the BBC, had written that 'the Corporation has added religious controversy to the other forms of controversy it broadcasts. It has stated in its duty towards the search for truth it must broadcast statements of unbelief as well as of differing beliefs.' Mitchell compares this statement with one made by Sir Hugh Greene seventeen years later. Haley had referred to Britons as 'citizens of a Christian country', and had reaffirmed that 'the BBC—an institution set up by the State—bases its policy upon a positive attitude towards Christian values'. Greene made no reference to Britons as Christians or to Christian values.[29]

It was not only the sense of context that had shifted, as Mitchell points out. The philosophy had changed too. Greene's searching after 'basic moral values' had little in common with the Christian quest for truth. By the time of the Annan Report both context and philosophy had shifted still further. Britain was now a 'pluralist' and 'multicultural society'; and two of the new projected guidelines of CRAC were (1) 'to seek to reflect the worship, thought and action of the principal religious traditions [note the plural] represented in Britain, recognising that those traditions are mainly, though not exclusively Christian' and (2) 'to seek to present to viewers and listeners those beliefs, ideas, issues and experiences in the contemporary world which are directly related to a religious interpretation or dimension of life' (Annan Committee 1977: 319).

Unlike Muggeridge, Mitchell would never have been tempted to talk of 'irresponsibility' in relation to these substantive changes. His own charge was expressed in very different language:

I am immensely impressed as any unprejudiced reader of these addresses [Haley's and Greene's] must be by the care with which these spokesmen of broadcasting have examined the ethics of their profession. Nevertheless I am not entirely sure that they have seen the problem with complete clarity. (Church of England 1973: 89)

The fifth feature of British religious broadcasting deserves far more extensive treatment than is possible in this context. What is remarkable is that the amount of time devoted to religious broadcasting did not decline in the 1960s and 1970s between the publication of the Pilkington Report and that of the Annan Report. Nor did the scheduling change. In 1976 as in 1962 the BBC was broadcasting two and three-quarter hours a week on television and about eight hours a week on radio; and in 1976 ITV's output remained consistent at about two and a half hours a week. There was no significant shift either in audience size. The Annan Committee recognized that there was a contrast between viewing and listening on the one hand and religious attendance on the other, though it talked in general terms about 'ecumenicism', a subject in itself in the history of broadcast religion, and 'speculation about myth and ritual'.

The sixth feature of religious broadcasting—its appeal to those outside the organized life of the Churches—which is the most interesting of all its features, deserves a monograph in itself. Christians of all sects were as divided in their attitudes towards it as they had been in their attitudes to evangelizing Victorian Britain, perhaps the greatest missionary effort ever undertaken.

This brief study should not end without an epilogue, the right word given its weekly significance in the history of broadcasting; and rightly it should focus on Reith.[30] However deeply interested he was in religious broadcasting as such, he was even more interested in the kind of issues concerning 'general standards' that preoccupied Muggeridge in his 1976 lecture. Before Muggeridge interviewed him in a remarkable television broadcast of 1967, Reith asked me whether he ought to accept the invitation, and I had no doubt that he should do so. I knew at once that as far as matters of religion were concerned, they would be on the same wavelength. For all Reith's Calvinist upbringing, which deeply influenced him as a son of the manse, his attitude towards religion had more in common with that of Muggeridge than with that of his father, the Revd George Reith, who became Moderator of the General Assembly of the United Free Church of Scotland. John Reith no more judged on the basis of sectarian commitment than did Muggeridge, and he was equally scornful of the values of late-twentieth-century secular society.

In 1968 he provided a brief foreword for a little book called *Religion by Radio*, almost the only book of its kind.[31] It was written by Melville Dinwiddie, also a son of the manse and from

1933 to 1957 Director and Controller of the BBC in Scotland. It was Dinwiddie who in 1939 launched the programme *Lift up your Hearts*. In his foreword Reith described 'religion by radio', somewhat surprisingly at first sight, as 'probably relatively the most ineffectual or anyhow the most inefficient—in an engineering or commercial sense of effort to result—of all the sectional activities of broadcasting'. Thereafter—and this was *his* summary—he lambasted 'the Churches—all denominations and confessions'—for their failure to follow up religious broadcasting programmes which 'from the beginning, and against indifference, ridicule, opposition' had been given a position of 'privilege and protection in the broadcasting service, which—circumstances having been otherwise and as might have been expected—no protest or petition by the Churches (on eventual recognition of what was happening) could have secured for them'. 'Millions of pounds worth of advertising had been done for them free.' They had not taken advantage of it.[32]

Reith's sharpest critique, not mentioned in this foreword—although he did refer in it to the protection not only of the Churches but of the sabbath—was reserved, as was Muggeridge's, for the over-all quality of BBC programmes, as he judged them, in the 1960s, the great decade of social and cultural change. He had always insisted, as his biographer Andrew Boyle (1972: 24) put it, on 'the intrinsic value of Christian values in any system of public broadcasting—no matter what his private relationship might be with God'; and it was in the light of this general judgement that, after a brief honeymoon period with Sir Hugh Greene (ibid. 342), he criticized the BBC, which, he maintained, 'particularly in television has utterly discounted everything I did'.[33]

Television for Reith was itself a 'pernicious' medium; but the BBC, too, became in his opinion a pernicious instrument, 'the leader of agnosticism and immorality among young people particularly'.[34] Like Muggeridge, he was dismayed by 'the corrupt misguided' society in which it had to operate, though he would never have gone so far as Muggeridge once did in generalizing that 'the media as a whole, and curiously enough the BBC in particular, represent the greatest instrument the Devil has ever found in the history of the world'.[35] After all, he had been its progenitor. Not surprisingly, Curran protested strongly against Muggeridge's judgement; there was talk of legal action; and Curran received an apology from the editor of the Catholic paper in which Muggeridge's article had appeared.

There was to be a further epilogue to this epilogue, an epilogue in two parts. The last paragraph of Boyle's biography refers to a visit by Muggeridge to Reith's bedside just before he died (Boyle 1972: 351). The last pages of Stuart's edition of Reith's diaries describe instead a final exchange of letters between Reith and Curran, who had not hesitated to tell Reith that he had underestimated 'the decisive influence on our present work [in the BBC] of the foundations which you so truly laid'. 'We have changed', Curran went on, 'but I do not think all the change has been for the worst. Much has been simply the change of times.' Leaving on one side divergent interpretation of what 'the change of times' really meant, Reith replied to Curran in 1971 in the month of his death, 'I only want to say that I think your letter is as impressive and delightful as I ever received' (Stuart 1975: 523–4).[36]

Notes

1. He had appeared on *Meeting Point* as early as 28 Oct. 1956, and had subsequently taken part in many programmes. In 1981, he was to present an autobiographical series, *Muggeridge: Ancient and Modern*.
2. About the inquiry, which made an effort to estimate qualitative as well as quantitative responses, see Briggs 1979: 796—800.
3. 'Though the Church is able to use the means of mass-communication, it does so only marginally—marginally both to its only total communication which still relies on the nexus of pulpit and pew, and on religious literature, and marginally to the total content of the mass-media as a whole' (Wilson 1966: 41).
4. There has been talk of 'rinsing the colour of controversy out of the tapestry of the faith' (*Church of England Newspaper*, 3 Feb. 1956), of 'phoney religion' (*Daily Herald*, 18 Mar. 1957), and even of the BBC actually 'doing harm to religion' (*Guardian*, 13 Nov. 1962). A rationalist critic, H. J. Blackham, complained in the *Ethical Record*, Oct. 1966, of what he called 'secularized Christianity': the Bishop of Woolwich had performed the non-miracle of converting wine into water. The Annan Committee quoted the National Association for the Protection of Family Life as saying that religious programmes were 'remarkable for their non-religious content', and quoted a clergyman

broadcasting on Radio 4 who said, 'Stop all this Jesus, Jesus stuff which I must say is counter-productive.'

5. Note too the subtitle of Wolfe's (1984) book, *The Politics of Broadcast Religion*.
6. At its peak, the programme reached 30 million viewers. It ran until 1957.
7. *Hansard*, House of Lords Debates, vol. 519, no. 86, 16 May 1990, col. 296.
8. Ibid. 295.
9. Lang, who had much to do with the statement, joined the BBC in 1964, straight from Emmanuel College, Cambridge, where he was chaplain. He served as Assistant Head of Religious Broadcasting from 1964 to 1967 and as Head of Religious Programmes, Radio, from 1967 to 1971, before becoming Head of Religious Broadcasting, staying in this post until 1980, when he became dean of Lichfield.
10. See Kenneth Lamb's lunch-time lecture on *Religious Broadcasting* (BBC Publications, 1965).
11. *Daily Telegraph*, 31 July 1922.
12. *Radio Times*, 17 Dec. 1926.
13. *Western Daily Press*, quoted in Briggs 1965: 227.
14. See ITA, *Annual Report and Accounts, 1955–1956* (London), 23–4.
15. See Slack 1962. This publication includes a number of revealing articles on the religious activities of the commercial companies. See also Sendall 1982.
16. See ITA, *Annual Report and Accounts, 1962–1963* (London), 29. There is a brief account of the issues in Weddell 1968. Weddell, who had been first Secretary of the Board for Social Responsibility established by the Church of England, was Secretary of the ITA from 1961 to 1964.
17. *BBC Annual* (London, 1935), 66–7.
18. See e.g. a letter from A. L. Kensit in *English Churchman*, 15 Mar. 1957, with a reply from the BBC's Secretary.
19. See e.g. a letter from W. Greenhouse Allt of the Church Music Society in *Church Times*, 8 Nov. 1957.
20. See Lambert 1940: 33. Lambert was editor of the *Listener* from 1929 to 1939.
21. 'Clericus', *BBC Religion* (London, 1942), 3. 'Clericus' also drew on the argument of Sir Ernest Benn (1941). The relationship between 'monopoly' and 'democracy' was controversial.
22. Central Advisory Committee, Minutes, 24 Oct. 1952.
23. *Two Worlds*, Feb. 1961.
24. *Daily Express*, 7 Jan. 1955.
25. *Daily Telegraph*, 7 Jan. 1955.

26. IBA news release, 'The Future of the Closed Period', in *BBC Handbook* (London, 1977), 34–5.
27. See Briggs 1970: 131 ff. For a different religious reaction to wartime broadcasting, see Dakers 1943.
28. K. Passingham (ed.), *The Guinness Book of TV Facts and Facts* (Enfield, 1984), 166. The programme was first broadcast on 17 Apr. 1969.
29. *Christian Broadcaster*, 1965.
30. The word 'epilogue' was chosen by Basil Nicolls, then London Station Director of the British Broadcasting Company, to describe the brief religious broadcast that on Reith's initiative brought Sunday broadcasting to a close. The first epilogue was broadcast on 26 Sept. 1926. There were no 'epilogues' on television after the 1950s.
31. See also, however, McKay 1964. McKay was Head of Religious Broadcasting from 1955 to 1963.
32. Dinwiddie 1968: 7–9. On Dinwiddie's retirement, he was paid warm tributes in the General Assembly of the Church of Scotland; but one critic of BBC religious broadcasting described it as 'too velvet gloved', adding that there was too much 'theatricalness' (*Scottish Daily Mail*, 22 May 1957).
33. Reith Diary, 7 Sept. 1963; reprinted in Stuart 1975: 509.
34. Ibid., 6 Aug. 1975; reprinted in Stuart 1975: 517.
35. *Catholic Herald*, 2 Aug. 1974.
36. Letter from Curran, 26 May 1970; letter to Curran, 24 June 1970.

References

Adler, R. P. (1981) (ed.), *Understanding Television: Essays on Television as a Social and Cultural Force* (New York).
Annan Committee (1977), *Report* Cmnd. 6753 (London).
Barnouw, E. (1975), *Tube of Plenty, The Evolution of American Television* (New York).
Benn, E. (1941), *The BBC Monopoly* (London).
Boyle, A. (1972). *Only the Wind will Listen, Reith of the BBC* (London).
Briggs, A. (1961), *The Birth of Broadcasting* (Oxford).
—— (1965), *The Golden Age of Wireless* (Oxford).
—— (1970), *The War of Words* (Oxford).
—— (1979), *Sound and Vision* (Oxford).
British Broadcasting Corporation (1975), *Religious Broadcasting* (London), with a Foreword by Sir Charles Curran.

Church of England (1973), *Broadcasting, Society and the Church, A Discussion Paper on the Report and General Synod Debate* (London).

Dakers, A. (1943), *The Big Ben Minute* (London).

Dinwiddie, M. (1968), *Religion by Radio* (London).

Evans, I. (1957), 'Prospero's View, The Religious Opportunities of Television', *Tablet*, 30 Mar.

Fore, W. F. (1987), *Television and Religion: The Shaping of Faith, Values and Culture* (Minneapolis).

Gerbner, G., Gross, L. *et al.* (1984), *Religion on Television* (New York).

Hadden, J. K., and Swann, C. E. (1981), *Prime-time Preachers: The Rising Power of Televangelism* (Boston).

Haley, W. (1949), 'Moral Values in Broadcasting', Address to the British Council of Churches, 1948 (Wembley).

Horsfield, G. (1984), *Religious Television, the Experience in America* (New York).

Klapper, J. T. (1949), *The Effects of the Mass Media* (New York).

Lambert, R. S. (1940), *Ariel and all his Quality* (London).

McKay, R. (1964). *Reflections on Religious Broadcasting* (London).

Muggeridge, M. (1977), *Christ and the Media* (London).

Paulu, B. (1981), *Television and Radio in the United Kingdom* (London).

Pilkington Committee on Broadcasting (1962), *Report of the Committee on Broadcasting* Cmnd. 1753 (London).

Reith, J. C. W. (1924), *Broadcast over Britain* (London).

Sendall, B. (1982), *History of Independent Television in Britain*, Vol. 1: *Origin and Foundation, 1944–1962* (London).

Silver, R. J. E., McKay, R., and Reindorp, G. (n.d.), *Religion on the Air* (London).

Slack, K. (1962), 'Progressing from the Religious Ice Age', in *Religion on Television, A Television Mail Publication*, June.

Stuart, C. (1975) (ed.), *The Reith Diaries* (London).

Thomson, D. C. (1937), *Radio is Changing Us* (London).

Weddell, E. G. (1968), *Broadcasting and Public Policy* (London).

Wilson, B. (1966), *Religion in Secular Society* (London).

Wilson, B. (1967) (ed.), *Patterns of Sectarianism* (London).

Wolfe, K. M. (1984), *The Churches and the British Broadcasting Corporation, 1922–1956* (London).

16

Crowds, Time, and the Essence of Society

RICHARD FENN

If a consensus is ever reached about the secularization of modern societies, it may read something like this: The most virulent demonstrations of charismatic authority in war and politics have slowly become domesticated over many centuries. As spiritual substance is drained from public discourse, politics turns into administration. The public sphere is thereby impoverished, and becomes empty of ultimate significance. None the less, there is a certain civility in modern societies. Individuals and groups no longer need to 'act like victors' at the expense of others. Dramatic displays of triumph in the religious or political sphere gradually yield to more rational controls over the administration of power and the management of conflict. Local, grass-roots movements still act out their claims to authority in ways that may be temporarily disruptive; but these displays, like the people themselves, are marginal to the basic structures and processes of modern societies.

Protest becomes entertainment as charismatic leaders become histrionic rather than serious protagonists in a public drama. Charisma becomes domesticated in the routines of everyday life, in which individuals display themselves as though on a very small, local stage. These displays are a far cry from the platforms on which heroic figures like Titus celebrated their triumphs in antiquity. Modern-day triumphs are therefore everyday and virtually banal, although, to those on the margins of modern societies, triumphs over decay and chaos are serious business indeed. The domestication of charisma has replaced ugly displays of triumph with the more predictable controls of social life in the home, the community, and in the state itself. If such a consensus on the process of secularization is ever reached, it will be heavily indebted to the work of Bryan Wilson.

There is something both tragic and ironic in Wilson's view of social life. The tragedy lies in the inexorable power of the centre, the central principle of order. *The system* always has a rationality of its own. It does not matter whether priests or chiefs are running things. They will provide order, coherence, purpose, and a certain logic to work, politics, and the affairs of everyday life. The inevitable side-effects of any such principle of order are the source of tragedy. Local cults become anomalies, no matter how long they have survived in their native place. Even the family and the local community become sources of static or noise in the system unless in some way they also serve its purposes.

As the traditional or customary forms of social life become threatened by the encroachment of Church and State, those who depend on these forms may become anxious or get nasty, but these responses are essentially hopeless rearguard reactions to the central principle of order. In the end, the forces of reaction are easily co-opted. Students, for instance, who demonstrated passionately outside the gates of one college during the 1960s seemed only too glad to be invited in for sherry. The tragedy culminates, however, in the drying-up of the very grass roots which nourished the larger society and provided it with willing and serviceable citizens possessing commitment, civility, and even the spirit of sacrifice. Without these sources of moral and emotional support, Bryan Wilson notes, modern societies will be unable to maintain and reproduce themselves; chaos or chronic conflict are predictable, alternative scenarios.

From the vantage-point of such a theory on the structural exchanges between centres and peripheries, one can see why time makes ancient good, as it were, uncouth. The element of tragedy is due not to the fates or the times working themselves out, but to the predictable consequences of a drive for centrality, significance, and power. With irony, one is faced with a somewhat more difficult task: not of explanation (as in the case of tragedy) but of interpretation. Irony suggests that 'we' know what is going on, whereas others are too caught up in the events themselves to appreciate what is 'really' happening. What may look to them like the fullness of time or a revelatory moment of *kairos* looks from the later vantage-point of the sociological observer like the beginning of a long process whereby the times become relatively empty and *kairos* is replaced by the dull cares of *chronos*. It is precisely such irony, however, that typifies Wilson's interpretation of the process of secularization. Time, intensified by the expectation of the millennium, becomes an extended period of time in which expectation gives way to calculation, significant event yields to planned strategy, and momentous occasion becomes merely the playing of games.

The process of secularization, then, is quite literally about time. On the one hand, societies that are confronted by an overwhelming colonial power, like many of those studied by Wilson, are indeed running out of time. That is why, I would argue, they seek to 'buy time', as it were, by appealing to times that have passed away: to the times of their ancestors, whose return gives the society a new lease on life, and time in which to recover, prosper, and vanquish their enemies. Moreover, it is characteristic of the masochist, Reik tells us, not only to indulge fantasies of triumph, but to engage in a 'flight forward' to the promised time of victory over the enemy. I would suggest that millennial movements engage in precisely such magical thinking about time, as if the promised day could be precipitated by marching to a particular drumbeat and by the sound of the proper bugles. Paradoxically, then, the process of secularization begins with the intensification of the experience of time. To understand that experience of time and to show how otherwise apparently unrelated social processes are aspects of the same process of intensification of the experience of time is part of the task of interpretation.

Note that secular time is the time that is thought to be 'passing away', that is, headed for death and extinction. David Martin's early study of the semantics of the word 'secular' preserved this meaning alone, after others were more easily eliminated for their contradictions and redundancies. It is in keeping with the usage of the New Testament, moreover, to understand the secular world as the world whose time is running out: the age, saeculum, or aeon that is on the way out. On the strength of this understanding of the term, then, I would make four assumptions:

1 That as social systems encounter increasing threats or surprises, their members will experience their situation as one in which time is running out.
2 That as time becomes scarce in such societies, some religious movements will seek to turn the clock back, as it were, to buy time, while others will seek to accelerate time toward an anticipated moment of victory.

3 That in the ideology of such religious systems, it is the opposing
   social system that is pictured as running out of time; that is, part
   of an epoch or aeon, a saeculum, that is passing away.
4 That these ideological concerns were typical of the encounters of
   the Roman centre with the Palestinian periphery in the first
   century.

Beyond these more general assumptions, however, I am making
the further assumption that the experience of time is construed
differently in institutions than in movements, among élites than
among the dispossessed or disenfranchised, and in structured
groupings than in crowds or mobs. I introduce these latter terms
particularly to suggest the social contexts in which time was
construed in pre-70 CE Palestine. One such context is the crowds
that gathered during the early stages of the Jesus movement, both
before and after the death of Jesus. Another such context, I will
argue, is the massed soldiery of the Roman legions as they engaged
guerrilla movements and the civilian population in Palestine in the
events initiating the civil war of 66–70 CE. Both these contexts, I
will suggest, were significant enough to have made a lasting
impression on the Judaeo-Christian community experience and
social construction of time.
    In this chapter I shall argue that students of the New Testament
have several reasons to explore the significance of the crowd. First,
the crowd was a major institution in antiquity: the third leg, as it
were, of the stool of the social system, the other two legs being the
institutions of tribal community and the state. The crowd's sense of
time or timing was therefore 'of the essence' of the social system.
Second, the crowd can become not only pivotal but revolutionary
under certain conditions; note especially the crisis in succession that
marked the Herodian dynasty at the death of Herod. The crowd's
sense of time could therefore mark a *kairos*, a decisive moment in
the life of the nation. Third, the crowd embodies the environment
of the social system: that is, the set of surprises and threats and
opportunities for new relationships with other systems or for the
avoidance of such relationships. Therefore, control of the crowd in
antiquity was of prime importance in controlling the pace of social
change. The crowd's sense of time was therefore crucial for
determining the notion that time might be running out and coming
to an end. Various religious movements in antiquity were shaped by

the type of crowd which they embodied. The crowd's sense of time is therefore important for determining whether the society's clock will be set backward (to an ancestral time) or speeded up toward the end of the epoch and the beginning of the millennium.

There are also other questions that arise from this approach. The attempt to domesticate the charisma of the crowd involves an attempt to limit the public sphere, to encapsulate the crowd in a circle of disciples and within the household. On the other hand, the attempt to domesticate the charisma of the crowd also seeks to embody certain vital, egalitarian, and unconstrained aspects of social life characteristic of the crowd. To what extent does this twofold attempt to limit the public sphere and yet to embody its dynamic aspects characterize the ambivalent relationship between religion and politics in societies historically associated with the Christian community and the Church? In modern democracies that have domesticated the crowd through various electoral procedures, the polling of public opinion, and the institutions of representative government, does the Church's attempt to domesticate the charisma of the people still retain its former political implications and significance? Or, under modern political conditions, does the Church's attempt to domesticate the charisma of the crowd reduce itself to relatively constrained performances—that is, to aspects of theatre and entertainment in the private sphere?

1. THE CROWD OF ANTIQUITY: THE ESSENCE OF SOCIETY

No one who has witnessed the enormous gatherings that have demanded the removal of Communist leaders from Eastern European governments in recent months can underestimate the political significance of the crowd even in 'modern' societies. They are clearly a political phenomenon even now; none the less they will disappear once routine political processes have reasserted themselves. *The opposite was the case in antiquity, where the crowd was itself an institution*: a pivotal political institution that often held the balance of power between colonial and local regimes (cf. Gluckman 1965). If we are to understand the significance of the crowd in the New Testament, then, we will have to stretch our sociological imagination beyond the scenes with which we are familiar. Crowds in the modern West fill the interstices and gaps of social order: the moments in which a government can reign but cannot rule. They often gather outside the usual hours of work: for example, the weekend 'marches' on Washington or the crowds in eighteenth-century England that demanded reform during lunch hours or after work in the evening. *The crowds in first-century Palestine occupied a more central place in the social order.*

Of course, some crowds were multitudes, and others were mere gatherings. The point, however, is that the crowd embodied the public sphere. It was a face-to-face gathering in which the most personal concerns took on public significance; indeed, the crowd is an early form of the 'cloud of witnesses', in which interaction between individuals became part of the public record. In pre-70 CE Palestine a crowd, of whatever size, was likely to have a few spies and informers, Herodians and Pharisees, to observe the words and gestures of those whose loyalties were suspect. That is another reason, I shall argue, why it was necessary to domesticate the charisma of the crowd of Palestinian antiquity. Like the demons who stirred up the Gadarene pigs, there were those listening to the Church's—or Jesus's—preaching who were *agents provocateurs.*

The modern crowd is an eruption of private persons into the public sphere, but the notion of a private sphere is very difficult to apply to antiquity. For instance, Nicolet (1975: 873) argues that the Roman state was obligated to keep under surveillance a wide range of acts and behaviour that, to us in the modern West, would seem to belong to the private sphere. Moreover, we must be careful, if we wish to apply such concepts as 'the crowd' to antiquity, to take into account certain differences between, say, the late Republic and the modern state. What we would regard as either a political or an economic issue would hardly be differentiated in that society; on the contrary, even the most practical or strategic concern was embedded in an undifferentiated public sphere which was understood as a whole, whether in metaphysical terms or as part of a sacred order. The point is particularly well taken in the case of crowds, whose persistent appearance in the Roman Empire suggests that they were a permanent institution rather than a form of collective behaviour signifying the breakdown of social order; they were part of that order itself.

It is nevertheless possible, especially in view of the recent transformation of Eastern Europe, to find a few parallels between the crowds of antiquity and modernity. Some of the earliest mass demonstrations were relatively quiet, like the communion feast near the Shrine of Our Lady of Czestochowa, where the Pope declared the support of the Catholic Church for the Solidarity movement; that movement had begun in the extensive strikes at steel plants and ship yards, notably Gdanzk, where everyday life and work were suspended in mass protest against the state. More recent European crowds have not been as orderly or as quiet; their solidarity consisted either in pursuing a head of state to his death, as in Romania, where the crowd's enthusiasm for revolution was sustained by the repeated portrayal of Ceauşescu's execution on public television, or in the mass flight of the population across the borders of East Germany. Whether in fight or in flight, in mass refusal to work or in communion feast, the public has declared itself the prime mover of European politics, not through the routine channels of the state but in the streets. In this respect the modern crowd does resemble those of antiquity, at least in Republican Rome. According to Moses J. Finley,

it would not be far from the truth to say that the Roman *populus* exercised influence not through participation in the formal machinery of government, through its voting power, but *by taking to the streets*, by agitation, demonstrations and riots, and this long before the gangs and private armies of the civil-war century. (1983: 91; emphasis added)

None the less, the differences are more important than the similarities. The crowd of antiquity was an institution, whereas the modern crowd appears only occasionally to do its work. The solidarity of workers in Poland and their sense of mutual obligation to one another are giving way to a market economy that rewards individual entrepreneurship; the tearing down of the Berlin Wall has dissipated the crowds in East Germany, and the execution of Ceauşescu has satisfied the hunger of Romanian crowds for victory.

The crowd of antiquity therefore represented a public concentration of face-to-face interaction. That interaction, however, was so highly coded that words and gestures, dress and eating, forms of address and appeal, all typified the social system, which was reproduced in symbolic interaction between persons. Any deviations from the norm would therefore have public and political meaning, just as the body politic could be said to reproduce itself whenever two or three gathered together according to the norms for the occasion. On the other hand, crowds could suspend the customary forms of deference, and blend persons of very different ranks into a cohesive and powerful social order. That is why it was essential to control the crowd at festivals and games, celebrations and funerals.

These public rites at which crowds gathered were not the leisure-time activities of the modern world, but civic occasions on which the community was honoured, its leaders legitimated, and benefits bestowed on the people in the form of rents, wages previously withheld, food, rebates from taxes, the release of prisoners, or public baths, libraries, and schools (cf. Hopkins 1983: ii. 249). Smaller gatherings, however, also had the shape and substance of rituals. The failure of the crowd to exhibit the requisite deference and decorum at collective meals or on the streets could be taken as evidence of seditious intent. Manners were morals, and morals were in the public rather than private sphere. The crowd was an embodiment of the public sphere and a major threat to the social order. Its times were indeed of the essence of society.

The crowd in first-century Palestine was thus a major element and actor in the public sphere; yet the significance of the crowd for Christian origins has yet to be determined. On the one hand, crowds were confronting Roman governors, procurators, prefects, and imperial emissaries; they were the sole court of last resort and also a primary source of confrontation, disruption, and collective action. Crowds attended the earliest Christian preaching after the death and resurrection, in scenes that may well have been reminiscent of critical moments in the life of the Jesus movement. To understand the political and social context of first-century Palestine, as well as to understand and perhaps explain the origins of the Jesus movement, it is therefore essential to have at least a rudimentary grasp of the crowd as a pivotal and potentially revolutionary aspect of the social system. To assess the political role of the crowd in pre-70 CE Palestine is one purpose of this chapter, as a preparation for asking certain questions about Christian origins and the process of secularization in societies that have been shaped or informed by the intensification of time in the Judaeo-Christian tradition.

2. THE MAGICAL KINGDOM: THE FULLNESS OF TIME

There can be something magical about a crowd, but not about a mob, without a leader, without sustained direction or purpose, and without a sense of solidarity beyond the moment or occasion. A crowd can sense its own unity, and be filled with anticipation both of unprecedented benefits and of imminent dangers. I use the word 'magical' to refer to the sense of omnipotence, of extraordinary entitlement, and of fusion with others experienced by the infant who has not yet discovered separation, limits, frustration, and disappointment. Freud speaks of this state of mind as a magical kingdom, and calls it 'narcissism'. What is more narcissistic than the relation of a leader to a people, the leader seeing his or her own reflection in the gestures of the crowd as arms are raised, and hearing his or her own echo in the voices raised in response to each chant or cry?

For some scholars the crowd is religious by definition, because it is unconsciously entranced by mysterious and supernatural powers and is willing to subordinate every wish or claim to them, even to the point of death (cf. Le Bon 1986: 84). For others, however, the crowd is only an expression of the same tendencies that underlie religious belief and devotion: a desire to surrender to a powerful leader. The charismatic nature of mass collective action leads to a sense of the 'fullness of time'; that is why Weber and others see the process of secularization in certain, more routine or rational expressions of collective enthusiasm: in combat, sports, theatre, and finally in the games of children (cf. Wilson 1973). For still other sociologists (e.g. Durkheim), the crowd is a source of religious enthusiasm and conviction because it is exterior to the individual, superior, constraining, and awesome.

Without reducing religion to a mere manifestation or consequence of collective behaviour, and without reducing collective behaviour to a mere expression or outcome of religious tendencies, we can still ask, 'What was the relation of the crowd of antiquity to the origins of the Jesus movement and of early Christianity?' We ask that question, of course, within the general problematic sketched out in the sociology of religion that seeks to describe, interpret, and explain the collective sources and expressions of religious movements.

On the face of it, there is an intimate relationship between the Jesus movement and crowds. Indeed, the fifth chapter of Matthew's gospel places the giving of Jesus's teaching on a hillside, from which he addresses crowds. The crowds are hardly incidental; in fact, 'When Jesus saw the vast crowds he went up the hillside' (Matthew 5: 1).[1] Note, however, that his teaching to the crowds neutralizes and reverses some of the very tendencies towards magical thinking, fantasies of omnipotence, and delusions of extraordinary entitlement that I have just mentioned. The beatitudes enjoin humility and suffering, warn against enmity and revenge, encourage reconciliation with enemies and outsiders, discourage publicity in either prayer or charity, and recall the binding authority of the Law and the Prophets: hardly an encouragement to revolutionary or violent action, towards exclusiveness or domination of any kind. The solidarity of the crowd, however, its intimacy and the equality of its members, are taken to be hallmarks of the faithful, who are enjoined to disregard social distinctions in everyday life, just as such distinction and privilege disappear within the crowd itself. To make the experience of openness, solidarity, and equality a domesticated way of life is to make possible the fullness of time at all times and places.

If this interpretation seems strained, consider the first encounters of Jesus when he comes down from the hillside, as 'large crowds followed him' (Matthew 8: 1 ff.). His meetings are entirely with outsiders, a leper and a centurion; the leper is placed within the Law, and the centurion combines the virtues that Jesus has just enjoined upon the crowd: respect for authority combined with a radical faith that breaks through distinctions between insiders and outsiders. Indeed, the healing of the centurion's servant occurs within the home, although Jesus remains outside. *The fullness of time is indicated in these extraordinary, revelatory encounters with outsiders, so long as the crowd is present.*

The crowds are still present when, 'on coming into Capernaum', Jesus encounters the centurion whose servant he heals without actually entering the centurion's house. The fullness of time occurs, as it were, without Jesus's physical presence: a point that could hardly be lost on the Christian community after Jesus's death. The key factor is faith, and a greater faith than can be found in Israel. Further domestication of the crowd's intensification of time occurs when, 'on coming into Peter's house', Jesus heals Peter's mother-in-law. Still the crowds are very much present; they bring him people possessed of evil spirits, which he expels 'with a word'.

I am arguing that it is the collective power and virtue of the crowd, the gathering of the people, which is being domesticated. Matthew makes that very clear in a later reference to Jesus's healing of a paralytic on his return 'to his own town'. It is 'when Jesus saw the faith of those who brought him' that he told the paralytic that his sins were forgiven and that he should 'go home' (Matthew 9: 2 ff.).

The crowd is the framework within which faith enables Jesus to heal; therefore the absence of crowds must interfere with the revelatory movement, and deprive the experience of time of its relative intensity. Lest the reader miss the point of the contrast, Matthew notes that it was 'When Jesus had seen the great crowds around him' that 'he gave orders for departure to the other side of the lake' (Matthew 8: 18). The other side of the lake provides a set of symbolic contrasts with the Capernaum side where the people (the crowd) are gathered. Across the lake a herd of pigs, possessed by the demons whom Jesus has expelled from the so-called Gerasene demoniac, engages in uncontrolled and destructive behaviour and rushes to its death in the lake. Conversely, a crowd of townspeople, disturbed by the exorcism, seek to drive Jesus out of their country. The wildness of the herd of pigs contrasts with the orderliness of the crowd in Capernaum; the town's lack of faith contrasts with the faith of the crowd. Clearly the contrast is between the revelatory moment and the emptiness of time in the absence of faith. Where collective faith is lacking and cannot be domesticated, the Son of Man has no home and is driven out by the people, who are like pigs—that is, animals who are only partially domesticated and can be possessed by evil spirits.

A structuralist would easily find in this narrative the opposition between order and disorder, structure and anti-structure. Those writing in the vein of Victor Turner, moreover, would find liminality in the presence of the lake; its shores symbolizing the threshold between structure and the threat of anti-structure to any society. On the 'other side' are those, like the Gadarenes of no faith, who do not understand the fullness of their times. Anthropologists who see Israel's animal metaphors as codes for prohibited or problematical relationships would see in the herd of pigs a metaphor for the Gadarenes themselves: outsiders who are too close to nature, too uncultivated, and too unclean to participate in the revelatory moment of Israel (cf. Eilberg-Schwartz 1988). These spatial metaphors, with their emphasis on boundaries and differentiation, point to the early Jewish-Christian community's attempt to preserve its own boundaries. For instance, in Syrian Antioch, Jews were frequently exposed to loyalty tests by the Gentiles. Only the exceptional Gentile, therefore, could be admitted to fellowship, while the common herd remained beyond the threshold of the faithful. Moreover, in the crowds gathering around the disciples during the years after Jesus's crucifixion, even boundaries that had remained relatively stable were as permeable as were the social boundaries in the crowds that attended Jesus during his lifetime. Finally, *I am arguing that the link between the two situations is precisely the crowd itself; that it perpetuates the magical kingdom and recalls the past into the present. That is why the times remained 'full' even after the death of Jesus.*

I would therefore hypothesize that societies in which the crowd is a pivotal social institution tend to intensify the experience of time. They may intensify time by drawing on the future or the past either to precipitate or prepare for a decisive moment of conflict and testing. Whether crowds seek the assistance of ancestors for the time of testing or call on charismatic leadership, the intensification of time makes every decision and each moment extraordinarily significant and even decisive for the survival and continuity of the system. Under these conditions, therefore, pressures also intensify on the people to act like victors; a demand that is reinforced by appealing to triumphant ancestors or messianic heroes.

There is a wide range of conditions, of course, under which a crowd may be driven to intensify the experience of time. One such condition is invasion or domination by an external force: Rome, for instance, in the case of first-century Palestine. Another is pressure by the political or cultural centre on the periphery, which makes the communities of the periphery unsure of their ability to survive. A third such condition is the pressure of the periphery on the centre, as in the case of the 'invasion' of Jerusalem by 'armies' of pilgrims from the Galilean fringe and from the diaspora. Poverty, civil disruption, famine, and other disasters can also produce acute anxiety about the ability of a community or society to reproduce itself. Under these conditions millennial expectations arise. The experience of time is thus intensified, and the people are called upon to face the threat of death with the sure and certain hope of triumph—that is, to act like victors.

To intensify time is precisely to become aware of a world that is heading for a decisive test or conflict. To take the stance of the victor, furthermore, is to understand that it is the world of the other, the enemy, that is destined to pass away; one's own epoch, the era being initiated, is to last for ever. Secularity, then, is the by-product of the intensification of time.

It is one thing to interpret, but quite another to explain, the process of secularization in terms of the intensification of time. With regard to the modern world, Luhmann (1987) has argued that the rapidity of communication makes time run out faster than in pre-modern societies. There is heightened pressure on decision-makers to cope with an environment that is full of threats, surprises, and opportunities for new relationships. On the other hand, modern societies, Luhmann notes, have become sufficiently complex to adapt to uncertain environments, including developments from within that pose sudden threats and opportunities. The result is a process that speeds up time, combined with structures that allow a society to temporize. Borrowing a phrase from Charles Dickens' notes on his visit to the United States, I would suggest that secularity under these conditions is less intense: an 'eternal foreground', as Dickens put it, to describe, in spatial imagery, a horizon that constantly recedes. The decisive moment of testing, the final conflict, is constantly postponed.

Of course, not all pre-modern societies are alike, and, like Palestine, any society changes markedly over time. The intensification of time, then, will take different forms according to whether a society traces its origin to decisive moments or to the actions of primordial figures. It is clear that Israel traced its origins to decisive moments, for example, confrontations with enemies, or constitutive events in which the people came together: to an exodus or to a gathering at Shechem. The intensification of time would therefore take the form of a prediction of another decisive confrontation or gathering: a *kairos* rather than the *chronos* that typifies the dating of significant events by modern societies (e.g. the date on which the Second World War was ended in Europe, when the atomic bomb dropped on Japan).

A society, like Palestine, which also traces its origins to the actions and movements of primordial figures like the patriarchs, would intensify time as being the future intended or foretold in earlier times—namely, that their descendants would prosper, multiply, and be a blessing to the nations. In contrast to this unfolding and development, in which the present is the fulfilment of the past, a more complex society may experience time as a form of duration in which anniversaries of patriarchal decisions are observed; for example, the two-hundredth anniversary of the Founding Fathers' framing of the American Constitution. Time in modern societies is partially intensified through the observance of chronology and the experience of duration; under these conditions time passes away slowly, and secularity is chronic and of low intensity compared with the more critical and acute experience of the passing away of an age as promised times come and decisive events precipitate or anticipate the end or rebirth of the society as a whole. Certainly, time is socially constructed, like other aspects of social reality. More important for present purposes, however, is the question of whether time is of the essence of social life rather than one of its by-products.

3. CROWDS AS THE INTERNAL ENVIRONMENT: CONTROLLING THE PASSAGE OF TIME

Christianity originated in a society in which revolution attacked the fundamentals of the social system by accelerating the passage of time. The time experience of the crowd also became normative for the people. In the time-frame of the crowd, social life is egalitarian and autonomous; by domesticating the crowd, furthermore, the Jesus movement sought to reduce the consistent and heavy weight of social obligation. By substituting its own sense of time and its experience of social life as potent, egalitarian, and full of possibility, the movement undermined the stability of larger organizations and of the society itself; it challenged not merely the system of tribute, which was taxing in every sense of the term, but also the nature of political authority itself.

I am suggesting that the crowd is not merely a threat to social order; rather, it is the pivotal institution that determines the 'times' of the social system. Gluckman puts it this way:

Every king during his reign tries to increase the power of his house. But if he oppresses the masses they *may turn to his successor. There is a balance, but it is 'precarious', and 'is written in rivalries, feuds, intrigues, and revolts, which threaten the peace of the country. . . . And out of this situation, to show yet another parallel to ancient Rome, or to London in medieval times, emerges the power of the city mob. . . .*

We are a long way from that differentiation of the economy which appears to eliminate the dynastic struggle as the focus of political intrigue, and which accompanies the clear rule of succession denoting one heir. . . . These West African states were tribute-organizing states, in which much use was made of the labour of slaves. The ancient Mediterranean states are better parallels . . . But they also show some parallels with the working of feudal political systems as a whole. (Gluckman 1965: 194–5; emphasis added)

The crowd in antiquity took on the quality of an environment for the society as a whole. Here is Luhmann's helpful statement about the system's environment:

Environments do not exist exclusively of various other systems. They also contain (and this is extrememly important) the *chance* to seek or avoid relation with other systems. Equally significant facets of any environment are: forms of interdependence, temporal relations, the degree of reliable 'normality', the frequency of surprise, and so forth. (Luhmann 1987: 232)

The crowd, I would suggest, typically is full of surprises; its judgements are not easily foretold. It was therefore risky for the Jesus movement to take its case to the city, where a hastily invoked crowd could well become the final court of appeal. None the less, as a movement, the 'crowd' itself was a source of surprises to every facet of the social system. Crowds broadened the range of what might be considered normal behaviour in their forms of address, methods of eating and celebration, and in face-to-face interaction. They insisted on broadening the range of social relationships to which they would have access. They were an environment in action: outsiders who became sources of pressure, demand, and judgement on the system as a whole.

I do not mean to ignore the usual motives of desire for wealth and power, but only to suggest that these were minor compared to the crowd's rebellion against the weight of an oppressive system itself. There is ample evidence in recent work on the social background of early Christianity to suggest that the duties of a Jew—even of a not very well-off Jew—were exceedingly burdensome during the first century. Gager (1975: 34) notes, therefore, Christian 'tendencies to minimize or even abolish traditional status distinctions': a tendency he ascribes to the levelling effects of groups that were relatively deprived of various forms of comfort and distinction. However, I trace these effects to the institution of the crowd itself.

The crowd is therefore a prototypical sect, and resembles what Wilson once described as the 'Marching Rule' movement. The movement had 'contradictions and oscillations ... entirely to be expected among a people at a low level of cultural development experiencing dramatic cultural contact' (Wilson 1973: 471): a mixture of material interests in cargo with even more critical concerns for regaining cultural integrity and self-respect in the future. In this regard, the members of the movement resemble the crowd of antiquity in the Jewish-Christian community: far less concerned with its own affluence, despite the visible economic interests of many members of the movement, than with the sense that time is running out on the whole community. Indeed, the material riches (should they arrive) would not be merely 'material' but tokens of collective spiritual well-being and virtue: a source of abundant life for the whole society in the messianic future.

Wilson's description of the type of society that was conducive to the Marching Rule movement also sheds some light on the circumstances of first-century Palestine; here the emphasis is on a social world entailing heavy traditional obligations: in which time is indeed of the essence of society. The obligations are inherited, of course; but they are imposed by a society whose organization is expressed through the minutiae of face-to-face relationships:

In societies in which local entrepreneurship is hampered by lack of individual capital, by traditional obligations of reciprocity between leaders and supporters which impede capital accumulation by individuals and restrict personal innovation and initiative, new economic opportunities can be realized only through quasi-political reorganization or community cooperatives. The development of a consciously new form of social organization can occur most easily when the existing social structure has been disrupted—by war, as in the case of the Solomons. (Ibid. 474)

As Wilson has reminded us, moreover, sects in traditional societies are not only radical but conservative 'in attempting to revive what they regard as uncorrupted religious performances, or an earlier pattern of organization which they believe to have been divinely warranted' (1982: 105–6): that is, to restore lost times. The Jewish-Christian community, like Qumran, maintained a belief in such an earlier 'pattern of organization': a people's court that would fulfil and complete the nation, restore the Kingdom, represent the peoples, worship God, and (especially in the case of Qumran) pass judgement on the peoples of the world (cf. Charlesworth 1985: 125–8). The crowd, I have argued, was precisely that: a people's court, and may well be the prototype of the popular imagination of an eschatological court of the people as it stands in judgement over history.

If secularization is indeed the dominant trend in Western societies, it is due to the capacity of these societies to domesticate the charisma of the crowd in the courtroom, the electorate, the stadium, and in the congregation. Each of these contexts has its separate times and calendar and its distinct seasons of memory and aspiration. The 'environment' of antiquity, the crowd, has become one of several modern 'contexts': places of limited opportunities, limited threats and surprises, and of relatively limited moment to the society as a whole. The 'times' of the political system no longer coincide with those of the religious or judicial systems. The 'times', even if not always out of joint, are therefore never full.

Note

1. All quotations of Scripture are from the RSV.

References

Burkert, W. (1979), *Structure and History in Greek Mythology and Ritual* (Berkeley, Calif.).
Canetti, E. (1978), *Crowds and Power*, trans. C. Stewart (New York).
Charlesworth, J. (1985), *Jesus within Judaism* (New York).
Cornfield, G. (1982) (ed.), *Josephus: The Jewish War* (Grand Rapids, Mich.).
Eilberg-Schwartz, H. (1988), 'Israel in the Mirror of Nature: Animal

Metaphors in the Ritual and Narrative of Ancient Israel', *Journal of Ritual Studies*, 2: 1–30.

Finley, M. I. (1983), *Politics in the Ancient World* (Cambridge).

Freud, S. (1956), *Delusion and Dream, and Other Essays*, ed. P. Rieff (Boston).

Gager, J. (1975), *Kingdom and Community: The Social World of Early Christianity* (Englewood Cliffs, NJ).

Girard, R. (1987), *Job: The Victim of his People*, trans. V. Freccero (Stanford, Calif.).

Gluckman, M. (1965), *Politics, Law, and Ritual in Tribal Society* (New York).

Hopkins, K. (1983), *Death and Renewal* (Cambridge).

Johnston, H. (1989), 'Toward an Explanation of Church Opposition to Authoritarian Regimes: Religio-Oppositional Subcultures in Poland and Catalonia', *Journal for the Scientific Study of Religion*, 28: 493–508.

Le Bon, G. (1986), *The Crowd, A Study of the Popular Mind* (London).

Luhmann, N. (1987), *The Differentiation of Society* (New York).

Neusner, J. (1987), *Self-Fulfilling Prophecy: Exile and Return in the History of Judaism* (Boston).

Nicolet, C. (1975), 'Economie, société, et institutions au II siècle av. J-C: De la lex Claudia a l'ager exceptus', *Annales: Economies, sociétés, civilisations*, 35/5: 871–94.

Rank, O. (1971), *The Double: A Psychoanalytic Study* (Chapel Hill, NC).

Theissen, G. (1971), *Sociology of Early Palestinian Christianity*, trans. J. Bowden (Philadelphia).

Wilson, B. R. (1973), *Magic and the Millennium* (London).

—— (1982), *Religion in Sociological Perspective* (Oxford).

Bibliography of Bryan Wilson's Works

1. 'Apparition et persistence des sectes', *Archives de sociologie des religions*, 5 (1958): 140–50.
2. 'The Origins of Christian Science: A Survey', *Hibbert Journal*, 225 (January 1959): 61–70.
3. 'An Analysis of Sect Development', *American Sociological Review*, 24/1 (February 1959): 3–15. This paper has been frequently reprinted in, among other things, S. M. Lipset and N. J. Smelser, *Sociology: Progress of a Decade* (Englewood Cliffs, NJ: Prentice-Hall, 1961); F. Fürstenberg, *Religionssoziologie* (Neuwied: Luchterhand, 1964); W. M. Newman, *The Social Meaning of Religion* (Chicago: Rand McNally, 1974).
4. 'The Pentecostal Minister: Role Conflicts and Contradictions of Status', *American Journal of Sociology*, 64/5 (March 1959): 494–504. Reprinted in B. McLaughlin (ed.), *Studies in Social Movements* (Glencoe, Ill.: Free Press, 1969).
5. 'Mass Media and the Public Attitude to Crime', *Criminal Law Review*, 345–432 (June 1961): 376–84.
6. *Sects and Society* (London: Heinemann, 1961, and Berkeley & Los Angeles: University of California Press, 1961; reprinted Westport, Conn.: Greenwood Press, 1978).
7. 'Analytical Studies in Social Institutions', in A. T. Welford *et al.* (eds.), *Society: Problems and Methods of Study* (London: Routledge & Kegan Paul, 1962), 99–110.
8. 'The Teacher's Role', *British Journal of Sociology*, 13/1 (March 1962): 15–32. This paper has been reprinted in *Education*, 14/2 (March 1965), in New Zealand; in Peter I. Rose (ed.), *The Study of Society* (New York: Random House, 1967); in K. Betzen and K. E. Nipkow (eds.), *Der Lehrer in Schule und Gesellschaft*, (Munich: Piper, 1971); in Donald E. Edgar (ed.), *The Competent Teacher* (Sydney, Australia: Angus and Robertson, 1974); and in H. R. Stub (ed.), *The Sociology of Education: A Sourcebook*, 3rd edn, (Homewood, Ill.: Dorsey Press, 1975).
9. (with Malcolm Bradbury) 'Artists without Art', *Texas Quarterly*, 5/4 (Winter 1962): 11–21.
10. 'Millennialism in Comparative Perspective', *Comparative Studies in Society and History*, 6/1 (October 1963): 93–116.
11. 'On the Fringe of Christendom', *Rationalist Annual*, 1963, 40–50.
12. 'Typologie des sectes dans une perspective dynamique et comparative',

Archives de sociologie des religions, 16 (1963): 49–63. Reprinted in translation in R. Robertson (ed.), *The Sociology of Religion* (London: Penguin, 1969).

13. 'Sectarians and Schooling', *School Review* (Chicago), 72/1 (1964): 1–21.

14. 'The Needs of Students', in Marjorie Reeves (ed.), *Eighteen Plus* (London: Faber, 1965), 44–88.

15. 'The Paul Report Examined', *Theology*, 68/536 (February 1965): 89–103.

16. 'Religion and Career', *School Review* (Chicago) 73/2 (1965): 156–72.

17. 'A Sociologist's Postcript', in Margaret Phillips, *Small Social Groups in England* (London: Methuen, 1965), 292–306.

18. *Religion in Secular Society* (London: Watts, 1966). Subsequently published in paperback (London: Penguin, 1969); Spanish edition (Barcelona: Editorial Labor, 1969).

19. *The Social Context of the Youth Problem*, The Charles Russell Memorial Lecture for 1965 (London: Charles Russell Memorial Trustees, 1966).

20. 'The Migrating Sects', *British Journal of Sociology*, 18/3 (1967): 303–17.

21. (ed.) *Patterns of Sectarianism* (London: Heinemann, 1967) (reprints items 3 & 4 above, and includes three original contributions: Introduction, 1–21; 'The Exclusive Brethren: A Case Study in the Evolution of a Sectarian Ideology', 287–337; and (with Gordon Willis) 'The Churches of God: Pattern and Practice', 244–86).

22. 'Sectarianism, Establishment and Partisanship', *Sociological Review*, 15/2 (1967): 213–20.

23. Foreword to H. E. Rhee, *Office Automation in Social Perspective* (Oxford: Blackwell, 1968).

24. 'Religion and the Churches in America', in W. McLoughlin and R. N. Bellah (eds.), *Religion in America* (Boston: Houghton Mifflin, 1968), 73–110.

25. 'Religious Organization', in *International Encyclopedia of the Social Sciences* (New York: Macmillan & Free Press, 1968).

26. 'Youth Culture, the Universities and Student Unrest', in *British Universities Annual for 1968* (London: Association of University Teachers, 1968), 90–104.

27. 'The Challenge to the Universities in Britain', in *La Révolte de la jeunesse* (Madrid: CEDI, 1969), 79–97.

28. 'A Typology of Sects', in *Types, dimensions et mesure de religiosité*, Acts of the Tenth International Conference for the Sociology of Religion (Rome, 1969), 31–56.

29. 'Unbelief as an Object of Research', in R. Caporale and A. Grumelli,

(eds.), *The Culture of Unbelief,* Proceedings of the First International Symposium (Rome, 1969); Berkeley & Los Angeles: University of California Press, 1971), 121–31 and 247–69.

30. *The Youth Culture and the Universities* (London: Faber, 1970) (includes, among other things, items 5, 8, 14, 19, and 26 above).

31. *Religious Sects* (London: Weidenfeld & Nicholson, 1970; Munich: Kindler, 1971; New York: McGraw-Hill, 1971; Paris: Hachette, 1971; Madrid: Guadarrama, 1971; Stockholm: Aldus/Bonniers, 1971; Tokyo: Heibonsha, 1973).

32. (ed.) *Rationality* (Oxford: Blackwell, 1970) (includes original introduction).

33. 'Sociology and History', *Proceedings of the Royal Historical Society,* 5th series, 21 (1971): 101–18.

34. (with Malcolm Bradbury) Introduction to Robert Escarpit, *Sociology of Literature,* 2nd English edn. (London: Cass, 1971).

35. 'Christian Science', in *Encyclopaedia Britannica,* new edn. (1972).

36. 'Mormonism', in *Encyclopaedia Britannica,* new edn. (1972).

37. 'Pentecostalism' (review article), in *Religion: Journal of Religion and Religions,* 2 (1972): 154–8.

38. 'American Religion: Its Impact in Britain', in A. J. N. den Hollander (ed.), *Contagious Conflict: The Impact of American Dissent on Europe* (Leiden: Brill, 1973), 233–63.

39. *Magic and the Millennium* (London: Heinemann and New York: Harper Row, 1973; London: Paladin paperback edn., 1975).

40. 'Jehovah's Witnesses in Kenya', in *Journal of Religion in Africa,* 5/2 (1974): 128–49.

41. 'American Religious Sects in Europe', in C. W. E. Bigsby (ed.), *Superculture: American Popular Culture and Europe* (Bowling Green, Oh.: Bowling Green State University Press and London: Elek, 1975), 107–22.

42. 'The Debate over Secularization: Religion, Society, and Faith', *Encounter,* 45/4 (October 1975): 77–84.

43. (ed.) *Education, Equality and Society* (London: Allen and Unwin, 1975) (with original Introduction, pp. 9–38).

44. Foreword to Marie-Louise Martin, *Kimbangu: An African Prophet and his Church* (Oxford: Blackwell, 1975).

45. *The Noble Savages: The Primitive Origins of Charisma and its Contemporary Survival* (Berkeley, Los Angeles, and London: University of California Press, 1975); Dutch translation: *Charismatisch leiderschap* (Utrecht: Het Spectrum, 1978); Japanese translation (Tokyo: Orion Press, 1982).

46. 'Sect or Denomination: Can Adventism Maintain its Identity?', *Spectrum: Quarterly Journal of the Association of Adventist Forums* (Athena, Oregon) 7/1 (Spring 1975): 34–43.

47. 'Aspects of Secularization in the West', *Japanese Journal of Religious Studies*, 3/4 (December 1976): 259–76.
48. *Contemporary Transformations of Religion* (Oxford: Clarendon Press, 1976); Italian translation (Rome: Edizioni Borla, 1981); Japanese translation (Tokyo: Jordan Press, 1978).
49. 'Modernization of Religion: The Case of Western Christianity', *Truth and Creation* 9 (1976); 81–96 (in Japanese).
50. 'New Religious Movements—Millennial Visions in Worldwide Context', *Shiso* (Tokyo: Iwanami Shoten), no. 621 (March 1976): 312–27 (in Japanese).
51. 'Recent Trends in the Sociology of Religion in Britain', *Journal of Religious Studies* (Japanese Association for Religious Studies), 51, no. 228 (June 1976): 67–94 (in Japanese).
52. 'Theories of Sects', *International Religious News*, 15/1–2 (January–June 1976): 9–28 (in Japanese).
53. 'Aspect of Kinship and the Rise of Jehovah's Witnesses in Japan', *Social Compass*, 24/1 (1977): 97–120 (also in Japanese, in *Kokusai Shukyo Nyuzu*).
54. 'De jeugdcultuur', *Kultuurleven* (Louvain), 44/6 (1977): 498–504 (in Dutch).
55. 'Zit Godsdienst op de dood?' (an interview given to F. Damen), *Kultuurleven* (Louvain) 44/4 (1977): 336–48 (in Dutch).
56. 'Becoming a Sectarian: Motivation and Commitment', in D. Baker (ed.), *Religious Motivation: Biographical and Sociological Problems for the Church Historian*, Studies in Church History, vol. 15 (Oxford: Blackwell, 1978), 481–506.
57. 'The Church and Social Change', in *The Church in a Changing Society*, Proceedings of the Commission internationale d'histoire ecclésiastique comparée conférence in Uppsala 1977, Stockholm: Swedish Society of Church History, NS 30 (1978): 181–6.
58. 'The Church, the Denominations, and the Idea of the Modern State', in *The Church in a Changing Society*, Proceedings of the Commission internationale d'histoire ecclésiastique comparée conférence in Uppsala 1977, Stockholm: Swedish Society of Church History, NS 30 (1978): 177–9.
59. 'The New Religions: Some Preliminary Considerations', in Acts of the Conférence internationale de sociologie religieuse (Tokyo, 1978), 112–30, Reprinted in E. Barker, (ed.), *New Religious Movements: A Perspective for Understanding Society* (New York: Edwin Mellen Press, 1982).
60. Foreword to Suzanne Campbell-Jones, *In Habit: An Anthropological Study of Working Nuns* (London and Boston: Faber and Faber, 1979), 11–16.
61. 'The Functions of Religion in Contemporary Society', *Toyo Gakujutsu*

Kenkyu (Journal of Oriental Science), Institute of Oriental Philosophy, Tokyo, 18/3 (1979): 14–36 (in Japanese).

62. 'On Millennial Sects', *Encounter*, 53/6 (December 1979): 50–8.

63. 'The Return of the Sacred', *Journal for the Scientific Study of Religion*, 18/3 (1979): 268–80.

64. (with Karel Dobbelaere) 'Jehovah's Witnesses in a Catholic Country: A Survey of Nine Belgian Congregations', *Archives de Sciences Sociales des Religions*, 50/1 (1980): 89–110.

65. 'The Academic Position of the Sociology of Religion in Modern Science', *Toyo Gakujutsu Kenkyu* (Journal of Oriental Science) 20/2 (1981): 2–32 (in Japanese). Subsequently reprinted with four critical responses and a Riposte, all in English, in *Japanese Journal of Religious Studies*, 9/1 (whole issue entitled 'Bryan Wilson in Japan') (1982): 9–40, 89–98.

66. *The Brethren: A Recent Sociological Study* (Melbourne, Australia: Alanby Press, 1981). Reprinted as *The Brethren: A Current Sociological Appraisal* (Sheffield: Duplicopy, 1981).

67. 'Morality in the Modern Social System', *Actes de XVI conférence internationale de sociologie des religions* (Lausanne, 1981), 340–60. Reprinted as 'Moraali ja nykyaikainen yhteiskuntajärjestelmä', in Juha Pentikäinen (ed.), *Uskonto, kulttuuri ja yhteiskunta*, (Helsinki: Gaudeamus, 1985).

68. (ed.) *The Social Impact of New Religious Movements* (New York: Rose of Sharon Press, 1981) (including Introduction, v–xvi, and 'Time, Generation, and Sectarianism', 217–34).

69. Preface to D. and H. Parker, *The Secret Sect* (Sydney: MacArthur Press, 1982), vii–xiii.

70. *Religion in Sociological Perspective* (Oxford: Oxford University Press, 1982), Italian translation (Bologna: Il Mulino, 1985). Japanese translation (in preparation).

71. 'Sect', in *Dictionary of Christian Theology* (London: SCM Press, 1983).

72. 'A Sect at Law: The Case of the Exclusive Brethren', *Encounter*, 60 (January 1983): 81–7.

73. 'Secularism', in *Dictionary of Christian Theology* (London: SCM Press, 1983).

74. 'Secularization', in *Dictionary of Christian Theology* (London: SCM Press, 1983).

75. 'Sympathetic Detachment and Disinterested Involvement', *Sociological Analysis*, 44/3 (Fall 1983): 183–7.

76. 'Rational Society and the Concept of Peace', in J. Cowan (ed.), *Peace is our Business* (London: Nichiren Shoshu United Kingdom, 1984), 49–67. Reprinted in *International Journal on World Peace*, 3/2 (1986): 67–82.

77. (with Daisaku Ikeda) *Human Values in a Changing World* (London: Macdonald, 1984), Japanese edition (Tokyo: Kodansha, 1987), Portuguese-language edition (Rio de Janeiro: Editora Record, 1987), American edition (New York: Lyle Stuart, 1987), Thai edition (Bangkok: Kled Thai Co., 1988).

78. 'Aims and Visions of Soka Gakkai', *Religion Today*, 2/1 (1985): 7–8.

79. 'Morality in the Evolution of the Modern Social System', Hobhouse Memorial Lecture for 1985, *British Journal of Sociology*, 36/3 (September 1985): 315–32.

80. 'Secularization: The Inherited Model', in Phillip E. Hammond (ed.), *The Sacred in a Secular Age* (Berkeley & Los Angeles: University of California Press, 1985), 9–20.

81. (with K. Dobbelaere) 'Het sektarisch antwoord op het begrip vrije tijd: het tijdsbudget van Belgische Moonies: een Gevalstudie', *Vrijetijd en Samenleving*, 4/2 (August 1986): 133–65.

82. 'Factors in the Failure of New Religious Movements', in David G. Bromley and Phillip E. Hammond (eds.), *The Future of New Religious Movements* (Macon, Ga.: Mercer University Press, 1987), 30–45.

83. Introduction to Anthony J. Gittins, *Mende Religion: Aspects of Belief and Thought in Sierra Leone*, Studia Instituti Anthropos no. 41 (Nettetal: Steyler Verlag-Wort und Werk, 1987), 11–18.

84. 'Religion nach englischem Recht', in J. Neumann and M. W. Fischer (eds.), *Toleranz und Repression: Zur Lage religiöser Minderheiten in modernen Gesellschaft* (Frankfurt-am-Main: Campus Verlag, 1987), 136–51.

85. 'Secularization', in *Encyclopedia of Religion* (New York: Macmillan, 1987), xiii, 159–65.

86. 'Secularization and Non-Western Countries', in *Actes de XIX Conférence internationale de sociologie des religions, 1987* (Lausanne: CISR, 1987), 169–75.

87. 'Secularization and the Survival of the Sociology of Religion', *Journal of Oriental Studies*, 26/1 (1987): 5–10.

88. 'Soka Gakkai', in *Encyclopedia of Religion* (New York: Macmillan, 1987), xiii. 405–7.

89. (with K. Dobbelaere) 'Unificationism: A Study of the Moonies in Belgium', *British Journal of Sociology*, 38/2 (June 1987): 184–98.

90. 'The Functions of Religion: A Reappraisal', *Religion*, 18 (1988): 199–216.

91. 'Methodological Perspectives in the Study of Religious Minorities', *Bulletin of the John Rylands University Library, Manchester*, 70/3 (1988): 225–40.

92. 'The Roots of Secularization', *Trinity Occasional Papers* (Brisbane, Queensland), 7/1 (1988): 3–7.

93. 'Secularization: Religion in the Western World', in S. Sutherland *et al.* (eds.), *The World's Religions* (London: Routledge, 1988), 953–66.

94. (edited with B. Almond) *Values: A Symposium* (Atlantic Highlands, NJ: Humanities Press, 1988) (includes Introduction, 1–10, and 'Values and Society', 31–45).

95. 'American Influences on the Development of Religion', in (no editor given) *Perspectives on Culture and Society*, The Provost's Lecture Series 1987–88 (Muncie, Ind.: Ball State University Press, 1989), 101–18.

96. 'Religion as a Community Resource', in (no editor given) *Perspectives on Culture and Society*, The Provost's Lecture Series 1987–88) (Muncie, Ind.: Ball State University Press, 1989), 82–100.

97. 'Sects and Society in Tension' in Paul Badham (ed.), *Religion, State and Society in Modern Britain* (New York and Lampeter: Edwin Mellen Press, 1989), 159–84.

98. 'The Westward Path of Buddhism', *Journal of Oriental Studies* (Tokyo), 28 (1989): 97–113 (in Japanese), Subsequently published in the English-language edition of *Journal of Oriental Studies* (Tokyo), 2 (1989): 1–10, and in (no editor given) *Buddhism Today: Views from Contemporary Scholars* (Tokyo: Institute of Oriental Philosophy, 1990), 49–62.

99. 'New Images of Christian Community', in John Manners (ed.), *The Oxford Illustrated History of Christianity* (Oxford: Oxford University Press, 1990), 572–601.

100. 'Old Laws and New Religions', in Dan Cohn Sherbok (ed.), *The Canterbury Papers* (London: Bellew Publishing, 1990), 210–24 (translation of item 84 above).

101. *The Social Dimensions of Sectarianism: Sects and New Religious Movements in Contemporary Society* (Oxford: Clarendon Press, 1990.

102. 'Culture and Religion', *Schweizerische Zeitschrift für Soziologie, Revue Suisse de Sociologie*, 3 (1991), 433–49.

103. 'The Changing Functions of Religion: Toleration and Cohesion in the Secularized Society', *The Journal of Oriental Studies*, 4 (1992), 71– 83.

104. 'The Flowering and Deflowering of Protestantism in Latin America', in John Fulton and Peter Gee (eds.), *Religion and Power, Decline and Growth* (London: British Sociological Association Sociology of Religion Study Group, 1991), 15–27.

105. (ed.) *Religion: Contemporary Issues* (London: Bellew Publishing, 1992).

106. 'Reflections on a Many Sided Controversy', in Steve Bruce (ed.), *Religion and Modernization: Sociologists and Historians Debate the Secularization Thesis* (Oxford: Oxford University Press, 1992).

107. 'Historical Lessons in the Study of Cults and Sects', in David G. Bromley and Jeffrey K. Hadden (eds.), *Handbook of Cults and Sects in America* (Greenwich, Conn., JAI Press, forthcoming).
108. 'Sects', in *The Routledge Dictionary of Theology* (London: Routledge, forthcoming).
109. 'Secularization', in *The Routledge Dictionary of Theology* (London: Routledge, forthcoming).

Index